The

Syon Abbey Herbal

*

The Last Monastic Herbal
in
England

c. AD 1517

𝕺rate pro anima 𝕿home 𝕭etson de 𝕾yon

The Syon Abbey Herbal. The Last Monastic Herbal in England, c. AD 1517

© Copyright AMCD (Publishers) Limited 2015.

No part of this publication may be reproduced, stored in a retrieval system, or transmitted in any form or by any means, electronic, mechanical, photocopying, recording or otherwise, without the prior permission of the relevant copyright holders.

The rights to the text of Thomas Betson's Notebook, St. John's College, Cambridge Manuscript 109 (E.6), rest with the Council of St. John's College, Cambridge, which has kindly given its permission to reproduce the text and images of the manuscript contained in this volume.

Plate iv from Joseph Strutt, Bibliographical Dictionary (1785), is © copyright The British Library Board, 7868.d.10 Vol.1 (image 4).

Reproduction of Folio 135v from MS H491 of the *Scala Perfectionis* by William Hilton, is courtesy of the Rosenbach Foundation.

The front cover is taken from MS Nova 2644, the *Tacuinum Sanitatis*, courtesy of the Österreichische Nationalbibliothek.

The authors assert their moral rights to be known as the authors of this work.

ISBN: 978-1897762-69-1

Printed and bound by CPI (UK) Group Ltd CR0 4YY.

Dustjacket design by Spiffingcovers, Colchester, CO7 9AZ.

The

Syon Abbey Herbal

*

The Last Monastic Herbal
in
England

c. AD 1517

by
Thomas Betson,
Last Librarian at Syon Abbey.

From
St. John's College, Cambridge Manuscript 109 (E.6).

Edited by
John Adams & Stuart Forbes

AMCD (Publishers) Ltd.
London
MMXV

'Ye shal be called Ladyes
for bycause that ye shall be spoused
to the Kyng of all kynges.
Whan ye shal go to your garden
&
seen the herber & grene trees,
smellynge þ^e floures, & fruytes with theyr swetnesse,
Mervaylle the grete power
of god
in his creatures.'

Thomas Betson, AD 1500.

From:
*A Ryght Profytable Treatyse Drawen
out of Dyuerse Wrytynges to Dyspose Men
to Be Vertuously Occupyed
in Theyr Myndes and Prayers.*

Published at Westminster by Wynkyn de Worde, AD 1500.

Acknowledgements

Kathryn McKee and her staff at the Library of St. John's College, Cambridge, the home of the Betson Notebook Manuscript 109 (E.6), source of this herbal, were unfailing in assisting us in our enquiries. The Council of St. John's College, Cambridge, were also most kind in granting us permission to produce this edition, together with images from Betson's notebook. Dr. Wolfgang Undorf and Anna Wolodarski, at the National Library of Sweden, were also most helpful in pointing us to their sources for the Syon Abbey mother house at Vadstena, and its library.

We are also grateful for assistance in assembling the Latin sections of *disiecta membra spiritualia,* in Betson's at times difficult handwriting, to Dr Winston Black and Emily Reiner at Saint Louis University, Jessica Henderson at the University of Toronto, Thomas O'Donnell, University College London and particularly to Iolanda Ventura at the Université d'Orléans. For the Middle English sections we are grateful to Tekla Bude, Research Fellow at Cambridge University, and Linne Mooney, Professor of Medieval English Palaeography at York University; and to Alla Babushkina at the University of Toronto and to M. Teresa Tavormina, Michigan State University, for assistance with both the Latin and English; to Mark Spencer at the Natural History Museum in London for commenting on Betson's *Herbarium* section of plant-names. Christina Stapley of Heartsease kindly looked at the efficacy of Betson's remedies in the light of modern herbal usage.

The drafting of our Introduction was much assisted by the illuminating comments of Professor Vincent Gillespie, J.R.R. Tolkien Professor of English Literature and Language at Lady Margaret Hall, Oxford, as well as Dr Ian Doyle, Honorary Reader in Bibliography at Durham University, and Karen Reeds, Department of History and Sociology, University of Pennsylvania.

Marie Addyman kindly wrote the Appendix on William Turner's 1548 audit of the gardens at Syon House, and Topher Martyn, Head Gardener at Syon, reviewed this audit to show the situation in mid-2014.

The Mediaeval Library Catalogues sponsored by the British Library and the British Academy were invaluable (in particular Professor Vincent Gillespie's volume on the Syon *Registrum*), as was the University of Michigan's on-line versions of the Middle English Dictionary, the Latin *Incipits* of Thorndike-Kibre, and the Middle English *Incipits* of Voigt-Kurz. The University of Edinburgh's eLALME, '*A Linguistic Atlas of Late Mediaeval English*' was of great use in identifying Betson's dialect as probably that of Billericay in Essex, and is courtesy of the authors, M. Benskin, M. Laing, V. Karaiskos and K. Williamson. The identification of Betson's plant names would have been impossible without the *Plant Names of Mediaeval England* by Dr Anthony Hunt of St Peter's College Oxford; Dr Hunt also kindly commented on the individual entries of Betson's *Herbarium*.

The authors would like to thank Laurie Elvin, Richard Farrant and Sigrid Padel as fellow members of SARA (Syon Abbey Research Associates), and Chris Hunwick, Archivist to the Duke of Northumberland, for their support and encouragement over the past two years. We are also indebted to our wives and families for their support and forbearance.

We should not of course forget the guidance of John Bray, physician to King Edward III, John Mirfield at St Bartholomews ('Barts') Hospital and Priory in London, John of Gaddesden and his *Rosa Anglica*, and John Lydgate, along with Bartholomaeus, Ricardus and Gilbertus, all *anglici*, and the Northumbrian William Turner, the father of English botany, as well as Michael Scot from Fife and Alfred Shareshill from Lichfield, mediaeval translators of medical texts from Arabic into Latin in Toledo.

But to the elderly monk from Essex, who led us gently but purposefully out of his library, into a mediaeval English herb garden, to botanise, and marvel at God's creation, in the chosen company of Greek, Latin, Arab and English herbalists, must go this last and greatest acknowledgement.

John Adams & Stuart Forbes
Syon Abbey Research Associates

All Souls' Day, 2014.

Contents

	Page
Forewords: Sister Anne Smyth, Last Abbess of Syon Abbey.	11
The Duchess of Northumberland.	13
Health Warning.	15
Introduction: Syon Abbey, Thomas Betson, and his Herbal.	17-63
List of Illustrations between pages 64 and 65.	64
St John's College, Cambridge MS 109 (E.6): Contents, Format, Description of the Binding, Paper, Vellum and Watermarks.	65-73
Text of the Syon Abbey Herbal:	75-297
(a) *Herbarium*: List of plants, with Latin, French and Middle English Names, and John Bray's Sinonoma.	75-209
(b) The Herbal Remedies in Latin and Middle English.	211-297
Appendices:	299-336
1. Tentative Linnaean Names of Betson's Plants.	299-308
2. A List of Diseases in MS 109 (E.6).	309-318
3. Plants at Syon House in 1548, listed by William Turner, Physician to Protector Somerset, by Marie Addyman.	319-332
4. Text of Rosenbach Foundation H491, *Scala Perfectionis*, folio 135v, written by James Grenehalgh of Sheen Priory for Joanna Sewell of Syon Abbey.	333-334
5. Text accompanying an Engraving of Thomas Betson in Joseph Strutt's *Bibliographical Dictionary* (1785).	335-336
Select Bibliography and List of Manuscripts consulted.	337-355
Index.	357-376

Foreword
by
Sister Anne Smyth O.Ss.S.

Syon Abbey, Its Library and Herbal.

In 2015 we celebrate the 600th anniversary of the founding of Syon Abbey by King Henry V, by a charter dated 3rd March 1415. Interest in the community of Syon (originally comprised of both men and women), its religious life, its library and its meticulous librarian, Thomas Betson, continues even to the present day. This first edition of the herbal section of Thomas Betson's notebook also casts light on the history of medicine. It allows us to measure the improvements in the alleviation of suffering which have been made since he wrote in the early 1500s.

The English Bridgettines of Syon Abbey are the only pre-reformation community to have weathered the tempests of the Dissolution in 1539. We look back to the constancy and determination of perhaps our greatest Abbess, Katherine Palmer, who in 1559 ensured that continuity by leading the sisters from Syon to Flanders, through many hardships, until her death in 1576. The sufferings and privations continued as the sisters made their way to France and later to Lisbon, arriving there in 1594. The community remained in Lisbon, surviving both fire and earthquake, until 1861 when the sisters returned to England, the brothers having died out in 1695.

Sadly, in September 2011 the community life of the sisters came to an end. Much of our library, including precious manuscripts and many volumes which the sisters brought to England from Lisbon, have now been lodged for safe-keeping at Exeter University. Thomas Betson, as a brother of Syon, would surely have been proud that of the over 1700 volumes he catalogued, including Books of Hours, some still remain. They continue to bear quiet witness to the silence, prayer and devotion of the community, sustained over the past six centuries.

Sister Anne Smyth O.Ss.S.   60th Abbess of Syon Abbey, 1976 – 2011.

7th June 2014

Foreword
by
The Duchess of Northumberland.

Looking at Syon House today, with its elegant Adam-style rooms, and its pleasant gardens landscaped by Capability Brown, it is difficult to imagine the stern and austere life of the religious community at Syon Abbey, founded six hundred years ago in 1415. Reconstructing that past is made all the more difficult by the absence now of any physical remains of the Abbey – the Church, the Library, the Infirmary and any Herb Garden. All lie buried somewhere beneath the lawns.

It is therefore my great pleasure to welcome this edition of the Herbal of Syon Abbey, compiled by its librarian Thomas Betson. I have a personal affinity with this elderly monk who, like me, clearly not only loved plants and trees, but valued them for their powers. The remedies listed in the Herbal range from the scientific application of Millefolium for the purging a wound, to the bizarre use of powdered owl for gout.

In Thomas Betson we have a modest person who had probably never left England, marvelling at the wealth of herbs and plants from many parts of the world. Here are Pomegranate trees, Cloves, Mulberries, even Amber, along with the more homely English Blackthorn sloes and Dog roses. Many of these varieties still flourish in the Syon parkland, wherein the mortal remains of Thomas Betson also lie. This volume illuminates the last flowering of the monastic tradition. We are all the richer for it.

12th Duchess of Northumberland.
October 2014

Health Warning.

Thomas Betson, who compiled this list of plants and remedies at Syon Abbey around 1500, was not a herbalist, apothecary, surgeon or physician, but an elderly church lawyer. This herbal was most likely written, not from observation, but at his librarian's desk. He was probably working in haste between other duties, in fading light, using at times badly written, derivative and corrupt manuscripts, perhaps (given the number of mis-readings) without the benefit of spectacles.

Furthermore, the naming of minerals, plants and illnesses in English had not yet stabilised in the Tudor period – so that a *foxglove* in Betson may not be a modern English *foxglove*, and was certainly not known by its modern Linnaean scientific name of *Digitalis purpurea*. Betson was drawing on a variety of sources, going back at least to Dioscorides in the first century AD. His flora come therefore from many different habitats – Southern and Northern Europe, the Eastern Mediterranean, the Middle East, even India. So there is therefore no guarantee that any mediaeval name used by Betson can be identified with certainty today.

These considerations can also be applied to the naming of illnesses. TB and Malaria were known, but by other names; their means of transmission were not understood. And mediaeval treatments could be crude in the extreme: it was not until 1536 that surgeons ceased pouring boiling oil into the relatively new gunshot wounds.

Other remedies in Betson are simply poisonous (e.g. using powdered lead), or involve herbs which are lethal if wrongly applied. Not for nothing were some plants named *'mortifer'* (the bringer of death) *'maliciosus'* (evil) *'viduam faciens'* (the widow-maker), and even *'insana... for the use therof is perilous.'* The modern idea that 'Nature' supplies 'natural remedies' takes little account of plants in an English hedgerow that can kill in a few hours. A number of Betson's plants are also dangerous in the extreme if used in pregnancy; others may provoke allergic reactions in varying degrees in susceptible people. And some have now been found to have imperceptible long-term noxious effects, for example leading to kidney failure.

This book is therefore not a medical or herbal guide, but only for historical interest. The modern identifications of Betson's mediaeval plants, minerals and diseases are always tentative.

As Betson himself said, in a moral context: *'Honey licked from thornes is bought dear.'*

INTRODUCTION

INTRODUCTION

Syon Abbey: A Brief History.

The reasons for the unlikely founding of a Swedish abbey of 60 nuns and 25 brothers to the west of London by Henry V in 1415 are to be sought in the bitter struggle between France and England during the Hundred Years' War. This war had effectively begun in May 1337, with the seizure of the continental possessions of Edward III of England by Philippe VI of France. This act led directly to the Battle of Crécy in 1346, in which Edward III destroyed the French army, killing many of the nobility. It was probably following this battle that Bridget of Sweden (1303-1373), a powerful and inspired voice in the Europe of the time, claimed to have received guidance from Christ himself, calling for a dynastic marriage between the French and English royal houses, so that the dual inheritance would fall to a legitimate heir, and thus end the war.[1]

This appeal, which was sent to Pope Clement VI, was transmitted to England by King Magnus of Sweden in 1348.[2] But it was picked up and used by English polemicists as supporting England's claim to France. Bridget's Revelations had in fact assigned the *maiorem iusticiam* to Edward III, though both he and the French king were also described as ravenous beasts. The particular Revelations were furthermore incorporated into *The Regement of Princes,* a guide to good governance prepared for the future Henry V in 1410-1411.

The Revelations also underpinned Henry's failed marriage negotiations with France in early 1415, and this moral support for his claim to France also motivated his foundation of Syon Abbey. Bridget of Sweden had added an appeal for the Kings of France and England to establish religious houses, based on her own foundation at Vadstena, and it was to this model that Henry V turned – the so-called Bridgettine Abbey of Syon.

Another ostensible motivation for Henry was to complete by prayer the penance of his father, Henry IV, for his seizure of the throne, and starving to death of the rightful king, Richard II, in 1400.

---

[1] Birgitta of Sweden, *Revelationes*, Book IV, Chapters 103-105. See Alicia Spencer-Hall, (2013) and Neil Becket (1993) for details. The relevant text in Chapter 105 is spoken by Christ: '*Quod per matrimonium fiat pax, et sic regnum per legitimum heredem poterit pervenire.*'

[2] See also Morris (1999), pp.79-80 for details.

Henry V came to the English throne in 1413 and rebuilt the royal residence at Sheen. The site was on the Thames at Richmond, and Henry proposed to construct near it three monastic houses of strict religious observance, to provide unceasing prayer around his residence. The orders chosen were the Carthusians, Celestines and Bridgettines. The houses were to be named Bethlehem, Jerusalem and Syon respectively. The building of Syon first went ahead on a site near the present Twickenham Bridge, and the foundation stone was laid by Henry V on 22nd February 1415. The Battle of Agincourt was only eight months away. By 1420 Henry was regent of France, and married to the French King's daughter. The throne of France appeared within his grasp, when he suddenly died, perhaps of dysentery, in 1421.

Henry V guaranteed Syon an initial income of 1,000 marks annually (c.£666, or about £500,000 now, an expensive royal investment) and in 1417 he also endowed it with lands taken from 'alien' (i.e. French) priories in England. The site at Twickenham, however, soon proved too small and damp for habitation, and new quarters were sought at what is now Syon House. The new foundation stone was laid in 1426 and occupation commenced in 1431, in what must have still been basic accommodation.

Bridgettine monasteries, being double houses of men and women, were of a unique design, and St Bridget's *Revelationes* were specific about size and layout. They were to be plain and simple, and although archaeological evidence at Syon has revealed no more than the footprint for the church and sisters' accommodation, and perhaps the brothers' reredorter (communal latrine), this evidence suggests that Syon was closely modelled on the mother house at Vadstena.

Funds for building were short in the early years. Henry VI had come to the throne in 1421, and his building priorities were not Syon, but Eton and King's College, Cambridge. Consequently, in 1440 he diverted Syon's lucrative source of income from St Michael's Mount in Cornwall to his own educational projects. Syon, however, gradually became known for its learning and piety and it attracted patrons and postulants, particularly from nearby London and its surrounds. These were among the educated, well connected and wealthy, who donated volumes to its growing library and funds for its endowment.

When in 1461 Edward IV came to the throne, St Michael's Mount and the other appropriated properties were finally restored to Syon, and spending on the abbey's buildings, which had been at a trickle, was able to resume in earnest. Building accounts for the twenty years from 1461 up to 1481 show almost £12,000 (perhaps £8mn today) was spent on the 'newe chirche' and cloisters, of which over

£5,000 (£3mn) was spent from 1479-1481.[3] The final consecration of the monastery and the dedication of the high altar, situated unconventionally at the west end of the church according to the Bridgettine requirements, was on 20th October 1488.

Syon seems to have avoided involvement in the political infighting that characterised the War of the Roses. The invasion of Henry Tudor (later Henry VII) in 1485 and Richard III's death at the Battle of Bosworth, followed by Henry's marriage in 1486 to Elizabeth of York, (Edward IV's eldest daughter), finally brought an end the Roses' conflicts, and ushered in a period of relative stability.

Syon Abbey was then to enjoy comparative peace and patronage. It became a centre for pilgrimage, preaching and learning, and the publishing of printed devotional books. Given its status, it is not surprising that it eventually became enmeshed in the political upheavals generated by the divorce of Catherine of Aragon in 1533, the Oath of Supremacy to Henry VIII in 1535, and the Dissolution of the major monastic houses in 1539. Syon was closed down in November of that year, Thomas Cromwell having apparently engineered a case of *Praemunire* (infringement of the royal legal jurisdiction) in collusion with the Bishop of London.[4] Syon Abbey did not lack courage in this unequal struggle. One of its priest-brothers, the gifted Richard Reynolds, was executed in 1535 for his opposition to the Oath of Supremacy, and one quarter of his body displayed on the Syon Abbey gatehouse.

A group of sisters went in 1539 to a sister house at Termonde in Flanders, returned briefly under Mary I, only to be exiled again in 1558 under Elizabeth I. It was, however, Syon's proud claim that it had never given up the seal or keys of the Abbey, nor signed away the deeds. The order returned to England finally in 1861, from their residence in Lisbon. They were the sole English religious order to survive the Dissolution. They were finally disbanded in 2011, because of falling numbers and ill-health, a few years short of the 600th anniversary of their foundation in 1415.

Thomas Betson, Last Recorded Librarian of Syon Abbey:
His Library Catalogue, Notebook, Herbal and Engraved Portrait.

In the summer of 1481 Thomas Betson, probably from near Billericay in Essex, and aged about 45, a church lawyer, ordained priest, and for the previous 15 years rector of the small parish of Wimbish in Essex, left the world and joined Syon

---

[3] On an *historic standard of living value* for purchase of goods and services, as adjusted by historic UK Retail Price Index calculations. See *http://www.measuringworth.com/index.php*

[4] For details see Jones and Walsham (2010) p.68.

Abbey.[5] He joined an enclosed order with a theoretical maximum (as stipulated by Saint Bridget) of some 60 nuns and 25 brothers. By Betson's time it was one of the largest and best endowed religious institutions in England, with a deserved reputation for learning, religious fervour and strictness.[6] Both the men and women within its enclosure were subject to its Abbess, who answered only to the Pope.[7]

Betson was fortunate to arrive when a reforming Confessor General, Thomas Westhaw, appears to have taken the library in hand.[8] Betson was given the duty of librarian (*custos librarie*), and in his spare moments in the newly-built library room, he perhaps began to write out a herbal in his Notebook.[9] He first made a neat quasi-alphabetical list of 700 herbal plant names, many not native to Britain, in transcribed Greek, Latin, French and Middle English, which he called a *Herbarium*. He then added a random selection of herbal remedies, with one chapter wholly in Latin on the use of urine for diagnosis, particularly of women's conditions, and another chapter on herbal essences, preserved in distilled alcohol.

Betson's purpose in compiling the *Herbarium* was perhaps straightforward. It provided him with reference book to the various names of plants in his several herbals in the medical 'B' section of the library. As a librarian he would perhaps have been questioned by his fellow monks on the meaning of difficult entries in the other herbals. One might also speculate that, if as seems likely, Syon called in physicians to prescribe medicines, and apothecaries to dispense their prescriptions, then the *Herbarium* provided a guide as to what exactly these herbs might be.

Betson went to the trouble of heading up his alphabetical entries in the *Herbarium* with synonyms (Latin or English) in groups, either by using brackets to link these together, or else by underlining header words and marking them with a red sign. His remedies however are much less well organised. They appear to be in no order, but certain words are underlined, capitalised, indicated with a pointing hand (*manusculus*) or simply by the letters *NB*. None of these systems can be said to be a good finding aid for a particular illness or remedy.

---

[5] See: Doyle, A. L. (1956a). See also ODNB entry by W. N. M. Beckett, and *Linguistic Analysis of Betson's English Text* below.

[6] The full complement was sixty sisters thirteen priests, another four 'deacons' (in fact also ordained priests, of which Betson was one), and eight lay-brothers. The size of the community varied over time.

[7] See the excellent summary of the legal position in Makowski (2011), pp. 160-167.

[8] See Gillespie (2001) pp. xlv-xlvi for details.

[9] St John's Cambridge MS 109, E.6. Notebook of T. Betson of Syon.

The Notebook is a desk study, with no reference to the habitat or appearance of the plants cited, no illustrations, no indication of when to gather or how to store a plant, nor the length of time of its efficacy. There is also no *'quid pro quo'* section, which was an addition to herbals, allowing unavailable plants to be substituted by another. Such substitutions were often the province of the apothecary, and therefore their presence in a herbal was neither obligatory nor uniform.[10] We have in fact no evidence that Betson, or any other member of the Syon Abbey community, male or female, had any practical knowledge of herbalism, botany or medicine.

Betson's Notebook is therefore more likely to be a personal reference document, not intended for reading by others. It also contains, apart from the *Herbarium* and herbal remedies, some sources on canon law, English history, even some star maps. There are long sections (omitted from our text) on the preparation and use of multiple mirrors to somewhat magical kaleidoscopic effect; on codes, secret writing and inks; and on methods to burn coloured lettering into steel knives. These are copied from a variety of sources, principally the anonymous *Secretum Philosophorum*.[11] It reveals Betson as someone with wide-ranging and perhaps rather boyish enthusiasms. He liked practical jokes and included one to convince people that an apple is possessed: it involved secreting a stag beetle inside a hollowed-out apple, so that the apple moved around his desk.

The Notebook is small and almost square, only some 5¾ inches long by 4¼ inches wide (14.6 x 10.8 cm). The skin on the wooden boards is off-white, but beneath it, particularly against the inside rear wooden board, lies what may be typical Syon deep pink binding, now much faded. The text is on paper, with a few added sheets of vellum, and in handwriting varying from the neat to the illegible. This is not surprising if it was compiled over a 36 year period (1481 to 1517) by an increasingly elderly Betson. There may however perhaps have been more than one writer at work in the Notebook. This is uncertain, since Betson was skilled in penmanship, and used a number of different styles.

The Notebook, with its varied handwriting and rapid shifts of style and language, also draws on a variety of medical sources. Betson had available almost the whole panoply of mediaeval and much of the classical *corpus* of medical, medical astrology and herbal literature beside him in the library, in the section marked 'B'. He was intimately acquainted with these books, having also been given the task of

---

[10] We are grateful to Christina Stapley for drawing this to our attention.

[11] Anonymous, c.1300, no copy listed at Syon, and still not yet in print.

compiling, or perhaps updating, the library catalogue *(Registrum)* of over 1,700 manuscript and printed volumes, each containing multiple titles.[12]

Had Betson incorporated some of these medical sources, both printed and manuscript, into his own text? Why are there no descriptions of any plant or habitat? Did he know any Greek and especially Greek plant names, as a result of the new wave of learning sweeping across Britain and Europe? Where did he acquire the strange remedies – such as dead dog stuffed with frogs, for gout? Before we answer these questions, let us look first at what kind of person Betson was. We need to bear in mind the great length of time he was at Syon, from around 1481, to his death in February 1517.[13]

Despite the instability in England leading up to the death of Richard III in 1485, Betson was fortunate to see great continuity at Syon, in serving under two long-lived abbesses - Elizabeth Muston (1456-1497), and Elizabeth Gibbs (1497-1518). He probably also served under only four Confessors-General: Thomas Westhawe (d.1488), William Falkley (d.1497), Stephen Saunders (d.1513), and finally John Trowell (d. 1523), all of whom were graduates with previous experience of administration. Between them these Confessors-General gave nearly 100 volumes to Syon Abbey library.

We do not know what duties, apart from being *custos librarie*, fell to Betson at Syon. It was a double monastery, and may have had its own special arrangements for the priest-brothers, who were by the 1470s and 1480s a male community in which graduates predominated.[14] The usual mediaeval monastic practice in *single* monasteries was for the duties of the librarian to fall to the Precentor, one of the major officials after the Abbot and the Prior, and who acted as a kind of registrar for official documents.[15] But we have no direct evidence that Betson ever carried such a title at Syon, or fulfilled that role.

The tasks which we know that Betson undertook, such as preparing the library *Registrum*, and copying the Rule for the Brothers suggest that at least some of the

---

[12] The Syon *Registrum* has been edited by Bateson, (1898), and Gillespie, (2001).

[13] 1516 old style. For legal and most other purposes the mediaeval year did not end until Lady Day, 25th March.

[14] See Cunich, Peter, (2010).

[15] For more details on the early (c. AD 1295) role of the Precentor and Librarian see: Clark, (1897) pp. 59 -69; and Crossley, Fred, (1949), p13. The BL *Corpus* Volume 5 affirms that John Whytefield, who compiled the 1389 catalogue at Dover Priory, was probably also Precentor. Stoneman, (1999).

typical Precentor's duties fell to him.[16] It may be that some of the entries in the Syon *Martyrologium* (list of deceased religious and patrons) are in his hand. He may have been in correspondence with religious houses elsewhere, requesting their prayers.[17] He copied out, though he did not invent, the guide to hand signs in the monastery for the times of silence.[18] The sign for 'sleep' or 'dormitory' is still in common use today – both hands joined, and placed against the head, inclined to one side.

Betson was also entrusted with writing the first recorded book to be published by Syon, entitled *A Ryght Profytable Treatyse* printed in 1500 by Wynkyn de Worde. Part of the draft for this is in his Notebook (not included here). Its English style and grammar (examined below reveals that Betson's original dialect and place of origin were probably near to Billericay in Essex (see pp.49-50 below).

Apart from Betson's Notebook and Library catalogue, he is blessed with a third miraculous and fragile survival: a print from the copper plate used perhaps for a printed indulgence, that contentious reformation issue. We have what seems to be an undated engraved portrait of Betson, by an unknown artist, on a broadsheet which contains Latin verses, possibly by Betson, entitled *'Oratio de omnibus sanctis'* (a prayer to all the saints).[19]

This is the sort of ephemeral piece of paper that might have been given to pilgrims who attended the famous Syon Pardon at Lammastide on August 1st. It shows the kneeling image of Betson, heavily tonsured, in Bridgettine habit with a small circular emblem over his heart. As one of the four Syon deacons, Betson was entitled, according to the Syon Additions to the Rule to 'bear on their mantles a white circle, for the incomprehensible wisdom of the four doctors whose figure they bear, in which circle, four little red particles in manner of tongues shall be sewed, for the Holy Ghost enflamed them.'[20]

---

[16] British Library MS Additional 5208, fols 3v -18v. *The Rules of St Saviour and St Augustine.*

[17] See also Doyle, 1956b and 2004 who states Durham University Library MS Cosin V.iii.16 to be: 'A copy of a letter from one convent of nuns to another.... The letter could have been composed by the spiritual director of a nunnery, and its style and script resemble those of Thomas Betson, brethren's librarian at Syon Abbey.'

[18] Previously St Paul's Cathedral MS 25,524 and now in the London Metropolitan Archives. For text see: https://archive.org/details/ryghtprofytablet00betsuoft (CUP 1905).

[19] Joseph Strutt, Bibliographical Dictionary (1785), plate iv, British Library shelfmark G.4421, cited by Erler (1992).

[20] Saint Gregory the Great, Saint Ambrose, Saint Augustine, and Saint Jerome. Syon had a formal preaching role, and these were the models to emulate, and the orthodox sources to use.

Betson is identified at the foot of the illustration by his monogram 'TB' and the words *De Syon*.[21] He is shown below an image of a standing Virgin and Child, a crescent moon at her feet. One verse of the text refers to *Thomas, spes Anglorum*, probably Thomas à Becket reflecting a little glory on his namesake, Thomas Betson. It is however extremely strange that an enclosed devout monk might choose such a self-celebratory image – perhaps Betson had no say in the matter. Could it be a piece of publisher's blurb, to promote the publication in 1500 of Betson's *Treatyse* ? Or was it in fact printed after Betson's death in 1517, as some sort of preliminary move towards his beatification?

The Later History of Syon

Betson overlapped for four years at Syon with its most famous son, and the only martyr of the Bridgettine Order, Richard Reynolds.[22] Reynolds was perhaps 50 years younger than Betson. He was a fellow of Corpus Christi College, Cambridge, and entered Syon in 1513. He donated 94 books to Syon library, some at his profession, others perhaps later. He is said to have known Hebrew, Greek and Latin. He was dismembered at Tyburn on 4th May 1535 for opposing the supremacy of Henry VIII as Head of the Church in England. One quarter of his body was exposed on the gatehouse at Syon Abbey. His sister, Edith, a nun at Syon, remained there until her death in June 1538.

Betson died on 20th February 1517, and was interred in a brick vault at the west end of the south aisle of the church, on the brothers' side of the monastery, and to the east of the present Syon House. Archaeology has since pinpointed his grave, but not his bones, so thoroughly was all trace of the church at Syon Abbey dismantled at the Dissolution. Opposite, further east, is also buried an Agnes Betson, possibly a relative. She appears only at the end of her life, in the *Martyrologium*: 'Agnes Betson, soror' and died on 22 April 1510. We know nothing about her, nor, if related, she ever chose to meet Thomas Betson at the grated windows, for the permitted whispered conversations with relatives – which more strictly observant nuns were encouraged to forgo.

Betson and Herbs.

We have little to indicate what Betson was like as a person – the collection of passages in the Notebook are mainly conventional and utilitarian. He must have been trusted at Syon as sufficiently conservative and orthodox to run the library and

---

[21] According to Erler (1992) this may refer to the origin of text, rather than to Betson himself.

[22] For details and sources, see entry in ODNB by Virginia R. Bainbridge.

to publish a book. But in his Notebook doodles he reveals a little more of himself. Most are penwork, or intricate little swirling knot patterns pricked out in the vellum with guidemarks for the ink. However, on one page there are also two small pike swimming in the top margins (image 39, folio 43v and 44r) accompanied by some lines of a favourite quotation: –

> *Si tibi defidant medici, medici tibi fiant*
> *Hec tria: mens leta, labor, moderata dieta.*
>
> If so be that lechys do thee fayll,
> Make this thi governans, if that it may be:
> Temperat dyet and temperate traveyle…..
>
> (Lydgate's Translation in *Dietarium rithmizatum in Anglicis*)

This quotation is from the influential and widespread School of Salerno *Regimen Sanitatis* – believed, perhaps incorrectly, to be dedicated to Robert, son of William the Conqueror (c. 1054-1134), copies of which were probably in the Syon *Registrum* at B.11 (SS1.88) or B.29 (SS1.106). According to Gillespie there also seems to have been a rhyming version of this in English by Lydgate - the *Dietarium rithmizatum in Anglicis* at B.29 (SS1.106d). The English version cited above is lines 9-11 of this latter. The English ends with the charming line, pertinent to this book and to Betson's herbal: 'this prescription comes from no apothecary.'

But the above lines also appear in a text on fishing, contemporary with Betson: *Treatyse of Fysshynge Wyth an Angle*, (written before 1450, with a printed version by 1496). It would be a pleasant thought, but completely without foundation, to imagine Betson at his desk in the Brothers' Library, a private copy of the *Treatyse of Fysshynge* to hand, longing to be out by the nearby Thames, all the while idly sketching little pike into his Notebook.[23] Or perhaps there was fishing at a '*stew*' or fishpond at Syon, as at the motherhouse at Vadstena in Sweden, to satisfy the house's needs of meatless Fridays and for fasting in Lent.[24] The fact that an unidentified *Oleum Benedictum*, rubbed on fishermen's nets, can attract fishes also caught Betson's eye:

> *Oleum benedictum: si piscatores unxerint retia sua, multitudinem piscium congregabunt.* (Image 115 left, folio 110v, lines 28-30).

---

[23] At the top of his Image 39, folios 37v and 38r.

[24] Betson omits the charming *angle-twitch* for *worm*, which is in Bray at Sloane 521, Fol. 172v, Col C.

And finally, it may be that we have Betson's own fingerprint in ink, rather blurred, in the central gutter of image 110, folios 105v and 106r, a strange extra-textual physical presence across five centuries. But Betson, as a Librarian, would doubtless not have been pleased by blots on one of his own Syon library books – he had, after all, finished his *Ryght Profytable Treatyse* with words of admonition to new postulant nuns: 'Lerne to kepe your bokes clene.'

Although we have Betson's *Herbarium* and his Remedies, we do not really know what he himself thought of herbs and their uses. We do have one reference, however. In his *Ryght Profytable Treatyse* he has the following strange connection regarding greed, diet, medicines and lettuces:

> It is wryten in the lyf of saynt Benet that a religious woman with a gredenes, receyued a wycked spiryte in etynge of letuse in the gardeyn.

There may be more to this than at first appears: lettuce seems to have had a mixed name in herbal history. Galen had rated 'lettuce' as cold in the first (weakest) degree - just below springwater, and having little effect. But Avicenna had noted its value as a food, and changed its degree of coldness to the second – this is picked up by Betson's source: *Letise is colde and moist in the second degree'* (image 95 right, folio 91r, lines 24-25). Macer Floridus still saw in lettuce a cure for 'polucion of the sperme', that is, night pollution (lines 20-25, on p90 of the Frisk edition). Perhaps we are hearing in Betson echoes of a very old debate.

Also, it has to be remembered that our modern Romantic sensibility in approaching 'Nature' is still some centuries away. Betson's approach to the delights of nature in a garden is to move immediately to encourage his female readers to conventional mediaeval religious sentiments. Addressing the novice nuns, he writes:

> Whan ye shal go to your garden & seen the herber & grene trees, smellynge the floures, & fruytes with theyr swetnesse, meruaylle the grete power of god in his creatures & thenne labour & engendre in your mynde, or talkynge of devocion & lyfte vp your herte to heven & thynke verely that the maker of them that is your spouse in heven is vnspekable fayre, swete, delectable, and gloryous.

Syon Abbey Gardens: After The Dissolution of 1539.

It is not clear from the written records if there was a monastic herb garden at Syon, and its location has not been revealed by the series of archaeological digs in the past decade. We do know that both Protector Somerset (d.1552) and the 'Wizard'

Ninth Earl of Northumberland (d.1632) rearranged the gardens of Syon House.[25] There was further landscaping of the park and lakes in 1760 by Capability Brown.

This probably means that a process of erasure has taken place many times. The recent Birkbeck archaeological digs revealed large circular structures to the East to the site of the church, interpreted as raised flower beds. Perhaps traces of herb gardens can be recovered too, along with the brothers' and sisters' infirmaries which they may have served. The infirmary sewer at Soutra Aisle in Midlothian was found to be full of medicinal seeds.[26] If the same were to happen at Syon, this might cast further light on the Syon Abbey Herbal.

Jackson (1910) in his guide to the trees and shrubs of Syon House notes the variety of Cypress mentioned by William Turner in 1548 (*Cupressus sempervirens*) was still present.[27] Gerarde in his herbal of 1597 also says that then there were Cypress trees at "Syon, a place neare London, sometime a house of nunnes." These slow growing trees may have been monastic in origin – they were presumably already sizeable enough for Turner to remark on them. Jackson also states, without giving sources, that in 1910:

> Near the eastern front of the house some Mulberry trees still remain, which were planted there by the Lord Protector Somerset under Turner's direction. The botanic garden laid out by Turner was probably in front of the house, between it and the river [Thames], where the old prints show a walled garden, but the site is not known for certain.
>
> The Mulberries at Syon are of especial historical interest, from the fact that they include what is reputed to be the oldest tree in England, said to be introduced from Persia in 1548. A remarkable specimen is growing from a small mound near the flower garden, and, though evidently of great age, it still bears fruit.

Jackson identifies the above as the *Morus nigra* or Black Mulberry. *Morus alba* or White Mulberry was then (1910) also present at Syon, on the south side of the Lake. This latter is the natural habitat of the silk worm. It seems unlikely that silk was ever prepared at Syon, the accepted date for the first and unsuccessful attempt being in 1609 under James I. Turner did not mention Mulberry trees in his audit of

---

[25] See M. Addyman, Appendix 3 for details.

[26] See Moffat (1987-1998).

[27] Jackson, A. Bruce (1910).

Syon gardens in 1548, so we can at least assume that they post-date the 1539 Dissolution.

It is not known if bees were kept at Syon. We know that Richard Reynolds gave to the library, at B.21 (SS1.98e), a Palladius *de Re Rustica* and *de Institutione*, in the Bologna edition of 1494 which dealt, inter alia, with gardening, cattle raising, bee-keeping and dovecotes. Bees in the orchards and gardens would have been ideal for both pollination of fruit trees, for producing wax for candles, and for honey.

The requirement that the candles used at mass should be only of beeswax seems to be a recent formulation, but the usage may in fact be ancient. The many altars at Syon, and lighting for the choir stalls, must also have consumed large amounts of wax, but one would be hard pressed today to find any mediaeval beeswax in quantity. We do however have what may be one small drop of Syon beeswax. On folio 71r of a copy of the *Mirror of Our Lady* in English, owned by Sister Elizabeth Moncton, there is small drop of bright yellow beeswax, with perhaps the indentation of a tiny fingernail.[28] No other Syon MS of the many we have examined seems to have wax gutterings, certainly none with this intimate and perhaps slightly guilty personal signature from somewhere between 1518 and 1539.

Dating the Syon Abbey Herbal.

When did Betson start his task of compiling the herbal, and when did he lay down his pen? One indication of dating is at the very end of his notebook, where, in tiny handwriting, almost hidden, he wrote down a prophecy that 'all flesh would perish by fire in 1500.' [29] This could of course have been written by Betson at any time prior to 1500. If the Notebook had already been made up before 1500, an endnote on the back cover would be a good place to secrete a dangerous prediction.

Firmer dating is perhaps provided by publication in 1500 of Betson's *A Ryght Profytable Treatyse*. What look like the draft 'foul papers' for this publication appear very early in the Notebook and before the Herbal, at images 15 and 16, folios 10v to 12r. If we conclude that everything after these folios is post-1500, then the Herbal would presumably have been written after 1500, but before Betson's death in February 1517. We need, however, to assume that the Notebook was bound up in the order it was written, though this is not necessarily the case. It may even be possible

---

[28] Aberdeen University Library: MS.134 . Last Leaf: '*This booke belongyth to syster Elizabeth Monton*' identified as Elizabeth Mountayne or Montague (professed 15 August 1518 – perhaps deceased by 1539, and in the *Martyrologium* as 17 July).

[29] Image 131, left: inserted into the space in a capital letter P, on an endpage, an unnumbered reused sheet from a breviary or hymnal.

that the herbal text was compiled *before* Betson joined Syon Abbey, and when he was still a secular cleric in Wimbish. This might explain his many notes on pregnancy and women's illnesses, given that it is unlikely that a brother at Syon would be involved in the care of sick sisters.[30]

The world did not however end in 1500. Betson lived on into his 80s to February 1517. In October of that year, Luther posted his 95 theses on the doors of Wittenberg Castle Church, attacking the indulgences such as those which Betson had perhaps endorsed. But the world would indeed end for Syon Abbey in 1539, with its closure and demolition. Betson's precious library was cast to the winds. Of the 55 volumes listed in the medical section 'B' of the *Registrum*, only two are known to survive; of the 1,747 in the library as a whole, only 43 have ever been found. And this is the picture for practically every religious house in Britain. According to Ker, of perhaps more than 120,000 titles in over 600 British cathedrals, abbeys, convents, colleges and hospitals, perhaps a meagre 6,000 or 5% are now identifiable.[31]

Syon Abbey Church was dismantled stone by stone. The lead from the roofs was probably melted *in situ* and shipped away, and the great bell tower was demolished. Some time after 1547 the Duke of Somerset, Protector to the Protestant boy-king, Edward VI, moved into what buildings remained, laid out new gardens, and brought in his entourage his physician, William Turner. Turner was, like Somerset, also a Protestant, and is seen as the father of English botany. He had fled abroad under Henry VIII, returned under Edward, and after the latter's death, had to leave England again when Catholic Mary I came to the throne.

In the late 1540s Turner was at Syon and noted the plants; this is a unique post-Dissolution audit.[32] He found amongst other things a Pomegranate tree. This was both a symbol of fertility, and the emblem of Catherine of Aragon, a frequent visitor to Syon Abbey. She however bore no living male issue in her six pregnancies, when Henry VIII still loved her.[33] But, as Turner writes, in a twist of politics, religion and

---

[30] Vincent Gillespie, Pers. Comm. August 2014.

[31] Ker (1964).

[32] See Appendix 4. John Tradescant, in Parkinson's *Theatrum Botanicum (1640)*, is credited incorrectly with introducing the pomegranate into England, but nearly a century later. There was still a Pomegranate tree at Syon at the time of Forrest's 1831 audit, classified under Hardy Trees at page120: *Punica Granatum, I v. flavescens*.

[33] See British Library Royal MS 11 E XI, given to Henry VIII, which contains the image of a pomegranate tree within *Felix Anglia* as a sea-girt castle, below sprigs of the Lancastrian and Yorkist red and white roses. From Flanders c.1516.

gardening, '*There are pomegranates in my Lord Somerset's garden in Syon, but their fruit cometh never to perfection.*'

There is an intriguing footnote to Turner's stay at Syon. An inventory for Syon House prior to its 1594 acquisition by Henry Percy, 9th Earl of Northumberland, records one unidentified room as being 'Master Morgayns Potticary.' The inventory lists nothing of significance, but a Hugh Morgan (c.1530-1613) was apothecary to Queen Elizabeth from 1583 onwards. Morgan also knew Turner, and had been given some roots of Hedge Hyssop, *Gratiola officinalis*, by him.[34] Perhaps therefore a garden which specialized in growing medicinal herbs continued to exist at Syon, from before the Dissolution and up to at least the 1580s.

Vadstena and its Daughter Houses.

Syon's motherhouse, the convent at Vadstena in Sweden, had been gifted to St Bridget in 1346, but was not consecrated until 1384. Because of difficulties over recognition of a new double order of both men and women, for nearly half a century Vadstena did not found any daughterhouses, until in 1393 with a house at Utrecht, 1394 at Florence and 1396 at Marbrunn in Danzig. Two houses founded in 1410 at Genoa and at Mariendal in Denmark preceded Syon' foundation of 1415. Maribo, also Denmark, followed in 1416, and Valencia in 1419. In all there were 27 European houses before the Reformation, the last being in 1464 at Dendermonde (Termonde).

Monastery Finances, and Numbers of Nuns in England to 1539.
At the Dissolution in England, (1536 to 1539), Jacka (1917, p2) lists 123 nunneries in England alone, with a total number of women religious of 1,198. She notes that the Dissolution also included nunneries in Ireland (3), Wales (3), and the Isle of Man (1), possibly Calais (1) as well as the Gilbertine double order with 139 nuns. At the end, Syon had 51 nuns, but Shaftesbury in Dorset had more, at 57. Next came Amesbury, Wiltshire with 33, and Barking, Essex with 30. Syon's income was £1,944. 11s. 5¼d, in properties in twelve counties, from Cornwall to Lancashire.[35] This was doubtless an administrative and accounting nightmare, requiring a bailiff for each manor.

By way of comparison, Shaftesbury had an annual income of £1,208.6s.0d, while Glastonbury Abbey, the richest, had £3,301. 7s 4d. But most nunneries, in Jacka's telling phrase, were 'as poverty stricken as they were aristocratic.........that

---

[34] See ODNB entry John Bennell, 'Morgan, Hugh (*c*.1530–1613)', *Oxford Dictionary of National Biography*, Oxford University Press, 2004; online edition, Jan 2008.

[35] About £1.1mn on an *historic standard of living value* for purchase of goods and services, as adjusted by historic UK Retail Price Index calculations. See http://www.measuringworth.com/index.php

any nun was ever drawn from a class below the rich bourgeoisie is extremely doubtful, and the dominant class in the nunneries was the country gentry.'

The Medical Section Books in Syon Abbey Library.

Before turning to the Syon Abbey Herbal proper, we need to look at the books available to Betson in Section B of the Syon Library. Up to perhaps the 1520s the books represented donations by both those joining Syon and lay people. It is generally thought that the donations have a random quality, representing the individual collections of the donors, perhaps from their university days. Several points are immediately noticeable in looking at Syon's holdings of medical books:

- Syon had most current European medical, medical-astrological and herbal classics. Despite the random nature and extended period of their donation, the 55 listed volumes of both printed books and manuscripts in the 'B' section of the *Registrum* at Syon, and the over 250 titles they contain, are similar to most of the British and major European holdings in religious houses.[36]

- Syon also held copies of many books which had for some time been part of the required reading at the main medical universities abroad, such as Paris and Montpellier, as well as the astrological and astronomical texts known to have been required by the University Bologna. For example, at Paris by 1422 apothecaries were required to have the *Antidotarium Nicholai*, the *Circa Instans* of Platearius and the *Cinonima Correcta* (Serapion's Synonyms).[37] Syon had the first two of these, and possibly also the Serapion in an omnibus edition.

- These holdings may indeed reflect the academic interests of their donors, rather than any official acquisitions policy, though the range, at least in medicine is surprisingly wide. Some books were perhaps already dated by the time they came to be accessioned at Syon. But the last 100 or so printed books (medical and medical-astrology) donated by Richard Reynolds both before and after his profession, reflect the wider world of what may be called early modern neo-platonic humanism.[38]

---

[36] See Appendix 1 for transcription of the *Registrum* from Gillespie (2001).

[37] See Trease (1959) p47, footnote 194.

[38] For an excellent background paper, and further notes on Betson as librarian, see: Gillespie, Vincent (2010). *Syon and the English Market for Continental Printed Books: The Incunable Phase* in *Syon Abbey and Its Books: Reading, Writing and Religion, c.1400 – 1700*. Boydell Press, Woodbridge.

- Syon seems to have acquired a considerable number of books in its medical section which appear unique in Britain. Its library often has the only copy of a medical book in Britain, as listed in the British Library *Corpus of Mediaeval Libraries*.[39] However, the fragmentary nature of other extant monastic library records, as evidenced in the BL *Corpus*, make it difficult to assert Syon's pre-eminence with complete confidence.

- Syon's collection of medical books in *English* also appears unique in Britain. The BL *Corpus* lists only about 60 mediaeval library books as being definitely in the English language, out of perhaps 9,000 titles.[40] Of these, some ten are from Syon, and five are medical. This stark picture is only marginally improved by Ker, whose list of surviving attributable books in English in all British houses is only around 100, out of his total of some 6,000 survivors.[41]

- Syon is curiously paralleled by holdings of English devotional books across the River Thames at the Carthusian house at Sheen. Of these, four survive (Ker, 1964, p 178). Could there have been a relationship at work here, with Sheen copying books in English, to be passed to Syon novices?

Despite this rich resource, Betson seems to have used almost none of the medical, astrological or herbal books in his library in compiling his own herbal. Instead Betson used the following sources, which were not in the library:

1. For his *Herbarium*, Betson used the *Sinonoma de nominibus herbarum* of John Bray, Physician to Edward III (d.1381). It is preserved in six MSS. Of those examined, the closest to Betson seems to be BL Sloane MS 282, fols. 167*v*–173*v*, which tallies closely with Betson's *Herbarium*.[42] Betson also seems to have had access to the remedies contained in the British Library Sloane MS 521, mainly using an anonymous and general collection of remedies at folios 189-275. This

---

[39] Edited by Sharpe, Professor R. (1990-2013).

[40] The search terms include translations into English (26), and the catalogue terms: *Anglica, Anglice, Anglicis, Anglico, Anglic., Englishe,* and *lingua vernacula.* The total includes two texts in Old English.

[41] Jones, (1999b) cites the growing number of translations into English of medical and scientific books from 1375 onwards - see pp. 434-435. Some were 'of unimpeachable academic quality.'

[42] British Library, Sloane MS 282, fols. 167*v*–173*v*: '*sinonima de nominibus herbarum secundum magistrum Iohannem Bray*'; Cambridge, Magdalene College MS Pepys 1661 pp. 245-66; Cambridge University Library Dd.II.45; Cambridge Trinity College MS O. I. 13 (1037) ff. 37v-44r (incomplete);; Durham University Library: DUL MS Cosin V.III.11; Glasgow University Library, MS 185, ff. 1-6v. The Glasgow and Durham MSS have not yet been examined.

is slightly curious, since Sloane 521 also contains Bray's *Practica Medicinae*, at Fols.128-159v, but this does not seem to have been used by Betson.[43]

2. It is less clear what text of Betson had in front of him when compiling his list of Remedies. Certainly his wording follows closely that of Bray in Sloane MS 521 on numerous occasions, but he omits a considerable amount of Bray material. Betson does however insert symbols into his text at the points where he departs from Bray – usually two strokes as //, or else a paragraph mark as Π. This seems to suggest that Betson had several sources open in front of him, and was inserting chosen remedies, in some kind of order which is no longer apparent to us.

3. For example, he included remedies from Sloane MS 3285, a Middle English collection which according to eLALME linguistic analysis (see below) originated somewhere close to the northern border of Sussex with Kent.[44]

4. Betson also uses recipes found in Dawson's *Leechbook*.[45] Perhaps further research may reveal the relationship to Betson of Sloane 282, 581 and 3285 as well as the *Leechbook*.

5. Betson's section *de Urinalibus* ('on urine flasks') draws on two widely circulating texts of the early Middle Ages, *Urina Rufa* (Reddish Urine) and *Colamentum sanguinis* (Cleansing of the Blood*).* These two texts originated in a 12th-century uroscopy treatise that has been called by German scholars, '*Der kurze Harntraktat*' (The Short Treatise on Urine). The text was mistakenly attributed to Johannes Vitalis (d.1327) in both the manuscript (1300s) and printed version (1531) of his *Pro Conservanda Vitae*.

6. Betson may also have used a copy of the *Breviarium Bartholomaei* of John Mirfield (fl.1390) of St Bartholomew's Hospital in London.[46] Betson's recipe for an *aqua ardens* at lines 15-19 below is almost identical to Mirfield's

---

[43] Sloane MS 521 is tiny – 5 inches high, by 2 ½ wide, (13cm x 7). It is confusingly paginated three times, but is probably about 300 folios long, and contains about 105,000 words in very small but perfect handwriting.

[44] Mackintosh, Samuels & Benskin (2013). Edinburgh University Electronic Linguistic Atlas of Late Mediaeval English. http://www.lel.ed.ac.uk/ihd/elalme/elalme.html

[45] Dawson, Warren R., (1934). *A Leechbook or Collection of Medical Recipes from the Fifteenth Century*. The text of Medical Society of London MS No. 136.

[46] Probably at B6 c, (SS1 82) in the *Registrum*

Breviarium, folio 262r, col A, line 48. But other *'aqua ardens'* texts in Betson differ greatly from Mirfield. The number and coverage in Mirfield's *Breviarium Bartholomaei* is extensive, with fifty different distilled waters. The overlap with Betson is small, suggesting that another source, which we were unable to identify, must have been used by Betson. The same is the case with the sixty *'Oleum'* recipes in the *Breviarium Bartholomaei*, which bear little relationship to those of Betson.

7. There are also some similarities in Betson with the sections on various *Aquae Vitae* in the *Tractatus Mirabilium Aquarum (de Preciosa Aqua ad Oculos)* by Petrus Hispanus, c.1205-1277, who was perhaps identical with Pope John XXI (*sedit* 1276-77). The Latin text of Betson (image 112 right, folio 108r, line 1 to image 113 right, folio 109r, line 8) follows it, with some variations in BL Sloane 1754, which is from St Augustine's, Canterbury, c. AD 1300.

Analysis of Betson's *Herbarium* and the Remedies.

The two sections of Betson's Herbal fall neatly apart into the *Herbarium* list of plants (copied from Bray Sloane MS 282), and the list of remedies (assembled by Betson himself). The *Herbarium* is a reference work, designed by John Bray, as befits a physician to the king, to be a guide to a pharmacopeia of herbs. Bray's list of plant names illuminates a number of difficulties in deciphering the text of Betson, who was perhaps working from a slightly corrupt version. To chose one of many examples, Betson has what looks like *'connarasses'* which gives no clue as to its real meaning. Bray has the more intelligible *'toun cress'* which is a form of watercress.

It looks however as though Betson had access to other sources, also used by Bray. For example with regard to *Anacardus*, a cashew-like nut, Bray quotes a source in English: *Anacardus is the lous of an elephant & sume sey that hit ys the fruyt of a tree.* Betson had access to the same quotation, but in Latin - *Anacardus est pediculus elephantis; secundum quosdam est fructus cuiusdam arboris.* This *canard* does not appear in antiquity, but it is in the 12th century *Circa Instans*, which actually debunks the 'louse origin.' It is also in the late 13th century *Clavis Sanitatis* by Simon of Genoa.[47] So Betson and Bray were drawing on different language versions of the same source.

There appears to be no correspondence between the plants cited in the *Herbarium* by Betson, and those listed in his Remedies. This is probably because, as mentioned above, Betson draws many of his remedies from sources other than Bray. Betson's *Herbarium* has nearly 700 entries, many being rather rare and exotic plants. But there are only 130 or so plants listed in his Remedies. Even when Betson cites a common English plant in the *Herbarium* – such as St John's Wort (nine times), this

---

[47] 'Simon online': http://www.simonofgenoa.org/index.php5?title=Anacardus (accessed 31 May 2014).

only translates into one mention in his remedies. Henbane, an important analgesic and soporific, also has nine mentions in the *Herbarium*, but only three in the remedies. Furthermore, of the 130 or so named herbs in the remedies, 44 are used in only one or two remedies, despite being relatively common in Britain.

There is considerable variation between herbs used in mediaeval herbals within the same basic recipe. Hargreaves in *'Some problems in Indexing Middle English Recipes'* (1981) points out the variety in remedies in the 200 or so manuscripts he examined. He mentions 40 variants, for example, of Betson's 'For clensing of *the* head' (image 100, folio 96r, line 14 onwards). He notes that variants tend to omit and simplify, or even change the ingredients. For example *'Peletre of Spayne'* is retained in full by Betson, but often becomes in other manuscripts elsewhere simply *'Peletre'*). Betson's remedy required five days to work. In Hargreaves, most of his 40 examples for 'cleansing the head' required only three or four days. In Betson these variants can be shown in the mentions of *Pestilencia,* the Plague. He has three very different remedies for the plague, with about 7 ingredients each, and only two ingredients overlap, Feverfew and Knapweed. Hargreaves gives several explanations for this variation in what is essentially the same remedy: scribes copying the same recipe several times a day, ultimately from memory; miscopying, simplifying and editing; and translating from a Latin or French original.

Hargreaves looked for example, at 25 different recipes for 'headache'. Betson lists another 14 (including some in Latin), but of these only two appear to be the same as in Hargreaves' samples. So there is, as one might well expect, not only variations within remedies, but also, as perhaps today, completely different remedies available for the same complaint. These variations may also be attributed to the fact that a pharmacopeia was driven both by a list of diseases, and a list of herbs arranged according to their various uses and applications.

Betson has, for example, eight mentions of gout, including one at Image 104 left, folio 99v, lines 13-21, which involves taking an owl, baking it to powder, before turning it into an ointment. This striking recipe is fairly widespread across manuscripts, time, and English dialects, and is memorable for its weirdness.[48] As with many such strange remedies, the modern reaction is to believe that it might just work. This possibility is perhaps called into question by Sloane 3285, folio 43, lines 6-13, which cites almost the same recipe as a cure for the *falling sickness* (epilepsy) but involves reducing a *Raven* to powder. Feckenham, last Abbot of Westminster, has a

---

[48]Also in the *Liber de Diversis Medicinis* (Thornton MS, Lincoln Cathedral A.5.2) ed. Ogden, Margaret Sinclair, EETS OUP 1938, at folio 306v lines 30-35, p63, and note on p.110. Similar recipes occur in Dawson p206, para 655; Henslow MS A, line 15, p19; Sloane 3285 Fol.3v, lines 14-32; and also in Culpeper's Last Legacy as late as 1671.

powdered *Jay* for the same illness at Remedy 348 in his *Sovereign Remedies*.[49] In BL Royal 12 B XII 'Cancre' is cured by the head, feet and intestines of a baked *Crane*.

Betson and his contemporaries used not only animal ingredients but also chemical and mineral materials. It was not realized that some of these chemical and mineral ingredients could be harmful, particularly if used over a long period. For example, a Betson recipe to whiten women's skin (Image 114 Left, folio 109v) called for various compounds of lead, made aromatic with camphor. Curiously, one of Betson's ingredients was still trading under its mediaeval name of *Litargirio*, and being sold to the Latino community in the US as late as 2003 as an anti-perspirant. It was one third ground lead, and was the subject of a US government health warning as a source of poisoning.

Mediaeval herbals are also full of citations that a particular remedy works. We find in the margins of Betson's text the set phrase '*Expertum est*' implying that the recipe had been tried and tested successfully. This occurs for example at Image 115 right, folio 111r, line 22, in another cure for gout. It required the production of an ointment from a very old and very thin dog which had been killed and stuffed with frogs between two feasts of the Virgin, i.e. August 15th (Assumption into Heaven) and September 8th (Birth of the Virgin). This was perhaps linked in the popular mind with the Dog Days around this period. The application of frogs and frogs' legs to cure gout is ancient, Betson's cure being only one more variant.

Betson contains not only remedies involving the consumption of animals, he also cites solutions for dealing with various creatures: to get rid of moles, put an onion in their runs; use St John's Wort to seize snakes without being bitten; burn Asafoetida to have a rout of wild animals follow you; and avoid bee or wasp stings by applying juice of Mallows. These are of course the stuff of general folklore, ancient and modern.

As an afterthought, it is of course all too easy for us in the enlightened 21st century to make fun of the more exotic elements in Betson's selection of remedies – dried bees for baldness, dead dogs, frogs and baked owls for gout, an *Aqua aromatica ad nobiles et matronas*. From what we know of Betson, we should be careful before we assume that the joke is on him – he too may have smiled wryly as he glanced at his source material. But of unassailable seriousness, and more worthy of our sympathy, are the pills and potions '*contra pestilenciam*' at a time when the Plague was still a real and constant threat, against which there was little that could be done, except, as the

---

[49] See Lalor (1995) and Macgill (1990).

Vadstena manuscripts tell us, to implore the assistance of heaven by prayers and masses.

One way to endorse a recipe was to cite it as having been used by royalty, both as a ploy to gain prestige, and also perhaps on the not unlikely assumption that royalty had access to the best advice and could afford the best ingredients. Betson does this only once, at image 111, folio 107r, line 12, for Tyngewich's *Aqua Nobilis* recipe for the eyes, requiring about 20 ingredients. Tyngewich was physician to Edward I, though Betson or his source changes this to Edward III. Bray was of course Physician to Edward III, and this may account for the error.

More practically, some of the ingredients in Betson's Remedies are often an element to make them palatable, or to act as a preservative. Honey is a good example of both, and appears 20 times in the Betson recipes, for example to remove the bitterness of *Spurges* or *Mustard*. Various gums e.g. *Storax*, are also commonly used to bind ingredients into pills, while perhaps also having a supposed medical effect.

Dangerous herbs seem to have been avoided by Betson or his sources in the Remedies – no Hemlock, Mandrake or Aconite. The latter two are not even in Betson's *Herbarium* list, though Bray has *Mandragora*. There are only three minor uses of Henbane in Betson (e.g. as a pain reliever for toothache and headache) and only one mention for Deadly Nightshade, in an *aqua vite* (Image 113 Right, Folio 109r, Line 12 onwards). Hellebore, which can also have dangerous repercussions, occurs only twice, as a laxative and to provoke purging. Its psychotropic effects, known from antiquity, are not mentioned. Pennyroyal, which can have an abortifacient effect, is mentioned 6 times in Betson though without any mention of its dangers, and once as actually aiding conception. The role of delivering a dead foetus is allocated to Rue and Mugwort, at image 95, folio 90v, line 9 and folio 91v, line 17.

Betson cites several kinds of pain-killers – two from poppies, one from Henbane, and one from *Quinquiracium*, whose identity is now uncertain. Henbane was of course well known in the mediaeval period, and formed the basis of John Arderne's surgical interventions for the *fistula in ano* – fistula in the anus, a condition doubtless rendered more painful by continuous riding on horseback. Henbane was also one of the major finds in the infirmary drains at Soutra Aisle in Scotland.[50]

Quinquiracium, which occurs in both Betson and Bray with the opiates, is extremely rare as a term, and does not seem to have been picked up by Hunt (1989)

---

[50] See Moffatt, (1987-1998).

in the 64 MSS of *Synonima* from the 11th to the 15th century which he examined.[51] It does however occur in Mirfield's *Sinonoma Bartholomaei,* and it seems probable that this was the ultimate source for both Betson and Bray. The exact identity of *Quinquiracium* appears to be lost, but its name is ultimately derived from Cyrenaica, now in Libya. A variety of the name, *Quirinacium,* is in the *Latin Galen* (Everett 2012), but the term seems to have been an invention of the Middle Ages. It has a parallel and perhaps precedent in another place-name among the opiates: *Opium Thebaicum,* from opium poppies originally grown at Thebes in Egypt. This term is in both Betson and Bray, and is fairly common in herbals.[52]

By the 15th century trade in spices was well established. Betson has chosen a number of recipes or remedies that call, for example, for Nutmeg (14 in all, if Mace is included), as well as Cinnamon (7). Cloves only feature in three recipes, and the supposedly ubiquitous mediaeval Cumin is also only in four samples. Garlic (while not strictly a spice) is also relatively absent, with only 3 mentions, while Saffron is rarely used at all.

Finally, we see once in Betson's Remedies the herbalist explaining his craft and prescription, not in any abstract terms of a plant's degrees of heat or cold, or of humours, or the motions of the stars, but in a straightforward description of its action on the patient:

'*Et nota quod Bugula tenet plagam apertam, Millefolium purgat, Sanicla sanat.*'[53]

[Note that Bugle keeps the wound open, Millefolium purges it, and Sanicle heals it.]

And it is certainly the herbalist speaking down to the surgeon when he goes on to state in the same paragraph that his cure is achieved solely by means of a potion:

'*sine instrumento sirurgico, et sine ferro, et sine ligno, et sine tenta.*'

[Without the use of a surgical instrument, or a knife, or any wooden implement, or of a probe.]

---

[51] Image 84 Left, Folio 79v, Col. A, Line 27. An unidentified plant. EMED gives '**Quirinaik,** the gum resin of the Old World *silphium*'. It is equated in Mowat, SB p.32 to *Ferula foetida,* Asafoetida. Its location in Betson's *Herbarium* next to *opium* suggests another opiate, perhaps its original use.

[52] In Mowat Alphita at p.129 as *Opium thebaicum idem succus papaveris albi.*

[53] Image 117 right, folio 113r, lines 12-15.

Betson's Choice of Remedies.

Betson's use of John Bray's *Sinonoma*, as one of the best available, meant that there was very little leeway for choice in the names of plants for his *Herbarium*. But the choice of remedies might have been more under Betson's control. Yet it is an eclectic collection, in which cosmetics and distilled aromatics, such as rose water, take up much space, and jostle for attention with serious medical conditions. This was however standard practice in the herbal from classical times to the Renaissance.

Betson lists around 450 remedies for various complaints. By far the largest number is for eye complaints (24 remedies). This probably reflects the easy transmission of some eye infections and the lack of clean water. It may also have been caused by the general smokiness of an environment where candles were the main form of lighting, and wood (or charcoal) the main form of fuel for heating and cooking. Perhaps reading religious books and missals in poor light, was also an added strain on the eyes, 'sore eyen' being the principal sub-category. The lack of spectacles, or use of unsuitable lenses may also have been another contributory factor. Spectacle frames were in fact found in the recent Syon Abbey archaeological excavations, though the glass was missing.[54]

Stomach problems also loom large, with 21 remedies, perhaps a reflection of the monastic life, and a poor, restricted and unbalanced diet, and continuous fasting. There are also several remedies for those with 'no talent to mete' meaning loss of appetite. Gout figures largely in the remedies, with 9 remedies, while 'dropsy' probably resulting from a variety of causes, but also related to diet, has 13 herbal treatments. There is also a range of remedies associated with strokes, such as loss of speech, palsy, apoplexy and paralysis. Fever, at 21 remedies, also cover a wide range, and interestingly these include both the tertian and quartan fevers, which are both characteristic of malaria, covered below in the case studies of this Introduction.

Occasionally Betson seems to have chosen a particularly luxurious recipe, such as that of Nicholas of Tynechewik (d.1339), image 111 right, folio 107r, lines 9-23. Here the recipe requires 18 ingredients, distilled over three days, and including the urine of a young boy, and breast milk. Not surprisingly it is an *'aqua aquarum nobilissima, pro omni causa et omni vitio oculorum'* [a most noble water of waters, for every purpose and every defect of the eyes.] Betson's *'Pomum Ambre'* (pomander) recipe is marked *'pro divitibus'* (for the rich – there were other lesser varieties for the poor), and has nine ingredients, including amber and exotic aromatic gums.

---

[54] See Bibliography: Wessex Archaeology, October 2003.

Another recipe at image 110 right, folio 106r, lines 1-15 differentiates between the wealth of different patients, *'secundum divitias et pauperitates patientis.'* It goes on to provide a long and involved recipe for a rich patient for a distilled water, which takes six days to make, and is to be stored in a gold or silver vase. The crown however must go to Betson's *Aqua vita perfectissima*, which has 37 ingredients, many exotic. It is immediately followed by a less expensive version of 13 ingredients, made from the more usual native British plants.[55]

One puzzling aspect is why Betson chose to place so much emphasis on female complaints which would not have presented themselves in an enclosed community of nuns. He lists over two dozen herbal applications, from conception to delivery, by way of lactation, inflammation of the nipples and diagnosis of pregnancy by uroscopy. For equal measure, there are a good number of complaints associated with the male genitalia. It is of course possible that the Herbal was compiled before Betson entered Syon Abbey, and was still fulfilling the functions of a parish priest in Wimbish in Essex. The range of required remedies would in that case have naturally been wider and have applied to both sexes.[56]

But we have in fact no indications when and why Betson wrote his Herbal. It may have merely reflected his wide range of interests. It might have been a way for him to check on the names of herbs being sold to the monastery by apothecaries, or recommended by physicians. We might also speculate (and it is no more than that) that it might have been a draft book to pass through the '*rota*' to the sisters side. This, however, seems rather unlikely, given the large amount of difficult Latin in the text. It also seems unlikely that his herbal was a draft for external publication. The market had moved on, and there was by 1500 a good supply of high quality herbals, illustrated with woodcuts, coming into England from the continent, for example the *Hortus Sanitatis* of which Syon had a copy, and which Betson as librarian may have seen.[57]

The Naming Of Plants.

1   Pagan Charms and Christian Names.

There appear to be no charms or spells in Betson, unlike those found in many mediaeval herbals. In fact, Betson chooses not to repeat a charm present in Mirfield's *Sinonoma Bartholomaei* (Mowat p.189) under 'Mullein':

---

[55] Image 107 right, folio 103r, line 12 onwards.

[56] We are grateful to Professor Vincent Gillespie for this suggestion. *Pers. Comm. August, 2014.*

[57] Syon *Registrum*, SS1.109, B.32. The *secundo folio* indicates a publication date between 1497 and 1517.

Tapsus Barbatus Maior....Molena...Pistatus cum pane grosso tritici, postea elixatus in vino rubeo et emplastratus circa manus ab intrante, domo eius inimicus exiet.

[Mullein..... if it is ground with large breadcrumbs, then added as an elixir in red wine, and used as a plaster around one's hand on entering a house, the enemy *(perhaps Devil)* will depart.]

These spells and charms could have a long lifetime. Gilbertus Anglicus had them, and noted that some believed that wounds could be cured by a charm (*divino carmine* - see Getz 1998 p.41). Even as late as the 1580s John Feckenham, the former Benedictine Abbot of Westminster Abbey, disgraced but miraculously alive as an orthodox and conservative Catholic, incorporated them into his *Sovereign Medicines*.

With regard to names of plants there are over seven hundred entries in Betson's *Herbarium* but surprisingly only a very small number of the names carry Christian connotations. These latter are most likely to be the popular names, or at least those popularised by the Church, and sometimes perhaps replacing pagan or obscene names. There are also a small number of names where a reference to the gods and goddesses of antiquity are retained, but these tend to be the 'learned' names, derived from classical pre-Christian sources.

Clearly deriving from Christianity is the ubiquitous 'St John's Wort', *Hypericon*, though several other plants bore this name. St John's Wort comes into flower around the summer solstice, close to the Eve and Nativity of St John the Baptist (23rd and 24th June). But Gilbertus Anglicus, at folio cccxix in the British Library copy of the *Compendium Medicinae* has a receipt for '*Oleum benedictun: in vigilia beati iohannis baptistae, collige iusquiamum in magna quantitate*' [Oleum Benedictum, on the vigil of St John the Baptist, gather henbane in great amounts] where it is plainly Henbane that is to be collected. St John's Wort was therefore only one of the herbs collected at that festival. There was also a sermon in the Syon library *de maleficiis in vigilia sancti Iohannis Baptiste* This is the intriguing but now untraceable '*Concerning Witches on the Eve of St John.*' which is attributed to St Augustine in the *Registrum* at N.64 (SS1.918).

Given its ancient name of *fuga demonum* and its high modern reputation, it is perhaps disappointing to find that Betson cites only one unlikely use for St John's Wort – *Ut Serpentes manu capias sine dampno: unge manum tuam cum succo Herbe Sancti Johannis Baptistis et non nocebis.* (To seize snakes by the hand without hurt, anoint your hand with the juice of the herb of St John the Baptist, and you shall take no harm.)[58]

Another contender for a religious name might be Betson's *Barba Aaron*, or *Arum maculatum*, lords and ladies. This plant had a more obscene folk name as an aphrodisiac, 'priest's pintle', still lurking in 'cuckoo pint' in modern English. The other old name, 'Wake Robin' is likewise a reference to the male organ and *Arum's* irritant effect.[59] *Barba Aaron* might be seen as a biblical reference, but perhaps it conflates Aaron of the Bible and his luxuriant beard, with a possible name from Dioscorides of *Aron*.

For those who like to beat the Oxford English Dictionary on earliest recorded dates for a word, or the University of Michigan Middle English Dictionary on entries, we have Samphere (modern Samphire) in Betson – not recorded in the EMED in this form, and not in the OED before 1542, (it is in *King Lear* by 1608). In the OED it is said to be a form of the French '*Saint Pierre*', but is also perhaps a variant of '*perce pierre*' - a stone crop name. Betson also has *Powder Holland*, as sort stomach settler. It is not in the EMED, and appears only in the OED in 1534. The problem with dating these entries is that parts of the Notebook may have been written post-Betson's death in 1517 – there is a suggestion of other unidentifiable hands at work.

Hemlock was also called *Herba Benedicta*, the blessed herb, and there may be an element here of not speaking the name of a particularly dangerous plant: it was a potent painkiller which could also bring death in its wake. Similarly Deadly Nightshade had its potency concealed and its name Christianised in Betson as *Herba Sancte Marie, Seynt Mary Bery*. In this context it is interesting to note that the vernacular name '*dwale*' meaning to stupefy, and used in Turner both for an anaesthetic drink containing Hemlock, and also as a name for Deadly Nightshade, does not occur in Betson. It is frequent in many mediaeval herbal texts, including Betson's source, Bray in Sloane MS 521, in a recipe for Dwale, where Hemlock, Henbane and Bryony (wyld nepe) appear, but Deadly Nightshade is omitted.[60]

There is also some mild clerical humour in naming – Cowslips are called *Herba Paradisi* - the flowers were seen as similar to the bunch of keys to the pearly gates of

---

[58] Image 99 right, Folio 95r, lines 1-3. See also Reeds (2012) for fuller discussion of *Hypericon perforatum L.* in folk medicine.

[59] See Grigson, (1958), pp.429-431 (*Arum maculatum*) and pp.290-291 for Deadly Nightshade and Dwale.

[60] Voigts, L. E. & Hudson R. P. (1992), pp. 34–56. See also Sloane MS 521 Folio 229/225/29v., Line 21.

paradise held by St. Peter, – hence the French and German folk names 'clef de Saint Pierre', 'Peters Blume'.[61]

But the main surprise in Betson is the number of plants listed by their classical Latin names – with Venus coming out as the main inspiration. The modern *Umbilicus rupestris*, Pennywort, was *Umbilicus veneris*; *Vervena officinalis*, Vervain, was *Herba Veneris*; while *Achillea millefolium*, Yarrow was *Supercilium veneris*. One 'Venus' name has survived into modern scientific usage: *Adiantum capillus-veneris*, or Maidenhair fern in the modern vernacular. It was *Capillus Veneris* in Betson.

Plant names also tend, like other words, to become obsolete and fall out of use. Betson and Bray both have variants of the now incomprehensible *Yekersteys* for cuckoo pint – *Yeke* being 'cuckoo', while '*tarse*' was a term for the 'penis' and still in use in 1530 (OED); but, like '*yerde*' and '*pint*' these terms have long since been replaced. Betson uses the word '*pintle*' for Sloane 3285's '*yerde*'. The use of '*pintle*' was however probably declining, and would be obsolete by 1600; the use of '*yerde*' would go on for another two centuries. It is therefore noticeable that Betson shows no hesitation in including words now considered vulgar from his text sources. But he uses less direct terms to refer to the female genitalia, using '*muliebria*' as a polite Latin alternative. This is not the case in other technical writers of the time: EMED carries a number of explicit mediaeval terms.

Celandine, *Chelidonium majus* had the English name 'Tetterwort', tetters then being a skin disease such as eczema and impetigo, supposedly cured by this plant. The meaning of 'tetters' is today no longer generally recognised, though 'wort' retains its place in herbal medicine as a suffix for curative herbs, just as the 'banes' are poisonous (Henbane, Wolfsbane and Cowbane). 'Wort' occurs throughout plant names in both Bray and Betson; 'bane' is present only as 'Henbane.'

2   Betson and the Greek Names of Plants.

There were few books in Greek in the library at Syon, none of them medical and it is fairly clear that Betson had little in the way of Greek language or reading skills.[62] Doyle (1956) gives a few examples of what he calls Betson's 'would-be Greek' and 'Greek by ear,' but there is no sustained written Greek text by Betson. He could manage the common χ *chi* symbol as in Palma Xti (Christi), and Hastula Sancti

---

[61] Image 77, Left, Folio 72v, Col. A, Line 3.

[62] See Bateson (1898), p.viii. The Greek texts were Erasmus's New Testament, the Psalter and Aratus, *Phenomena*; and the text of Proclus's *Sphaera* in Greek and in Linacre's Latin translation. See also Doyle, A. I. (1956).

Xtofori (Christofori). He was however dependent on his unreliable sources for latinised versions of the Greek names of plants. As a result, Betson can occasionally be seen struggling with the spelling of Greek terms, with variants appearing in the margins of his text. For example, at image 112 right, folio 108r, Betson has copied out *Diaconithon*, and then added in the right margin *Diacathicum*. His probable source was no help, since Sloane MS 1754 also appears to be corrupt at this point. Perhaps the text should have read '*Diacatholicon*', a purge or universal remedy, containing *inter alia* Senna and Rhubarb. It was in the *Antidotarium Nicholai*, at Betson's elbow, but according to the OED, did not arrive as a word in written English before 1562.[63]

Betson's uncertainty can also be partly ascribed to John Bray, his major source for the plant names in the *Herbarium*, who had been writing about a century before, in 1400, well before knowledge of Greek became more common in England. Even as late as 1538, in his *Libellus de Re Herbaria*, Turner was still complaining about the lack of Greek learning in the botanical area, and only one herbal in English – '*all full of unlearned cacographees* [mis-spellings] *and falselye naminge of herbes.*'

Betson, in compiling his herbal, perhaps died too early to benefit from the efforts of Thomas Linacre (*c*.1460–1524), who translated seven works by Galen into Latin from the original Greek. None of these had been previously published. These appeared from 1517 to 1524, after Betson's death (in February 1517). Fewterer, the Confessor- General, donated a copy of the earliest book to the library, a *Galienus de sanitate tuenda, cum aliis*, in an edition from Paris dateable to 1517 on *secundo folio* grounds, at B.23 (SS1.100).

3 Betson and Bray's List of Plant Names.

It is also beyond the scope of this book to look at the history of plant-names from the Greeks to Betson. What follows is a short summary of some of the more interesting uses to be found in Bray and Betson. The English herbalists of the early 1500s were dealing with five linguistic inheritances – Greek, Latin, Norman or Anglo-French, native English, and to a much lesser extent Arabic. Their ability in these languages varied (Arabic, Greek and French being their weakest), as did the range and ability of the languages themselves to handle technical matter. Greek and Latin had the advantage of accepted technical terms, a long tradition, but with many corruptions of spelling, compounded by misunderstanding of the differences in flora between the Mediterranean and Northern Europe. English was still developing its technical terms, and did not of course have the international intelligibility of Latin.

---

[63] This late date may reflect the lack of early medical texts in the OED noted by Hunt: the term appears in the Middle English translation of Guy de Chauliac c.1425.

It is also very likely that Betson and Bray had never seen a number of the more exotic plants they cite, which may have been rare in London at that time. They are thus reduced to repeating old tales about a world of mysterious possibilities. It still seemed possible to them that the legendary stone, the *Lapis Lyncis*, was fossilized Lynx urine or faeces; these were probably belemnite fossils. Mirfield similarly mocks those who assert that 'amber' came from whales – of course it came from trees. Perhaps he had seen neither amber nor ambergris. And he also affirms, like many others, that the Narcha fish, some sort of electric eel, gave rise to the term 'narcotic'.[64] And perhaps, as Betson asserts, cashew nuts really were elephant lice, or was this just an apothecary's misunderstood witticism?

Given the large influence that writers in Arabic, both Christian and Muslim, had on western medicine in the period, it is surprising not to find more Arabic terms in Betson or Bray. Even where these occur, Bray seems to have adopted a corrupt form of the Arabic terms. This can be seen in two examples. Bray has *Libleb* and Betson *Lablis* for Dog's Mercury (Mercurialis perennis).[65] Simon of Genoa (fl. circa 1200), with perhaps better access to Arab sources, is more informative: under '*Alhulbub*' he states: '*yelbub est mercurialis et iebub et halbub.*' Again, looking at Betson's '*Binni robenet*' and Bray's '*Ben iubium*', these on closer inspection turn out to be the Arabic for Red and White '*Behen.*'[66] These plants are completely different and non-native to Britain. They both happen to be astringent, and are thus lumped together in our text.

4   English Names in Betson and Bray.

With regard to English plant names, most of Betson's (derived from Bray) in the *Herbarium* are well attested from other sources, such as the 64 MSS cited by Hunt. The main problem is the lack of any standardisation of spelling and use of names. Hunt regularly cites four or more possible modern names for one mediaeval name. Mediaeval *Scabiosa* has five mediaeval names. This could be critical, since *Morel* might be the dangerous *Atropa belladonna*, Deadly Nightshade, or the less noxious *Succisa pratensis*, (Moench), Devil's Bit Scabious. It took several more centuries after Betson before the flora could be identified and named in a scientific fashion.

---

[64] Mowat, Alphita, p.123, and Image 83, right, Folio 79r, Col. A, Line 13. The Greek term from which 'narcotic' is derived means to benumb, deaden. OED.

[65] Image 83, left, folio 78v, col. A, line 31.

[66] Image 77, left, folio 72v, col. B, lines 21-23. The white is *Centaurea Behen*, White Behen. The red is *Statice Limonium*, Sea Lavender or Red Behen

5   **Latin Names.**

Betson and Bray were drawing on a Latin tradition which ultimately goes back to Pliny's *Natural History*, of which there was copy in Syon library. But many new Latin works had been created in the intervening period, including some by translation into Latin from the Greek via Arabic.

Betson probably had better Latin than Bray: Bray produces the extraordinary Latin spoonerism - *Fecula cotidia* for *Cotula fetida*, Mayweed. Betson has the correct term for oak apple – *pomum quercinum*, while Bray or his copyist has *pomum porcinum*, perhaps by analogy with *Rostrum porcinum*, Sowthistle. The Bray variant does not appear to be attested elsewhere and is most likely an error. Sometimes Latin and French names appear intertwined: *malum granatum* and *pomme garnet* for our modern pomegranate.[67] And finally there is the charming *Herba Luminaria*, the Latin name for Mullein (*Vebascum thapsus*). This refers to the use of Mullein as a wick, soaked in fat, for a kind of torch. Mowat cites a number of such Mullein names, including 'Torches' and '*Candela Regia*' - an unexpected insight into the use of one plant in the past.

6   **French Names.**

French, and Norman French are generally absent from Betson, and he does not attempt to transmit the French names found in Bray. Even in Bray's time knowledge of French must have been limited: Mistletoe is cited by Bray in perhaps a 'heard' version, as Wilde Cheyn, (= French *gui de chêne*, oak mistletoe). Meanings have also shifted: the French *Pee de pulayn* (meaning *coltsfoot*) is used in Bray for *Arum maculatum*, whereas our modern English 'Coltsfoot' is now *Tussilago farfara* – a completely different plant with different uses. Dandelion of course occurs in Bray and Betson, but in the French spelling only (Dent de lyon). It had the additional mediaeval Latin name of *Caput Monachi* – Monk's Head, referring to its baldness (and the monk's tonsure) once its seeds have blown away. Bray and Betson march in complete agreement in their texts, with *Caput Monachi*, *Dens Leonis*, Lyons Toth and Dent de Lyon.[68]

Both Betson and Bray use variants of the French '*Chastaynes*' for the modern word 'Chestnut'. The OED shows that modern 'Chestnut' is only recorded from 1519, so was perhaps just gaining ground at the time of Betson's death. Similarly, modern 'Mustard' is absent from Bray and Betson, but variants of '*senevei*' (from Latin via Old French; cf. modern German 'senf') are used.

---

[67] Image 79 right, folio 75r, col. B, lines 25 and 27.

[68] Image 77 right, Folio 73r, Col. B, Line 14.

Both Bray and Betson carry variants of what appears to be the Norman French *'Tutsan'* for *agnus castus*.[69] *'Tutsan'* is now used for *Hypericon androsaemum* in modern French. Turner (1548) uses *Tutsan* in this French sense, so perhaps the two uses had co-existed in England in the mediaeval period and up to the Renaissance. He states: *'Androsaemon is the herbe (as I dooe gesse) whiche we call totsan, and the Poticaries falsly cal Agnus castus.'* (OED).

Linguistic Analysis of Betson's English.

The web-based University of Edinburgh eLALME project allows for over 400 linguistic markers, differentiated by both grammar and spelling, to be plotted onto a map of Britain, against a large database of similar documents in Middle English from 1350 up to about 1450. Betson is somewhat later – perhaps 1440s to 1517. But it seemed worthwhile to make the attempt, since many of Betson's speech habits will have been in part laid down within the eLALME timespan.

Two sets of Middle English texts were used to triangulate Betson's dialect – (i) the complete English text of the remedies, and (ii) the text of the Ten Commandments at image 15 left, column A, folios 10v to 11v. (not included in this book). We have assumed that the latter is Betson, writing in his own voice.

Betson was certainly not the author of the text of the remedies, and there is some doubt as to whether he was the writer of all these sections. But the doubtful inscriptions are few and short, and should not affect the overall outcome. The result from eLALME shows a strong correlation between two points on the map. These are, in the first place, Essex locations around Billericay, and Sudbury in Suffolk. We do not know if Betson came from Essex, but it *may* be significant that, according to Ian Doyle, someone of the same name was Rector of Wimbish in Essex from 1466 (i.e. prior to Betson joining Syon Abbey in 1481). If this is correct, then eLALME may indicate that Betson was still using some dialect and writing conventions acquired early in his life, and changing his manuscript sources to a written form of his own dialect.

The other eLALME cluster for the English remedies is around Rochester in Kent: this may in fact be indicative of the dialect influence of Sloane 3285, which seems to have been a major Betson source for Remedies, or at least to share a common ancestor with Betson's text. Sloane 3285 is described as coming in part from Sussex, 'somewhere close to the northern border with Kent'. Care must be exercised here, because the analysis of Sloane 3285 was also carried out using

---

[69] See Image 75 left, Folio 70v, Col. B, line one; Toteseyn in Betson, Tutsayne in Bray.

eLALME.⁷⁰ But if correct, it looks as if in this case Betson simply copied this particular text, rather than amending it to suit his own speech habits.

From the above, it does not seem that Betson, despite having practised as a lawyer for several years, had approximated his writing to the new Chancery Standard English. Its use was expanding from the 1470s onwards under the influence of books printed by Caxton from 1473, then Wynkyn de Worde, and more elegantly, by Pynson from 1491, with all three aiming at a form of more widely intelligible English.

The second source for Betson's English is a religious miscellany in the Notebook, including the Ten Commandments, This seems to be part of the foul papers for Betson's *Ryght Profytable Treatyse Drawen out of Dyuerse Wrytynges to Dyspose Men to Be Vertuously Occupyed in Theyr Myndes and Prayers* (Wynkyn de Worde, c.1500). Analysis of Betson's own Notebook text at images 15 and 16, folios 10v to 12r by means of eLALME also suggests a location in Essex, at Billericay. Betson can then be fairly confidently identified as being from Essex.

Syon and the Care of its Sick:
Case Studies of Diseases and Forms of Treatment.
The differing rules of the Brothers and the Sisters at Syon both contain sections on the management of their mutual infirmaries (whose locations at Syon have yet to be uncovered by archaeology).⁷¹ These were only for the community – there is no suggestion of care for outsiders. For both sides the emphasis is on the spiritual as well as the physical healing: the Brothers' Keeper , for example, should 'styre, exhorte, and comforte them *(the sick)* to be confessyd *and* receive the sacraments of holy chirche.' He is also responsible for setting out the items needed for the last rites 'whan any brother is to anelyd...' [*to be anointed*.]

This is in addition to being 'strong and mighty to lift and move them...often change ther bedding and other clothes, ley to her [*their*] plasteres, give hem ther medicyns and mynster unto them mete and drynke, fyre water and other necessaryes nyght and day after the counsel of the physician....'

There is a fine character portrait of the qualities needed in a Keeper to treat both physical and mental illnesses: 'not squames [*squeamish*] to handle hem and wash hem; not angry nor unpaciente, though one have the vomett, another the flyxe, another the frensy - now cryeng, now syngynge, now chidying, now fyghtyng. For

---

⁷⁰ Loen-Marshall, Maria-Helena (2005).

⁷¹ Chapter lvii, pp.126-128 in Hogg (1980) and *Rule Of Our Most Holy Saviour* (1914).

ther be some maner of sekeness that provoke the seke to angyr, and when the matry is drawn into the brayn, it alyeneth ther mendes [minds].'

The sick brother, if he recovered, was required to do public penance ('take hys veyne') for his absence from services during his sickness. This was a common feature in monastic rules (also in the Benedictine), though strange to our modern way of thinking, where illness is generally not seen as divine punishment for sin. The Additions for the sisters give further details on how the recovered nun is to behave: *'...kneeling before the Abbess she shall say "Mother, with your leave I have been for some time in the Infirmary, and I have transgressed in meat, drink and many other ways, not keeping the regular times of eating, drinking and sleeping and the like, wherefore I do crave mercy and pardon." And then the Abbess shall impose upon her some penance......'* (1914 translation)

Finally it is worth noting that personal hygiene was not ignored. The Remedies section of Betson's Notebook contains several recipes for soap. One in particular is for making a bushel at a time. This is around 80lbs or 36 kilos and probably enough to provide the Syon community with one pound of soap each at each making.[72] There are also recipes for making a coarser black soap – presumably for cleaning rooms rather than for personal use.

1 Malaria.

We have no direct evidence of Malaria at Syon Abbey, but the disease was at that time endemic in parishes along the River Thames and in the coastal marshes in Essex and Kent. Its distinctive symptoms allow it be identified as far north as Lancashire and the Solway Firth on the West Coast, and in Lincolnshire on the East, even as late as the beginning of the 20th century.[73] We know also that the first foundation of Syon at Twickenham was abandoned after a short time because of the unhealthiness of the location.

The British variety of Malaria was not the deadly *P. falciparum*, but two lesser varieties which debilitated rather than quickly killing their victims. Dobson, in his article *The History of Malaria in England*, identifies five British species of mosquito capable of carrying the parasites, and one in particular which lived in close proximity to humans (*A. atroparvus*) as the likely culprit in transmitting *'vivax malaria'* – the so-called 'benign' form in Britain. Betson and the authors of his herbal sources are unlikely to have identified mosquitoes as a source of malarial fevers. More likely they saw only the miasma, damp and fogs of the Thames.

---

[72] Image 94 left, Folio 89v, Lines 3-27.

[73] See: Dobson, M. J. (1989) for summary and bibliography on this topic.

Malaria was generally diagnosed in the Middle Ages by the periodicity of the three fever symptoms – 'quotidian' 'tertian' and 'quartan'. Quotidian occurred every 24 hours, tertian had a 48 hour periodicity (i.e. recurred every three days), and quartan with a periodicity of 72 hours, was classed as occurring every four days. These periodicities are now known to be associated with the lifecycle of the individual malarial parasites.[74]

Another symptom of Malaria is enlargement of the spleen. It is interesting to note therefore that both 'tertian' and 'quartan' fevers, and illnesses of the spleen, appear regularly in Betson's remedies. Two of the herbs in his *Herbarium* are qualified by the *Sinonoma Bartholomei* as being useful against the 'quartan' (*'Camedreos'* - Germander Speedwell and *Gramen amcaste* – Couch Grass). Camomile is cited as good 'for the hede ake and brennyng (burning) ague' probably malarial and producing alternate hot and cold agues.[75] Betony and Parsley are cited against the 'Fever Tercian', Vervain for both tertian and quartan.[76] Basil is stated to be useful for quartan fever, and may indeed reduce fever.[77]

The modern *Tanacetum parthenium* or 'Feverfew' is not specifically identified by Betson with 'tertians' or 'quartans', but he has the annotation '*febrifu*' against Henbane perhaps as a generic treatment for fevers, rather than an alternative name for Henbane.[78] *Tanacetum*, as *Febrifuge Maior* is only mentioned by Betson in the context of the Plague (image 117 left, folio 112v).

Malaria did not of course spare the noble or the rich: Catherine of Aragon, when still Dowager Princess of Wales (i.e. before her second marriage, to Henry, in 1509) was believed to have had 'tertian ague' or acute fever at one stage, perhaps contracted in England. The Surgeon to Henry VIII for many years, Sir William Butts died of a complicated variety of the fever, diagnosed as 'dooble febre quartanz.' Henry VIII himself is said to have had an attack of 'ague' just before he died.

---

[74] "Quotidian fever, with a periodicity of 24 hours, typical of *Plasmodium falciparum* or *Plasmodium knowlesi* ; Tertian fever (48 hour periodicity), typical of *Plasmodium vivax* or *Plasmodium ovale* malaria; Quartan fever (72 hour periodicity), typical of *Plasmodium malariae* malaria". Wikipedia, 7 July 2014

[75] Image 97 left, Folio 92v, Line 33.

[76] Image 97 left, Folio 92v Lines 8-9, 13 & Image 97 right, Folio 93r, Line 11.

[77] Christina Stapley of Heartsease, *Pers. Comm.* Aug 2014

[78] Image 79, Right, Folio 75r, Col. B, Line 2.

Urine could be used for diagnosis of Malaria. In the *Harntraktat* text cited by Betson there is the chilling comment '*Urina Nigra*: *In quartarna semper est mortalis et mala*'. And also '*Urina lucida sicut cornu* (urine transparent like horn) *significat indispositiones splenis et indispositiones quartarne*'. [79]

Blood-letting was used regularly as one of the means treating fevers. Quotidian, tertian and quartan fevers are all included in the 15th century Gonville and Caius MS 176/97 on phlebotomy, which has the added interest of being early, in English and of a technical nature.[80] Lines 161-162 state that: '*the 3^{en} (tertian) wiche ofte tymes is curid of phlebotomie…..*'(by bloodletting). The tertian and quartan fevers are covered in some detail in lines 189 to 206, with recommendations for herbal treatment – '*electuary frigidum and confortative of the stomach, as succar ros(arum) & triasandalis.*' This casts a somewhat different light on Betson's several recipes for preserving roses, if it is suggesting that they may have been administered against malarial fevers.

By way of comparison, it is noticeable that Feckenham in his *Sovereign Medicines* (early 1580s) also has a considerable number of remedies aimed at the quotidian, tertian and quartan agues (remedies 74-83). His audience was the poor without access to physicians, and his remedies are consequently for the most part homely and inexpensive, such as snail shells, Mouse-ear Hawkweed (*Pilosella officinarum*), nettles and cobwebs.

2 The Sweating Sickness and Syon.

In 1552, on the occasion of the fifth (and final) outbreak in England of the Sweating Sickness, the renowned physician John Caius published a short book on the topic, setting out his views on the causes, preventative measures and remedies.[81] This was the first book to appear in English dedicated to one disease. He noted that the illness seemed to have appeared with the arrival from France of the future Henry VII at Milford in Wales on 7th August 1485, and killed numerous people in London by October of that year, sparing neither aristocracy nor bourgeoisie. There were subsequent visitations in 1488, 1506, July to December 1517, and May to July 1528.

The Sweating Sickness may have visited Syon in 1488, when there is a run of increased mortality recorded in the Syon *Martyrologium*. The brothers were first to suffer: lay brother Robert Bryde on 16 May, the Confessor General Thomas Westhawe on 1 June, Brother Robert Derham on 4th June and lay Brother Robert

---

[79] Image 89 left, Folio 84v, Line 4, and Image 89 left, Folio 84v line 5.

[80] Voigts, Linda E., & Mcvaugh Michael R. (1984).

[81] See: https://archive.org/stream/thesweatingsickn33503gut/33503.txt

Hall on 7 June. It then affected both the brothers and the sisters - Robert Frynge, priest, and Sister Alice Hutton (aged c.80), died on 10 June, Sister Isabel Lambourn on 15 June, Sister Catherine Dymock on 17 June, Sister Marion Cross on 4 July, Sister Catherine Fogg on 2 October and Sister Joan Payne 20 October.[82] There is another peak in deaths at Syon between March and August 1508, which may possibly have been associated with a recurrence of the Sweating Sickness.[83]

The Syon mortality figures imply deaths of about 10% of the sisters, and perhaps a similar mortality for the male religious, including priests and lay brothers. Dyer's study of 1997 gives an estimate of only between 1.2 and 2.2% mortality in England in those parishes where records have survived. He does however have one peak at Farnworth in Lancashire of over 10%, and possible other samples at 5% and 7%. Perhaps inclusion of data from the enclosed religious communities might have yielded higher figures overall. If the Sweating Sickness was, as some suggest, a highly infectious pulmonary condition, then joint male and female attendance at church services, and even closer auricular confession of the sisters by the confessors might have provided the vector route.

There is no mention *per se* of the Sweating Sickness in Betson, and none of the ingredients cited by Caius in his cures seem to match any remedy in Betson. The link between Syon's increased mortality in 1488 and the Sweating Sickness cannot therefore be affirmed with certainty, though it seems a probable cause.

3 Toothache.

Toothache is the only condition picked out in red in the Syon copy of Gilbertus Anglicus.[84] Betson has seven mentions of teeth and rotting gums, treated variously with Lesser Celandine tied to the finger, powdered Roses, a distillation of Cloves (probably useful as a pain-killer), Garlic or Yarrow. There is also a teeth whitener, *farinam ordei, sal, mel et acetum (barley meal, salt, honey and vinegar)*. Loose teeth are to be fixed by an application of horse dung.[85] Clearly dentistry was an area of medicine in its infancy.

---

[82] Strangely, she is not recorded as being buried like the other sisters in the abbey church at Syon.

[83] John Colet, Dean of St. Paul's, realising he had the Sweating Sickness, retired to Sheen Priory (Carthusian), opposite Syon Abbey, and died there on the 16th of September 1519. British History on-line: The Priory of Sheen, citing Wood's *Athenæ Oxonienses* (Bliss), i. 26.

[84] Bodarwé (2002, p260), cites arrangements for the pulling of teeth.

[85] See Appendix 3, 'Teeth and Gums', for text references.

4 Breast Cancer.

The well-researched higher incidence of breast cancer among nuns seems to have first been described clinically in 1713 by Bernardo Ramazzini in his book on occupational diseases.[86] Monica Green also draws attention to one mediaeval explanation of breast cancer in women, based on the corruption of blood: '*The unexpelled menstrual blood was diverted up to the breasts through special veins that connected them to the uterus…*'. [87]

Betson mentions '*kancur*' only once in this context, at image 105 left, folio 100v, lines 1-4.

> For the kancur in a Woman's pappis: Take the penns [*wing feathers*] of the white gose [*goose*] and the juse of Cellidony [*Greater Celandine*] and bray [*crush*] them well to gider, and ley therof to the sore pappe.

Greater Celandine (*Chelidonium maius*), powdered with rose petals, and mixed with vinegar, is also cited in *Circa Instans* as being useful against cancers in the mouth or those external to the body. But the plant is categorised as a 'powerful irritant' by Grieve in her herbal.[88] Another suggested use by Betson and his sources on the eyes is therefore of considerable danger.[89]

5 Tuberculosis (TB).

TB would have a been a constant risk in large monastic communities with a hundred or more individuals attending church services, eating and sleeping in close proximity to each other. 'Thisic' – probably TB, is one of the first illnesses noted in Betson.[90] The illness, it is claimed, produces '*urina rubea*' (image 34 right, folio 30r, line 2), though this colour of urine is also cited as a sign for eight conditions in all, including death, and so a reminder that urine may not have been a very accurate diagnostic tool. It is also in the same text associated with *Periplimonia:* abscesses on the lungs, again perhaps TB. Betson has palliative remedies for '*thisicis*' involving

---

[86] Ramazzini, Bernardo (1713).

[87] Green, Monica H. (2010).

[88] See on-line version at: http://botanical.com/botanical/mgmh/c/celgre43.html

[89] Image 106 left, folio 101v, lines 7-17 and Image 111 right, folio 107r, line 24 onwards.

[90] Betson lacks the detailed descriptions of TB contained, for example, in the *Breviarium Bartholomaei* of Mirfield under *De Ptisi*. See Hartley and Aldridge (1936) pp.74-89 for Latin and English text of symptoms and treatment.

distilled alcohol and camphor (image 113 left, folio 108v, line 10), which might have alleviated the coughing.

The 'perilose kogh', as perhaps one of the symptoms of TB (see EMED entry), receives two mentions, at image 101 right, folio 97r, lines 15-19, and image 112 right, folio 108r, line 4. Here the remedies are Rue, Pepper, Sage, Milk of Almonds and Wild Celery, again perhaps as palliatives. There are also two remedies for 'spitting blood' (image 101 left, folio 96v, lines 25-30), which involve Betony, Rue, Wild Celery, Mint and goat's milk. Against this there is the unhygienic practice mentioned at Image 98 Right, folio 94r, line 23, of adding sputum and mercury to a remedy for skin complaints.[91]

Finally, in the Additions to the Rule there is an injunction, unconnected to TB, which prohibits spitting on the steps going up to the dormitory, unless one stubs it out with one's foot. This perhaps was a safety measure, born of experience of slippery stone stairs in the dark.

6   A Case of Leprosy at Syon c.1487.

Carole Rawcliffe (2006, p279) draws attention to a case of leprosy at Syon around 1487, when the then Abbess, Elizabeth Muston, (1456-1497) petitioned Rome for permission to remove immediately Nicholas Edward, a leprous monk, for fear that the infection might spread to the rest of the community. The papal reply allowed her to remove both Nicholas Edward, and any other member of the community (nun or brother) who might in future be afflicted with leprosy or any other contagious disease, to a place assigned to receive them.[92] This approach by the Abbess to Rome was of course necessitated by the nature of the perpetual vows of the sufferer, who was not permitted to leave the monastery without dispensation.

Betson, who may have been aware of this case, has four references to Leprosy in his Remedies, including an oil, *Oleum Leprosorum*, made from violets or using a live snake.[93] In this context, Rawcliffe (2006, p279) also notes a case of Leprosy at Sempringham Priory (Gilbertine double monastery, 1131-1538), where the novice mistress was shunned, because she had massaged a leprosy sufferer with an ointment.

---

[91] fasting spattill: 'the spittle of one observing a fast or eating sparingly.' EMED.

[92] Calendar of Papal Registers , Papal Letters Vol XV, 1484-92, p42, Item 76, 29 July 1487, *Reg. Lat. 846 A, folios 24 1r – 24 1v.*

[93] Image 109 left, folio 104v, lines 3-6; image 112 right, folio 108r, lines 16-17 & 18-24; image 109 left, folio 104v, lines 4-5 & *Oleum Leprosorum*: image 121 right, folio 117r, line 21.

Betson's sources also suggest the use of calamine or zinc ore, presumably for its soothing effect. There is also a very long and complicated *Aqua Mirabilis*[94] for lepers involving 13 ingredients, mainly metals-based, and only for the rich. A cheaper variety was available for the poor. Betson's source indicates that this remedy is also good for *Lepra non vera* or 'false leprosy', showing perhaps the difficulty of diagnosing this disease correctly. Betson also cites an *Aqua vite perfecta* which seems to have been a cure-all, including leprosy of the face. This was the part of the body where leprosy was most frequently noticed, as being the most difficult to conceal.[95]

7   Blood-Letting.

Detailed accounts of blood-letting (*minutio*) in male monastic orders in around 1300 are given in Clark[96] (1897) pp.lxi – lxxiii. The authority for this practice was Galen, the most respected and available of the ancients, in his *de curandi ratione per venae sectionem*. The purpose was not only to relieve illness, but also to prevent it, by reducing the amount of surplus blood which might turn into 'corrupt material'. For women there was the added concern that failure to menstruate allowed corrupt blood to remain in the body and cause illness. Even animals were not exempt – horses were also blooded on St Stephen's day (26th December).

Blood-letting took place in some orders by organised rota, in others by personal choice. The frequency of bleeding varied – the Cistercians were bled four times a year and the Augustinian Canons eight times. We do not know the frequency of bloodletting at Syon, nor if it varied between the brothers and the sisters.

Betson and Bray mention only one location in the body for bloodletting (at image 86 left, folio 81v, col. B,) the Salvatelle, involving four veins, which occur in both the foot and the hand. In Bray's precise terms it is 'Bytwene the litel finger & the next fenger & upon the foote in the same place'. The left vein on the left side of the body was believed to affect the spleen, and on the right the liver.[97]

Most medical books of the time had fuller sections on blood-letting than Betson, the most popular being the *Regimen Sanitatis Salerni*, which existed in most mediaeval libraries in Britain. (It is in six houses in the BL *Corpus*). Syon had an AD 1480 printed copy from Cologne at K.13 (SS1.623c), and possibly another at B.29

---

[94] Image 110 right, folio 106r, lines 11-13.

[95] Dietary and medical treatments, including herbs, are given in Rawcliffe (2006), pp. 213-251.

[96] Also on web: http://archive.org/stream/observancesinuse00claruoft/observancesinuse00claruoft_djvu.txt

[97] Clendening, (1960) p286-287.

(SS1.106), with an unidentified phlebotomy at B11 (SS1. 88g) by Maurus of Salerno. Vadstena had a *Phlebotomia,* partly in Swedish, at MS UU C19.

It is unclear as to how, and by whom, the blood-letting was performed at Syon. If it was carried out on a regular but restricted basis (in order not to affect attendance at services adversely), then a month of daily blood-letting might allow all 60 sisters to be both bled and to recuperate for three days in small batches of five or six. This would need to be repeated for a whole month four times a year. It suggests that blood-letting by a trained brother or sister would be more efficient than calling on an external practitioner, but we do not know the practice at Syon.

Finally, it may be worth mentioning in this context that the leech or blood-sucker, *sanguisuga,* is not mentioned in Betson despite his inclusion in the *Herbarium* of animals of the witches' brew, such as bats and newts.[98]

Whatever the situation with regard to blood-letting at Syon, medical treatment of the sisters by a resident physician seems, according to the Additions to the Rule, to have been unlikely: 'If any suster be so seke that sche may not be couered with oute medicine, sche schal be brought to the crates to the physician'.[99] This exception was expressly permitted by the papal decree *Beata Clara*[100] under Pope Boniface VIII (1294-1303): *A doctor is excluded from the above law (prohibiting entrance to a convent), on the grounds of serious illness (in a nun).*

8 Other Arrangements for the Sick at Syon.

There is extant a papal dispensation for Richard Wyot at Syon, of 3 Sept 1457, who had, when subjected to the strictness of the rule fallen 'often and gravely ill'. He was allowed to transfer to another order of milder observance.[101] A similar permission was granted to on John Pinchbeck on 8 Jan 1462, who could no longer 'with a quiet mind and a good conscience dwell' at Syon, to take himself to some mendicant order. A similar papal letter of 27 March 1501 carries an intriguing insight into the Syon pardons and treatment of the sick.[102] 'The faithful of those

---

[98] Leeches are recommended in Avicenna's *Canon of Medicine*, Sections 1037-1043, p.512, Gruner, 1929. See also EMED for medical citations.

[99] The 'crates' were either the iron grating around the public area of the church, or a grating between the external and internal part of the monastery, and not necessarily the grille within the church.

[100] Cited in Bodarwé (2002, p259 and footnote 135).

[101] *Papal Letters*, Vol. 11, 1455-1464, pp. 151-2

[102] *Papal Letters*, p97, no.91, Reg. Vat. 844, fos 89v-92r

parts are singularly devoted to it [Syon Abbey], and a great multitude flock to it.' The Confessor-General may therefore 'appoint some places for the healthy, others for the sick and aged' to hear mass at a portable altar. There is of course no suggestion or evidence that Syon or its nuns cared for the sick in a formal fashion on these occasions, or in any general way.

It may also be worth mentioning in the context of healthcare that a number of nunneries took in as sisters (presumably against a cash payment) those who were deformed or insane. Jacka cites a number of houses where the episcopal visitation turned up sisters who were *'lunatica'*, *'ideota'*, or *'a fole'*, as well as deaf and dumb, or an *'idiot fool'*.[103] Again we have no evidence for this at Syon

There are no mentions of smallpox or syphilis in Betson, nor of any plants associated with their treatment or cure, though both diseases were known.

9   Uroscopy.

Neither Dioscorides nor Galen appears to have used urine as a means of diagnosing diseases, apart from for urinary tract infections. But diagnosis of disease and prognosis of its course by the examination of urine was one of the basic tests introduced to the west by the Salerno School of Medicine. In particular the *de Urinis* of Maurus of Salerno (c.1130-1214) was one of the major works to which physicians of the 12th and 13th century referred. It was present in at least three houses in Britain, but appears to be absent from the Syon library catalogue.

Syon had however around twenty titles on uroscopy, in some 10 volumes, including most of the classic texts. These included a copy of Theophilus (fl. ? 7th century), *de Urinis*, at B.30 (SS1.107e), in a Latin translation. This was a common text, recorded in at least a dozen British houses or colleges according to the BL *Corpus*.

Theophilus served as a source of Giles de Corbeil's poem of the same name, *de Urinis,* also present at Syon at B.5 (SS1.82x and SS1.82cc), but probably in manuscript form. This too was a popular work – 15 recorded copies in Britain. The commentary by Gilbertus Anglicus on Corbeil's *de Urinis* was also at Syon, one of five copies recorded in Britain. There was also a copy of the *Liber urinarum* by Isaac Iudaeus, translated by Constantinus Africanus, and printed at Lyon in 1515. Bateson notes that this title was used in the Paris medical course, and its popularity is shown by its presence in at least a dozen British houses.[104] Finally, Syon had the sole recorded copy in Britain of Walter Agilon's *Compendium urinarum* at B.5 (SS1.82z). Despite

---

[103] Jacka (1917, chapter 1, p7-8).

[104] Bateson (1898) p14, footnote 3.

this selection of useful academic works, Betson's main source of information on uroscopy in his Notebook, as we have already noted, was the *Harntraktat*, (image 88 right to image 90 right, folios 84r to 86r), which was probably not at Syon Abbey.

Although there is no indication of the use for diagnosis at Syon, uroscopy could no doubt also act as a protection for an abbey against unsuitable female candidates seeking to become novices. Vitalis' diagnostics allow for both a virginity test (image 89 right, folio 85r, lines 25-27) and a pregnancy test (lines 12 – 19, applicable even in the first few months of pregnancy), as well as detection of recent sexual intercourse with a man (lines 27-29). Similar urine diagnostics for virginity, pregnancy, and intercourse are repeated at image 34 right, folio 30r, lines 7-15. [105]

Finally although the era relied regularly on with diagnosis by urine, Gilbertus Anglicus was aware of the symptoms of diabetes, such as 'continual thirst, dryness of the mouth, emaciation, inordinate appetite, frequent and profuse urination' but he does not mention the taste of sugar in the urine. Certainly diagnosis by the smell of urine is often mentioned by practitioners as one of the signs for diabetes.[106] It may be because tasting and touching the urine had been rejected by Avicenna as "objectionable".[107] Apart from his long citation of the *Harntraktat*, Betson also cites several other examples of the diagnosis by the use of urine. For example, at image 104 right, folio 100r, line 28 onwards:

> Recipe urine of him that is seke, and kast it on a Rede Netill at ones whan he hath pist, and come agen at the morrow, and if the Netill be not dede, it is a token of lif. And if it be dede, he shal dy.

This strange diagnostic technique, which occurs in other herbals, seems to lean towards charms (of which Betson is singularly free). The 'rede netill' is probably the Red Dead Nettle, *Lamium purpureum,* a dead Dead Nettle, with no sting.

Menstruation is beyond the scope of this text. It is covered in detail by Green (2005). Betson shows no hesitation in mentioning it in his Notebook, and uses the standard terms '*flouris*' and *menstrua.*

---

[105] See Green (2011) p179, *de Urinis Mulierum* for further discussion of the source of this text.

[106] *per odorem* – see Image 34 Right, folio 30r, line 3 for the other signs.

[107] See Avicenna, *Canon of Medicine,* Inspection of Urine, Section 606, p325, Gruner, 1929.

20   Mental Health and Syon – A Case Study in Love.

We know little of the passions and frustrations which may have driven some of the religious, male and female, of this community. There is however one outstanding example. In 1915 Margaret Deanesly unpicked the doomed literary relationship of James Grenehalgh, professed 1495 as a monk at Sheen Priory (Carthusian, 1414-1539) just across the River Thames, and Joanna Sewell at Syon who was professed in 1500.[108] Bateson suggests that the two had met during Sewell's year's novitiate, which would have customarily been spent outside Syon, before her profession.

Grenehalgh gave Sewell a number books that he had laboriously copied out (including the perhaps ambiguous *Incendium Amoris* - The Bonfire of Love), and added their intertwined initials, with IG and IS forming IGS. Of these five still survive.[109] There is some evidence that they may have met together on Thursday, 13th February 1504, the Vigil of St Valentine's Day, though, as Sargent points out, this would have been contrary to both Bridgettine and Carthusian discipline.

Grenehalgh also gives advice on diet to Sewell. He selects a passage from Hilton's *Scala Perfectionis*: 'That manner of food that least checks and least troubles the heart, and may keep the body in strength – be it flesh, be it fish, be it bread, be it ale – that I believe the soul chooses to have, if it may come by it.'   Grenehalgh, who as a Carthusian was forbidden meat, adds for Sewell's benefit: 'Follow not the book in this, but rule according to discretion, and take counsel.' [110]

But it is Grenehalgh's copy of the *Scala Perfectionis* which takes on a more ominous note of counsel. It contains a text addressed directly to the devil and almost in the form of an exorcism - *'Discede, liquesce.'* [111] (*Go thy way and melt to nought* in one elegant mediaeval translation).[112] There is also a sketch of a church building, presumably that at Syon, in which the name of Joanna Sewell is placed in

---

[108] Deanesly (1915). See also Sargent (1984), and Kerby-Fulton, Hilmo, and Olson, 2012.

[109] British Library BL Add 24661, Richard Rolle, *Incendium Amoris*. 15 c. Copied by Grenehalgh for Joanna Sewell. Cambridge University, Emmanuel College: MS 35 (I.2.14); Oxford University, Bodleian Library, MS Lat. Th. D. 27, ff. 196v-200v; Philadelphia, and Rosenbach Foundation H491, all with intertwined monograms.

[110] Sargent (1984) p.106 and p.94.

[111] Now Rosenbach Foundation H491, Walter Hilton's *Scala Perfectionis* (*The Ladder of Perfection*) (Wynkyn *de* Worde, Westminster 1494, STC 14042).

[112] William Flete '*De Remediis contra Temptaciones*' in The *Digital Index of Middle English Verse*.

the transept, protected by the Saviour, Mary, St Bridget and St Augustine. (See Illustration between page 64 and 65, and Appendix 4 for full text).[113]

This is a complicated document to untangle. We can assume from its context that it was intended to be sent to Sewell by Grenehalgh. The text beginning '*O tortuose serpens*' is taken, slightly disordered, from a long hymn by Prudentius (d. ?413), sung as part of the Office before retiring to bed. The hymn has as its theme divine protection from night terrors and temptations to impurity.

Someone evidently noticed the exchange of books and the intertwining of initials. Grenehalgh was questioned by his superiors, removed from Sheen to the Coventry Carthusians in 1507 or 1508 and then, on remaining 'obdurate', was sent to their Kingston-upon-Hull house.[114] The trials of a contemplative vocation for someone of Lancastrian origins, now in a Yorkist stronghold, at a time when England's weather was dominated by wet summers and freezing winters, does not bear too close examination. He was dead by about 1530. We do not know his age, but he was perhaps 60, having had half a lifetime to reflect on his errors.

But Joanna Sewell remained at Syon, dying in 1532 – perhaps in her 50s, and was interred there with her sisters, *iuxta gerras*, beside the church grating made from cast iron. We do not know whether she was publicly upbraided for her '*defautes*' in the chapterhouse of the Abbey, in front of the Abbess and full body of her sisters.[115] But we do know from the Syon Additions to the Rule what happened by way of '*Bodily Discipline*' to those sisters who committed serious errors. The erring sister was required to bare her back, and then:

> Ther scahl not be yeven for the discipline but five lasches [lashes], but yf the defaute be of the more grievous defautes, or els that sche or they schewe any token of rebellion, then the discipliners schal not cese till the abbesse chargeth them to cese. And the laches in disciplines owe not to be to softe or to esy, but moderately scharpe, after the commandment of the abbes.

Betson has a number of recipes for mitigating the effects of beatings. Black Bryony, for example, was long known for treating bruises. But tucked away in his notes, at image 86 left, folio 81v, col. B, Betson, who may have known of the scandal,

---

[113] See also Krug (2008) for an interesting coverage of this text.

[114] See Sargent (1984), Volume 1, p79

[115] According to the Brothers' Rule, the sending out of 'any lettres of carnal affection' was classed as one of the most 'grevous defautes' of *lechery and the synne against nature.* Aungier, (1840), pp. 255-256,

has a gentler comment: Fatua is at gode for them that ben love sike. (Sycamore Figs are good for those who are love sick).

Fatua generally referred to the insipid-tasting Sycamore fig, which is restricted to sub-Saharan Africa and the Middle East. But at Syon it may have been understood as the Mulberry. The more exotic but practical remedies for lovesickness of the *Viaticum*, translated by Constantinus Africanus, were totally inappropriate for religious - wine women and song.[116]

The final offending Grenehalgh volume is strangely poignant.[117] It is the '*Incendium Amoris*' (The Bonfire of Love) by Richard Rolle of Hampole, an early Yorkshire mystic, whose own innocent relations with women had also apparently attracted criticism. It contains again on fol. 18v the combined monograms of Joanna Sewell and James Grenehalgh (the 'IGS' symbol). There are also a number of allusive catchwords, featuring '*amoris*' (love) and perhaps also too many illuminated 'S' letters (Sewell) for coincidence. On the vellum of the last page is written in a firm hand, '*Amor Dei Vincit Omnia*' *(The love of God overcomes all things)*, which for English readers can only bring to mind Chaucer's rather flighty prioress, whose pendant bore a similar motto. Then at the end of the book there appears in Latin: '*Mens est tibi*' - 'My thoughts are with you'. The book has been closed while these words were still wet, leaving a ghostly reversed images on the opposite pages.

And then in a less clear feminine hand appears: '*Gentle Jesu have mercy on me, Joanna*' And below that, but curtailed, is '*anno domino millesimo quin….*' (In the year of the Lord 15…..), perhaps 1500, the year of Joanna's profession as a nun of Syon. And a few more lines of handwritten text, but with the ink wiped away, wet and blurred, made forever illegible.[118]

Finis.

---

[116] See Wack, Mary F., (1990). *Lovesickness in the Middle Ages*

[117] British Library BL Add 24661, Richard Rolle, *Incendium Amoris*.

[118] Both Power (1922, pp. 53-54) and Jacka (1917, pp. 59-69) cite cases where celibacy fell below the required standards. The Nun of Watton provided a disturbing 11th century precedent in a double Gilbertine monastery. Cromwell and his visitors were however unable to find any such cause against Syon in the late 1530s.

List of Illustrations between pp. 64 and 65.

1   **Image of Thomas Betson**, (TB) below Virgin and Child, tonsured and in the garment of a Deacon of Syon. From Joseph Strutt, *Bibliographical Dictionary* (1785), plate iv. See Appendix 7 for a transcription of the text.

From the Thomas Betson Notebook, St John's College, Cambridge, MS 109 (E.6):

2   Folio 70r: **Beginning of the *Herbarium*** (List of Plants) at 'Alleluia' (*Oxalis acetosella*, Wood Sorrell) and ending at 'apium domesticum' See Image 74 right, folio 70r, col. A, page 80, to Image 74 right, folio 70r, col. B, page 83.

3   Folio 86r: End of the text on **Urine, *De Urinalibus***, at Image 90 right, Folio 86r, page 222, and beginning of **Remedies**, *Pro matrice take Rubarbe.*

4   **Fingerprint**, between Folios 105v and 106r, Image 110 left and right. It is not known if this is indeed the inky fingerprint of Betson, who finished his *Ryght Profytable Treatyse* with the words of admonition to new postulant nuns: 'Lerne to kepe your bokes clene.'

5   **Pike**, on Folios 34v and 35r, Image 39. There were probably fishponds at Syon to provide fish for Fridays and other days of fasting. It is not clear if these 'doodles' can be attributed to Betson, but the other penwork looks typical of his hand.

6   **Watermark**, at folio 83v, Image 88 left. This watermark, one of seven or perhaps eight identified, appears to show a single inverted cow's horn (to the left) with a stem ending in a star. It is Watermark style 4. See page 68 for details.

7   **Prayers written by James Grenehalgh for Joanna Sewell** in Rosenbach Foundation H491, the *Scala Perfectionis* by William Hilton, folio 135v. See Appendix 5 for transcription and translation of the Latin.

8   **Hypothetical reconstruction of the interior of a Bridgettine Abbey Church**, such as Syon, from a Dutch woodcut of 1500. It shows the typical interior, with orientation reversed from the norm. From left to right: Brothers' sunken choir at west end of the church; windows for Sisters' confession set in north wall; Priest-Brother's thirteen altars on steps including the western raised high altar; grill (of iron at Syon) surrounding the nave and separating the religious from the laity, who entered the church by two doors at east end; Sisters' choir raised on columns, facing east to their elevated altar, with door from choir accessing north into their cloister at first floor level. *Kunliga Bibliotheket, (National Library of Sweden, Stockholm).*

ST JOHN'S COLLEGE MS.109 (E.6): DESCRIPTION OF THE BINDING, PAPER, VELLUM AND WATERMARKS

Cambridge University, St John's College MS.109 (E.6): Thomas Betson Notebook. Description of the Binding, Paper, Vellum and Watermarks, with Weblinks.

1   **Contents:** A full list of the contents is set out in the St John's College Catalogue – see weblinks at end below. These are principally notes on Canon Law, and from Folio 70 to 115 (over one third of the text), a list of plants (called an '*Herbarium*' by Betson) and of herbal remedies. There are also sections on practical jokes, astrology (including rough two star charts), uroscopy, and enamelling. These can be traced to specific texts copied out by Betson – see 'Introduction – Betson's Sources' below.

2   **Size**: 5 ¾ inches long x 4 ¼ wide x 1¼ deep (14.6 x 10.8 x 3.2cm); ff124 +8, perhaps 50,000 words on both vellum and paper.

3   **Folios:** ff124 +8

4   **Cover:** Dark varnished leather on wooden boards. Leather is white on inner sides of boards, but appears to be over another pink cover, also perhaps of leather. Where the second inner cover is exposed on the back board, it is not pink, but a darkish brown. There are Compass marks on the front cover in the common geometric 'circle and flower' pattern. These have penetrated and damaged the leather cover.

5   **Inscriptions**: On front cover at top right, inscribed in ink: 'Thos CS' (*Thomas, Comes Southamptoniensis,* (Thomas, Earl of Southampton). According to the James catalogue entry: 'Was in possession of Henry Wriothesley, Earl of Southampton *(1573-1624),* then to Thomas Wriothesley, then to St John's, Cambridge.'

At image 6 right, Folio 2r. '*Orate pro anime Thome Betson de Syon*' (Pray for the soul of Thomas Betson of Syon).

On pastedown of rear board. 'Anno *Domini 1500 peribit omnis caro per ignem.*' (In the year of the Lord 1500, all flesh will perish by fire).

6   **Catch:** is missing. There remains its attachment to the cover, probably iron, at front in middle of board, secured by with triangular-headed brass nail; a clip present on back cover – 7/16 inch, (0.2cm), perhaps brass.

7   **Binding**: Three double strings at back and front set into the boards. These are still creamy and clean, and look perhaps like plaited reeds.

8   **Collation:** a⁴, 1¹⁰ 2¹⁰ 3⁸ 4¹² 5⁸ - 11⁸ 12¹² 13⁸ 14⁸, b⁴. The collations have paper pastedowns, except for Gathering 14. The gatherings themselves have five stitches, at approximately ¼, 1¼, 3, 4½ and 5½ inches (0.6, 3.2, 7.6, 10.2 and 14cm).

9   **Watermarks:** The text was examined using a 'light-sheet'. The resulting images were then photographed, and then compared the entries in Briquet.[119] The patterns are in fact rather common, and it was not possible to identify any one source in particular. It would be interesting to know how Betson, as a monk sworn to poverty, acquired the paper – was it for example from Wynkyn de Worde's printing house, which had a close association with Syon?

There are eight **watermarks** visible in the text, excluding vertical and horizontal lines on the paper. But four of these watermarks appear to be severed halves of each other (discussed below.) The watermarks have been categorised roughly after Briquet. Their locations are in the second section below.

> **Watermark Style 1** occurs only once, but is somewhat indecipherable. It consists of two circles and wavy lines. It is present at image 12 right, folio 8r, at top left. It is 1¼ inches (3cm) deep and 2 ¾ inches (7cm) wide.
>
> **Watermark Style 2:** Tête de Boeuf, a schematic bull's head, also occurs once only; at Image 17 right, folio 8r, top left, the head is inverted and at an angle.
>
> **Watermark Style 3:** again a Tête de Boeuf, which occurs seven times and is a distinctive head with large eyes and both nostrils well delineated, at image 58 right, folio 54r; image 73 right, folio 69r; image 86 right, folio 82r; image 95 left, folio 91r; image 104 right, folio 100r; image 114 right, folio 110r; image 124 right, folio 120r.
>
> **Watermark Style 4**: is a bull's horn next to a long stem, ending in an X shaped star. It looks as though this may in fact be a truncated part of Tête de Boeuf Style 3 above, where several examples show the beginning of a stem in the centre of the bull's head. There are seven example of this version, so that the paper may in fact been cut along the line of the Bull's head with stem and star, creating the two watermarks. It occurs at image 59 right; folio 55r; image 76 right, folio 72r; image 87 right; folio 83r; image 94 right; folio 90r; image 105 right; folio 101r; image 115 right, folio 111r; image 121 right, folio 117r.
>
> **Watermark Style 5**: only one occurrence at image 34 right, folio 30r: a crescent (like a croissant pastry), and a curved line, at top left; 1 inch (2.4cm) deep.

---

[119] Briquet, Charles Moïse, (1907).

Watermark Style 6: is a bunch of grapes, with two examples at image 66 right, folio 61r and image 67 right, folio 62r.

Watermark Style 7: is a distinctive lower half of a bull's body. This also appears to have once been a single watermark, and now severed in two. It occurs at image 82 right, folio 78r.

Watermark Style 8. Probably the lower half of Style 7, and is also present only once, at image 83 left, folio 79r.

These are common types of watermarks in Briquet, who has over 1250 examples of the Bull's head (Tête de Boeuf). Grapes, as at Style 6 above, are also a common theme. It has not therefore been possible so far to identify any example or dates. The several variants suggest that the sheets were from different sources.

10   Gatherings, Vellum, Paper and Watermarks

Flyleaves at Front: Four vellum flyleaf Folios of music and hymns.

Gathering 1: Ten Folios from image 005 right, folio 1r, to image 15 left, folio 10v.

> **Vellum:** Image 009 right, folio 5r, to image 11 left, folio 6v, in centre of the gathering.
>
> **Watermark Style 1**, image 12 right, folio 8r at top left.
>
> **Paper**: downstrokes and lateral ribbing in watermark.

Gathering 2: Ten Folios from image 15 right, folio 11r, to image 25 left, folio 20v.

> **Vellum**: image 19 right, folio 10r to image 21 left, folio 12r.
>
> **Watermark Style 2**, image 17 right, folio 8r, top left, Tête de Boeuf, head only, inverted and at an angle.
> **Paper**: downstrokes and lateral ribbing in watermark.

Gathering 3: Eight folios with pastedown in middle, from image 25 right, folio 21r to image 33 left, folio 28v.

> **Paper**: downstrokes and lateral ribbing in watermark. No other watermarks.

Gathering 4: 12 folios with vellum at start and in centre from image 33 right, folio 29r, to image 45 left, folio 40v.

Watermark Style 5: image 34 right, folio 30r, a crescent (shaped like a croissant pastry), and a curved line, at top left. It is 1 inch (2.4cm) deep, and is the sole example.

Paper: downstrokes and lateral ribbing in watermark.

Gathering 5: Eight folios. Image 45 right, folio 41r to image 53 left, folio 48v.

Paper: at image 45 right, folio 41r the paper changes to plain with no downstrokes and no lateral ribbing in watermarks. No other watermarks.

Gathering 6: Eight folios with pastedown in middle. Image 53 right, folio 49r, to image 61 left, folio 56v.

Watermarks:
(i)Watermark at top left in **Style 3**, Tête de boeuf, head only, about 1 inch (2.4 cm) deep at image 58 right, folio 54r.

(ii)Watermark **Style 4**, with horn and star, at top left; about 5 cm visible at image 59 right, folio 55r.

Paper: at image 57 right, folio 54r downstrokes and lateral ribbing visible in watermark.

Gathering 7: Eight folios with pastedown in middle. Image 61 right, folio 57r, to image 69 left, folio 64v.

Watermark: Bunch of grapes, Watermark **Style 6** at top left, one inch, (2.5 cm) long at image 66 right, folio 61r and image 67 right, folio 62r

Paper: image 57 right, folio 53r downstrokes and lateral ribbing visible in watermark.

Gathering 8: Eight folios with pastedown in middle. Image 69 right, folio 65r to image 77 left, folio 72v

Watermarks:
(i)Tête de boeuf, **Style 3**, about ½ inch (1.2) visible, top left at image 73 right, folio 69r.

(ii)Watermark **Style 4**, horn and star, top left, about 2 inches (4.8 cm) visible at image 76 right, folio 72r.

Paper: at image 69 right, folio 65r paper changes, no vertical lines or horizontal ribbing in the watermark.

Gathering 9: Eight Folios with pastedown in middle. Image 77 right, folio 73r to image 85 left, folio 80v.

Watermarks:
(i) Watermark **Style 7**, at top left of image 82 right, folio 78r. Four legs of bull and pizzle, well drawn, possibly the other half of next entry below (Watermark Style 8). About ¾ inch deep, and 2 inches long (1.5 cm and 5 cm).

(ii) Watermark **Style 8** at image 83 left, folio 79r. Inverted image of a bull, with head, back and an 'S' shaped tail, but no legs, and no 'stem and star' between horns. Well drawn. About ¾ inch deep, and 2 inches along the back, including tail and head (1.5 and 5 cm).

Gathering 10: Eight folios with pastedown in middle. Image 85 right, folio 81v to image 93 left, folio 88v.

Watermarks:
(i)Tête de boeuf, **Style 3**, at image 86 right, folio 82r, but with head only, top left. About 1 inch (2.5 cm.).

(ii)Watermark **Style 4,** horn and star, image 87 right, folio 83r, top left,. Length of image: 1½ inches (3.5 cm.).

Gathering 11: Eight folios with pastedown in middle. Image 93 right, folio 89r, to image 101 left, folio 96v.

Watermarks:
(i) Watermark **Style 4**, horn and star, top left at image 94 right, folio 90r. Visible length of section: 1½ inches (3.6 cm.).

(ii) Tête de boeuf, Watermark **Style 3**, head only, top left at image 95 left, folio 91r. Visible image about 1 inch (2.5 cm.).

Gathering 12: Twelve Folios, with pastedown in middle.
Image 101 right, folio 97r to image 113 left, folio 108v.

Watermarks:
(i) Image 104 right, folio 100r shows a Tête de boeuf, **Style 3**, head only, at top left in gutter, with stem of star in centre of head. Visible length about ¾ inches (2 cm).

(ii) Image 105 right, folio 101r, Watermark **Style 4**, horn and star, at top left in gutter. Visible length about 1 ½ inches (3.6cm).

Gathering 13: Eight folios with pastedown in middle. Image 113 right, folio 109r to image 121 left, folio 116v.

Watermarks:
(i) Image 114 right, folio 110r, Tête de boeuf, **Style 3**, head only, top left in gutter. Visible image is about ¾ inch (2 cm) long, with beginning of stem for star in centre of head at top.

(ii) Image 115 right, folio 111r, Watermark **Style 4**, horn and star, at top left in gutter. Visible length is 1 ½ inches (3.5cm) to top of stem.

(iii) Image 121 right, folio 117r, Watermark **Style 4**, horn and star, at top left in gutter. Visible length is 4cm to tip of stem.

Gathering 14: Eight folios with pastedown in middle, which is vellum; image 121 right, folio 117r, to image 129 left, folio 124v.

Watermark: Image 124 right, folio 120r, Tête de Boeuf, Watermark **Style 3**, head only, at top left in gutter. Ears visible, but no horns or 'star on stem'. Visible section is about ½ inch (1.2 cm) long.

Flyleaves at end: Four re-used flyleaf vellum folios of music at end of book.

11   Weblinks:

St John's College Catalogue entry:
http://www.joh.cam.ac.uk/library/special_collections/manuscripts/medieval_manuscripts/medman/E_6.htm
M.R. James, St John's College catalogue entry:
http://ia600404.us.archive.org/16/items/catmanustjohscol00jamesuoft/catmanustjohscol00jamesuoft.pdf

THE SYON ABBEY HERBAL

I THE HERBARIUM

Abbreviations and Symbols

Π : In Betson this sign marks the main entry of a group of synonyms or remedies.

BB: *Breviarium Bartholomaei,* BL Harley MS 3 (John Dee's copy).

eLALME: *An Electronic Version of a Linguistic Atlas of Late Mediaeval English.* The University of Edinburgh, 2013.

EMED: Electronic Middle English Dictionary. University of Michigan.

EPN: English *Plant Names from the Tenth to the Fifteenth Century,* Earle, J. (1880) OUP.

eTK: THORNDIKE, Lynn & KIBRE, Pearl (1963). *A Catalogue of Incipits of Mediaeval Scientific Writings in Latin* (Cambridge, MA, Mediaeval Academy.) and supplements.

eVK: VOIGTS, Linda Ehrsam and KURTZ, Patricia Deery (2000). *Scientific and Medical Writings in Old and Middle English: An Electronic Reference CD* . University of Michigan Press.

HUNT, Tony, (1989). *Plant Names of Mediaeval England.* DS Brewer.

ISTC: Incunabula Short Title Catalogue: see http://www.bl.uk/catalogues/istc/index.html

'i.' or 'id' : Latin 'idem' – meaning ' the same.' Here usually the same plant by another name.

MBDS: KRÄMER, Sigrid, & BERNHARD, Michael (1989). *Mittelalterliche Bibliothekskataloge Deutschlands und der Schweiz.* C.H. Beck'sche Verlagsbuchhandlung, München.

MLGB: *Medieval Libraries of Great Britain* (1964 -1987). Volumes I-V and Supplement. Ker, N. R., edited by Andrew G. Watson. London. The Royal Historical Society.

Mowat: *Sinonoma Bartholomaei, Alphita, and Synonyma Antidotarii Nicolai,* (1882). Edited by J.L.G. MOWAT. Clarendon Press.

ODNB: Oxford Dictionary of National Biography, online version.

OED: Oxford English Dictionary, on-line version.

OF: Old French.

SAN: *Synonyma Antidotarii Nicolai,* taken from Mowat, above.

SB: *Sinonoma Bartholomaei,* taken from Mowat, above.

ssp. : sub-species.

Tr.: Translation, in general from Latin into English.

Transcription conventions for Betson's Latin and English Text

We have attempted to create a legible text for readers who may be unfamiliar with Latin abbreviations and Middle English letters.

Latin: Betson's ā, ē, ī, ō, ū, have benn expanded to 'a*m*, e*m*, i*m*, o*m*, u*m*', and similarly for abbreviations with the letter 'n'. The use of the 'u' in Latin has been replaced by the letter 'v' where appropriate, in order to assist comprehension; for example 'ova' for 'oua', meaning 'eggs'.

Middle English: Thorn 'þ' as in 'þe' (*the*) has been replaced by italicised '*th*' and 'Þē' becomes the more intelligible '*them*' or '*then*' depending on the context. Betson also very occasionally seems to use simply a 'd' as in 'fedur' *feather*, 'modur' *mother*, and 'turnid' for *turneth*. We have retained Betson's spelling since the cross bar to the 'ð' or 'eth' is missing, and the 'eth' had in any case largely disappeared from Middle English by 1300.

Betson also uses the 'yogh' letter 'ʒ'. We have replaced it with the modern letter 'y', so that 'sore eiʒen' for example, becomes 'sore eiyen,' equivalent to the modern 'sore eyes.'

Betson has three forms of the modern letter 's', namely ß, ʃ, σ. His use of these is not consistent (though ß usually only appears at the end of a word). We have therefore replaced all three with the letter 's'. Similarly 'ff' in initial position has been replaced by a single capital letter (Fenell for ffenell, etc). '℞'has been expanded to 'Recipe' meaning 'Take' (the following list of ingredients.)

We have also added punctuation and capital letters, where this aids the sense. This is particularly the case with lists, viz: 'Caraway, Fenell, Spkykenard, Anice, Synamome, Galang*ur*' etc. Where words are continued over a line-break, we have added a hyphen for the sense, e.g. 'quanti-/ te'. Betson's own text in fact adopts this convention towards the end. Other mediaeval Latin and English abbreviations, which are signalled in the original text by a confusing variety of symbols, have been expanded.

The pages are numbered by folio number – that of the St John's catalogue, which is M. R. James from his catalogue[120]. We have also included the image numbers from the St John's microfilm, which shows two pages at a time. Here we have distinguished each individual page by its Image Number and by *left* (which are the verso pages of the previous folio) and *right* (which are the recto pages). Betson's double columns on each page of his *Herbarium* are then listed as 'A' or or 'B.' This Image numbering system includes the sheets of music pasted into the covers at front and rear, and which have no folio numbers in the James catalogue.

We have followed Hunt for the identification of plants. He often cites a number of alternative identifications, using over 60 MSS. We have retained these alternatives, since Betson was using a number of sources, and there may well have been no consistency of naming between the sources.

---

[120] See James, M. R. (1903). *Descriptive Catalogue of the Manuscripts in the Library of St John's College, Cambridge.* Cambridge University Press.

Text of Betson's *'Herbarium'*: Introduction

From Image 74 right, folio 70r, col. A, to Image 87 left, folio 82v, col. B.

This section of the notebook, which Betson at the very end entitles an *'Herbarium'*, comprises a list of about 700 medicinal plants, animals and minerals, with many repetitions. It is in rough mediaeval alphabetical order, which omits the letters J and W. It follows closely a similar list produced by John Bray, (d.1381), physician to Edward III, which he called the *Sinonoma de nominibus herbarum*. Bray's list is preserved in six extant manuscripts. Of those we have examined, Betson's seems to be closest to BL Sloane MS 282, fols. 167v–173v.[121]

There are also a few marginal notes in Betson, which may be taken from the *Sinonima Bartholomaei* of John Mirfield (fl. 1390), of St Bartholomew's Priory and Hospital in London. Betson's list of plants, probably compiled around 1500, was therefore already a century old, and has not benefitted from the new Greek learning of the period, nor the contemporary publication of standard printed herbal texts (such as, for example, the 1492 *Lumen Apothecariorum*, which was in the Library at Syon).

Both Bray (in Sloane 282) and Betson employed a system of bracketing their entries in groups of different names for the same plant. It was not possible to reproduce the bracketing systems in the text.

---

[121] We have not yet examined Durham DUL MS Cosin V.III.11, and Glasgow University Library, MS 185, ff.1-6v. A full list of the extant Bray MSS is at end of this book.

Betson's *Herbarium*:
From Image 74 Right, Folio 70r, Col. A, to Image 87 Left, Folio 82v, Col. B.

Ihus
[Jesus]

Image, Folio and Line Numbers.	Betson Entry. [The alphabetical letters A-Z below are for reference only, and are not in Betson].	The Synonoma of John Bray: BL Sloane MS 282, with folio number and column.	Possible Modern Names, mainly Linnaean, and taken from Hunt (1989). Non-Linnaean names are indicated.
Image 74 Right, Folio 70r, Col. A			
1.	[A] Π Alleluya.	Sloane 282, Folio 167v, Col. A Alleluya. Panis cuculi, pain de kukell.	*Oxalis acetosella,* Wood Sorrell. *(Hunt, p298, has pain de coucou).*
2.	Panis cuculi	Panis cuculi,	As above.
3.	Wodesour	Wodesour	As above.
4.	Chemerek		As above. Name not found.
5.	Stevenwort		As above.
6.	Π Amantilla	Amantilla, potentilla, , matinella, valeriana, ffeu, valerian	*Valeriana phu* or *V. officinalis,* Valerian. *V. officinalis* is a British native; phu is not native and scarcely grown now, but may have been formerly.
7.	Potentilla	Potentilla	As above.
8.	Maturella	Matinella *(not in Hunt).*	As above. Hunt (p.294) gives Maturell as 'fu'.
9.	Valeriana		As above.
		Bray text:- Allipiados. Lanceola. Herba Catholica. Lanceolearius. Semen dicitur Coconidium.	
10.	Π Alleum.	Alleum	*Allium vineale,* Crow Garlic.

80

Image, Folio and Line Numbers.	Betson Entry. [The alphabetical letters A-Z below are for reference only, and are not in Betson].	The Synonoma of John Bray: BL Sloane MS 282, with folio number and column.	Possible Modern Names, mainly Linnaean, and taken from Hunt (1989). Non-Linnaean names are indicated.
11.	Scordion	Scordeon	*Allium ursinum,* Ramsons, Wild Garlic, Crow Garlic.
12.	Tiriaca rusticorum	Tyriaca rusticorum	*Allium sativum,* Garlic.; or *?Allium porrum,* ?Leek.
13.	Ayle Gallice; Gallik, Anglice	ayl, anglice Garlek.	French 'Ail', Garlic.
14.	Π Arthemesia.	Arthemesia, Heymoyse.	*Artemisia vulgaris,* Mugwort. Heymoyse *is not in Hunt. Perhaps a form of Arthemesia. cf. also Ermoyse in SB, Mowat p.20 and Hunt p.36.*
15.	Matricaria	Matricaria	As above.
16.	Mat*er* herb*arum*	Mater herb*arum*	As above.
17.	Mugwort c. sic*us* (?)	anglice mugworth	As above.
18.	Π Arthemesia silv*estris*.	Arthemesia sylvestris, Fyvefing*er*	As above. Fyvefing*er*: *perhaps for Fyuefever, Feverfew, see Hunt p.37.*
19.	Febrifuga	Febriffuga.	As above.
20.	Febrifue.		As above.
21.	Π Altia.	Altea	*Althaea officinalis,* Marsh mallow. Ray: *Alcea rosea,* Hollyhock.
22.	Bismalva	Bismalva	As above.
23.	Bruscus		*Ruscus aculeatus,* Butcher's Broom, but perhaps here *Althaea officinalis*, Marsh mallow. *Betson seems to have mis-read Bruscus for Eviscus, which latter makes more sense here in the Mallows section. See Hunt p.112.*
24.	Malvaviscus	Malva viscus	*Althaea officinalis*, Marsh mallow; *?Anthemis Cotula,* Mayweed.

Image, Folio and Line Numbers.	Betson Entry. [The alphabetical letters A-Z below are for reference only, and are not in Betson].	The Synonoma of John Bray: BL Sloane MS 282, with folio number and column.	Possible Modern Names, mainly Linnaean, and taken from Hunt (1989). Non-Linnaean names are indicated.
Image 74 Right, Folio 70r, Col. B			
1.	Wyemawe.	Wyemalve	As above.
2.	Merchmawe.	Merche Malve	As above.
3.	Holihok	Holikokke	*Althaea officinalis*, Marsh mallow, Hollyhock.
4.	Π Arnoglossa.	Arnoglossa	*Plantago major*, Greater Plantain.
5.	Plantago M*ajor*	Plantago maior	As above.
6.	Playntengu*m* Weibrede	Planteyne or Weybrede	As above.
7.	Avencia	Avancia	*Geum urbanum*, Herb Bennet.
8.	Pes leporis	Pes Leporis	As above.
9.	Gariophilata.	Gariophilata	As above.
10.	Sana munda.	Sanamunda	As above.
11.	Harefote Avence.	Harefote or Avence	As above.
12.	Adiantos	Adiantos	*Adiantum capillus-veneris*, Maidenhair fern.
13.	Politricum.	Pollitricum	As above.
14.	Pes Nisi	Pes Nisi	?*Adiantum capillus-veneris*, Maidenhair fern; or ?*Asplenium trichomanes*, Maidenhair Spleenwort; or ?*Asplenium adiantum-nigrum*, Black Spleenwort.
15.	Sperhaukesfote	Spa*r*hawkyffote	?*Adiantum capillus-veneris*, Maidenhair fern.
16.	Atriplex	Attriplex	*Atriplex hortensis*, Garden Orach.
17.	Crisolocana	Crislocanna	As above.
18.	Arage	An*glice* Arage	As above.
19.	Urtica nettill		*Urtica dioica*, Stinging nettle.

Image, Folio and Line Numbers.	Betson Entry. [The alphabetical letters A-Z below are for reference only, and are not in Betson].	The Synonoma of John Bray: BL Sloane MS 282, with folio number and column.	Possible Modern Names, mainly Linnaean, and taken from Hunt (1989). Non-Linnaean names are indicated.
20.	Achalaffe vide Urtica		As above. Hunt p.3 has Acalephe and variant spellings in three other MSS.
21.	Semen azizon dicitur Anglice:		Perhaps *Lamium purpureum*, Red Dead Nettle, as below. But Daems #498, p.273 has Azizon as *Rumex acetosa*. The 'Aison' and 'Aizoon' variants in Hunt at p.12 are not for *Lamium purpureum*.
22.	Rednettull		
23.	Archangelica	Archangel	As above.
24.	Blyndnettill	Blynd netle	As above.
25.	Agrimonia	Agrimonia. Egrymoyne, Garschyve	*Agrimonia eupatoria*, Agrimony. (Hunt p11 has Garscleve).
26.	Apium domesticum.	Apium. Ther beth v spices [species] of hem, viz apium domesticum.... [Bray names only four, not five, species of Apium below].	*Apium graveolens* Wild Celery
Image 75 Left, Folio 70v, Col. A			
1.	Π In margin: Detrahit fevrum a vulnere. Supposita capiti dormientis, continuat sompnum.	Tr: Withdraws the fever from a wound. Placed under the head of a sleeping person, prolongs their sleep.	A similar text is found in Alphita, Mowat, p.3 under 'Agimonia vel Agrimonia'.

Image, Folio and Line Numbers.	Betson Entry. [The alphabetical letters A-Z below are for reference only, and are not in Betson].	The Synonoma of John Bray: BL Sloane MS 282, with folio number and column.	Possible Modern Names, mainly Linnaean, and taken from Hunt (1989). Non-Linnaean names are indicated.
2.	Apium ranarum	Apium ranar*um*	*Ranunculus scelaratus,* Celery-Leaved Buttercup, Crowfoot.
3.	Apium risus	Apium risus	*As above.*
4.	Apium amoraidarum	Apium emoiroid*arum*	*Ficaria verna,* Lesser celandine, Pilewort, crowfoot.
5.	Ache merche	Ache merche	*Levisticum officinale,* Lovage.
6.	Smalache	et Smalache	*Apium graveolens,* Wild Celery, Smallage.
7.	Abrotanum	**Folio 167v, Col. B** Abrotanu*m,* Averoyne	*Artemesia abrotanum,* Southern Wormwood.
8.	Sotherwode (*sic*)	Ang*lice* Sotherenwode	*As above.*
9.	Π <u>Anetium.</u>	Anetium	*Perhaps for Anetum, as in Anethum graveolens,* Dill, *below at line 11.*
10.	Absintheum	Absinthiu*m* dulce	*Artemisia absinthium, rather than A. pontica,* Wormwood.
11.	Dille dulce	Dile, Ang*lice*	*Anethum graveolens,* Dill
12.	Avens agneti (?)		*As above, Anethum graveolens,* Dill. *Image 86 Left, Folio 81v, Col. B, Line 29 gives* Dill *as 'Agnetum.'*
		Bray: Aloes, *th*ere beth iii Aloes evatik, Aloes cicotrinum, thes ben put on medicines; Aloes caballinu*m,* he is put on plastres; Aloes ligni est *tha*t cometh out of paradys and *tha*t ys oyt that cometh out of Indes (?), de India.	

Image, Folio and Line Numbers.	Betson Entry. [The alphabetical letters A-Z below are for reference only, and are not in Betson].	The Synonoma of John Bray: BL Sloane MS 282, with folio number and column.	Possible Modern Names, mainly Linnaean, and taken from Hunt (1989). Non-Linnaean names are indicated.
13.	Π Anagallis	Anagallis	*Symphytum officinale,* Common Comfrey.
14.	Anagallicum	Anagallicum	*As above.*
15.	Consolida m*a*ior	Consolida maior	*As above.*
16.	Exsimphicum (?) rad*ix* ma*ior*	And the rote of hym is y cleped Simphoni*tum*	*As above.* SB, Mowat, p.39 also has '*Simphicum*'.
17.	Confery	Conferie	*As above.*
		Bray: Consolida media, Wryngynwort, (*Hunt pp. 87 and 315*), Myddel Consoude, Consolida minor, Brusewort or Dayseye. These are all *Bellis perennis*, Daisy.	
18.	Π <u>Aquileria</u>	Aquileria	Either: *Ranunculus sceleratus,* Celery-Leaved Buttercup or Crowfoot. Or *Melissa officinalis*, Balm, or *Filipendula ulmaria,* Meadowsweet. See Hunt p31, (*Aquilaris and Aquileia 1 & 2*)
19.	Columbaria	Columbina	*?As Balm above.*
20.	Colu*m*byn	Colu*m*byne	*?As Balm above.*
21.	Π Auricula lepori*n*a	Auricula leporis	*Sedum telephium,* Orpine.
22.	Harisworth Orpy*n*	Hariswort, Orpyn	*As above.*
23.	Π Aron	Aaron, Barba Aaron, Pes vituli, Pee de pulayn	*Arum maculatum,* Lords and Ladies.
24.	Pes vituli.	Pes vituli	*As above.*
25.	Yeksterys	Yekersteys	*As above.*
26.	Π Aquilaria	Aquilaria,	*Ranunculus sceleratus,* Celery-Leaved Buttercup or Crowfoot.

Image, Folio and Line Numbers.	Betson Entry. [The alphabetical letters A-Z below are for reference only, and are not in Betson].	The Synonoma of John Bray: BL Sloane MS 282, with folio number and column.	Possible Modern Names, mainly Linnaean, and taken from Hunt (1989). Non-Linnaean names are indicated.
27.	Celidonia	Celidonia	*Chelidonium majus*, Greater Celandine.
28.	Tetereworth	Anglice Celidoigne, Tete*r*wort	*Ranunculus sceleratus*, Celery-Leaved Buttercup or Crowfoot, or Greater Celandine (*Chelidonium majus*), EMED.
29.	Π Aritemis	Anthemis	*Chamaemelum nobile*, Sweet Camomile.
30.	Camomilla	Camamilla	*As above.*
31.	Camemilla	Anglice Camamille	*As above.*
32.	ΠAbsintheum	Absinthemu*m*, Aloyne, Anglice Wermode or Symon	*Artemisia absinthium*, rather than *A. pontica*, Wormwood. Hunt p.2 has Aloyne and Symount.
33.	Wormode		*As above.*
34.	Π Agnus Castus	Agnus Castus	*Vitex agnus-castus*, Chaste Tree.
35.	Calix *(sic for Salix)* marinus	Calx Marinus	*As above.*
Image 75 Left, Folio 70v, Col. B			
1.	Toteseyn.	Tutsayne	*As above.*
2.	Π <u>Anisium</u>	Anisu*m*	*Pimpinella anisum*, Aniseed.
3.	Ciminum dulce	Ciminu*m* dulce	*As above.*
4.	Aneys	Aneis	*As above.*
5.	Π <u>Andrago</u>	Andrago	*Portulaca oleracea*, Green/Golden Purslane.
6.	Portulaca	Portulaca	*As above.*
7.	Purslane	Porcelane	*As above.*

Image, Folio and Line Numbers.	Betson Entry. [The alphabetical letters A-Z below are for reference only, and are not in Betson].	The Synonoma of John Bray: BL Sloane MS 282, with folio number and column.	Possible Modern Names, mainly Linnaean, and taken from Hunt (1989). Non-Linnaean names are indicated.
		Alica, Spelta, Spelt	*Hunt p.16 has 'Alitum', identity unknown.*
8.	Π Anacarus	Ancorus,	*Sanicula europaea,* Sanicle. *Hunt p.24.*
9.	Saincls	Saniculus	*As above.*
10.	Sanicle	Sanicle or	*As above.*
11.	Wodemerch	Wodemerche	*As above.*
12.	Ambrosia	Ambrosia	*Teucrium scordonia,* Wood Sage.
13.	Hindhal Anglice Hendhale	Hyndehale,	*As above.*
14.	Wildsauge.	Wildesauge	*As above.*
15.	Eutoporium	Eupatorium	*As above.*
16.	Ambrose.	Ambrose	*As above.*
17.	Salvia agrestis	Salvia agrestis	*As above.*
		Bray Fol 168r, Col. A	
18.	Π Ambra sperma cete [whale]	*Ambra* sperma ceti	Ambergris.
19.	Ambre	Ambre	Amber
20.	Azarabaccera	Azarabaccara	*Asarum europaeum,* Asarabacca, *'but variously applied'* Hunt.
21.	Garriofilata agrestis	Gariofilata agrestis	*As above.*
22.	Azarus	Azarus	*As above.*
23.	Π Ayson·	Ayson	*Sempervivum tectorum,* Houseleek.

Image, Folio and Line Numbers.	Betson Entry. [The alphabetical letters A-Z below are for reference only, and are not in Betson].	The Synonoma of John Bray: BL Sloane MS 282, with folio number and column.	Possible Modern Names, mainly Linnaean, and taken from Hunt (1989). Non-Linnaean names are indicated.
24.	Barba iovis	Barba iovis, Jovis Barba	As above.
25.	Semperviva		As above.
26.	Iubarbe	Iubarbe	As above.
27.	Herworth	Herwort	As above.
28.	Senygrene.	Synegrene	As above.
29.	Housleke		As above.
30.	Π Astula regia.	Astula regia	*Galium odoratum*, Wood-ruff.
31.	Herba muscata	Herba muscata, Hastula regia	As above.
32.	Woderof	Woderove	As above.
33.	Π Acetosa.	Acetosa	*Rumex acetosa*, Sorrel.
Image 75 Right, Folio 70v, Col.A			
1.	Sorrel. Souredok	Sorel, Asedula, Souredokke	As above.
2.	Π Agrediadema	Agradiadema id est hofe.	*Glechoma hederacea*, Ground Ivy. Hunt p.11, with 'hofe' variants in 6 MSS. It is not in Henslow or Mowat.
3.	Hofe		As above.
		Appollinaris, Closewort.	Neither word is in Betson. Hunt p30 gives Appollinaris, Glofwort or Closewort as: *Convallaria majalis*, Lily of the Valley; or *Digitalis purpurea*, Foxglove; or *Mandragora officinarum* Mandrake, or *Solanum nigrum*, Black Nightshade.
		Archapiaris id est melde.	Neither in Betson. Hunt p33 gives it as *Atriplex*, Orache, with 'melde' in 4 MSS. Daems #16, p.102 also has Archaposcis as *Atriplex*.

Image, Folio and Line Numbers.	Betson Entry. [The alphabetical letters A-Z below are for reference only, and are not in Betson].	The Synonoma of John Bray: BL Sloane MS 282, with folio number and column.	Possible Modern Names, mainly Linnaean, and taken from Hunt (1989). Non-Linnaean names are indicated.
4.	Π Annotana	Annotana	*Bryonia dioica*, White Bryony.
5.	Brionia.	Brionia	*As above.*
6.	Scicida.	Sicida	*As above.*
7.	Wildnep	Wildnepe or	*As above.*
8.	Wildvyne.	Wildevyne	*As above.*
9.	Π Aspaltios	Aspaltios	*Potentilla reptans*, Creeping Cinquefoil.
10.	Quinque folium	*Quinque*folium	*As above.*
11.	Pentafilon	Pentafilon	*As above.*
12.	Fyveleved-gresse	Fyvelevede gras	*As above.*
13.	Π Aristologia.	Arestologia	*Aristolochia rotunda / longa*, Round-rooted and Long-rooted Birthwort. *Daems #494, p.272 gives (the poisonous) Aristolochia clematis.*
14.	Smerworth	Smerewort	*? Aristolochia rotunda as above. OED gives 'perhaps annual mercury, Mercurialis annua (family Euphorbiaceae).' EMED gives 'One of several kinds of plants, including Aristolochia rotunda, Chenopodium Bonus-Henricus, and Mercurialis annua.'*
15.	Algea	Algea, also Alga, Sewort	*Probably Glyceria fluitans, which is a grass, not an algae. See Hunt p.14.*
16.	Floteworth	Flotwort	*As above.*
		Arnoglossa, Centinarvia, Signa aretis, Pla*n*tago maior	

Image, Folio and Line Numbers.	Betson Entry. [The alphabetical letters A-Z below are for reference only, and are not in Betson].	The Synonoma of John Bray: BL Sloane MS 282, with folio number and column.	Possible Modern Names, mainly Linnaean, and taken from Hunt (1989). Non-Linnaean names are indicated.
17.	Π Atramentum.	Bray: Atramentum is a veyne of the erthe of the which there beth thweyn; one the white, other blakke that ys y clepid coperose & the other grene coperose gr. vitriale hit is i clepid.	
18.	Vitriole.		'Any of certain glassy mineral salts of sulfuric acid used esp. in alchemy or medicine, vitriol; also, sulphuric acid' EMED.
19.	Coperose.		A metallic sulphate, as of iron (green), of copper (blue), or of zinc (white); vitriol. EMED
20.	Π Alipiardos	Cf. Bray's Allipiados above.	Daphne laureola, Spurge Laurel.
21.	Lauriole		As above.
22.	Semen Cinsoni.	semen dicitur Coconidium	As above - the seed.
23.	Cocnindium	semen dicitur Coconidium	As above - the seed.
24.	Π Affoddillus	Affoddillus	Allium ursinum, Ramsons, Wild Garlic, Crow Garlic.
		Bray Fol. 170r., Col. B Hermodactilus ys an herbe the which the rote is commendable to medicines. As above	
25.	Centum capita	Centum capita	As above.
26.	Π Alla gallica	Allogallica	Gentiana amarella, Gentian.
27.	Gentiana	Genciana, Gencian	As above.
28.	Baldemoyn		As above.
29.	Π Antera semen rosarum		Rosa species.

Image, Folio and Line Numbers.	Betson Entry. [The alphabetical letters A-Z below are for reference only, and are not in Betson].	The Synonoma of John Bray: BL Sloane MS 282, with folio number and column.	Possible Modern Names, mainly Linnaean, and taken from Hunt (1989). Non-Linnaean names are indicated.
30.	Π Arnoglossa		*Plantago major*, Plantain.
31.	Cent*e*rimsia.?	Centinaria	*As above.*
Image 75 Right, Folio 71r, Col. B			
1.	Signa Ariet*is*	Signa aretis	*As above.*
2.	Plantago mi*n*or		*Plantago lanceolata*, Ribwort Plantain.
3.	Agni li*n*gua		*As above.*
4.	Π Alexander	Alexander	*Smyrnium olusatrum*, Alexanders, Horse Parsley.
5.	Π Aron		*Arum maculatum*, Lords and Ladies.
6.	Barba Aaron		*As above.*
7.	Iarus. Pes Vituli.		*As above.*
8.	Yextere		*As above.*
9.	Π Absintheum	Bray Fol. 168r, Col C.	*Artemisia absinthium* rather than *A. pontica*, Wormwood.
10.	Ponticum	Absinthium ponticum	*A. pontica*, Wormwood.
11.	Semen		*As above* - seed
12.	Sentonica Wormod		*As above.*
13.	Π Acantium	Acantum	*Urtica dioica*, Seed of the Stinging Nettle
14.	Ozimu*m*		*As above. See Hunt, p.188.*
15.	Virida.		*Perhaps 'virida' goes with Ozimum.*
16.	Π Agaldo (?)	Agalido (?), Ozimum, Ygia	*Agaldo & Agilido not found. Ozimum is in Hunt at p188, Nettle; Ygia is at Hunt, p.267 as Nettle-seed.*

Image, Folio and Line Numbers.	Betson Entry. [The alphabetical letters A-Z below are for reference only, and are not in Betson].	The Synonoma of John Bray: BL Sloane MS 282, with folio number and column.	Possible Modern Names, mainly Linnaean, and taken from Hunt (1989). Non-Linnaean names are indicated.
17.	Semen urtice	Semen urtice	*As above*
18.	Π Asedula	Asedula	*Rumex acetosa*, Common Sorrel. *Hunt pp4-5*
19.	Herba acetosa		*As above.*
20.	Panner (?)		*?As above. Not found. Hunt p4 has anglice 'rammes' in one MS.*
21.	Ox. lappacium		*As above. See Hunt p.195.*
22.	Surrell		*As above.*
23.	Sourdok		*As above.*
24.	Π Acis ylder		*Sambucus nigra*, Elder. *More usually Actis. See Hunt, p.7.*
25.	Sambuci		*As above*
26.	Π Acus muscata minor	Acus muscata minor, Crowbille	*Erodium moschatum*, Musk Storks Bill, Crowbill, Herb Robert, Ground Needle Storks Bill.
27.	Ozonpill		*Perhaps a misreading of Crowbill? In Hunt at p.8.*
28.	Acus muscata major		*As above.*
29.	Herbrobert Major		*Geranium robertianum*, Herb Robert.
30.	Agrimulatum	Agrimulatum	*Agrostemma githago*, Corn Cockle or *Lolium temulentum*, Darnel.
31.	Gith. Melancium	Gith. Melancium	*As above.*
Image 76, Left, Folio 71v, Col. A			
1.	Nigella	Nigella, kokel	*Agrostemma githago*, Corn Cockel.

Image, Folio and Line Numbers.	Betson Entry. [The alphabetical letters A-Z below are for reference only, and are not in Betson].	The Synonoma of John Bray: BL Sloane MS 282, with folio number and column.	Possible Modern Names, mainly Linnaean, and taken from Hunt (1989). Non-Linnaean names are indicated.
2.	Π Acmalici semen	Acmalici idem semen saxifragii	*Saxifrage* ssp., Saxifrage; or *Pimpinella saxifragia*, Burnet Saxifrage
3.	Saxifrage		*As above*
4.	Π Acride	Acride	*Pastinaca Sativa* Wild Parsnip, *Hunt p6*
5.	Pastinaca	Pasinaca	*As above.*
6.	Bauci	Baucia	*As above.*
7.	Pastnepe	Parsenepe	*As above.*
8.	Π Adiantos	Adiantos, Alocon	*Adiantum capillus-veneris*, Maidenhair fern. *For variants see Hunt pp12, 13 & 15, and Daems #548, p.285: Alacon Aiacon, & Algon.*
9.	Alacio		*As above.*
10.	Capillus veneris	Capilli veneris	*As above.*
11.	Maidenhere	Maydenhere	*As above.*
12.	Π Agon	Agon	?*Adiantum capillus-veneris*, Maidenhair fern; or ?*Asplenium trichomanes*, Maidenhair Spleenwort; or ?*Asplenium adiantum-nigrum*, Black Spleenwort.
13.	Pollitricum	Pollitricum	*As above.*
14.	Sparowisfote	Sperhaukesfote	*As above.*
15.	Π Adriangus	Adriagnis Fol.172 r., Col C.	*Portulaca oleracea*, Green / Golden Purslane. *Hunt p24 Andrago, and Daems #357, p.223, Adragnis, Andraginis.*
16.	Portulaca alba	Portulaca, Aglaba	*As above. 'Aglaba' not found.*
17.	Glapes pulli	Pes pulli	*As above. A mis-reading of 'Pes Pulli' – Purslane; see Hunt p.205.*

Image, Folio and Line Numbers.	Betson Entry. [The alphabetical letters A-Z below are for reference only, and are not in Betson].	The Synonoma of John Bray: BL Sloane MS 282, with folio number and column.	Possible Modern Names, mainly Linnaean, and taken from Hunt (1989). Non-Linnaean names are indicated.
18.	Π Allium		*Allium ursinum*, Ramsons, Wild Garlic, Crow Garlic.
19.	Tiriaca rusticorum		*As above.*
20.	Garlek		*As above.*
21.	Π <u>Albos</u> Coriand*er*	Albos Coriander	*?Coriandrum sativum*, Coriander. Hunt p.13, as '*Albor*'
22.	Alexandri*um*	Alexander, at f.168r, Col B.	*Smyrnium olusatrum*, Alexanders, Horse Parsley.
23.	Olexaton	Olexatrum	*As above.*
24.	Petrocillum	Petrocillinu*m* maior	*Smyrnium olusatrum*, Alexanders, Horse Parsley; or *Petroselinum crispum*, Wild Parsley.
25.	Macedonium	Macedonicum	*As above.*
26.	Π <u>Alphita</u>	**F.168v, Col A** Alphita nome*n* ordei feyynede orge, barlich mele	*Hordeum ssp.* Barley
27.	Farina dei		Barley meal ?
28.	Farina ordei		Barley meal
29.	Π Alleuala ?	Allenala	Neither in Hunt. In Betson it is bracketed with Lingua avis below.
30.	Lingua avis	Sophir, Lingua avis. Sophir is not in Hunt.	*Fraxinus excelsior*, Ash Tree Keys; or *Stellaria holostea*, Stitchwort.
31.	Π Amarisca fetida	Amarisca fetida	*Anthemis cotula*, Stinking Camomile, Mayweed.
32.	Cotida	? *As above.* Bray has *Fecula cotidia* for *Cotula Fetida* – see Hunt p.91.	

Image, Folio and Line Numbers.	Betson Entry. [The alphabetical letters A-Z below are for reference only, and are not in Betson].	The Synonoma of John Bray: BL Sloane MS 282, with folio number and column.	Possible Modern Names, mainly Linnaean, and taken from Hunt (1989). Non-Linnaean names are indicated.
33.	Masmaratrum	Masmaratrum	Hunt p.171 has Peucedanum officinale, Hog's Fennel.
34.	Peucedenum	Peucedanum	As above.
Image 76, Left, Folio 71v, Col B			
1.	Feniculus porcin*orum*	Feniclus porcinus	As above.
2.	Amerok	Folio 168v, Col. C Amerok	Anthemis cotula, Stinking Camomile or Mayweed, Hunt p.19.
3.	Hundefenell	Houndfenel or	As above, and in Hunt p.19.
4.	Matyn.	Ma*th*pen	As above and in Hunt p.19.
5.	Maraviscus		Althaea officinalis, Marsh mallow. Ray: Alcea rosea, Hollyhock.
6.	Amaricio cimbrium	Amaracus, Amaricon, Cimbrium	Majorana hortensis or vulgare Marjoram. See Hunt p19, and Daems #317, p.209
7.	Sansuc*us* olimbrium	Sanscus olimbriu*m*	As above. See Hunt p227 'Samsucus'.
8.	Maiorana.	Maiorana	Origanum vulgare Marjoram.
9.	Michworth	Muchewort	Origanum vulgare Marjoram; or Artemisia vulgaris, Mugwort.
10.	Π Amphoricon	Amphoricon	Hypericum perforatum, St John's Wort.
11.	Yp*er*ycon	Ypericon	As above.
12.	Herba Ioha*nn*is	Herba Ioha*nn*is	As above.
13.	Herba p*er*forata	Herba p*er*forata	As above.
14.	Scopa regia.	Scopia regia	As above.
15.	Fuga demonum	Fuga demonum	As above.

Image, Folio and Line Numbers.	Betson Entry. [The alphabetical letters A-Z below are for reference only, and are not in Betson].	The Synonoma of John Bray: BL Sloane MS 282, with folio number and column.	Possible Modern Names, mainly Linnaean, and taken from Hunt (1989). Non-Linnaean names are indicated.
16.	Seynt John Worte	Anglice St Jon Wort	As above.
17.	Π Antiframacum.	Antyfernatum	Aquilegia vulgaris, Columbine. See Hunt p26 & 261 Antifarmacum. Daems #473, p264, points to next entry 'vincetoxicum' about which there is confusion.
18.	Vicetoxicum	Vincetoxicum	?Gentiana amarella, ?Felwort Or: ? Mercurialis Perennis ?Dog's Mercury Or ?Potentilla Erecta, ?Common Tormentill. See Hunt p.261.
19.	Turmentill.	Anglice Tormentille & hit is gode agyn fenym (venom).	Potentilla erecta, Common Tormentill.
20.	Π Ardillus	Ardillus	Allium ursinum Ramsons, Wild Garlic.
21.	Porcisuaticum	Porrum silvaticum.	As above. See Hunt p33. Betson or his source seems to have misread Bray.
22.	Ramsey	Anglice Rammeson	As above.
23.	Aloes epatis.	Aloë esp. succotrina, Aloes, Liverwort. Sometimes referred to as Socotrine Aloes. Bray: Aloes, the beth iii Aloes evatik, Aloes cicotrinum, thes ben put on medicines; Aloes caballinum, he is put on plastres; Aloes ligni est that cometh out of paradys and that ys oyt that cometh out of Indes de India.	
24.	Aloes galbarbium	Caballinum above	?As above.

Image, Folio and Line Numbers.	Betson Entry. [The alphabetical letters A-Z below are for reference only, and are not in Betson].	The Synonoma of John Bray: BL Sloane MS 282, with folio number and column.	Possible Modern Names, mainly Linnaean, and taken from Hunt (1989). Non-Linnaean names are indicated.
25.	Aloes cucotrinum	(Aloes cicotrinum, thes ben put on medicines;)	*Aloë* esp. *succotrina*, Aloes, Liverwort. *Sometimes referred to as Socotrine Aloes*
26.	Aloes lignum paradisi	(Aloes ligni est *tha*t cometh out of paradys and *tha*t ys oyt that cometh out of Indes de India.)	*Aloë* L ssp. Aloes.
27.	Anacardus, es*t pedicul*us elephantis; *secundu*m quosdam est fructus cuiusda*m* arboris.	Anacardus is *the* lous of an elepha*n*t & sume sey *that* hit ys *the* fruyt of a tree.	*Semecarpus anacardium,* Marking Nut. *It is closely related to the cashew nut.*
Image 76, right, Folio 72r, Col. A			
1.	Aspaltu*m* bitume*m* iudiacum.	Aspaltum, bitumen iudaicum	Asphalt, bitumen.
2.	Albestio calx viva.	Albeston, calx viva, quik lyme	Quicklime.
3.	Ambra.		Ambergris.
4.	Sperma ceti		*As above.*
5.	Ambre		Amber.
6.	Π Acetosum		Vinegar.
7.	Aysel, vynager		Vinegar; *Aysel* is the Middle English form.

97

Image, Folio and Line Numbers.	Betson Entry. [The alphabetical letters A-Z below are for reference only, and are not in Betson].	The Synonoma of John Bray: BL Sloane MS 282, with folio number and column.	Possible Modern Names, mainly Linnaean, and taken from Hunt (1989). Non-Linnaean names are indicated.
8.	Π Arilli Kirnellis	Arilli be*th* kernels of reyso*n*s	*Vitis vinifera*, Grape-seeds. *Hunt p.34.*
9.	of reysyns		
10.	Π Attramentum		Vitriol (EMED)
11.	White copur		Cupronickel, or copper-nickel.
12.	Vitriole grene copor		
13.	Π Acacia juce of slon	Acacia is *the* juce of the lytil smale wild slon *the* which be*th* not follich rype	*Prunus spinosa,* Sloe, Blackthorn.
14.	not fullich ripe		*As above.*
15.	Π Allogallica *vel* genci*an*a		*Gentiana* ssp. esp. *lutea,* Gentian.
16.	Π Antera sede of rosis		Anthers, Rose seed.
17.	Π Amidum agreste		*Peucedanum officinale,* Hog's Fennel. *Hunt p25, Anetum agreste. See also Daems #314 p.207.*
18.	Amydoyn the jeus of	Amidum, Anidoyne, *the* tare of whete.	*Not found. 'Amidum' is usually late latin for Starch. Bray's Amidum is at Daems #55, p.114.*
19.	Anagadum *sumak*	Folio 168v, Col. B Anagodam, Sumac	*'A part or parts of the shrub sumac Rhus coriaria'* EMED, *Sicilian Sumac or 'Anagodan'.*

Image, Folio and Line Numbers.	Betson Entry. [The alphabetical letters A-Z below are for reference only, and are not in Betson].	The Synonoma of John Bray: BL Sloane MS 282, with folio number and column.	Possible Modern Names, mainly Linnaean, and taken from Hunt (1989). Non-Linnaean names are indicated.
20.	Π Antale	Antale *idem* amentu*m* dulce	Soapstone. *Mesue: 'similis est lapis durus'. Opera de medicamentorum purgantium.*
21.	Π Amictum dulce	Amentum dulce	As above
		Acinum *idem* hyndbery: Hunt p.5, *Rubus idaeus,* Raspberry	
22.	Π Antifoly is *the* gr*e*te clow founden amo*n*g other clowis	Antifolii is the grete clowe y founde amonge clowis	*Eugenia caryophyllata,* Thunb. Cloves.
Image 76, right, Folio 72r, Col B			
1.	**[B]** Brassica caul*u*s	Brassica Caulus	*Brassica oleracea,* Wild Cabbage.
2.	Olus colex	Olus Choler	As above.
3.	Caule wortis	Cowl, Anglice Wortes.	As above.
4.	Π Branca urcine	Branca urcina	*Acanthus mollis,* Acanthus, Bear's Claw.
5.	Branche Urscine	Branc de Ursine	As above
6.	Π Brachios	Bracheos	*Juniperus savina,* Savine, Savin Juniper.
7.	Savina	Savina	As above
8.	Savyne	Saveyne	As above
9.	Π Brionia	Brionia	*Bryonia dioica,* White Bryony.
10.	Scicides	Sicides	As above, also *'Squirting cucumber'* Sicyos. See Hunt pp.80, 233 and 237.
11.	Wildnep	Wildenepe	As above.
12.	Cucurbita agrestis	Cucurbita agrestis	As above.

Image, Folio and Line Numbers.	Betson Entry. [The alphabetical letters A-Z below are for reference only, and are not in Betson].	The Synonoma of John Bray: BL Sloane MS 282, with folio number and column.	Possible Modern Names, mainly Linnaean, and taken from Hunt (1989). Non-Linnaean names are indicated.
13.	Buglossa	Buglossa	*Anchusa arvensis*, Bugloss.
14.	Lingua silvana	Lingua silvana	*Anchusa arvensis / officinalis*, Bugloss / Alkanet ?
15.	Lingua bovis	Lingua bovis	*Anchusa arvensis / officinalis*, Bugloss / Alkanet ? Or: *Picris echoides*, Bristly Ox Tongue; or: *Borago officinalis*, Borage.
16.	Lange de bef	Lang de beof	*As above.*
17.	Π Bardona	Bardana	*Arctium lappa*, Burdock.
18.	Glis, Lappa, Clote.	Glis, Lappa, Anglice Clote	*As above.*
19.	Bedegar	Bedegar, Vulnis	*Rosa rubiginosa*, Eglantine; Or: *Rosa canina*, Dog Rose. *Bedegaur or robin's pincushion, is a gall on the rose not the rose itself.*
20.	Bulinam ?		Not found. Context suggests as above.
21.	Eglenter	Engleter (sic)	*Rosa rubiginosa* Eglantine.
22.	zhebreer	zeobrere	*Here probably Rosa rubiginosa, Eglantine; or: Rosa canina, Dog Rose. But see also Hunt p49, Bedegar, for other possibilities.*
23.	Birula. birle	Berula, Biler	*Veronica beccabunga*, Brooklime.
24.	Bariche.	Burith	*Saponaria officinalis*, Soapwort.
25.	Saponaria.	Saponaria	*As above.*

Image, Folio and Line Numbers.	Betson Entry. [The alphabetical letters A-Z below are for reference only, and are not in Betson].	The Synonoma of John Bray: BL Sloane MS 282, with folio number and column.	Possible Modern Names, mainly Linnaean, and taken from Hunt (1989). Non-Linnaean names are indicated.
26.	Crowpsope (sic)	Crowsope, Cardinis fullonis, Savener	As above.
27.	Balsamita.	Balsamita	*Mentha aquatica,* Water Mint; or: *Mentha longifolia,* Horse Mint.
28.	Baume	Bawme	*Melissa officinalis,* Balm.
29.	Π Broncus.	Bruncus Fol 170r., Col A: Cruncus, Podadria Lini, Cuscuta idem est.	*Cuscuta europaea,* 'Large Dodder'; Or: *Cuscuta epithymum,* 'Common Dodder'; Or: *Cuscuta epilinum* (Weihe); Flax Dodder.
30.	Cuscuta. podrag*a*	Cuscuta	*Cuscuta epilinum* Weihe, Flax Dodder.
31.	Lini dodur	Lini Dodir	As above
32.	Π Butalmon	Butalmon	*Leucanthemum vulgare,* Ox-eye Daisy.
33.	Oculus bovis	Oculus bovis	As above.
Image 77, Left, Folio 72v, Col. A			
1.	Oyle de Beff	Oil de Beof	As above.
2.	Herba par*a*lesis	Herba Paralesis	*Primula veris,* Cowslip; or *Primula elatior,* Oxlip; or *Primula veris* L. x *vulgaris* Huds. Common Oxlip.
3.	Herba par*a*disi		As above.
4.	Couslop	Anglice Cowsloppes	*Primula officinalis, P. veris*; English cowslip. EMED

Image, Folio and Line Numbers.	Betson Entry. [The alphabetical letters A-Z below are for reference only, and are not in Betson].	The Synonoma of John Bray: BL Sloane MS 282, with folio number and column.	Possible Modern Names, mainly Linnaean, and taken from Hunt (1989). Non-Linnaean names are indicated.
5.	Π Borago	Borago	*Borago officinalis,* Borage.
6.	Borage	Borage	*As above*
7.	Π <u>Benedicta</u>.	Benedicta	*Conium maculatum,* Hemlock, Herb Bennet.
8.	Herb Benete	Herb Benet	*As above.*
9.	Hemelok	Hommelok	*As above.*
10.	Π Bugla bugle	Bugla, Bugle	*Ajuga reptans,* Bugle.
11.	Wodebrounien	Anglice Wodebrowne	*As above.*
12.	Π <u>Broscus.</u>	Bruscus	*Ruscus aculeatus,* Butcher's broom.
13.	Fracin bruskis	*As above. Old French fressun, fresçon for Butcher's Broom.* **Bray:** *Fagrum, unobholein, Bruske See Hunt p56, where Fagrum is given as a 'gallice' variant, and 'unobholein' as probably an errant writing of 'knee holly'.*	
14.	Π Basilica.	Basilica	*Gentiana amarella,* Gentian. or: Dragonwort, *Dracunculus vulgaris; any of several other plants, such as the cuckoopint (Arum maculatum).*
15.	Basilicon.		*Polygonum bistorta,* Snake root, Bistort; or *? Dracunculus vulgaris,* Dragon Arum.
16.	Dragancia.	Dragancia	*Dracunculus vulgaris,* Dragonwort.
17.	Serpentina.	Serpitian	*As above.*
18.	Dragance.		*As above.*

Image, Folio and Line Numbers.	Betson Entry. [The alphabetical letters A-Z below are for reference only, and are not in Betson].	The Synonoma of John Bray: BL Sloane MS 282, with folio number and column.	Possible Modern Names, mainly Linnaean, and taken from Hunt (1989). Non-Linnaean names are indicated.
19.	Π Baucia.	Baccia	*Pastinaca sative,* Parsnip; Or: *Sium sisarum,* Skirret.
20.	Pastineca	Pastinaca	*As above.*
21.	Pastnake pastnep	Pastinake Pasternepe	*As above.*
22.	Π Baccara.	Baccara	*Asarum europaeum,* Asarabacca, Hazelwort.
23.	Azarabaccara	Azarabaccara	*As above.*
24.	Spewyngworth	Spywi*ng*wort	*As above.*
25.	Π Balsamita.	Balsamita	*Mentha aquatica,* Water Mint; Or: *Mentha longifolia,* Horse Mint.
26.	Menta aquatica	Menta aquatica	*As above.*
27.	Ortensis menta.	Ortensis	*Mentha,* 'Garden Mint'.
28.	Sisinbriu*m* mente	Sisimbrium	*Mentha silvestris,* Horsemint; *Menta aquatica,* 'Water Mint'.
29.	Π Barbastus	Barbastus	*Vebascum thapsus,* Mullein. *Forrest (1831) p.196 lists 13 varieties of Vebascum at Syon House.*
30.	Tapsus	Tapsus	*As above.*
31.	Barbastus flosmus	flosmus	*As above.*
32.	Pentafilion	Ponfilon, Herba lu*m*enaria	Here probably 'Pantifilagos' *Vebascum thapsus,* Mullein, rather than 'Pentafilon' *Potentilla repens,* Creeping Cinquefoil.
33.	Moleyn		*As above.*
Image 77, Left, Folio 72v, Col. B			
1.	Π Branca lauri	Bacca Laure	*Laurus nobilis,* Bay Tree Berry.
2.	Fructus lauri	Fructus Lauri	*As above.*
3.	Daumocokci	Da*m*pno cocci, Da*m*pno costi	*As above.*

Image, Folio and Line Numbers.	Betson Entry. [The alphabetical letters A-Z below are for reference only, and are not in Betson].	The Synonoma of John Bray: BL Sloane MS 282, with folio number and column.	Possible Modern Names, mainly Linnaean, and taken from Hunt (1989). Non-Linnaean names are indicated.
4.	Π Baccarum.	Fol. 168v, Col B Baccarum Edere	*Hedera helix*, Ivy berries.
5.	Edere, fruct*us* ede*re*	Fructus Edere	*As above.*
6.	Carpocissi.	Carpocisci	*As above.*
7.	Π Barba Ircina	Barba Ircina	*Cytinus hypocistis*, Cytinus.
8.	Ypoquistides	Ipoquistidos	*As above*
9.	Π Bitumen iudaicu*m*	Bitume*n* iudaicu*m*	'Jews' Pitch' or Asphalt.
10.	Aspintum	Aspaltu*m*	*As above ?*
11.	Π Bruscus	Bruscus	*Ruscus aculeatus*, Butcher's Broom.
12.	Bonworth	Bonewort, or kneholm	*As above.* 'Kneeholly'.
13.	Π Bursa Pastoru*m*	Bursa Pastoris	*Capsella bursa-pastoris*, Shepherd's Purse.
14.	Sanguinaria	Sanguinaria	*As above.*
15.	Stanche	Stanche	*As above.*
16.		Folio 168v, Col. C Bellirici marini	*Probably the Bellirici Marini of Mattheus Silvaticus (with similar wording as Line 17 below and SB, Mowat p.12). Perhaps Whelks - See London Encyclopedia (1829), p.778: 'a species of sea shells of an umbilical figure, sometimes of a white colour.' See also SB, Mowat, p.43 for 'umbilici marini' which is perhaps the original form.*
17.	Bellirici marini sunt albi p*ar*vi lapides	be*th* smale stones & whyte	
18.	inventi p*er* litus maris.	which be*th* fonden be *the* see brinkes.	

Image, Folio and Line Numbers.	Betson Entry. [The alphabetical letters A-Z below are for reference only, and are not in Betson].	The Synonoma of John Bray: BL Sloane MS 282, with folio number and column.	Possible Modern Names, mainly Linnaean, and taken from Hunt (1989). Non-Linnaean names are indicated.
19.	Bolus armoinic*us*	Bolus armenicus	Bole armeniac or Armenian bole. *Probably Azurite.*
20.	Π Bole armoniak	Bole of armonak	*As above.*
21.	Π Binni robenet It....	Ben iubiu*m*	*The Bray and Betson texts seems to be garbled forms of Been, Arabic Behen, as in "Been rub. radix quae in India invenitur. Been album in Egypto reperitur" in Alphita, Mowat, p.21 line 20. Hill, A History of the Materia Medica, 1751, p629, gives a complete description of the two plants and their uses.*
22.	is founden in ynde	Ys a rote wyche is founde on inde	
23.	& *the* rede *in* egipte.	& *the* white i*n* egipte	*The white is Centaurea Behen,* White Behen. *The red is Statice Limonium,* Sea Lavender or Red Behen. *Both are astringent, and hence grouped together here.*
24.	Π Brionia cucurbita		*Bryonia dioica,* White Bryony.
25.	agrestis ang*lice:* wildenep		*As above.*
26.	aliquantulu*m* assi*mi*latu*r* viti		
Image 77 Right, Folio 73r, Col. A			
1.	[C] Ciclamen.	Fol 169r, Col A Ciclamen	*Conopodium majus (Gouan) Loret,* Pignut, Earthnut; OR *Cyclamen hederifolium.* Cyclamen, sowbread.

Image, Folio and Line Numbers.	Betson Entry. [The alphabetical letters A-Z below are for reference only, and are not in Betson].	The Synonoma of John Bray: BL Sloane MS 282, with folio number and column.	Possible Modern Names, mainly Linnaean, and taken from Hunt (1989). Non-Linnaean names are indicated.
2.	Cassanum.	Cassanum	As above. See Hunt p72 - Cassamus
3.	Panis porcinus.	Panis porcinus	As above.
4.	Nux terre.	Nux terre, Nois de terre	As above.
5.	Malum terre.		As above.
6.	Erthe nuttis.	Anglice Erthe note	As above.
7.	Π Camedreos.	Camedreos	Veronica chamaedrys, Germander Speedwell. Hunt also gives: Teucrium chamaedrys, Wall Germander; Rhianthos cristi Galli, ?Yellow Rattle; Pedicularis palustris, ?Red Rattle.
8.	Germandria.	Germandrea	As above.
9.	Germandre.	Anglice Culerage	As above.
10.	Π Colophonia	Colofonia	Pine resin, Colophony.
11.	Pix greca.	Pyx greca	'Pix' here in the sense of 'resin','pitch'.
12.	Colophonie.	Anglice Colofoyne	As above.
13.	Π Cantabrum	Cantabrum	Triticum aestivum, Wheatbran.
14.	Furfur tritici.	Furfur tritici, Bran of whete, Berin de frument	As above.
15.		Capitellum lixivium , Lessive, Lye	
16.	Π Cervisa [Read: Cerusa].	Cerusa album (sic).	White Lead, Hydrocerussite.

Image, Folio and Line Numbers.	Betson Entry. [The alphabetical letters A-Z below are for reference only, and are not in Betson].	The Synonoma of John Bray: BL Sloane MS 282, with folio number and column.	Possible Modern Names, mainly Linnaean, and taken from Hunt (1989). Non-Linnaean names are indicated.
17.	Ceroisa		*As above.*
18.	Album plumbum		*As above.*
19.	Whitelede.	Blank plum, Whit leed.	*As above*
20.	ΠCaprifolium	Caprifolium	*Lonicera caprifolium,* Honeysuckle.
21.	Mater silve.	Mater silve	*As above.*
22.	Cherfole. Woodbynde	Chiverfoil, Wodebynde	*As above.*
23.	Π Caniclata.	Caniculata	*Hysocamus niger,* Henbane.
24.	Iusquiamus.	Iusquiamus	*As above.*
25.	Simphonica.	Simphonica	*As above. See Hunt p.239 for Simphoniaca.*
26.	Fistula henbane.	Fistula Chenil Henbane. *Hunt p.118 'Chenillé idem Henbane'.*	*As above, with a side reference to John Arderne's 'Fistula in ano' use of Henbane.*
27.	Π Centaurea.	Centaurea	*Centaurium erythraea* Rafn. Common Centaury.
28.	Fel terre.	Fel terre	*As above.*
29.	Centorye	Centorye eorthe	*As above.*
30.	Π Centrium Galli		*Salvia pratensis* or *sclarea,* Clary; or *Agrostemma githago,* Cockle; or *Lolium temulentum,* Darnel. *See Hunt p.77, Centrum Galli and Daems #146, p.147; #235, p.179, and #577, p.292.*
31.	Centregalle		*As above.*

Image, Folio and Line Numbers.	Betson Entry. [The alphabetical letters A-Z below are for reference only, and are not in Betson].	The Synonoma of John Bray: BL Sloane MS 282, with folio number and column.	Possible Modern Names, mainly Linnaean, and taken from Hunt (1989). Non-Linnaean names are indicated.
32.	Cellidonia deme*stica* (sic).	Celidonia, moun, celidoyn de mere	*Chelidonia majus,* Gtr. Celandine; Or *Glaucium corniculatum* 'Red Horned Poppy' Or: *Glaucium flavum,* Crantz, 'Yellow Horned Poppy'.
33.	m*a*jor Memiter*i*a		As above. See also Hunt p175 for Memita as *Glaucium flavum,* Crantz, 'Yellow Horned Poppy'.
Image 77 Right, Folio 73r, Col. B			
1.	Π Crassula	Fol 169r, Col A & B Crassula minor	*Sedum telephium,* Orpine.
2.	Vermclaris m*i*n*o*r	Vermiclaris	*Sedum acre,* Stonecrop.
3.	Stonhore	Stonore	As above.
4.	Π Crassula m*i*n*o*r		As above.
5.	Orpyu*m*	Orpyn	As above.
6.	Π Calamentum.	Calame*n*tu*m*	*Calamintha sylvatica* or *C. officinalis,* Wood Calamint or common Calamint; or *Nepeta cataria,* Catmint, Catnip.
7.	Calamynte.	Calamy*n*te	As above.
8.	Π Canabus	Canabus, Canarure	*Eupatarium cannabinum,* Hemp Agrimony.
9.	Hemp	He nepe (sic)	As above.
		Caballinus marinus, Ypotaneus	*Presumably 'sea horse'.*

Image, Folio and Line Numbers.	Betson Entry. [The alphabetical letters A-Z below are for reference only, and are not in Betson].	The Synonoma of John Bray: BL Sloane MS 282, with folio number and column.	Possible Modern Names, mainly Linnaean, and taken from Hunt (1989). Non-Linnaean names are indicated.
10.	Π Caticule	Caticula, Ranns (*Ramsons*)	*Allium ursinum*, Ramsons, Wild Garlic.
11.	Ramsyns		*As above.*
12.	Π Centrum grania	Centrum grana	*See Hunt p77 – not identified. Perhaps Centrum Galli: Salvia pratensis*, Clary; Or *Agrostemma githago*, Cockle; or *Lolium temulentum*, Darnel.
13.	Herba cancri	Herba cancri	*Calendula officinalis*, Pot Marigold; or *Delphinium ambiguum*, Larkspur; or *Leucanthemum vulgare*, ? Ox-Eye Daisy; or *Salvia sclarea*, ? Clary.
14.	Π Caput monachi	Caput monachi	*Taraxacum vulgare*, Weber; Dandelion.
15.	Dens Leonis	Dens Leonis	*As above.*
16.	Lyons toth	Lyon to*th*	*As above.*
17.	Dent de Lyon	Dent de Lyon	*As above.*
18.	Sowr*th*istill		Sow thistle Hunt,q.v., gives 20 possible equivalents. A 'Sonchus' species.
19.	Π <u>Cruciata</u> m*a*jor	Cruciata *t*hei be*th* ii of he*m*. Herba Croyse	*Galium cruciata?* Crosswort.
20.	Croise	Herba Croyse	*As above.*
21.	Π <u>Centinodium.</u>	Centinodium	*Persicaria aviculare*, Knotgrass.
22.	Lingua Passerum	Lingua passeris	*As above.*

Image, Folio and Line Numbers.	Betson Entry. [The alphabetical letters A-Z below are for reference only, and are not in Betson].	The Synonoma of John Bray: BL Sloane MS 282, with folio number and column.	Possible Modern Names, mainly Linnaean, and taken from Hunt (1989). Non-Linnaean names are indicated.
23.	Swynesgrece	Swynesgrace	*As above.*
24.	Π <u>Cepa Marina</u>	Alabu*m*, Cepa marina, Squilla, Squill.	*Drimia maritime,* Squill.
25.	Sqillis	Squillis, Squilla, Squill	*As above.*
26.	Π Cima rubi cinosus (?)	Cima rubi, cinons de rons	*Rubus fructicosus,* Bramble tops.
27.	*the* crop of *the* brembyll	Bremel croppe	*As above.*
28.	Π <u>Capillus veneris</u>	Capill ven*er*is	*Adiantum capillus-veneris,* Maidenhair fern.
29.	Maiden here	Mayden here	*As above.*
30.	Calendula	Calendula	*Calendula officinalis,* Garden Marigold.
31.	Solsequium	Solsequ*ium*	*As above.*
32.	Sponsa Solis, Rodone	Sponsa solis, goowe (=gold ?) Rodene	*As above.*
Image 78 Left, Folio 73v , Col. A			
1.	Colde ?		*As above –* read Golde. See Hunt p242, *Solsequium.*
2.	Π <u>Consolida</u> m*a*jor	Consolida *ther* ben *th*rei of he*m*	*Symphytum officinale,* Comfrey.
3.	Conferius	Comferie	*As above.*
4.	Wrenging-worth	**Fol 169r, Col C** Wringingwort Myddel Consoude.	*Bellis perennis,* Daisy. *See Hunt p.87 Consolida Media, for other possibilities and also ME variants.*

110

Image, Folio and Line Numbers.	Betson Entry. [The alphabetical letters A-Z below are for reference only, and are not in Betson].	The Synonoma of John Bray: BL Sloane MS 282, with folio number and column.	Possible Modern Names, mainly Linnaean, and taken from Hunt (1989). Non-Linnaean names are indicated.
		Consolida minor, Brusewort or Dayseye.	
5.	Daiseyen	Daiziee	*As above – Daisy.*
6.	Π <u>Camamilla</u>.	Camamilla, Camamille	*Chamaemelum nobile,* Sweet Camomile.
7.	Cyminu*m* dulce.	Ciminum dulce	*Pimpinella anisum,* Wild Cumin.
8.	Anyse camamyll	Aneys	*As above.*
9.	Cepe oynoins.	Cepe, Oynons	*Allium cepa,* Onion.
10.	Π <u>Calx viva</u>.	Calx viva	Quicklime.
11.	Lyme	Quik lyme	Lime.
12.	Π <u>Cucurbita</u>.	Cucurbita agrestis, Bryonie, Wildenepe	*Bryonia dioica,* White Bryony.
13.	Coule couell	Caulis agrestis, Coul chenel.	*Brassica oleracea,* Cabbage
14.	Π <u>Carduus Fullo*n*is</u>	Cardus fullonis	*Dipsacus fullonum,* Teasel. Hunt also gives *Saponaria officinalis,* Soapwort.
15.	Cavvener	Savvernere	*As above.*
16.	Crouesope.	Crousope	*As above.*

Image, Folio and Line Numbers.	Betson Entry. [The alphabetical letters A-Z below are for reference only, and are not in Betson].	The Synonoma of John Bray: BL Sloane MS 282, with folio number and column.	Possible Modern Names, mainly Linnaean, and taken from Hunt (1989). Non-Linnaean names are indicated.
17.	Π Cuscuta	Cuscuta	*Cuscuta epilinum*, Flax Dodder; or *Cuscuta europaea*, Large Dodder; or *Cuscuta epithymum*, Common Dodder.
18.	Dedere	*Idem* Dodi*r*	*As above.*
19.	Podagra lini	Podagra lyni	*As above.*
20.	Π Colubrina.		*Polygonum bistorta*, Snake root, Bistort. Or *Dracunculus vulgaris*, Schott. Dragon Arum, *(a Mediterranean plant).*
21.	Dragance		*As above.*
22.	Nedderworth		*As above.*
23.	Π Corona Regia.	Corona regia	*Melilotus officinalis*, Melilot, Sweet Clover; or *Trifolium pratense*, Red Clover.
24.	Mellilotum.	Mellilot*um*	*?As above.*
25.	Trifoliium.	Trifoliu*m*	*?As above.*
26.	Mellilote. Levedgras	Mellilote, *th*releved gras.	*?As above. (Betson appears to have mis-read his source).*
27.	Π Catapucia	Catapucia Fol. 169v, Col. A Elacterides iuce of catrepus, iuce of spurge.	*Euphorbia lathyris*, Seed of Caper Spurge.
28.	Spurge	Spourge	*As above.*
29.	Π Copiosa, herb copi		*Unidentified by Hunt, at p.88 though it occurs in five listed MSS. Also occurs in Bray.*

Image, Folio and Line Numbers.	Betson Entry. [The alphabetical letters A-Z below are for reference only, and are not in Betson].	The Synonoma of John Bray: BL Sloane MS 282, with folio number and column.	Possible Modern Names, mainly Linnaean, and taken from Hunt (1989). Non-Linnaean names are indicated.
30.	Π Crocus affrican*us*	Crocus affricanus	*Crocus sativus,* Saffron Crocus; or *Carthamus tinctorius,* Safflower, Bastard Saffron.
31.	Crocus ortensis	Crocus ortensis	*As above.*
Image 78 Left, Folio 73v, Col. B			
1.	Saffron	Safron de ort*orum*	*As above.*
2.	Π Custos ort*orum*.	Custos ort*orum*	See Palma Xpi below and Hunt pp. 96 and 196.
3.	Palma Xpi (*i.e. Christi*)	Palma Xpī	?*Leonurus cardiaca,* Motherwort; or ? *Ricinus communis,* ? Castor Oil Plant; or *Lithospermum officinale,* Gromwell; or *Artemesia vulgaris,* Mugwort; or *Lamium purpureum* 'Red Dead Nettle. *See Hunt p196 for variants Also Daems #393, p.235.* *But also in Daems, #729, p.326, where there are several citations of Palma Christi as Orchid varieties.*
4.	Π Chimolia	Chinolea, terra sigillata vel hispanica.	'A sort of fuller's earth.' *Alphita ,Mowat, p.38, footnote15.*
5.	Terra sigillata		*As above*
		Dactillis, Anglice dates	

Image, Folio and Line Numbers.	Betson Entry. [The alphabetical letters A-Z below are for reference only, and are not in Betson].	The Synonoma of John Bray: BL Sloane MS 282, with folio number and column.	Possible Modern Names, mainly Linnaean, and taken from Hunt (1989). Non-Linnaean names are indicated.
6.	Π Calcaticum	Fol 168v, Col C Calculum	Not found. "Perhaps chalcanth or calcanthum, used for the compound blue vitriol, and the ink made from it. The term was also applied to red vitriol and to green vitriol (ferrous sulfate)." Also simply for sulphuric acid. Chambers Cyclopaedia, 1728.
7.	Cardamonium	Cardamonium	Hunt p68 has Cardamomum, which is Rorippa nasturtium-aquaticum Hayek., Watercress, or Lepidum sativum, Garden Cress. See also Daems #337, p.216.
8.	Π Calcatum.	Calcantium	See Calcaticum above, Line 6.
9.	Attramentum	Attramentum	Vitriol EMED
10.	Vitriolum	Vitrolum	'Any of certain glassy mineral salts of sulfuric acid used esp. in alchemy or medicine, vitriol; ...also, sulphuric acid' EMED.
11.	Π Camophiteos	Camepiteos, medarattel See Hunt pp.64 and 217 for variants.	Ajuga chamaepitrys, Ground-pine; or Rhianthus crista-galli, Yellow Rattle; or Pedicularis palustris, Red Rattle, or Teucrium chamaedrys, 'Wall Germander.'
12.	Π Campherata	Camphorata	Artemesia abrotanum, Southernwood.
13.	Averoyn	Averoyne	As above.
14.	Sotherwode	Sothernewode	As above.
15.	Π Camcattis.		Sambucus ebulus, Danewort, Dwarf Elder.

Image, Folio and Line Numbers.	Betson Entry. [The alphabetical letters A-Z below are for reference only, and are not in Betson].	The Synonoma of John Bray: BL Sloane MS 282, with folio number and column.	Possible Modern Names, mainly Linnaean, and taken from Hunt (1989). Non-Linnaean names are indicated.
16.	Ebulus	Fol. 169v., Col. A Ebulus, Eble, Lythewort or Walwort	As above.
17.	Eble.		As above.
18.	Walworth	Walwort	As above.
19.	Π Camely	Camelee	*Potentilla reptans,* Cinquefoil.
20.	Qui*n*que folium	Qui*n*que foliu*m*	As above.
21.	Pentafoliu*m*.	Pentafilon	As above.
22.	Qui*n*yfole.	Qui*n*yfoile	As above.
23.	Π Camaleoncia.	Camaleonta ys a *th*istle i*d*em Reni*n*gwort.	*Sonchus* species, Sowthistle. See Hunt p.63, Cameleonta.
24.	Anglice thistill		As above.
25.	Π Cantarides	Cantarides	'A kind of beetle; esp., *Cantharis vesicatoria;* one of these beetles dried for medicinal use.' EMED.
26.	Grene wormes in	be*th* usyen grene wormes	
27.	asshis growi*n*g	growing in aisches	Presumably 'ash trees'. *Fraxinus excelsior.*
		Cancer marinus, Anglice a crabbe	
28.	Π Cardo thistill.	Cardo asinin*us,* Cardo co*mm*unis, Anglice a *th*ystel	*Cardo Asininus* may be *Onopordon acanthium,* Scotch Thistle (Hunt p.68).

Image, Folio and Line Numbers.	Betson Entry. [The alphabetical letters A-Z below are for reference only, and are not in Betson].	The Synonoma of John Bray: BL Sloane MS 282, with folio number and column.	Possible Modern Names, mainly Linnaean, and taken from Hunt (1989). Non-Linnaean names are indicated.
29.	Cardo benedicta	Cardo benedictus	*Cnicus benedictus*, Blessed Thistle.
30.	Labrum veneris	Labrum veneris	*Sonchus*, Sowthistle.
31.	Thowthistill (sic)	Vowethistel (See Hunt p.68.)	As above.
32.	Π Catholica lauriola.	Catholica idem Lauriola	*Laurus nobilis*, Bay Tree
Image 78, Right, Folio 74r, Col. A			
1.	Π Cariaca.	Cariaca	*Ficus carica*, Fig.
2.	Ficus sicca.	Ficus sica	As above.
3.	Dry fige.	Drie fyges	As above.
4.	Π Carei Porcini	Carei Porcini	*Daucus carota*, Wild Carrot. *The usual word 'pontici' is replaced here by 'porcini.'*
5.	Daukis.	idem Dauck	*Daucus carota*, Wild Carrot; or *Pastinaca sativa*, Wild Parsnip; or ?*Athamanta cretensis*, ?Cretan Carrot.
6.	Π Cardami	Cardami	*Lepidium sativum*, Garden Cress EMED.
7.	Connarasses (sic)	idem tuncarse seed (i.e. town cress – EMED).	*Lepidum sativum*, Garden Cress. See Image 83 right, folio 79r, col. A, line 27 for correct Bray citation.
8.	Catamatici	Cathamatici	Shaving from the horns of deer.
9.	Rasura	Est rasura cornuum cervi	As above.
10.	Π Cornu cervi.		As above.
11.	shaving of harts horns	**Folio 169 Col A** idem shaving of the hert horne	As above.

116

Image, Folio and Line Numbers.	Betson Entry. [The alphabetical letters A-Z below are for reference only, and are not in Betson].	The Synonoma of John Bray: BL Sloane MS 282, with folio number and column.	Possible Modern Names, mainly Linnaean, and taken from Hunt (1989). Non-Linnaean names are indicated.
12.	Π Caride miristice	Caride miristice	*Myristica fragrans,* Nutmeg.
13.	Nuces muscate.		*As above*
14.	Not muges. (*i.e. 'nutmegs'*)	Anglice Notemuge	*As above*
		Bray: Cassia Lignea, Xilocassia Cassia fistula is *the* fruyt of a tree, bot *[but]* cassia lignea is *the* rinde of *the* fruyt.	
15.	Π Castorium *the* balok	Castorium is the balok of a beste.	Castor, Beaver.
16.	of *the* best.		
17.	Π Cauda equina	Cauda equina	*Hunt p.73 gives Digitalis purpurea, Foxglove for 13 of his MSS – see next entry.*
18.	Foxisglove	Foxesglove	*Digitalis purpurea,* Foxglove.
19.	a padokpipe	Cauda Pulli , Paddokespipe	*Cauda Pulli in Bray suggests that Equisetum, Horsetail is likely here. See Hunt p.74.*
20.	Π Cauda pulli		*Hippuris vulgaris* Marestail.
21.	Π Celsus amara	Celsus mara maior.	*Centaurium erythraea,* Common Centaury; *But also ?Blackstonia perforata,* Yellow Wort.
22.	Maior centorie		*Centaurea erythraea,* Common Centaury
23.	Π Cristos ladder.	Cristes ladder	*As above.*

Image, Folio and Line Numbers.	Betson Entry. [The alphabetical letters A-Z below are for reference only, and are not in Betson].	The Synonoma of John Bray: BL Sloane MS 282, with folio number and column.	Possible Modern Names, mainly Linnaean, and taken from Hunt (1989). Non-Linnaean names are indicated.
24.	Π Centonica absi*n*th	Centonica Absintiu*m* Ponticum	*Artemesia maritima*, 'Sea Wormwood'
25.	Ponticu*m* wormod.	Ponticum, Wermode	*As above entry? Hunt p.212 gives Artemesia absinthium*, Wormwood.
26.	Centru*m* pulli.	Centrum Galli - *perhaps an error – pulli 'hen' , for 'cockerel'*	*Salvia pratensis*, or *sclarea*, Clary; or *Agrostemma githago*, Cockle; or *Lolium tremulentum*, Darnel.
27.	Gallitricum.	Gallitricu*m*	*As above.*
28.	Gallicrista.	Gallicrista	*As above. Daems #146, p.147, has Crista Galli.*
29.	Centum galle.	Centumgalle	*As above.*
30.	Centenaria.	Centinaria	*?Plantago lanceolata*, Ribwort, read '*centinervia*'.
31.	Plantago.	Pla*n*tago	*? As above.*
Image 78, Right, Folio 74r, Col. B			
1.	Arnoglossa	Arnoglossa	*Plantago major*, 'Lamb's tongue plantain'.
2.	Lingua agni	Lingua agni	*As above.*
3.	Lambis tong	Lambestonge	*As above.*
4.	Π Consolida ma*ior* Co*m*fery		*Symphytum officinale* Comfrey.
5.	Π Consolida mi*n*or daisey		*Bellis perennis*, Daisy.
6.	Cutulus (*for Dactulus*)	Dactulus acetosus	*Tamarindus indica*, Tamarind.
7.	Acetosus		*As above.*

118

Image, Folio and Line Numbers.	Betson Entry. [The alphabetical letters A-Z below are for reference only, and are not in Betson].	The Synonoma of John Bray: BL Sloane MS 282, with folio number and column.	Possible Modern Names, mainly Linnaean, and taken from Hunt (1989). Non-Linnaean names are indicated.
8.	Oxencia	Oxifenicia	As above.
9.	Finico*n* Tamaides	Finirco Taniarindes, Anglice Sorel	As above. Daems#189, p.161 has 'Finicus id est dactilus' for *Phoenix dactylifera*, Datepalm.
10.	**[D]** Daucus	Daucus	*Pastinaca sativa*, Wild Parsnip.
11.	Creticus.	Creticus	As above. See Hunt pp.97-98
12.	Trericus De*n*tdelion	Trericus Dent de Lyon	*Taraxacum officinale*, Dandelion. *Trericus is not in Hunt. It looks like a mis-spelt and misplaced version of 'Creticus' above.*
13.	Dragantum	Draggantu*m* the gume of a tre	*Astracantha gummifera*, Gum tragacanth.
14.	Gum of a tre		As above.
15.	Π Dragancia.	Dragancia	?*Sinapis arvensis*, Charlock; or: ?*Raphanus raphanistrum*, Wild Radish.
16.	Aragriofora (?)	Agirofera	Not found. As above ?
17.	Iapist*ru*m	Iapistrum	Read 'Rapistrum'. Charlock as above. See Hunt p.219.
18.	Chevlange (?)	Cherlok	*Bray is as above.*
19.	Dragraniscia (?)	Draguncia	*Polygonum bistorta*, Bistort Or *Dracunculus vulgaris* Schott, Dragon Arum. See Hunt p.102 for variants below.
20.	Columbrina	Colu*m*brina	As above. See Hunt p.102 for variants.
21.	Serpentaria	Serpentaria	As above.
22.	Cocodrilla.	Cocodrilla	As above.
23.	Basiliscus.	Basilicus	As above.

Image, Folio and Line Numbers.	Betson Entry. [The alphabetical letters A-Z below are for reference only, and are not in Betson].	The Synonoma of John Bray: BL Sloane MS 282, with folio number and column.	Possible Modern Names, mainly Linnaean, and taken from Hunt (1989). Non-Linnaean names are indicated.
24.	Nedduworth	Edderwort	As above. (Adderwort)
		Bray: Dascrista, epatica, liverwort. For Dacrista see Hunt p.97, Dascripta. Betson picks this up at Line 17 of image 79 left, folio 74v, col. A, below.	
25.	Π Danilion	Dampindos the tre of the lorel Dampinleon	Laurus nobilis, Bay Tree Berry.
26.	Olium laurinum	Olium laurinum	As above – Bay Oil.
27.	Dendrolibani	Dendrolibani	Rosmarinus officinalis, Rosemary.
28.	Labanitidos.	Libanitidos	As above.
Image 79 Left, Folio 74v, Col. A			
1.	Antos rosemary flour	Antos Ros marinus Fol 168r, Col C Bray: Antos is the flower of the rose marine. Also a eye with owt shelle *(an egg with no shell).* Hunt p.27.	
2.	Rosemarinus		As above.
3.	Rosemaryn	Rosmaryne	As above.
4.	Dens equi	Dens equi	Hunt p99 gives six possiblities, including: Cyperus rotundus or C. longus, Rush or Galingale, *which seems to fit with the next entry below.*
5.	Ciperus		As above
6.	Π Dematheam	Dimathian	Daemonorops draco, Blume ex Schult; Dragon's Blood (Resin); Dracaena draco L. Dragon Tree.
7.	Amiltus Datum.	Multis datum	As above.
8.	Sanguis draconis	Sanguis draconis	As above.

Image, Folio and Line Numbers.	Betson Entry. [The alphabetical letters A-Z below are for reference only, and are not in Betson].	The Synonoma of John Bray: BL Sloane MS 282, with folio number and column.	Possible Modern Names, mainly Linnaean, and taken from Hunt (1989). Non-Linnaean names are indicated.
9.	Π Diptamis	Dyptamnis	*Dictamnus albus,* Ditany.
10.	Ditandre	Ditayne	*As above.*
11.	Π Droptori	Droptori	*Dryopteris filix-mas* or *Polypodium* ssp., Male Fern, Polypody.
12.	Pollipodium	Polipodium	*As above.*
13.	Π Dionisia.	Dionisia	*Calendula officinalis,* Marigold.
14.	Flos Cicorie.	Flos cicorey	*As above.*
15.	The Flour of rodeum	The fluer of rodene	*As above.*
16.	[E] Epatica	Fol 169v Col A Epatica	*Marchantia polymorpha,* Liverwort; or *Anemone epatica.* 'Noble Liverwort'.
17.	Dascripta	Dascripta, Couper	*As above. (See Hunt p.97 and p.108).*
18.	Lyverworte	Lyverwort	*As above.*
19.	Π Epatorium	Eupatorium	*Teucrium scorodonia,* Wood Sage, Hind Heal, 'Sage-leaved Germander'.
20.	Ambrosium	Ambrosia	*As above.*
21.	Lilifagus.	Lilifagus	*As above.*
22.	Salvia agrestis	Salvia agrestis	*As above.*
23.	Hyndehale.	Hyndhale, Wildesauge	*As above.*
24.	Edera terrestris	Edera Terestris	*Glechoma hederacea* Ground Ivy.
25.	Heyhove; Tunhove.	Heyhove,	*As above. See also Hunt pp.42 and 132-33.*
26.	Elotropia	Eleutropia	Heliotrope. *Calendula officinalis*

Image, Folio and Line Numbers.	Betson Entry. [The alphabetical letters A-Z below are for reference only, and are not in Betson].	The Synonoma of John Bray: BL Sloane MS 282, with folio number and column.	Possible Modern Names, mainly Linnaean, and taken from Hunt (1989). Non-Linnaean names are indicated.
27.	Solsequium	Solsequium	*As above.*
Image 79, Left, Folio 74v, Col. B			
1.	Verucaria.	Verucaria	*As above.*
2.	Cicoria.	Cicoria	*As above.*
3.	Sponsa solis.	Sponsa solis	*As above.*
4.	Gira solis.		*As above.*
5.	Solsequile	Solsekile, Roden	*As above.*
6.	Π Elempnum.	Elempinum	*Inula helenium,* Elecampane, Horseheal, Scabwort.
7.	Enula campana.	Enula campana	*As above.*
8.	Horself	Horselve	*As above.*
9.	Π Elactorium the	Elacterium	*Euphorbia lathyrus,* Caper Spurge; or here: *Ecballium elaterium,* Squirting Cucumber.
10.	Juce of wilde cucumbre	The iuce of wilde cucumber	*As above.*
11.	Wilde popy	idem Wilde Papie	*As above.*
12.	Π Esbrinum flos salme	Esbrium the flower of sage	*Salvia officinalis,* Sage.
13.	Elixis bardana	Elixis bardana	*Arctium lappa,* Greater Burdock.
14.	Lappa eversa. Clote	Lappa eversa, Anglice Clote	*Arctium minus,* Lesser Burdock.
15.	Π Emathites.	Emathites	*Haematite, crystallized form of iron ore, was believed to staunch bleeding.*
16.	Lapis quondam	Lapis quondam	*As above.*
17.	Lapis sanguina.	Lapis sanguinarius	*As above.*

Image, Folio and Line Numbers.	Betson Entry. [The alphabetical letters A-Z below are for reference only, and are not in Betson].	The Synonoma of John Bray: BL Sloane MS 282, with folio number and column.	Possible Modern Names, mainly Linnaean, and taken from Hunt (1989). Non-Linnaean names are indicated.
18.	Π Es ustum	Fol 168v, Col C Es Ustum,	Copper. Oxide
19.	Calor. Omnenon ?	Calcetuminon,	*As above.* See EMED: '*calcecumenon quod est es vstum* Chauliac, 1425.
20.	Calceos, brent bras	Cathiceos Es ustum Calcecuminon, Calchitheos, Bras y brent.	*As above.* EMED: *Es vste .i. brent bras*, Chauliac, 1425.
21.	Π Edia troxima (read: 'Endivia')	Fol. 169v, Col. A Endiva troxima	*Chicorium endiva*, Endive; or *Sonchus oleraceus*, Sowthistle; or *Lactuca serriola*, 'Prickly Lettuce'.
22.	Endivia. Endyve.	Endive	*As above.*
23.	Π Eviscus altea.	Eviscus altea	*Althaea officinalis*, Marsh mallow.
24.	Malva viscus.	Malva viscus	*Althaea officinalis* Marsh mallow. ?*Anthemis Cotula* Mayweed.
25.	Bismalva.	Bismalva	*Althaea officinalis*, Marsh mallow.
26.	Wymawe.	Wuemalve, Anglice Hocke	*As above.*
27.	Π Eleborus Albus	Eleborus albus	*Veratrum album*, White or False Hellebore.
28.	Adarasta.	Adarasta	*As above.*
29.	Whyte Elebo	Whit Ellerne	*As above.*

Image, Folio and Line Numbers.	Betson Entry. [The alphabetical letters A-Z below are for reference only, and are not in Betson].	The Synonoma of John Bray: BL Sloane MS 282, with folio number and column.	Possible Modern Names, mainly Linnaean, and taken from Hunt (1989). Non-Linnaean names are indicated.
30.	Π Eleboeris niger	Eleborus ma*ior*	*Helleborus niger,* Black Hellebore.
31.	Clovetong	Clovetong	*Veratrum album,* White or False Hellebore.
32.	Blak Eleborum	Blak Ellerne	*Helleborus niger,* Black Hellebore.
Image 79, Right, Folio 75r, Col. A			
1.	Π Epitimu*m*.	Epithimiu*m* flours of Time	*Cuscuta epithymum,* Thyme Dodder.
2.	Flos of tyme.	*As above*	*As above*
3.	Π Eruca Skirewite	Eruca, Skyrewit	*Eruca sativa,* Garden Rocket; or *Sium* ssp., Skirret; or *Raphanus raphanistrum,* Wild Radish; or *Sinapis arvensis,* Charlok.
4.	Π Euforbrium	Euforbium	*Hunt p112 gives Euphorbium,* Spurge.
5.	Π Eufrobe gu*m*ma.	Euforbe, hit ys gume of a tre	*As above.*
6.	Π Eriscus. Colonne	Eriscus, Colofoine, Resina, Pyx greca.	Pine resin, colophony ? *'Eriscus' is not in Hunt or Mowat, though there is an entry for Colofonia under 'Erice' at Mowat, Alphita p.58*
7.	Resina pix greca.		Pine resin, colophony.

Image, Folio and Line Numbers.	Betson Entry. [The alphabetical letters A-Z below are for reference only, and are not in Betson].	The Synonoma of John Bray: BL Sloane MS 282, with folio number and column.	Possible Modern Names, mainly Linnaean, and taken from Hunt (1989). Non-Linnaean names are indicated.
	[F]	Faba a bene	
8.	<u>Fabaria</u> Favicle	Fabaria	*Veronica beccabunga*, Brooklime.
9.	Lem.	Lemyk, Faverole	*As above.*
10.	Π <u>Farina.</u> Alphita.	Farina ordei, Alfita	Barley Meal or Flour
11.	Flour of barlich.	Flour of Barliche	*As above.*
12.	Π <u>Fragaria.</u> Fraserus	Fragaria. Fraser	*Fragaria vesca*, Wild Strawberry.
13.	Streberiwise	Strewberywise	*As above.*
14.	Π <u>Fragra</u> strebery	Fragra, Strewberye*n*	*As above* – read *Fraga* ?
15.	Π <u>Flam</u>*m*ulus	Flamulus	MED: Sleepwort, lettuce (*Lactuca scariola* or *L. virosa*). Or perhaps: *Lactuca serriola*.
16.	Sleveworth	Shepeworth	*As above* ?
17.	Π <u>Fraximus</u> (sic) an*g*lice Ash.	Fraxinus ys a Ashe	*Fraxinus excelsior*, Ash Tree.
18.	Π <u>Fragrum</u> bruscus	Fragrum, Bruscus	*Ruscus aculeatus*, Butcher's Broom.
19.	Bonworte.	Bone Worte	*As above.*
20.	Π <u>Fageria</u>. Filix.	Falgeria, Filex	*Polypodium* ssp., Common Polypody; or *Osmunda regalis*, Royal Fern; or *Dryopteris filis-mas*, Male Fern.
21.	Frager Fern	Fengre, Anglice Fern	*As above.*

Image, Folio and Line Numbers.	Betson Entry. [The alphabetical letters A-Z below are for reference only, and are not in Betson].	The Synonoma of John Bray: BL Sloane MS 282, with folio number and column.	Possible Modern Names, mainly Linnaean, and taken from Hunt (1989). Non-Linnaean names are indicated.
22.	Π Febrifuga	Febrifuga,	*Probably Centaurium erythraea*, Common Centaury, *or perhaps: Tanacetum parthenium*, Feverfew.
Image 79, Right, Folio 75r, Col. B			
1.	Felterre Centaurea	Felterre Centaurea	*Centaurium erythraea*, Common Centaury.
2.	Simphonica. Febrifu.	Simfoinata, Fetherfoyee	*Hysocamus niger*, Henbane. *See Hunt p.238 for Simphoniaca*
3.	Π Fenugrecum	Fennigrecum,	*Trigonella foenum-graecum*, Fenugreek.
4.	Fenugrek	Fennigrek	*As above.*
		Fex, Drasces Fel, Galle	OF drache, 'dregs, sediment.'
5.	Π Feniculus. Semen.	Finiculus, Fenel	*Foeniculum vulgare*, Fennel seed.
6.	Maratrum fynkill	The seed ys y clepyd marastrum.	*Foeniculum vulgare*, Fennel.
7.	Π Ferula qui fit gal-	Ferula ys an herbe that of the iuce ys made Galbanum.	*Perhaps Ferula communis* or *Ferula gumosa* in the group Dorema ammoniacum (D. DON.) Listed in the British Pharmocopeia.
8.	-banum domesticum (?)		i.e. 'ordinary gum'
9.	Π Feniculus porcinus	Feniculus porcinus	*Peucedanum officinale*, Hog's Fennel.
10.	Peucedanum. Marisca	Peucedanum amarisca	?*As above.*

126

Image, Folio and Line Numbers.	Betson Entry. [The alphabetical letters A-Z below are for reference only, and are not in Betson].	The Synonoma of John Bray: BL Sloane MS 282, with folio number and column.	Possible Modern Names, mainly Linnaean, and taken from Hunt (1989). Non-Linnaean names are indicated.
11.	Hundesfennel	Houndesfenel	*Anthemis cotula,* Stinking Camomile, Mayweed.
12.	Π Filago Horworth.	Filago Horwort	*Filago vulgaris,* Cudweed; or *?Pilosella officinarum,* Mouse-ear Hawkweed; or *?Gnaphalium uliginosum,* 'Marsh Cudweed'.
13.	<u>Filipendula</u>	Filipendula	*Filipendula vulgaris,* Dropwort.
14.	Fisalidos stonewort	Fisalidos, Stonwort	*As above.*
		Finicon, Indi, Oxifencia, Tamar indi	*For Betson entry see: image 81 left, folio 76v, col. B , line 26.*
15.	Π <u>Flosmus</u> tapsus	Flosmus tapsus	*Vebascum thapsus,* Mullein.
16.	Barbastus Pentafilon.	Barbasus, Penfilon	*As above.*
17.	Herba luminaria Moleyn	Herba luminaria Molyne	*As above.*
18.	Π Flos ciriacus. Malwye	Flos ciriacus,	*Althaea officinalis,* Marsh Mallow.
	Flour of malvys	Flour of Malwes	*As above.*
19.	Flos rosmarini	Flos roris marini	*Rosmarinus officinalis,* Rosemary.
20.	Π Antos	Antos	*As above*
21.	Flor of rose mary	Flour of rose marine	*As above.*

Image, Folio and Line Numbers.	Betson Entry. [The alphabetical letters A-Z below are for reference only, and are not in Betson].	The Synonoma of John Bray: BL Sloane MS 282, with folio number and column.	Possible Modern Names, mainly Linnaean, and taken from Hunt (1989). Non-Linnaean names are indicated.
22.	Π Flos fraxini	Flos fraxini	?*Fraxinus excelsior*, Common Ash.
23.	Alphin	Alphur	As above. See Hunt p.18, Alpha as 'Ash-key ?'.
24.	Flour of assh	flour of *the* asshe	As above.
25.	Π Flos mali granati	Flos Maligranati	*Punica granatum*, Dried flowers of Pomegranate
26.	Balanustia	Balaustia	As above. Bray's Balaustia was the standard form. See Hunt p.44
27.	Flos of pome garnet.	Flowe of Pomme garnet	As above.
28.	Π Flos plumbi	Flos plu*m*bi	'a mixture of the carbonate and hydrate of lead' EMED.
29.	Ceruce	Ceruce	White Lead
30.	Blaunk plome.	Blanche plum	As above.
31.	Π Flos eris.	Flos eris	Brass
Image 80, Left, Folio 75v, Col. A			
1.	Verdegres	Verdgrece	Verdigris
2.	Π Flo*res* Valeriana	Fol. 169v., Col. B Fu Valeriana, Fumetere.	*Valeriana phu* or *V. officinalis*, Valerian. (*Betson has misread 'Fu 'as 'Fll' for 'flores'*)
3.	Potentilla.		As above.
4.	Π Fum*us*terre		*Fumaria officinalis*, Common Fumitory. See Hunt p.122.
5.	Camthor		*Perhaps here a variant of EMED q.v. for Fumitory.*
6.	Fumitoris		As above.

Image, Folio and Line Numbers.	Betson Entry. [The alphabetical letters A-Z below are for reference only, and are not in Betson].	The Synonoma of John Bray: BL Sloane MS 282, with folio number and column.	Possible Modern Names, mainly Linnaean, and taken from Hunt (1989). Non-Linnaean names are indicated.
7.	Π Fulfulabia	Filfulabiat	*Alphita, Mowat, p.69 gives 'fulful ebiat' as piper album, and 'fulful ebet' as piper nigrum. See Mowat footnotes for sources and variants; 'fulful abyad' is the Arabic for white pepper.*
8.	Pi*per* nigrum.	Piper nigru*m*	*Piper nigrum,* Black Pepper.
9.	Blak pepur.	Black Piper	*As above.*
10.	Π Fulfules	The unripe fruit seeds of *Piper nigrum*, Black Pepper. *Bray:* Fulfulesbeth, Pi*per* Albu*m*, Piper albu*m*, Fulfulabiat, Piper longu*m*, melanu*m*, nigru*m*, Fulfulesbeck. Hit is macro piper.	
11.	Beth. Piper album	*As above*	*As above.*
12.	White piper	White piper	*As above.*
13.	Π Furfur tritici	Furfur tritici	*Bran, hard outer layer of cereal grain.*
14.	Cantabrum	Cantabrium	*As above.*
15.	Bran of whete	Bran of Whete	*As above.*
16.	Π Fructus Iuni*per*	Fructus Iuniperi	*Juniperus communis,* Juniper.
17.	Armfractus.	Amyfructus	*As above.*
18.	Frute of juniper	Fruyt of Iunip*ery*	*As above.*
19.	Π Fructus de edera	Fructus Eder*e*	*Hedera helix,* Ivy.
20.	Corpotissa.	Capocisci	*As above*
21.	Baccarum edere	Baccarum Edere	*Hedera helix,* Ivy Berries.
22.	Bayes of yby.	Bayes of yvy	*As above.*

Image, Folio and Line Numbers.	Betson Entry. [The alphabetical letters A-Z below are for reference only, and are not in Betson].	The Synonoma of John Bray: BL Sloane MS 282, with folio number and column.	Possible Modern Names, mainly Linnaean, and taken from Hunt (1989). Non-Linnaean names are indicated.
23.	Π Frumentum	Frumentum	Wheat
24.	Whete.	Whete	*As above.*
Image 80, Left, Folio 75v, Col. B			
1.	[G] Π (G)Albanum	Galbanum ys the iuce of an herbe	*Ferula galbaniflua,* Galbanum.
2.	Galla.	Galla	Oak Apple.
3.	Pomum quercinum	Pomum porcinum *(perhaps in error for 'quercinum').*	*As above.*
4.	Sicidon. Alapasa	Scicidon, Alapsa	*As above.* *See also Hunt p.13, Alapsa.*
5.	Ox appull.	Oke appel	*As above.* *Betson to be read as 'Oak's Apple' ?*
6.	Π Galanga galinygal.	Galanga, Galingale	*?Alpinia officinalis,* Hance; Galangal – ginger. Or: *Cyperus longus,* Galingale, 'English Galingale'.
7.	Π Gallitricum	Gallitricum	*Salvia pratensis,* Clary; or *Agrostemma githago,* Cockle; or *Lolium temulentum,* Darnel.
8.	Centum galli	Centrum galli	*As above.*
9.	Π Gallicrista	Galli crista	*Hunt p124 gives Galli Cresta as Salvia sclarea,* Clary / Wild Clary.
10.	Π Gariophilus	Gariofilus	*Syzygium aromaticum – formerly Eugenia caryophillata,* Cloves.

Image, Folio and Line Numbers.	Betson Entry. [The alphabetical letters A-Z below are for reference only, and are not in Betson].	The Synonoma of John Bray: BL Sloane MS 282, with folio number and column.	Possible Modern Names, mainly Linnaean, and taken from Hunt (1989). Non-Linnaean names are indicated.
11.	Clovis	*idem* Clowes	*As above.*
12.	Π Gariofilata	Gariofilata	*Geum urbanum,* Avens, 'Clove Root'.
13.	Sana mu*n*da	Sanamu*n*da	*As above.*
14.	Pes Lepor*is*	Pes leporis	*As above.*
15.	Avencia avence	Avencia, Avence	*As above.*
16.	Π Gariophilus ag*r*estis	Gariofilus agrestis	*Eugenia caryophyllata* Thunb., Cloves; or *Dianthos caryophyllus,* Clove Gillyflower ; or ?*Geum urbanum,* ?Avens.
17.	Azarabara *(sic)*	Azabaccara	*Asarum europaeum,* Asarabacca.
18.	Π Gladiolus	Gladiolus	*Iris Pseudacorus,* Yellow flag.
19.	Gladiole	Gladiole	*As above.*
20.	Gramen amcast*is*	Gramen amesistis	*Elytrigia repens,* Couch grass. (Not in Mowat, but in Hunt, p.130).
21.	Quche grasse.	Anglice Cuchegras	*As above.*
22.	Π Grana solis	Grana solis	*Lithospermum officinalis,* Gromwell.
23.	Molen folia	Milium solis	*As above.* (Betson / source has misread entry)
24.	Gromole	Anglice Gromel	*As above*
25.	Π Gagates geth	Gagatis, Geeth	Jet.
26.	Glaucia	Glaucia	*Chelidonium majus,* Gtr. Celandine.
27.	Celidonia Celidon	Celidonia Anglice Celidoyne	*As above.*

Image, Folio and Line Numbers.	Betson Entry. [The alphabetical letters A-Z below are for reference only, and are not in Betson].	The Synonoma of John Bray: BL Sloane MS 282, with folio number and column.	Possible Modern Names, mainly Linnaean, and taken from Hunt (1989). Non-Linnaean names are indicated.
28.	Genesta	Genesta	*Cytisus scoparius*, Broom.
29.	Merica Brom	Mirica, Genet, Anglice Brome	*As above.*
30.	Genestula lyeth in brambles *with* white flo*ur*. (?)	Genestula, hyt ys lyche Brome, with a whit floure.	*As above.*
31.	Geniculata	Geniculata	*Persicaria aviculare*, Knotgrass.
32.	Poligonia	Poligonia	*As above.*
Image 80, Right, Folio 76r, Col. A			
1.	Π Gencia Allogalica	Gentiana Allogallica	*Gentiana amarella*, Gentian.
2.	Π Germandria	Germandria	*Teucrium chamaedrys*, Common or Wall Germander; or ?*Cymbalaria muralis*, ?Pennywort.
3.	Germandre	Germa*nd*er	*As above.*
4.	Π Gelena	Geleni	*Citrullus colocynthis*, Colocynth; or *Lagenaria vulgaris* Ser; Gourd.
5.	Colloquintida	Coloquintida	*As above.* Hunt p.85.
6.	Cucurbita	Cucurbita	*As above.*
7.	Alexandrina	Alexandrina	*As above.*
8.	Π Gersa.	Gersa	'Flowers of lead' Lead Oxide.
9.	Serusa gith	Cerusa	*As above.*
10.	Agrimulatu*m*	Gith & Agrimulatum.	*Agrostemma githago*, Corn Cockle; or *Lolium temulentum*, Darnel.
11.	Melanciu*m*	Fol. 170r., Col A	*As above.*

Image, Folio and Line Numbers.	Betson Entry. [The alphabetical letters A-Z below are for reference only, and are not in Betson].	The Synonoma of John Bray: BL Sloane MS 282, with folio number and column.	Possible Modern Names, mainly Linnaean, and taken from Hunt (1989). Non-Linnaean names are indicated.
		Nigella, Melancium	
12.	Kokkill	Anglice Kokkel	*Agrostemma githago*, Corn Cockel.
13.	Π Gira solis	Gira solis	*Leonurus cardiaca*, Motherwort.
14.	Custos Orti	Custos Orti	*As above.*
15.	Miracla.	Miracla	*As above.*
16.	Pentadactulus	Pentadactilis	*As above.*
17.	Palma Xtī (*i.e. Christi*)	Palma Xti	*As above.*
18.	Glicida, pionia.	Glicida, Pionia	*Paeonia mascula* or *officinalis*, Peony.
19.	Π Giron Lap*is* ematithes	Giron Lapis, Amatites	Magnet, Haematite.
20.	Π Glicia licoricia	Glicia, Licoricia	*Glycyrrhiza glabra*, Liquorice.
21.	Glis alexis (*sic*)	Glis, Elixis ,	*Arctium lappa*, Burdock.
22.	Lappa bardana.	Lappa Bardana	*Arctium minus*, Lesser Burdock.
23.	Illafeas clote	Illapheas, Clote	*As above.*
24.	Π Grisanatana	Crislocanna	*Atriplex hortensis*, Orache. (SB, Mowat, p. 17: Crisolocanna idem Atriplex)
25.	Atriplex agrest*is*	Attriplex agrestis	*Atriplex hortensis*, Orache; or *Beta vulgaris*, Beet
26.	Arage	Arache	*As above.*
27.	Π Gliconium	Gliconium	*Mentha pulegium*, Pennyroyal.

Image, Folio and Line Numbers.	Betson Entry. [The alphabetical letters A-Z below are for reference only, and are not in Betson].	The Synonoma of John Bray: BL Sloane MS 282, with folio number and column.	Possible Modern Names, mainly Linnaean, and taken from Hunt (1989). Non-Linnaean names are indicated.
28.	Pulegium regale	Pulegium regale	As above.
29.	Piloile riall	Puliol reale	As above.
30.	Π Glaucus	Gricus (?)	*Crocus sativus*, Saffron, Crocus; or *Carthomus tinctorius*, Safflower, Bastard Saffron.
31.	Crocus magnetis	Crocus	Probably 'crocus' Lapis magnetis is the next entry in Sloane 282. Betson seems to have run the two together.
32.	Saferon	Safran	*Crocus sativus*, Saffron, Crocus.
33.	Π Giro lapis		Magnet
34.	Π Gisasterios	Gisastereos	'A red pigment containing ferric oxide.'
Image 80, Right, Folio 76r, Col. B			
1.	Bolus armoracus	As above. Bray: Bolus Armenicus hit is a rede er*the* which is fu*n*de in Armanye.	
2.	Gum arabik	*A natural gum from Acacia tree.* Bray: Gum Arabice: when it ys y wryte simplich gum*m*e, it shal be understo*n*de gum*m*e of Arabik	
3.	[H] Hastula regia	Hastula regia vel	*Asperula odorata*, Wodruff;
4.	Hasta regia	Hasta regia	As above.
5.	Woderove	Anglice Woderove	As above.
6.	Π Hastula S*a*ncti Xtofori	Hastula S*a*ncti Xpofori	*Actaea spicata*, Baneberry, Herb Christopher.

Image, Folio and Line Numbers.	Betson Entry. [The alphabetical letters A-Z below are for reference only, and are not in Betson].	The Synonoma of John Bray: BL Sloane MS 282, with folio number and column.	Possible Modern Names, mainly Linnaean, and taken from Hunt (1989). Non-Linnaean names are indicated.
7.	Pollicaria minor	Policaria minor	*Pulicaria dysenterica* or *P. vulgaris* Common and Small Fleabanes.
8.	Scabbeworte	Scabwort	*Inula helenium*, Elecampane, Horseheal, scabwort.
9.	Π Herba benedicta	Herba benedicta	*Conium maculatum*, Hemlock.
10.	Cicuta incubus	Cicuta incubus	As above.
11.	Hemelok	Hemmelocke	As above.
		Herba paralisis	As line 12 below – See Hunt p.137
12.	Π Herba Sancti Petri	Herba Sancti Petri	*Primula veris*, Cowslip.
13.	Kowisloppis	Cowsloppe	As above.
14.	Π Herba Roberti	Herba Roberti	*Geranium robertianum* Herb Robert.
15.	Acus muscata	Acus muscata	As above.
16.	Pes Columbe	Pes Columbe	*Geranium ssp.*, Dove's foot Cranebill; or *Cruciata laevipes*, ?Crosswort; or *?Aquilegia vulgaris*, Columbine.
17.	Π Herba Iohannis	Herba Iohannis	*Hypericum perforatum*, St John's Wort.
18.	Π Herba perforata	Herba perforata	As above.
19.	Ypericon	Ypericon	As above.
20.	Fuga demonum		As above.
21.	Seynt Johns Wort	Seint Ion Wort	As above.

Image, Folio and Line Numbers.	Betson Entry. [The alphabetical letters A-Z below are for reference only, and are not in Betson].	The Synonoma of John Bray: BL Sloane MS 282, with folio number and column.	Possible Modern Names, mainly Linnaean, and taken from Hunt (1989). Non-Linnaean names are indicated.
22.	Π Herba Walteri	Herba Walteri	*Asperula odorata*, Woodruff; or ?*Potentilla anserina*, ?Silverweed.
23.	Herbe Water	Herbe Water	As above.
24.	Herba Acetosa	Herba Acetosa	*Rumex acetosa / acetosella*, Common or Sheep's Sorrel; or *Oxalis acetosella*, Wood Sorrel.
Image 81, Left, Folio 76v, Col. A			
1.	Acedula oxilapac*ium*	Acedula oxilapaciu*m*	*Rumex acetosa / acetosella*, Common or Sheep's Sorrel.
2.	Sorrel Sourdok.	Sorel or Sourdock	As above.
3.	Π Herba luminar*ia*	Fol. 170r., Col. B Herba l*umi*narie	*Vebascum thapsus*, Mullein.
4.	Tapsus barbastus	Barbastus	As above.
5.	Flosmus pontfelyon	Flosmus Ponfilion	As above.
6.	Molena Moleyn	Molenia, Molyne	As above.
7.	Π Herba cruciata	Herba cruciata	*EMED has* Crosswort (*Galium cruciata*).
8.	Herbe croise	Herb croise	As above.
9.	Π Herba medee	Herba mede	?*Melissa officinalis*, ?Balm. EMED.
10.	Medeworte	Medewort	As above.
11.	Π Herba Fullonu*m*	Herba fullonum	*Saponaria officinalis*, Soapwort; or *Dipsacus fullonum*, Teasel.
12.	Soponaria. (*sic*)	Saponaria	As above.
13.	Brith.	Berith	As above.
14.	Cousope (*sic*)	Crowsope	?*As above*.

Image, Folio and Line Numbers.	Betson Entry. [The alphabetical letters A-Z below are for reference only, and are not in Betson].	The Synonoma of John Bray: BL Sloane MS 282, with folio number and column.	Possible Modern Names, mainly Linnaean, and taken from Hunt (1989). Non-Linnaean names are indicated.
15.	Π Herba *Sancti* Pauli	Herba *Sancti* Pauli	*?Euphorbia*, Spurge; Or *?Spergula*, ?Spurrey.
16.	Sp*er*orgle	Sp*er*gula	As above
17.	Π Her*o*nia et Hirve*tt* (?)	Hironia et Yronea	*Equisetum*, Horsetail. See Hunt *'Hirema' p.143, and Daems#59, p.115 for variants.*
18.	Hiposeta	Hiposita	*As above, and Hunt p.143*
19.	Cauda caballina.	Cauda equine, Cauda caballina ys a row herb with *the* wych me*n* polisshen combes, bowes and coppis.	*As above. The Bray quotation is taken from Cambridge University Library version (Dd.II.45).*
20.	Π Herba Hirca est		*As above. But Daems has similar at #105, p.132 under Trapogon pratensis, Showy Goat's Beard.*
21.	cum quaedam hastae radiu*nt*ur		
22.	Hispia . ma*j*or mi*n*or	Hypia maior et minor	<u>Maior</u>: *Anagallis arvensis*, Scarlet Pimpernel or *Pimpinella saxifraga*, Burnet Saxifrage. <u>Minor</u>: *Stellaria media*, Chickweed.
23.	Hispia ma[ior] m[in]or est *(text repeated)*		<u>Minor</u>: *Stellaria media*, Chickweed.
24.	Morsus gallincia.	Morsus galline	*As above.*
25.	Chekynworte	Chikyn mete	*As above.*
26.	Hispia mi*n*or	Hippia minor	*As above.*

Image, Folio and Line Numbers.	Betson Entry. [The alphabetical letters A-Z below are for reference only, and are not in Betson].	The Synonoma of John Bray: BL Sloane MS 282, with folio number and column.	Possible Modern Names, mainly Linnaean, and taken from Hunt (1989). Non-Linnaean names are indicated.
27.	Selfhele	Selfhele	As above. Hunt p.149 cites several MSS where variant spellings of Selfheal are included in both Ippia major and minor.
Image 81, Left, Folio 76v, Col B			
1.	[I] *I*acia nigra	Iacia nigra	*Centaurea scabiosa / jacea*, Greater or Lesser Knapweed.
2.	Matfelon alba	Matfelon with a reed flou*r*	*Centaurea scabiosa*, Greater Knapweed; or ?*Potentilla anserina*. Silverweed.
3.	et Nigra		As above.
4.	Π Iacia alba.	Iacia alba	As above.
5.	Matfelon rede	Matfelon with a purpur flou*r*	MED: Knapweed, matfellon : (*Centaurea nigra*); also, greater knapweed (*Centaurea scabiosa*); ?lesser knapweed (*Centaurea jacea*).
6.	Π Iarus Pes Vituli	Iarus Pes vituli	*Arum maculatum*, Cuckoo-pint.
7.	Barba Aron	Barba Aaron, Zekesters	As above.
8.	Π Ilapeas.	Ilascas.	*Arctium lappa*, Burdock. *See Hunt p.146 for variant spellings.*
9.	Bardana	Bardana	As above.
10.	Lappa Clote	Lappa, Anglice Clote	As above.
11.	Insana	Insana	*Hysocamus niger*, Henbane.
12.	Iusqueam*us*	Iusquiamus	As above.
13.	Henbane	Anglice Hennebane	As above.

Image, Folio and Line Numbers.	Betson Entry. [The alphabetical letters A-Z below are for reference only, and are not in Betson].	The Synonoma of John Bray: BL Sloane MS 282, with folio number and column.	Possible Modern Names, mainly Linnaean, and taken from Hunt (1989). Non-Linnaean names are indicated.
14.	Π Jumelon alba	Ilk Viola alba	*? Viola*, Violet. *Hunt p.152.*
15.	White violet.	Whit violette	*As above.*
16.	Π Incubus cicuta	Incudus (sic)	*Conium maculatum*, Hemlock.
17.	Herba benedicta homelok	Cicuta, Herba Benedicta, Humbelok	*As above*
18.	Π Incuba sponsa solis	Incuba Sponsa soli	*Calendula officinalis*, Pot Marigold.
19.	Cicoria	Cicorea	*As above.*
20.	Mirra solis	Mirra solis	*As above.*
21.	Verucaria Rindene *(sic)*	Verucaria Roodyn	*As above. Hunt p.81 also suggests Cichorium intybus, Chicory, with 'Roddis' as one translation.*
22.	Π Indidictulus	Indi dactilis	*Tamarindus indica,* Tamarind. *See Hunt p.147 for Indi Dactilis*
23.	Acetosus oxifencia	Acetosus, Oxifencia,	*As above.*
24.	Thamarinides.	Tamarides	*As above.*
25.	Π Yperycon	Ypericon	*Hypericum perforatum*, St John's Wort.
26.	Herba Johannis herba perforatum	Herba perforate, Herba Iohannis	*As above.*
27.	Scopia regia et ts *(Iohannis ?)*	Scopia regia Seynt Ion Wort	*As above.*
28.	Π Ypia major	Ipia maior, Morsus galline,	*Anagallis arvensis,* Scarlet Pimpernell.

Image, Folio and Line Numbers.	Betson Entry. [The alphabetical letters A-Z below are for reference only, and are not in Betson].	The Synonoma of John Bray: BL Sloane MS 282, with folio number and column.	Possible Modern Names, mainly Linnaean, and taken from Hunt (1989). Non-Linnaean names are indicated.
		Folio 170, Col. C Chikenmete, Iria minor	
29.	Ulex. eyeworte.	Ulex or Heywort 'Wheywort' is in Hunt at p149, with 'Wayworte' as Ippia maior.	*Anagallis arvensis,* Scarlet Pimpernell or: *Stellaria media,* Chickweed.
30.	Ypoquintides	Ipoquistidos	Rose Gall
31.	a superfluitate *th*at g*r*ow*e*th oute	Is a sup*er*fluite growing on *th*e brere which *th*ei beth rosa canina	
Image 81, Right, Folio 77r, Col. A			
1.	of the breer and		
2.	Prat ? rosas caninas		*As above ?*
3.	Π Yris hath a p*ur*pul flo*ur*	Iris ha*th* a purpur flo*ur*	*Iris germanica,* Iris.
4.	Π Yreos ha*th* a whyte flor	Ireos a whyte floure	*Iris florentina,* Florentine Iris.
5.	And Gladiole ha*th* a yelu flour a safron	Ireos an oth*er* *th*at ys y clipid gladone. Hyt ha*th* a yelw flou*r*e liche safro*n*	*Iris pseudacorus,* Yellow Flag.
6.	Another is clepid spatula fedida and it ha*th* no flo*ur*.	A no*ther there* ys *th*at is y clipid spatula fetida he ha*th* no flour at al	?*Iris foetidissima,* ?Gladden, Stinking Iris.

140

Image, Folio and Line Numbers.	Betson Entry. [The alphabetical letters A-Z below are for reference only, and are not in Betson].	The Synonoma of John Bray: BL Sloane MS 282, with folio number and column.	Possible Modern Names, mainly Linnaean, and taken from Hunt (1989). Non-Linnaean names are indicated.
		Iunipus, Iunipeer	
7.	Π Iovis barba	Iovis barba	*Sempervivum tectorum*, Houseleek.
8.	Senegrene	Syngrene	*As above*
9.	Π Iringi	Iringi,	*Eryngium*, esp. *Eryngium maritimum*, Sea Holly.
10.	Secaul Iringes	Setacul, Yringes	*As above.*
11.	Π Ysyon centory	Ision, Anglice Centori	*Centaurium erythraea*, Centaury.
		Bray: Kalendula, Solsequium, Herba Sancte Marie, Anglice Rooden, Kufordafyn, Anamomum, Ranel	
12.	[K] Katariacum	Kateriacu,	*Shavings of deer horn for Ammonia.*
13.	*Rasura*	Rasura cornuum cervi	*As above.*
14.	Cornum cervi		*As above.*
15.	Shavyng of hartis horn	Shavyng of an hertes horne	*As above.*
16.	Π Kakabre Vernyssh	Kacabre Vernis	A type of varnish.
17.	Π Kalendula solsequium	Fol 169r, Col B Calendula Solsequium	*Calendula officinalis*, Pot Marigold.
18.	Π Kufordafin	Kufordafyn	*Cinnamomum zeylanicum*, Cinnamon.

Image, Folio and Line Numbers.	Betson Entry. [The alphabetical letters A-Z below are for reference only, and are not in Betson].	The Synonoma of John Bray: BL Sloane MS 282, with folio number and column.	Possible Modern Names, mainly Linnaean, and taken from Hunt (1989). Non-Linnaean names are indicated.
19.	Sinamomum	Cinamomium	*As above.*
20.	Canell.	Kanel	*As above.*
Image 81, Right, Folio 77r, Col. B			
1.	**[L]** *Labrusca*	*Labrusca*	*Vitis vinifera*, Wild Vine; or *?Bryonia dioca*, Bryony.
2.	*Labrum Veneris*	*Labrum ven*eris	*Sonchus ssp.*, Sowthistle.
3.	Cardo benedictus	Cardus benedictus	*Cnicus benedictus*, Blessed Thistle; or *Senecio vulgaris*, Groundsel.
4.	Semen eiusdem	Th*e* seed ys y clipped Seynt Marie seed	*As above.*
5.	Lactuca domes*tica*.	Lactuca domestica	*Lactuca sativa*, Lettuce.
6.	Letuse	Letuse	*As above.*
7.	**Π** Lapdanum a gumme	Labdanu*m* ys a gume	*Cistus ladanifer*, Gum Rockrose, or *Laudanum*, Labdanum.
8.	**Π** Lappa bardana	Lappa brandana (sic)	*Arctium lappa*, Burdock.
9.	Glis Gleton	Glis, Elixis, Gleton, Clote	*As above.*
10.	**Π** Lappatium gum*me*		*Rumex* ssp. esp. *sanguineus*, 'Red Veined Dock, or *Arctium lappa*, Burdock.
11.	Lappa Barba		*?As above*
12.	**Π** Lappatium rotundum	Lappaciu*m* rotundum	*Rumex* ssp. esp. *obtusifolius*, 'Broad-Leaved Dock' or *Arctium lappa*, Burdock.

Image, Folio and Line Numbers.	Betson Entry. [The alphabetical letters A-Z below are for reference only, and are not in Betson].	The Synonoma of John Bray: BL Sloane MS 282, with folio number and column.	Possible Modern Names, mainly Linnaean, and taken from Hunt (1989). Non-Linnaean names are indicated.
13.	*the* moch dok	*Bray:* Mechedok, Rumes, Parelle. Whan hit is y write simpullich of Lapacium acutum, hit shal be understonde Lapacium acutum. Liteldok *See Hunt p156. 'Rumes' is not given, but may be variant for 'Rumex' in Hunt at p.224 as 'muche dok'.*	
14.	Π Lappatium acutum		*Rumex aquaticus / sanguineus,* Dock, esp. Red-Veined Dock.
15.	*the* smale dok	Liteldok	*As above.*
		Bray: Lapis Lazuli ys a ston of *the* which azure is made	
16.	Π Lapis armoniacus	**Folio 170v, Col A** Lapis Armenicus i*dem*	*Probably Azurite.*
17.	Π Lapis calamiar*is*.	Lapis Calamaris Ben gode to medycines	Calamine or Zinc Carbonate.
18.	Π Lapis urrtis flynt ?	Lapis parietis, Silex idem est. Anglice Flyntes. The term 'Lapis parietis' could not be found, but perhaps 'wall stone' as flint is used for building.	*Perhaps burnt flint. See Image 109 left, folio 104v, Lines 27-33, for heating of flints for 'Aqua silicis'.*
19.	Π Lapis magnetis.	Lapis magnetis	

Image, Folio and Line Numbers.	Betson Entry. [The alphabetical letters A-Z below are for reference only, and are not in Betson].	The Synonoma of John Bray: BL Sloane MS 282, with folio number and column.	Possible Modern Names, mainly Linnaean, and taken from Hunt (1989). Non-Linnaean names are indicated.
20.	Lodestone giron.	Githon, Lodestone	As above.
21.	Π Lanceola		Plantago lanceolata, Ribwort Plantain.
22.	Plantago minor		As above.
23.	Quinconervia		As above.
24.	Ribbeworte		As above.
25.	Lannceole		As above.
26.	Π Lapis linxcis	Lapis Lincis cometh of the urine of a wolf y pissed in the hills & muntaynes crudded	Some kind of fossilised stone, perhaps Belemnites.
27.	Volpevemt (?)		Not found.
28.	Π Lapis agapitis	Lapis agapis	'Lapis Lazuli'
29.	Lapis iudiacus	Lapis iudaicus idem	As above.
30.	Π Litaridos (?)	Lactarides – this is bracketed by Bray with Catapucia and Anabulla below.	Euphorbia lathyris, Caper Spurge, or Daphne laureola, Spurge Laurel

Betson's Litaridos not found; SB, Mowat, p.93 has Lacterides. |
31.	Catapucia	Catapucia	As above.
32.	Anabula.	Anabulla	As above.
Image 82, Left, Folio 77v, Col. A			
1.	Π Lauriola	Laureola, Lepidon, Alipiados	Laurus nobilis, Bay Tree.

Image, Folio and Line Numbers.	Betson Entry. [The alphabetical letters A-Z below are for reference only, and are not in Betson].	The Synonoma of John Bray: BL Sloane MS 282, with folio number and column.	Possible Modern Names, mainly Linnaean, and taken from Hunt (1989). Non-Linnaean names are indicated.
2.	Concodium / semen ei est	The seed thereof ys conconidium	As above. See Hunt p.85 Coconidium.
3.	Π Laurencia, Bugla	Laurencia, Bugle	?*Lavandula officinalis*, Lavender. 'Bugle' appears to have been inserted in error, if *Ajuga reptans* is meant.
4.	Π Lavendula	Lavendula	*Lavandula officinalis / latrifolia*, Lavender, or French Lavender.
5.	Lavendure	Lavendure	As above.
6.	Π Laurus Loreltre	Laurus, a Lorey tree	*Laurus nobilis*, Bay Tree.
7.	Lentiscus arbor	Lentiscus ys a tree which swetyth out oyl of hym.	*Pistacia lentiscus*, Lentisk, mastik.
8.	Ex qua olium manat		
9.	Π Lempnius.	Lempinos	Arsenic.
10.	Orpement.	Orpiment	As above.
11.	Arcenik	Ersenek	As above.
12.	Π Levisticum	Levisticum, Lovestiche	*Levisticum officinale*, Koch; Lovage.
13.	Loveache.	Anglice Loveache	As above.
14.	Π Lenticula aquatica	Lenticula aquatica	*Lens culinaris*, Lentil.
15.	Lentigo	Vel Lentigo,	*Lemna minor*, Duckweed.

Image, Folio and Line Numbers.	Betson Entry. [The alphabetical letters A-Z below are for reference only, and are not in Betson].	The Synonoma of John Bray: BL Sloane MS 282, with folio number and column.	Possible Modern Names, mainly Linnaean, and taken from Hunt (1989). Non-Linnaean names are indicated.
	Lenteldow	Lentildew, Anglice Endemete.	*See Hunt p157 for variants.*
16.	Π Lectoria.	Lectoria	*Corylus avellana* or *C. maxima*, Hazelnut.
17.	Nux Coruli Avelana	Nux Corula, Avellana	*As above.*
18.	Nux	Nux perna (?)	*As above.*
19.	Filberdys nux parva	Fylberd	*As above.*
20.	Nux pontica	Nux pontica	*As above.*
21.	Π Battitura eris	Lempidos, Calcathis, Battitura eris	Sweepings of brass
22.	Shallis of bras	Shales of Bras	*As above.*
23.	Squama eris		*As above.*
24.	Π Leporina	Leporina, Prianinscus (?)	?*Hyacinthoides non-scripta*, Bluebell, Wild Hyacinth; or *Orchis*, Orchid. SB, Mowat, p. 35 has 'priapismus dicitur herba leporina, satirion idem'.
25.	Sutirion	Saturion	*As above.*
26.	Π Lepus hare ante (?)	Lepus silvestris an hare	*Lepus, leporis: Latin for the animal 'Hare'.*
27.	Π Leuco Piper album	**Folio 170v, Col B** Leuco piper Piper album	White Pepper: the unripe fruit seeds of *Piper nigrum*, Black Pepper.

Image, Folio and Line Numbers.	Betson Entry. [The alphabetical letters A-Z below are for reference only, and are not in Betson].	The Synonoma of John Bray: BL Sloane MS 282, with folio number and column.	Possible Modern Names, mainly Linnaean, and taken from Hunt (1989). Non-Linnaean names are indicated.
28.	Libanum Olibanum Thus	Libani, Olibani	*Boswellia thurifera,* Frankincense.
29.	Π Libanatidos	Thus Libanatides, Rosemarie	*Rosmarinus officinalis* ? Rosemary.
30.	Rosemaryn		*As above.*
31.	Π Ligustrum	Ligustrum	*Primula vulgaris,* Cowslip.
Image 82, Left, Folio 77v, Col. B			
1.	Wilde lylly. Primerose.	Wild Lylye	*As above. See Hunt p.159 Ligustrum.*
2.	Π Lilium lilly	Lillium, Lilye	*Lillium candidum,* White Lily.
3.	Lilifagus	Lilifagus	*Salvia officinalis,* Sage, or *Teucrium scorodonia,* Wood Sage.
4.	Salvia agrestis.	Salvia agrestis	*As above.*
5.	Ambrosia	Ambrosia	*As above.*
6.	Epatorium.	Eupatorium	*As above.*
7.	Hyndhale	Hyndhale, Wild Sauge	*Teucrium scorodonia,* Wood Sage, Hind Heal.
8.	Π Licosoma semen Saxifragi	Licosperma est semen saxifragie	*Hunt p.164 lists Betson's and Bray's entries under Lithospermon 'Saxifrage'. (Lithospermon officinale is now* Gromwell.)
9.	Π Linilion olium lini	Linilion, Olium Lini	*Linum usitatissimum,* Flax.
10.	Lynsede	Lynseed.	*As above.*
11.	Π Litodemonis blak		Jet.

Image, Folio and Line Numbers.	Betson Entry. [The alphabetical letters A-Z below are for reference only, and are not in Betson].	The Synonoma of John Bray: BL Sloane MS 282, with folio number and column.	Possible Modern Names, mainly Linnaean, and taken from Hunt (1989). Non-Linnaean names are indicated.
12.	stone of Ynde	*Bray:* Litodemonis ys a blak ston wich come*th* out of Ynde & thawse hym *with* frotyng & he drawy*th* to hy*m* straws. Anglice Gette.	
13.	Π Lymphea aquati*c*a	Limphia aquatica	*Nymphea alba / lutea,* White or Yellow Water Lily.
14.	Memphen (?)	Memphea	*As above.*
15.	Lillium aquaticum	Lilium aquaticum	*As above.*
16.	Nemifar (?)	Nenufare	*As above.*
17.	Wat*er* lily.	Water Lilye	*As above.*
18.	Π Lynochites.	Linochites	*Mercurialis perennis,* Dog's Mercury.
19.	Mercuriell	Mercuriale	*As above.*
20.	Π Lingua canis	Lingua canis	*Cynoglossum officinale,* Hound's Tongue.
21.	Hou*n*dis tong	Howndestonge	*As above*
22.	Π Lingua cervina	Lingua cervina	*Asplenium scolopendrium,* Hart's Tongue Fern.
23.	Scolependria	Scolopendria	*As above.*
24.	Hertisto*n*g	H*a*rtes to*n*ge	*As above.*
25.	Π Lingua bovina		*Anchusa officinalis,* Bugloss.
26.	Buglossa oxisto*n*g		*As above.*
27.	Π Lingua agnina	Lingua agnina	*Plantago major* or *lanceolata,* Great Plantain or Ribwort.
28.	Agnoglossa (*sic*) plantago	Arnoglossa	*As above.*
29.	Centudina	Centin*er*via,	*As above.*

Image, Folio and Line Numbers.	Betson Entry. [The alphabetical letters A-Z below are for reference only, and are not in Betson].	The Synonoma of John Bray: BL Sloane MS 282, with folio number and column.	Possible Modern Names, mainly Linnaean, and taken from Hunt (1989). Non-Linnaean names are indicated.
		Pantago (*sic for Plantago*)	
30.	Π Lingua avis.	Lingua avis	*Stellaria holostea*, Stichwort; *but also:* Fraxinus excelsior, Ash Keys (*semen fraxini*).
Image 82, Right, Folio 78r, Col. A			
1.	Stichwort	Stichewort	*Stellaria holostea*, Stichwort.
2.	Π Lingua ircina	Lingua Hircina	*Plantago lanceolata*, Ribwort; *but also Lepidium coronopus*, Swine Cress; *or ? Asplenium scolopendrium.* Hart's Tongue Fern.
3.	Plantago minor.	Plantago minor	*Plantago lanceolata*, Ribwort.
4.	Laciolata. (*sic*)	Lanceolata	*As above.*
5.	Π Lippotoma	Lippotomia idem male*factiō* sincopis	*Fainting from 'a defect in the motion of the heart'. EMED: Lipothymia*
6.	Manfocon	Malefcō	*As above.*
7.	Sinicopis		*As above. See EMED for Sincopis*
8.	Swoyning	Swonyng	*ME 'Fainting'.*
9.	Π Lynarye ? berith	Linarie purgi*th the* colour *the* wiche bere*th* a white flo*u*r	*? Linaria vulgaris* Mill. Wild Flax, Toadflax. *But the flower is yellow.*
10.	a white flo*u*r.		
		Linoyse i*dem* spynnache, *the* wiche bere*th* an	*Not found*

Image, Folio and Line Numbers.	Betson Entry. [The alphabetical letters A-Z below are for reference only, and are not in Betson].	The Synonoma of John Bray: BL Sloane MS 282, with folio number and column.	Possible Modern Names, mainly Linnaean, and taken from Hunt (1989). Non-Linnaean names are indicated.
		Fol.170v. Col C Ynde blew flo*r*	
11.	Π Longu*m* piper	Longu*m* piper	*Piper longum*, Long Pepper.
12.	Mac*ro* pep*er*.	Macro p*ip*er	*As above.*
13.	Agrimulatum Gith.	Agrumlatu*m* Gith	*Agrostemma githago,* Corncockle. OR *Lollium temulentum,* Darnel. See Hunt p.11, Agrimulatum.
14.	Π Lollium nigella	Lolliu*m*, Nigella	*As above.*
15.	Melancium kokkel	Melancium i*dem* kokkille.	*As above.*
16.	Π Lupines	Lupine	*Lupinus albus* or *L. luteus*, Lupin.
17.	Faba egypciaca.	Faba egipcia	*As above.*
18.	Marcilum lupynis	Marfilu*m* Lupines	*As above.*
19.	**[M]** Mabafematicon is *the* juse of wylde caule dried	Mabafematicon, *the* iuce of wilde caul y dryed	*Brassica* species, or *Crambe maritima,* Sea kale
20.	Macedonia seme*n*	Maces folium Macedonica, Alisandre	*Smyrnium olusatrum,* Alexanders, Horse Parsley.
21.	Alexandrie		*As above.*

Image, Folio and Line Numbers.	Betson Entry. [The alphabetical letters A-Z below are for reference only, and are not in Betson].	The Synonoma of John Bray: BL Sloane MS 282, with folio number and column.	Possible Modern Names, mainly Linnaean, and taken from Hunt (1989). Non-Linnaean names are indicated.
Image 82, Right, Folio 78r, Col. B			
1.	Π Magnetis *the* lodston*e*	Magnetis ys a ston *that* ys clyped a lodestone	Magnet
2.	Π Maculata trifoliu*m*	Maculata trifoliu*m*	*Trifolium* ssp., Clover.
3.	*th*e iij leved grasse	*Th*releved gras	*Trifolium* ssp , Clover.
4.	Π Maiorana Marc*u*s	Maiorana	*Origanum vulgare,* Marjoram.
5.	Amaricom Cimbrium	Amaricon, Amaracus Cimbrium	*Origanum vulgare,* Marjoram; or *Majorana hortensis,* Moench. Sweet Marjoram.
6.	Sansucus prosa (*sic*)	Sansucus persa	*Majorana hortensis,* Moench. Sweet Marjoram. Hunt p.227.
7.	Merchworte	Muchelwort	*As above.*
8.	Π <u>Malum macianu*m*</u>	Malu*m* macianu*m*	*Malus sylvestris,* Crab Apple.
9.	Malu*m* macidum	Malu*m* macid*u*m	*As above.* macid*u*m for macid*o*nicum ?
10.	Pomu*m* silvestre.	Pomu*m* Silvestre	*As above.*
11.	Wodecrabbis.	Wodecrabbes	*As above.*
12.	Π Malum punicu*m*	Malu*m* punicum	*Punica granatum,* Pomegranate.
13.	Malum granatum	Malu*m* granatum	*As above.*
14.	Pome g*a*rnett.	Pome granett	*As above.*
15.	Π Mala coctaita		*Cydonia oblonga,* Quince. See Hunt pp.84 & 166 for Mala Coctana etc.

Image, Folio and Line Numbers.	Betson Entry. [The alphabetical letters A-Z below are for reference only, and are not in Betson].	The Synonoma of John Bray: BL Sloane MS 282, with folio number and column.	Possible Modern Names, mainly Linnaean, and taken from Hunt (1989). Non-Linnaean names are indicated.
16.	Mala citorina		As above. Hunt has 'citonia' and 'citonica' p166
17.	Quencys		As above.
18.	Π Melano	Malonopiper piper nigrum	Piper nigrum, Black Pepper.
19.	Nigrum piper		As above.
20.	Π Malum terre	Malum terre	Conopodium majus (Gouan) Loret. Pignut, or Cyclamen hederifolium, Sowbread.
21.	Ciclamen	Ciclamen	?As above.
22.	Celsamus	Calsamus	?As above.
23.	Panis porcinus	Panis porcinus	As above.
24.	Erthnote	Erthe notes	As above.
25.	Π Macro piper longum		Piper longum, Long Piper.
26.	Π Malua voscus	Malua viscus	Althaea officinalis Marshmallow.
27.	Bismalva eviscus	Bismalva, Altea, Eviscus	As above.
28.	Π Matricaria	Matricaria	Artemisia vulgaris, Mugwort.
29.	Arthemisia	Arthentesia (sic)	As above.
30.	Mugwort	Muggewort	As above.
31.	Π Matrisilva	Matri silva	Lonicera Periclymenum, Honeysuckle
Image 83, Left, Folio 78v, Col. A			
1.	Caprifolium.	Caprifolium	As above.
2.	Oculus Lucii	Oculus lucii	As above.

Image, Folio and Line Numbers.	Betson Entry. [The alphabetical letters A-Z below are for reference only, and are not in Betson].	The Synonoma of John Bray: BL Sloane MS 282, with folio number and column.	Possible Modern Names, mainly Linnaean, and taken from Hunt (1989). Non-Linnaean names are indicated.
3.	Volubilis minor.	Volubilis maior	In Hunt as Convulvulus arvensis, Bindweed, but there was some confusion of ' maior', 'media' and 'minor'. Hunt p.265. Probably Honeysuckle.
4.	Caprificus.	Caprificus	As above: Lines 31 to 5 bracketed with 'Matri Silva'.
5.	Wodebynde	Wodebynde	As above.
6.	Π Marsilium	Marsilium	Lupinus ssp. esp. albus L., Lupin
7.	Faba lupine.	Faba lupina	As above.
8.	Faba egipciata	Faba egipciata	As above.
9.	Lupines	Aelagonglice (?) Lupine	Betson as above. Bray may have had a corrupted version of 'anglice lupine' – see Hunt p165.
		Several lines of Bray's Sloane 282, Fol. 171r, Col A, have been omitted here, and inserted where appropriate after the relevant Betson entries. These include Masmatrum, Feniculus porcinus, Houndefenel, Maratrum, Horhound, Manna, Mandragora, Melandria, Mede, Mel, Mellilotum and Corona regia.	
10.	Π Melissa	Melissa	Melissa officinalis, Balm.
11.	Citraria	Citrana	As above.
12.	Pigmentaria	Herba primentaria	As above. Hunt p.207
13.	Citrago.	Citrigo	As above.
14.	Π Mellones sunt mundificatores	Mellones beth mundificatices	Cucumis melo, Melon.
15.	Π Mellancium	Melancum, Gith, Agrimulatum	Agrostemma githago, Corn Cockle; Or Lolium temulentum, Darnel.

Image, Folio and Line Numbers.	Betson Entry. [The alphabetical letters A-Z below are for reference only, and are not in Betson].	The Synonoma of John Bray: BL Sloane MS 282, with folio number and column.	Possible Modern Names, mainly Linnaean, and taken from Hunt (1989). Non-Linnaean names are indicated.
16.	Gith. Nigella.	Nigella	*As above*
17.	Cokkill	Cokel	*As above.*
18.	Π Menta amana	Menta Anana	*Menta aquatica*, 'Water Mint'. Hunt has *Menta Anana* and *Amana* p.176.
19.	Fissh mente.	Fisshementes	*As above.*
20.	Π <u>Menta aquatica</u>	Menta aquatica	*As above.*
21.	Π Mentastum		'Mentastrum': Hunt p.241 has both *Mentha sylvestris* and *Mentha aquatica*, for this and for Horsemint and 'Water Mint'.
22.	Semibrium (?)	Sizimbrium	*As above. See Hunt p.241 Sisimbrium*
23.	Horsmynt	Horsmyntes	*As above.*
24.	Π Mentula Epi*scopi*	Mentula episcopi.	*Ficaria verna*, Lesser Celandine, Pilewort. Hunt p.176-77.
25.	Mede flou*r that* grow*eth*	Mede flour & hyt ha*th* a yolw flor & brode leves & hyt growth on wateres.	*As above.*
26.	in waters *with* a brode		
27.	lef and a *y*elow flou*r*		
28.	Π Mentula sacerdot*is*	Mentula sacerdotis	*Cichorium intybus*, Chicory, Wild Succory.
29.	Sacanus	Sircoure – *Hunt p.177 for variants*	'sacanus' not found. Sircoure is as line 28 above.

Image, Folio and Line Numbers.	Betson Entry. [The alphabetical letters A-Z below are for reference only, and are not in Betson].	The Synonoma of John Bray: BL Sloane MS 282, with folio number and column.	Possible Modern Names, mainly Linnaean, and taken from Hunt (1989). Non-Linnaean names are indicated.
30.	Mercurialis	Mercurialis	*Mercurialis perennis*, Dog's Mercury.
		Linochites, Parcenochidos	As above. See *Linozostis* in Hunt at p.163, and *Parthenocidos* at p.198. Daems #315, p.208 has similar variants – *Linozostis and perenotidos*.
31.	Lablis	Libleb. Bracketed with mercurialis; neither the Betson nor the Bray are in Hunt.	See Mowat, *Antidotarium Nicholai*, p.220 : 'Arab Ableb, Latin vero mercurialis' Simon of Genoa under 'Alhulbub' also has: 'yelbub est mercurialis et iebub et halbub.'
32.	Π Meu is an herb lik	Meu is an herbe that is lich houndfenel, but yt is more croked.	?*Anethum graveolens*, ?Dill; ?*Meum athamanticum*, Spignel, Meu, Baldmoney; or *Peucedanum palustre*, Hog's Fennel, Milk Parsley.
33.	Hondesfennel but it is not croked.		As above.
Image 83, Left, Folio 78v, Col. B			
1.	Π Menelata	Menelata	*Glebionis segetum*, Corn Marigold; or ?*Convolvulus arvensis*, ?Bindweed.
2.	Goldis boton	Goldesbomes puli, noef pomfles	As above. Hunt has 'goldysbothom' p.175.
3.	Π Mespilus		*Mespilus germanica*, Medlar.
4.	Merles	Melees	As above. See Hunt p177.

Image, Folio and Line Numbers.	Betson Entry. [The alphabetical letters A-Z below are for reference only, and are not in Betson].	The Synonoma of John Bray: BL Sloane MS 282, with folio number and column.	Possible Modern Names, mainly Linnaean, and taken from Hunt (1989). Non-Linnaean names are indicated.
5.	Π Meltrodatum (?)	Meltrodatum de machian (?)	*Not found.*
6.	Sanguis draconis	**Folio 171r, Col B** Sanguis draconis	*Daemonorops draco,* Blume ex Schult; Dragon's Blood(Resin); *Dracaena draco* L. Dragon Tree.
7.	Miconium white pop. [*poppy*]	Michonium, Micocodum, papaver album, Whit popy	*Papaver somniferum,* White Poppy.
8.	Π <u>Supercilium veneris</u>	Millefolium, venter apis, Supercilium veneris,	*Achillea millefolium,* Yarrow.
9.	Yarow	Anglice Yarowe	*As above.*
10.	Π <u>Meleum solis</u>	Millium solis	*Lithospermum officinale,* Gromwell.
11.	Granum solis	Grana solis	*As above.*
12.	Cauda porcina Gromyll	Cauda porcina, Anglice Gromyle	*As above.*
13.	Π Mirtus est frutex	Mirtus est fructus	*Vaccinum myrtilis,* Bilberry ?
14.	ben clepid Mirtels	*tha*t ys clyped myrtilles, Anglice Hortene	*As above*
15.	Hurtene	Hortene	*As above. Hortene and Hurtene are both in Hunt at p.179.*
16.	Π Mirta est frutex	Mirta est frutex *tha*t growth on mores, i*dem* Gaweil.	*As above ?*

Image, Folio and Line Numbers.	Betson Entry. [The alphabetical letters A-Z below are for reference only, and are not in Betson].	The Synonoma of John Bray: BL Sloane MS 282, with folio number and column.	Possible Modern Names, mainly Linnaean, and taken from Hunt (1989). Non-Linnaean names are indicated.
17.	ben clepid/myrtillis		*As above ?*
18.	Anglice witene (?) and it groeth		*As above ?*
19.	in marisse and galwill		*As above. See Hunt p.179 'Mirta '*
20.	Π Mira solis	Micarea solis, cicorea, Anglice Rooden.	*Calendula officinalis*, Pot Marigold.
21.	Ruden		*As above.*
22.	Π Mirabulanes est	*Bray:* Mirabolanes be*th* fruytes & *th*ey be*th* of v. divers maners. Videte Kebuli Indorum, Embilicorum, Citrinorum et Belliricorum. *Terminalia bellerica*, Belleric, Bastard Myrobalan.	
23.	Fructus kebuler Indo*rum*		*As above.*
24.	Emblicor*um* et belericor*um*		*As above.*
25.	Π Mirra, A*nglice* gum of a t*re*	Mirra, gume of a tre	*Commiphora myrrha*, Holmes; Myrrh.
26.	Π Mirica genesta bro*m*	Mirica, Genesta, Brome, Genet	*Cytisus scoparius*, Broom; or *Calluna vulgaris*, Ling Heather.
27.	Mora. blak berys	Mora, Blakberies or Dewberies	*Rubus fructicosus*, Blackberry.
28.	Π Mora celsi.	Mora celsi	*Morus niger*, Mulberry.
29.	Mulberys	Molleberis	*As above.*

Image, Folio and Line Numbers.	Betson Entry. [The alphabetical letters A-Z below are for reference only, and are not in Betson].	The Synonoma of John Bray: BL Sloane MS 282, with folio number and column.	Possible Modern Names, mainly Linnaean, and taken from Hunt (1989). Non-Linnaean names are indicated.
30.	Π Morella	Morella	*Atropa belladonna* Deadly Nightshade; or *Solanum nigrum*, Black Nightshade.
31.	Strignum	Strignum	As above.
		Solatrum, Herba Sancte Marie, Morel. Morsus demonis. Herbe coupe (Hunt p181)	*Perhaps incorrectly for Atropa Belladonna. Morsus diaboli (Hunt p181) is also 'reucoupe' as here. Probably Succisa pratensis,* Moench, Devil's Bit Scabious. *See Betson entry below, line 3, again 'Morsus demonis'*
32.	Seynt Mary bery	Herba Sancte Marie, *above*	As above.
Image 83, Right, Folio 79r, Col. A			
1.	Morsus galline	Morsus Galline	*Stellaria minor*, Chickweed. Also: *Anagallis arvensis*, Scarlet Pimpernell; or *Pimpinella saxifragia*, Burnet Saxifrage;
2.	Chikenmete. Ypia.	Ipia, Chykenmete	As above.
3.	Π Morsus demonis		*Succisa pratensis*, Moench. Devil's Bit Scabious.
4.	Π Malena. moleyn	Molena, Tapsus barbastus, Moleyne	*Vebascum thapsus*, Mullein.
5.	Π Muscata woderofe	Fol. 171r, Col C. Muscata, Hasta regia, Woderove	*Asperula odorata*, Sweet Woodruff.
6.	Π Muscus, humiditas	Muscus ys the hemedite ['humidity' or sweat] of a beste	Musk.

Image, Folio and Line Numbers.	Betson Entry. [The alphabetical letters A-Z below are for reference only, and are not in Betson].	The Synonoma of John Bray: BL Sloane MS 282, with folio number and column.	Possible Modern Names, mainly Linnaean, and taken from Hunt (1989). Non-Linnaean names are indicated.
7.	cuiusdam bestis		
8.	Π Mulsa is made of viii parties of water and	Mulsa is made of viii partes water & the ix parti of hony & y soden	*Mulsa – a form of honey drink.*
9.	ix parties of hony	the ix parti of hony	
10.	and sodun to the consumcon [consumption]	& y soden [boiled away, seethed] to the consumpcion	
11.	of the third parte	of the thridde parteye.	
		Mus is a best, a mous.	
12.	Π Mater silva Anglice wodbind		*Lonicera periclymenum*, Honeysuckle.
13.	**[N]** Π Nata a fissh.	Narcha is a fisshe that when he is drawen with hoke or line, yf the fisher put his honde uppon hit, hit maketh his honde onfredeabile [numb] & all the body after.	Mowat, Alphita, p.123: 'Narchos vel Narcha piscis, teste Aristotele, adeo stuporifere nature, vel saporifere nature ut medianmte ligno vel calamo vel hamo vel rethi reddat manum piscatoris insensibilem et totum corpus, nisi citius dimittit. Inde **narcoticum,** idem medicamen stuporiferum vel saporiferum.'

Image, Folio and Line Numbers.	Betson Entry. [The alphabetical letters A-Z below are for reference only, and are not in Betson].	The Synonoma of John Bray: BL Sloane MS 282, with folio number and column.	Possible Modern Names, mainly Linnaean, and taken from Hunt (1989). Non-Linnaean names are indicated.
14.	Π Nasale *vel*	Nasale is a	*Nasal spray.*
15.	Suppositorie *equivocum* ad pessarie.	Suppositor or a pissarie	
16.	Π Nasale is an instr-	Nasale Ys an instrument	As above.
17.	ument to cast in medicyns into the nose thirlis *(nostrils)*	To cast in medicine by *the* nostreles (sic)	
18.	Nasturtium aq*ua*ticu*m*		*Rorippa nasturcium- aquaticum,* Watercress.
19.	Water crassis		As above.
20.	Nasturtium ortulanu*m* Toun cressis	Nasturciu*m* ortulanu*m* an Touncressen	*Lepidum sativum,* Garden Cress.
21.	Watercrassis		As above.
22.	Nasturtiu*m* por*c*inu*m*	Nasturcium porcinum	*Capsella bursa-pastoris,* Shepherd's Purse.
23.	Sanguinaria	Sanguinaria	As above.
24.	Bursa pastor*um*	Bursa pastoris	As above.
Image 83, Right, Folio 79r, Col. B			
1.	Speperdis purs (sic)	Shepherdis purs	As above.
2.	Π Nasturtium agreste	Nasturcium agreste	*Lepidum sativum / campestre,* Garden Cress / Pepperwort.
3.	Wild cressis.	Wilde carse	As above.

Image, Folio and Line Numbers.	Betson Entry. [The alphabetical letters A-Z below are for reference only, and are not in Betson].	The Synonoma of John Bray: BL Sloane MS 282, with folio number and column.	Possible Modern Names, mainly Linnaean, and taken from Hunt (1989). Non-Linnaean names are indicated.
4.	Π Nardostanch-ium.	Nastancium	*Nardostachys jatamansi,* Spikenard; or *?Cyperus longus,* Galingale.
5.	Spiconard. spikenard	Spicanardi, Spikanarde	*As above.*
6.	Π Nemp (?)	Napta, petrolion, oleum of tile stones, Oleum benedictum	Naptha
		Napium, semen Sinapis, Mustard seede, Nardelion, oile of spikenard	
7.	Ungule cabilline.	Nenuphar, Menpheare, rote **Fol 171v., Col A** there of that is y cleped ungula caballina	*Nymphea alba,* White Water Lily; or *Nuphar lutea,* Yellow Water Lily.
8.	Π Nimphea	Nimphia	*As above.*
9.	Lilium aquaticum	Lilium aquaticum	*As above.*
10.	Π Nunphar Anglice water lily	Idem est Nenufa, Water Lilye	*As above.*
11.	Nepta calaminta minor	Nepta is the lasse *(lesser)* Calamente	*Nepeta cataria,* Catmint.
12.	Cattisment		*As above.*

Image, Folio and Line Numbers.	Betson Entry. [The alphabetical letters A-Z below are for reference only, and are not in Betson].	The Synonoma of John Bray: BL Sloane MS 282, with folio number and column.	Possible Modern Names, mainly Linnaean, and taken from Hunt (1989). Non-Linnaean names are indicated.
13.	Π Nigella kockill. Posita in aqua per noctem et mane teratur, naribus odoret et caput purgat et dolores aurium *(illegible)* quae sint in capite attrahit.	Nigella, Gith, Agrimulatum, Cockell	Here *Agrostemma githago,* Corn Darnel. *Hunt also gives*: *Nigella sativa,* Black Cumin; *and Lolium temulentum,* Darnel.
14.	Nitrum squens (?) et salis.	Nitrum is a veyne of the erthe or a kynde of salt	*'Native sodium carbonate, natron'* (EMED). SB, Mowat p.31 has: *'Nitrum lapis est albus et salsus.' Perhaps the Betson and Bray is a confusion of 'salsus'.*
15.	Π Nux maior walnote	Nux maior, Walnote	*Juglans regia,* Walnut.
16.	Π Nux muscata	Nux muscata, Nux mirista, Notemuge	*Myristica fragrans,* Houtt. Nutmeg
17.	Notmuges. (*i.e.* 'nut megs')		*As above*
18.	Π Nux vamica	Nux vomica	*Strychnos nux-vomica, 'Poison Nut' at Hunt p.188 which also had Castanea sativa, Chestnut.*
19.	Chastaynes	Chasteynes	*Castanea sativa,* Chestnut;
20.	Nux longa	Nux longa	*? Prunus amygdalus,* Bosch. Almond
21.	Almonds	Almondes	*As above.*

Image, Folio and Line Numbers.	Betson Entry. [The alphabetical letters A-Z below are for reference only, and are not in Betson].	The Synonoma of John Bray: BL Sloane MS 282, with folio number and column.	Possible Modern Names, mainly Linnaean, and taken from Hunt (1989). Non-Linnaean names are indicated.
		Nux Pontica, Avellana, Lectorica, Nux coruli, notes of hasel tree (Hazelnut)	*Corylus avellana* or *C. maxima*, Hazelnut.
22.	Nux pina	Nux pina	*Pinus pinea*, Pine Nut.
23.	Avelanna lactoria		*Corylus avellana* or *C. maxima*, Hazelnut.
24.	Nux coruli		As above.
25.	Hasilnott		As above.
26.	Nucheus pynes.	Nucleus, Anglice pynes	*Pinus pinea*, Pine Nut.
Image 84, Left, Folio 79v, Col. A			
1.	**[O]** Obtaratium	Obtarticum	'Sneeze herbs', as below.
2.	Sternutatorium	Sternucarium ys thing	
3.	do make men snese.	to make men snese	
4.	Π Obtalmiam	Obtalimicum	Hunt p188: ?*Calamintha ascendens* Jord. ?Common Calamint, *but see the next two entries.*
5.	Lapis calammaris	*Idem* Lapis Calamaris	See next entry
6.	Calamys	Calamyn	EMED gives 'An ore of zinc, cadmia, calamine; prob. both zinc carbonate and the hydrous silicate of zinc.' It notes that it is sometimes confused with <u>calaminte.</u>

Image, Folio and Line Numbers.	Betson Entry. [The alphabetical letters A-Z below are for reference only, and are not in Betson].	The Synonoma of John Bray: BL Sloane MS 282, with folio number and column.	Possible Modern Names, mainly Linnaean, and taken from Hunt (1989). Non-Linnaean names are indicated.
7.	Π Oculus Xpi oclis	Oculus Xi ys good for mannys yeen	*Calendula officinalis*, Pot Marigold; or *Delphinium ambiguum*, Larkspur; or *Leucanthemum vulgare*, Ox-Eye Daisy; or *Salvia sclarea*, Clary.
8.	Oculus bovis	Oculus bovis *idem* Bothon	*Leucanthemum vulgare*, Ox-eye Daisy.
9.	Bachum	Bothon	As above. See Hunt p.188.
10.	Π Oculus populi	Oculus populi	*Populus*, Poplar-bud.
11.	Burjuones of pepul	Borions of popler	As above. See Hunt p.190 for 'burgeon' varieties.
		Offei, gum edere; Ypocissi, gum of Yvy;	
12.	Π Olium leva	Olium lenti, Oleum olive	'Ordinary oil'
13.	Oly de olyf		*Oliva europeae*, Olive Oil.
14.	Π Olium commune	is commune oyle	As above.
15.	Π Olium de Luthion	Oleum lini, Linelion	*Linum usitatissimum*, Linseed oil (flax).
16.	Ole de lynsede	Oyl of Lynseed	As above
		Oleum lapidum, Oleum perleon, Oleum benedictum	

Image, Folio and Line Numbers.	Betson Entry. [The alphabetical letters A-Z below are for reference only, and are not in Betson].	The Synonoma of John Bray: BL Sloane MS 282, with folio number and column.	Possible Modern Names, mainly Linnaean, and taken from Hunt (1989). Non-Linnaean names are indicated.
17.	Π Omentum	Omentum, Abdumen, Sumen, Zirbus, Sagimen, Pinguedo, Fatnesse, or Grece. And when any of these foreseyd is put (Fol. 171 v., ColB begins) simplech bi himself, hit shal be undertstonde of swynces grece thenne. Ointment - see 'Axungia' below. Auxungia meant originally 'axle grease'.	
18.	Auxungia	Auxungia	As above.
19.	Hogges gres	'swynces grece'	Hog's grease.
20.	Π Olibanum	Olibanum	*Boswellia thurifera*, Frankincense.
21.	Libanum thus	Libanum thus	As above.
22.	Frankensens	Frankencens	As above.
23.	Π Olixatrum	Olixatrum	*Smyrnium olusatrum*, Alexanders.
24.	Alexandrum	Alexandrum Petrosilinum, Anglice Alesaundre	As above.
25.	Alexandrs		As above.
26.	Π Opium	Opium	*Papaver somniferum*, Juice of Opium Poppy.
27.	Quirinacium	Rare and not cited in Hunt's 64 MSS. An unidentified plant. EMED gives Quirinaik, the gum resin of the Old World silphium. It was equated to a form of Umbelliferae, esp. Ferula foetida, Asafoetida., as at SB, Mowat, p.32 'opium quirinacium'. From the name 'Cyrene' – Cyreniacum.	
28.	Juse of blak pope		*Papaver somniferum*, Juice of Opium Poppy.

Image, Folio and Line Numbers.	Betson Entry. [The alphabetical letters A-Z below are for reference only, and are not in Betson].	The Synonoma of John Bray: BL Sloane MS 282, with folio number and column.	Possible Modern Names, mainly Linnaean, and taken from Hunt (1989). Non-Linnaean names are indicated.
29.	Π Opium theobaicum	Opium theobaicum	'*Opium from Thebes*'. *The Cambridge Bray (CUL Dd.11.45) is the sole source cited by Hunt, though it also occcurs in Chaucer. The next entry below (Juse of whyte popy) seems to be an expansion on this term.*
30.	Juse of whyte popy	Is *the* iuce of whit popy, but is good for me*n* tha*t* mow not slepe, to be anointed *the*r with about the temples & i*dem the* pame *(palm)* of *the* hondes & on the sole of *the* fete.	?*Papaver rhoeas,* Corn Poppy.
		Opium quinaciu*m* is *the* iuce of blak popy	
31.	Opium iusqana *(sic)*	Opium iusquiami, spuim *(sic)* miconis, *the* iuce of Hen*n*ebane	*Hysocamus niger,* Henbane. *Miconium is generally Papaver somniferum the white poppy. Perhaps used here generically –* 'spume or froth from henbane.'
		Wha*n* Opiu*m* is put simple lich bi hy*m* silf, of Opiu*m* tedbaicu*m* hit shal be understonde *cum more.* '*Cum more*': '*it shall be understood according to customary usage.*'	
32.	Juse of henbane.	*As above*	As above.
33.	Opopunus is clepid [illegible]	Opoponak is the iuce of an herbe	?*Opoponax,* Opoponax, Sweet or Bisabol Myrrh.

Image, Folio and Line Numbers.	Betson Entry. [The alphabetical letters A-Z below are for reference only, and are not in Betson].	The Synonoma of John Bray: BL Sloane MS 282, with folio number and column.	Possible Modern Names, mainly Linnaean, and taken from Hunt (1989). Non-Linnaean names are indicated.
		Opopiris is clene bran fro the bran payn de mayne	*Opopiris seems to have been flour for bread of the highest quality (payn de mayne).*
Image 84, Left, Folio 79v, Col. B			
1.	Π Orpoba the juse of balsamum	Opobalsamus the iuce of bame	Gum of *Commiphora opobalsamum*, Balsam Tree.
2.	Π Orobus. Fech, apllu. (?)	Orobus Milan mous	*Lathyrus* ssp. Vetch, Tare. Hunt p.193 has various 'mousevetch.'
		Ordei, Barlich, Pece	
3.	Π Origonum, Oxiforus (?) Pilioreal, Wodemynt.	Origanum	*Origanum vulgare*, Marjoram; or *Mentha pulegium*, Pennyroyal; or *Thymus serpyllum*, Wild Thyme.
		Orgon, Orton, Veriena, Anglice Verveyne	*Probably all Verbena officinalis*, Vervain – see Hunt p193
		[Three words of Bray text illegibile] Os de corde cervii is a bon *[bone]* on the hert of an herte. *The cartilage found in the heart of a stag.*	
4.	Π Oxifencia	Oxifencia finico, Dactilus acetosus	*Tamarindus indica*, Tamarind.

Image, Folio and Line Numbers.	Betson Entry. [The alphabetical letters A-Z below are for reference only, and are not in Betson].	The Synonoma of John Bray: BL Sloane MS 282, with folio number and column.	Possible Modern Names, mainly Linnaean, and taken from Hunt (1989). Non-Linnaean names are indicated.
5.	Tamarindes	Tamarindes, Sorel	As above.
6.	Π Oxi venegus	Oxi vynegre	Betson not found. Perhaps vinegar ?
7.	Π Oxi rey	Oxiren	Vinegar : *Mowat, Alphita, p.133, Oxiren idem, forte acetum.*
8.	Strong vinigur	Stron vine*gar*	As above.
9.	Π Oxilappatium	Oxilappaciu*m*, Acedula, Rumen, Herba acetosa	*Rumex acetosa*, Sheep Sorrel. See Hunt *Oxilappatium* p.195
10.	Surelt, Surdok.	Souredokke, Sorel	As above.
11.	Π Oxicantium.	Oxicantu*m*	Perhaps *Berberis vulgaris*, Barberry.
12.	Berberies.	Verberys	*?As above.*
		Oximu*m*, semen basiliconis	
Lamium / *Urtica* ss., Npettle.	Π Ozimem *the* sede of netill.	Ozimu*m*, Igia, Acantu*m*, Urtica. A seed netel.	
Osmunda regalis, Royal Fern; or *Polypodium* ssp., 'Polypody'.	Π Osmunda boneworte	Osmunda Polipodie Fol. 171v., Col C *the* fern of an oke	
13.	Oscurtiu*m* alexandr (?)		*Perhaps for Olusatrum – Smyrnium olusatrum,* Alexanders

Image, Folio and Line Numbers.	Betson Entry. [The alphabetical letters A-Z below are for reference only, and are not in Betson].	The Synonoma of John Bray: BL Sloane MS 282, with folio number and column.	Possible Modern Names, mainly Linnaean, and taken from Hunt (1989). Non-Linnaean names are indicated.
14.	**[P]** Papaver album.	Papaver album	*Papaver rhoeas,* Corn Poppy.
15.	White popy. blak	Blank susement Whit popy	*Papaver rhoeas* Corn Poppy; and *Papver somniferum*, Opium Poppy.
		Papaver nigrum, noir susement, Blak popy.	As above. Blank & Noir Susement are only in Sloane 282, according to Hunt p.197.
16.	Π Palma Xpī	Palma Xpi	?*Leonurus cardiaca*, ? Motherwort; or ? *Ricinus communis*, ? Castor Oil Plant; or *Lithospermum officinale*, Gromwell; or *Artemesia vulgaris*, Mugwort; or *Lamium purpureum* Red Dead-Nettle.
17.	Cauda porcina	Cauda porcina	*Peucedanum palustre*, Hog's Fennel; or *Lithospermum officinale*, Gromwell; or *Sonchus oleraceus*, Sowthistle.
18.	Π Pampiris	Pamphinus	*Vitis vinifera*, Vine Leaf.
19.	Folium vitis	Folium vitis, the lefe of the vyne	As above.
20.	Π Panifiligos	Pamphiligos, flosmus tapsus barbastus	*Vebascum thapsus*, Mullein
21.	Moleyn	Moleyne	As above.
22.	Π Panis cuculi	Panis cuculi, Alleluia	*Oxalis acetosella,* Wood Sorrell.

Image, Folio and Line Numbers.	Betson Entry. [The alphabetical letters A-Z below are for reference only, and are not in Betson].	The Synonoma of John Bray: BL Sloane MS 282, with folio number and column.	Possible Modern Names, mainly Linnaean, and taken from Hunt (1989). Non-Linnaean names are indicated.
23.	Wodesoure	Anglice wodesoure	*As above.*
		Bray continues:- Panis porcinus, Ciclamen, Malum terre, Erthe notes, Plantago, Planteyne, or Weybrede, Planto Cimium montanum, Suremontayne	
24.	Alleluia		*Oxalis acetosella,* Wood Sorrell.
25.	Π Passarla	Passula, Passulus.	*Raisins*
Image 84, Right, Folio 80r, Col. A			
1.	Peysyns (*sic*)	Uva passa, reysones	*As above.*
2.	Π Pastinaca. Pastenep	Pastinaca, Baucia, Pasternepe	*Daucus carota,* Wild Carrot, or *Pastinaca sativa,* Wild Parsnip.
3.	Π Passerina Lingua	Passerina lingua	*Persicaria aviculare,* Knotgrass.
4.	Corigiola	Corigiola	*As above.*
5.	Cynuniglata (?)	Geniculata	*As above.*
6.	Proserpinia.	Prosperina	*As above.*
7.	Sweynes gresse	Poligo, Swynesgrece	*As above.*
8.	Π Prassium	Prassium, [porrus, leek] Prassium viride Fol. 172r., Col A.	*Marrubium vulgare,* White Horehound.
9.	Horehonde	Horehounde	*As above.*
10.	Π Marubium	Marubrium album	*As above.*

Image, Folio and Line Numbers.	Betson Entry. [The alphabetical letters A-Z below are for reference only, and are not in Betson].	The Synonoma of John Bray: BL Sloane MS 282, with folio number and column.	Possible Modern Names, mainly Linnaean, and taken from Hunt (1989). Non-Linnaean names are indicated.
11.	Morell	Marioll	*Morell is usually Solanum nigrum*, Black Nightshade. But here under Marubium it is perhaps Marioll as in Bray.
12.	Π P*a*ritaria. Pitary		*Parietaria officinalis / diffusa,* Pellitory of the Wall.
		Paritoria, Perciados (*?for Perniciades - in Mowat Alphita, p.134 under Paritaria*), H*e*rba vitriola, H*e*rba murialis (?), Paritorie, Stonhore, Walwort. *Hunt p201.*	
13.	Penticla cortex cit (?)	Pecula cortex, Cicrim, Pentafilon, Qui*n*quefoliu*m*	*Potentilla reptans,* Creeping cinquefoil
14.	Five leved gres	Fivelevede gras	*As above.*
15.	Π Pentadactulus	Pentadactulus	*As above.*
16.	Palma Xpi	Palma Xpi	*As above.*
17.	Swynestaile	Swynestayle	*Peucedanum palustre*, Hog's Fennel; or *Lithospermum officinale*, Gromwell; or *Sonchus oleraceus*, Sowthistle.
18.	Π Petrocillum	Petrociliu*m*	*Smyrnium olustratum*, Alexanders, Horse Parsley.
19.	Macedonu*m*	Macedoniu*m*	*As above.*
20.	Alexandris sede	Alexandris seed	*As above.*
21.	Π Pes ancipitris		*Geranium*, esp. ssp. *G. columbinum*; or *?Aquilegia vulgaris,* Columbine.
22.	Columbynd.		*As above.*

Image, Folio and Line Numbers.	Betson Entry. [The alphabetical letters A-Z below are for reference only, and are not in Betson].	The Synonoma of John Bray: BL Sloane MS 282, with folio number and column.	Possible Modern Names, mainly Linnaean, and taken from Hunt (1989). Non-Linnaean names are indicated.
23.	Petrolium olium de petra	Petrolinum, oleum de petra, oleum benedictum	*Presumably a form of mineral oil.*
24.	Olium benedictum	Oleum benedictum	*As above ?*
25.	Π Pes leporis	Pes leporis	*Geum urbanum,* Herb Bennet.
26.	Avence	Avancia	*As above.*
27.	Π Perechen-icion	Pericheminon, Mater silve, Caprifolium, Capistus, Oculus lucis, Volubilis maior	*Lonicera periclymenum,* Honeysuckle.
28.	Wodebynde	Wodebynde	*As above.*
29.	Π Peristerion	Peristerion.	*Verbena officinalis,* Vervain.
Image 84, Right, Folio 80r, Col. B			
1.	Columbaria verbena	Columbaria	*As above.*
2.	Culrage.	Culerage	*Polygonum persicaria* or *P. lapathifolium,* or *P. hydropiper,* Redshank, Pale Persicaria or Water-Pepper.
3.	Persicaria	Persicaria maior	*As above.*
4.	Dropeworth	Dropwort	*Filipendula vulgaris,* Dropwort.
5.	Pigaminis	Piganis,	*Ruta graveolens,* Rue, or *Thalictrum flavum,* 'Meadow Rue'.

Image, Folio and Line Numbers.	Betson Entry. [The alphabetical letters A-Z below are for reference only, and are not in Betson].	The Synonoma of John Bray: BL Sloane MS 282, with folio number and column.	Possible Modern Names, mainly Linnaean, and taken from Hunt (1989). Non-Linnaean names are indicated.
6.		Pulmonaria, Velpella.	*Pulmonaria officinalis*, Lungwort. 'Velpella' not found, but next entry in SB, Mowat p.35 is 'Pulpilla', for pupil of eye, so perhaps a mis-reading of this.
7.	Bellewede	Bellewort	Hunt p206 and pp216-7 has Bellewort as both Rue and *Pulmonaria officinalis*, Lungwort, as above.
8.	Π Persa maiorana	Persa maiorana cimbrium, Sansucus,	*Maiorana hortensis* Moench. Sweet Marjoram; or *Origanum vulgare*, Marjoram.
9.	Amaracus		As above.
10.	Methworth.	Muchwort	*Melissa officinalis*, Balm.
11.	Pepones. melones	Pepones, Melones	*Cucumis melo*, Melon.
12.	Pes nisi. Pollitricum	Pes nisi, Pulinona, Pollitricum	?*Adiantum capillus-veneris*, Maidenhair fern; or ?*Asplenium trichomanes*, Maidenhair Spleenwort; or ?*Asplenium adiantum-nigrum*, Black Spleenwort. Bray 'Pulinona' not found.
13.	Hawkisfote	Sperhaukesfote	As above.
14.	Pes vituli. Iarus	Pes vituli, iarus, Barba aaron, zekersterse,	*Arum maculatum*, Lords and Ladies.
15.	Pes corvi: ligatum ad digitum, aufert dolorem dentium	Pes corvi, Apium emoroidarum,	*Ficaria verna*, Lesser celandine, Pilewort, Crowfoot.

Image, Folio and Line Numbers.	Betson Entry. [The alphabetical letters A-Z below are for reference only, and are not in Betson].	The Synonoma of John Bray: BL Sloane MS 282, with folio number and column.	Possible Modern Names, mainly Linnaean, and taken from Hunt (1989). Non-Linnaean names are indicated.
16.	Crowisfote	Crowes fote.	*As above.*
		Fol.172 r., Col B Pes pulli, And*r*ago	
17.	Pes columbe	Pes columbe idem	*Geranium ssp.,* Dove's foot Cranebill; or *Cruciata laevipes,* ?Crosswort; or ?*Aquilegia vulgaris,* Columbine.
18.	Peucedanum	Peucedanum, finiculus porcinus,	*Peucedanum officinale,* Hog's Fennel.
19.	Houndesfenell	Houndefenel	*As above.*
		Penidie, Penetes, Picula, Pyx liquida, Anglice pitch *Varieties of pitch or tar.*	
20.	Pistasie. Be*n* fru*t*s	Pistacie be*th* fruytes y liche pynes	*Pistacia vera,* Pistachio.
21.	like pynes		'Like pine nuts'
22.	Π Pygamen	Pigamen, wild rewe	*Thalictrum flavum,* 'Meadow Rue'.
23.	Wilderwe (*sic*)		*Wild rue, as above*
24.	Pigla. lingua avis.	Pigla, Lingua avis, Pigle	Here *Stellaria holostea,* Stitchwort; but also: *Fraxinus excelsior,* Ash Tree Keys.
25.	Stichwort. Prigill	Stichewort	*As above.*
26.		*Bray:* Piper albu*m,* Fulfulabiat, Piper longu*m,* melanu*m,* nigru*m,* Fulfulesbeck. Hit is macro piper.	

Image, Folio and Line Numbers.	Betson Entry. [The alphabetical letters A-Z below are for reference only, and are not in Betson].	The Synonoma of John Bray: BL Sloane MS 282, with folio number and column.	Possible Modern Names, mainly Linnaean, and taken from Hunt (1989). Non-Linnaean names are indicated.
		'Fulful ebiat' above is in Mowat, Alphita, p.69 as piper album; 'fulfulsbeck' looks like another variant. Alphita has 'Fulful ebet' as piper nigrum.'	
27.	Pilobella *(sic)*	Pilosella	*Pilosella officinarum'* Mouse Ear Hawkweed.
28.	Peluet		As above.
29.	Chenet	Channet	As above. See Hunt p.207
30.	Moushere	Moushere	As above.
31.	Pigmentaria.	Pimentaria	*Melissa officinalis*, Balm.
32.	Mellilote	Melissa citrago, Melilot	*Trifolium* ssp. Melilots and Clovers.
Image 85, Left, Folio 80v, Col. A			
1.	At top of Page: Π Pimpinella pilos se*d* saxifragia no*n* ha*bet* ullos.		*Anagallis arvensis*, Scarlet Pimpernel; or *Pimpinella saxifraga*, Burnet Saxifrage; or *Sanguisorba officinalis*, 'Great Burnet'
2.	Π Psidia cortex ma-	Psydia cortex ma	Pomegranate rind.
3.	-li granati	-li granati	
4.	Π Psillium seme*n* aliq*uis* herbe	Psillium is *the* sede of an herbe	*Pulicaria dysenterica* or *P. vulgaris*, Common & Small Fleabanes; or *Plantago indica*, Fleawort.
5.	Piretrum	Peretru*m*, Peletre of Spayne	*Anacyclus pirethrum*, Pellitory; or *Parietaria judiaca*, Pellitory of the Wall.

Image, Folio and Line Numbers.	Betson Entry. [The alphabetical letters A-Z below are for reference only, and are not in Betson].	The Synonoma of John Bray: BL Sloane MS 282, with folio number and column.	Possible Modern Names, mainly Linnaean, and taken from Hunt (1989). Non-Linnaean names are indicated.
6.	Peletre of spayn.	Peletre of Spayne	*Veratrum album,* White or False Hellebore; or *Helleborus foetidus,* Bears Foot.
7.	Folium marinum	Pollium marinum	*Sempervivum tectorum,* Houseleek.
8.	Pulegium	Pulegium	*Mentha pulegium,* Pennyroyal.
9.	Puleim montanum	Pollium montanum	*Mentha pulegium,* Penny-Royal; or *Thymus polytrichus,* Wild Thyme.
10.	Pyliol montayning	Poleos, Pulyole montayne	As above.
11.	Π Propoleos alba cera	Propolis, whyte wex	'Propolis'. Here 'white wax', but now meaning the hard dark resin, collected by bees from the gum of certain trees, to glue up the hive.
12.	Π Pollicaria est herba	Policaria is an herbe & the sede ther of is y clipped psillium	*Pulicaria dysenterica* or *P. vulgaris,* Common & Small Fleabanes; or *Plantago indica,* Fleawort.
13.	cuius semem nomine psillium.		As above
14.	Π Pollicaria minor	Policaria minor	As above
15.	Skabworte.	Skabbewort	*Inula helenium,* Elecampane, Horseheal, Scabwort.
16.	Π Plumbum. Led	Plumbum leed	Lead.

Image, Folio and Line Numbers.	Betson Entry. [The alphabetical letters A-Z below are for reference only, and are not in Betson].	The Synonoma of John Bray: BL Sloane MS 282, with folio number and column.	Possible Modern Names, mainly Linnaean, and taken from Hunt (1989). Non-Linnaean names are indicated.
17.	Π Polipodum	Polipodium, Feugerole (*French: Feugerole de Chêne*)	*Polypodium* ssp., 'Polypody'; also *Thelypteris dryopteris*, Oak Fern.
18.	Everfern growing in oke	Overfern growing on oke	As above. These seem to be corruptions of 'oakfern' or everfern. See Hunt p.211.
19.	Π Podagra lini	Podagra lini, Cuscuta, Dodire	*Cuscuta europaea*, 'Large Dodder'; Or: *Cuscuta epithymum*, Common Dodder.
20.	Cuscuta Dogir	Cuscuta, Dodire	As above.
21.	Π Pes pulli	Andraginis, Pes pulli, Portulaca, Abaga.	*Portulaca oleracea*, Purslane; or *Tussilago farfara*, Coltsfoot; or ?*Nuphar lutea*, Yellow Water Lily; or *Ranunculus acris*, ?Meadow Buttercup; or ?*Ficaria verna*, Lesser Celandine. 'Abaga' not found
22.	Purcelana	Porcellana	As above.
23.	Purslane	Purcelane	As above.
24.	Pomum quercinum	Pomum quercinum, Galla Sciadon	Oak Apple
25.	Galla Alapsa	Alapsa	As above.
26.	Okappull	Anglice an oke appel	As above.
27.	Π Pomum citrine	Pomum citrinum,	*Citrus limon*, Lemon; or *Citrus aurantium*, Orange.

Image, Folio and Line Numbers.	Betson Entry. [The alphabetical letters A-Z below are for reference only, and are not in Betson].	The Synonoma of John Bray: BL Sloane MS 282, with folio number and column.	Possible Modern Names, mainly Linnaean, and taken from Hunt (1989). Non-Linnaean names are indicated.
28.	Π Pomecitrina	Pom*me* citr*ine*	
29.	Pomfilion	Ponfilon	*Vebascum thapsus*, Mullein. See Hunt p.197 – *Panphilagos*.
30.	Plasinus	Flosmus, Tapsus barbast*us*,	*As above*. Betson's source appears to have read '*Plasinus*' for '*Flosmus*'.
31.	Maleyn.	Molyne	*As above*.
Image 85, Left, Folio 80v, Col. B			
1.	Pulegium Gliconu*m*	Pulegium, Gliconium	*Mentha pulegium*, Pennyroyal; or *Thymus serpyllum*, Wild Thyme.
2.	Golena Puliol roial.	Golena, Puliol real	*As above*.
3.	Pulegium maris	Pulegium martis	*Origanum dictamnus*, Dittany of Crete, or *Dictamnus albus*, White Dittany.
4.	Diptanus, Dyptand (?)	Dyptamnus, Ditayne	*As above*.
		Plumbu*m* leed, Prima a plum*me*, Prunella ys a sloe	
5.	Pimpinella, Selfhele Hyacinthoides		*Anagallis arvensis*, Scarlet Pimpernel; or *Pimpinella saxifraga*, Burnet Saxifrage; Or *Sanguisorba officinalis*, 'Great Burnet' *'Selfheal' is now the common name for Prunella vulgaris.*
6.	*In the gutter*: *'Labria…' then illegible.*		

Image, Folio and Line Numbers.	Betson Entry. [The alphabetical letters A-Z below are for reference only, and are not in Betson].	The Synonoma of John Bray: BL Sloane MS 282, with folio number and column.	Possible Modern Names, mainly Linnaean, and taken from Hunt (1989). Non-Linnaean names are indicated.
7.	Bleddistong		*Galium aparine*, Cleavers. *Tongbledes is in Mowat, Alphita, p.157 under Rubea minor, Clivure.*
8.	Π Pilosella Moushere		*Pilosella officinarum*, Mouse Ear Hawkweed.
9.	Policaria contra puli / ces (against fleas).		*Pulicaria dysenterica* or *P. vulgaris* Common and Small Fleabanes.
10.	Persicaria		*Poligonum persicaria*, Persicaria, or *Poligonum hydropiper*, Water-Pepper
11.	**[Q]** Quercus an oke	Quercus an oke	Oak Tree
12.	Quercula maior		*Ajuga chamaeptys*, Ground Pine; or *Teucrium chamaedrys*, 'Wall Germander'.
13.	Quercula m*in*or	Quercula minor, Camedreos, Germand*er*	*As above.*
		Quercula maior, Camepiteos, mede ratill *(all bracketed in Bray)*	*As above.*
14.	Germander	*As above*	*As above.*
15.	Quinquerina	Quinquinerina	*Plantago lanceolata*, Ribwort. See Hunt p.218 for *Quinquenervia*

Image, Folio and Line Numbers.	Betson Entry. [The alphabetical letters A-Z below are for reference only, and are not in Betson].	The Synonoma of John Bray: BL Sloane MS 282, with folio number and column.	Possible Modern Names, mainly Linnaean, and taken from Hunt (1989). Non-Linnaean names are indicated.
16.	Plantago minor	Plantago Lanceolata	*As above.*
17.	Lanciolata ribwort	Ribwort	*As above.*
18.	Quinquefolium	Quinque folium, Pentafilon	*Potentilla reptans*, Cinquefoil.
19.	Cameleon	Camolee, Quintfoile, Fyveleved gras	*As above.* Hunt p.63 also gives: *Chamaemelum nobile*, Sweet Camomile; or *Anthemis cotula*, Stinking Chamomile, Mayweed; or *Anthemis arvensis*, Corn Chamomile.
20.	**[R]** Radix simple	Radix whan hit is put simpliche	Radish ssp.
21.	Raphanus radissh	Of Raphani, *idem* Radich hit shal be understode	*Raphanus sativus*, Radish; or *Armoracia rusticana* . Gaertn. Horse-Radish; or *Raphanus raphanistrum*, Wild Radish, White Charlock.
22.	Rapistum	Raphistrum, Dragancia	*Raphanus raphanistrum*, Wild Radish, White Charlock.
23.	Charlok	Cherlok	*As above.*
24.	Resta lini	Rasta lini, Podagra	*Cuscuta europaea*, 'Large Dodder'; Or: *Cuscuta epithymum*, 'Common Dodder'.
25.	Cuscuta	Cuscuta, Dodyr	*As above.*

Image, Folio and Line Numbers.	Betson Entry. [The alphabetical letters A-Z below are for reference only, and are not in Betson].	The Synonoma of John Bray: BL Sloane MS 282, with folio number and column.	Possible Modern Names, mainly Linnaean, and taken from Hunt (1989). Non-Linnaean names are indicated.
26.	Regina Moderwort	Regina aquilia, Anglice Roynet, Moderwort or Medewort	*Filipendula ulmaria* Meadowsweet. See Hunt p220
27.	Resta bovis *(as catchword at bottom of page).*	Resta bovis	*Ononis repens*, Restharrow. 'holding back the ox (bovis) at the plough.'
Image 85, Right, Folio 81r, Col. A			
1.	Resta bovis	Resta bovis	As above.
2.	Camlok	Cam*m*ok	As above.
3.	Rosina rosyn	Resina, Rosyne	*Rosin.* Sometimes also in ME as new or 'white' wax.
4.	Π Rami cedri.	Rama Cedri, Lignu*m* Iuniperi	'Cedar branches'
5.	Lignum Ienup*er*	Lignu*m* Iuniperi	*Juniperus communis*, Juniper.
6.	Π Pecoree	Recope, Recopie,	*Succisa pratensis*, Moench, Devil's Bit. See Hunt p181-2, *Morsus Demonis*.
7.	Morsus demoins (sic)	Morsus demonis	As above
8.	Forbiten	Forbytene	As above
9.	Π Resuris	Rasi, Rys	*Rheum raponticum*, Rhubarb
10.	Rubarbe	**Folio 172v, Col A** Rubarbe is a rote or *the* leves of Genet.	As above.

Image, Folio and Line Numbers.	Betson Entry. [The alphabetical letters A-Z below are for reference only, and are not in Betson].	The Synonoma of John Bray: BL Sloane MS 282, with folio number and column.	Possible Modern Names, mainly Linnaean, and taken from Hunt (1989). Non-Linnaean names are indicated.
11.	Π Radix minor		*Cytisus scoparius,* Broom.
12.	Genest		*As above.*
13.	Π Repontiphus		*As above.*
14.	Rosa rubea.	Rosa rubea, Reed Rose, Rosa alba, Whit Rose,	'The red rose' *Hunt has* 'Rodon, Rosa, anglice red rose'
15.	Π Rodaxigrou	Rodix ioron	*Not found*
16.	Oleum rosarum	Oleum rosar*um* or Wat*e*r of Rose	'Oil of Roses'
		Bray Sinonima continue: Ros marinus, Antos Dendrolibanus, Ros Ciriacus, Floures of Maythes.	
17.	Π Rostrum porcinum	Rostr*um* porcin*um*	*Sonchus oleraceus,* Milk- or Sow- Thistle.
18.	Thowisall (?)	Sow*t*histel	*As above.*
19.	Π Robelia.	Robelia, *the* commune pese	*Pisum sativum,* Pea; or *Lathyrus* ssp., Vetchling.
20.	Rubea Maior	Rubia maior	*Rubia tinctorum,* Madder.
21.	Warencia mather	Warancia, Mader	*As above.*
22.	Rubea Minor	Rubia minor,	*Galium aparine,* Cleavers.
23.	Hereve Cliten	Hayrif, Anglice Cli*t*hrone	*As above.* For *Clithrone* see *Hunt p.223.*
24.	Rubus rumex, Tr*i*bul*u*s	Rubus, Rumex, Tribulus	*Rubus fructicosus,* Blackberry, Bramble.

Image, Folio and Line Numbers.	Betson Entry. [The alphabetical letters A-Z below are for reference only, and are not in Betson].	The Synonoma of John Bray: BL Sloane MS 282, with folio number and column.	Possible Modern Names, mainly Linnaean, and taken from Hunt (1989). Non-Linnaean names are indicated.
25.	Ruba blak bery bremble	Bray: Bremel. Wyte hit wel that ther beth many bremles bote when Rubus is simplich y set of the bremle, that beryth blak beries hyt shal be understonde.	
26.	[S] Sagapium Serapium	Sagapinum idem Serapinum Sansucus, Amariscus, Amaracus,	?Maiorana hortensis, Moench. ?Sweet Marjoram.
27.	Maiorana	Maiorane	As above.
28.	Mecheworte	Muchelwort	(Filipendula ulmaria) Meadowsweet
Image 85, Right, Folio 81r, Col. B			
1.	Sambucus	Sambucus actis	Sambucus nigra, Elder.
2.	Eleer [elder]	Ellerne	As above.
3.	Sanguis draconis	Sanguis draconis, Multisdatum, Demathian	Daemonorops draco, Blume ex Schult; Dragon's Blood (Resin); Dracaena draco, Dragon Tree.
4.	Sankdragon	Sankdragon	As above.
5.	Π Salix sallinea	Salix,	Salix ssp., Willow; or Salix viminalis, Osier Willow.
6.	Welew tre	A withy tree	As above.
		Salinuca, Spica celtica,	
7.	Π Salvia sauge	Salvia, Salgia, Sawge	Salvia officinalis, Sage.

183

Image, Folio and Line Numbers.	Betson Entry. [The alphabetical letters A-Z below are for reference only, and are not in Betson].	The Synonoma of John Bray: BL Sloane MS 282, with folio number and column.	Possible Modern Names, mainly Linnaean, and taken from Hunt (1989). Non-Linnaean names are indicated.
8.	Salt gum*me*	Sal comen *idem* salt, but *th*er be*th many* maner of saltes.	*It appears that Betson's source has mis-heard 'sal comen', common salt, and run it together with 'Sal gemma', Rock Salt*
9.	Π Sal armoniak	Sal armoniak	*Ammonium Chloride. EMED*
10.	Π Sal geme	Sal gemme	*Rock Salt*
11.	Π Sal capodoxitu*m*	Sal capadociu*m*	*Not found.*
12.	Π Sal traceatum	Sal tracencium	*Mowat, Alphita, p.159 under 'Salis': 'sal tragesicon vel tragesion, quod nos habemus in Alexandro, et est sal [pensum] quod est fuligo nata in tectis balneorum...'*
13.	Π Sal ponsinus ?	Fol. 172v., Col A Sal pensum	*'Sal Pensum' : sal ammoniac, ammonium chloride.*
14.	Π Sal sacerdotale	Sal sacerdotale	*Not found.*
15.	Π Sal matelli. (?)	Sal mateli	*Not found*
16.	Π Sal catercutie (?)		*Not found*
17.	Π Sal nitrum	Sal nitri	*Native sodium carbonate, natron. EMED*
18.	Π Sal alkali	Sal alkali	*An alkaline substance obtained from the calcined ashes of plants. EMED*
19.	Π Sal tartari	Sal tartari	*Potassium Carbonate. EMED*

Image, Folio and Line Numbers.	Betson Entry. [The alphabetical letters A-Z below are for reference only, and are not in Betson].	The Synonoma of John Bray: BL Sloane MS 282, with folio number and column.	Possible Modern Names, mainly Linnaean, and taken from Hunt (1989). Non-Linnaean names are indicated.
20.	Π Saundres ben iii spics (three species)	Saundres: *ther* be*th* th*re* spices of he*m*	*This seems to be Santalum album, White Sandalwood; Pterocarpus santalinus, Red Sandalwood, and a yellow (citrine) variety.*
21.	White. rede et citrine	Whyte, reed & citrine	*As above.*
		Bray: Sanguinaria, Bursa pastoris, Sanicla, Sanicle, or Wodemerch; Sandix ys wode; Sanamunda, Pes Leporis, Gariofilata, Anglice Avance.	
22.	Sandonicum	Sandonicu*m*,	*Artemesia maritima,* Sea Wormwood; or *Santolina chamaecyparissus,* Lavender Cotton.
23.	Sewarmede		*As above, Sea Wormwood*
24.	Π Sandarica vinssh [*varnish*]	Sandarica, Anglice Vernishe	Mowat, Alphita p.161, *Sandarica idem quodam vernicis.* But also in Mowat, SB, p37 as *Sandarica, idem auripigmentum rubrum.*
25.	Π Sapa est novu*m* vinum	Sapa, new wyne	EMED: 'New wine boiled to a syrup.'
26.	in tempore vino*rum* musto	*The* time of *the* vine mat (?)	Perhaps '*in the time of the wine 'must' or fermentation'*
27.	Π Saponaria canaid (?)	Saponaria, Saveney,	*Saponaria ocymoides* or *officinalis* ? Rock Soapwort or Soapwort
28.	Crowsope	Crowesope, Netebroun	*As above.*

Image, Folio and Line Numbers.	Betson Entry. [The alphabetical letters A-Z below are for reference only, and are not in Betson].	The Synonoma of John Bray: BL Sloane MS 282, with folio number and column.	Possible Modern Names, mainly Linnaean, and taken from Hunt (1989). Non-Linnaean names are indicated.
29.	Π Saturion leporina Costirlos... ? [illegible entry in gutter]	Saturion, Priamuscus (?), Leporina	*Orchis ssp. esp. Anacamptis pyramidalis*; Pyramidal Orchid; or *Arum maculatum*, Cuckoo Pint; or *?Hyacinthoides non-scriptus*. Bluebell
30.	Satercia Savereyu (?)	Satireia, Tymbra, Anglice Savereye	*Satureia hortensis*, Summer Savory; or *Satureia montana*, Winter savory. In Hunt at pp.230 and 252
31.	Sarcocolla *the* gu*m*	Sarcocalla ys *the* gum*m*e of a tree	*Astrogalus fascislifolius*, Boiss. Gum Saracolla; or *Bryonia dioca*, White Bryony; or *Agrimonia eupatoria*, Agrimony.
32.	of a tre.		
		Savina, bracteos	Juniper. *Mowat, SB, p13: Brateos vel Brachteos idem Savina*
Image 86 Left, Folio 81v, Col. A			
1.	Scoriola silv.	Scariola silvestris	Possibly *Lactuca virosa*, Prickly Lettuce; or *Euphorbia* ssp., Spurge; or *Sonchus oleraceus*, Milk- or Sow-Thistle.
2.	Wilde letuse.	Ys wilde letuse	*?As above.*
3.	Stafisatis	Stafisagria	*Delphinium staphisagria*, Stavesacre, licebane.
4.	He*r*ba prinits	Herbe pinnetis & lyes (*for nits and lice*).	As above

Image, Folio and Line Numbers.	Betson Entry. [The alphabetical letters A-Z below are for reference only, and are not in Betson].	The Synonoma of John Bray: BL Sloane MS 282, with folio number and column.	Possible Modern Names, mainly Linnaean, and taken from Hunt (1989). Non-Linnaean names are indicated.
5.	Π Scamonia.	Scamonia, Diagradium	*Convolvulus scammonia*, Levant Scammony. *Diagradium or Diegradium was a preparation of Scammony by Galen used as a laxative. See EMED & OED (Diegradium)*
6.	Π Saxifragia	Saxifragia	*Saxifrage* spp., Saxifrage; or *Pimpinella saxifragia*, Burnet Saxifrage.
7.	Acinalia (?)	Acinalia	*Not found.*
8.	Π Statumcellus	Statumcellus	*Umbilicus rupestris*, Salisb., Pennywort.
9.	Umbilicus veneris	Umbillicus veneris	*As above.*
10.	Penyworte	Anglice Balarium (?), Penywort	*As above.*
11.	Speragon.	Speragiis, Alyon	*Not found.*
12.	Π Spatula fetida	Spatula fetida	*Iris foetidissima*, Gladden, Stinking Iris.
13.	Gladyn berith no flor	Gladyn, which berith no floure.	
14.	Π Setacul, Seholin	Fol. 172v, Col C Setacul, Yringes, Seholme	*Eryngium* esp., *E. maritinum*, Sea Holly. *For variants see Hunt p.237.*

Image, Folio and Line Numbers.	Betson Entry. [The alphabetical letters A-Z below are for reference only, and are not in Betson].	The Synonoma of John Bray: BL Sloane MS 282, with folio number and column.	Possible Modern Names, mainly Linnaean, and taken from Hunt (1989). Non-Linnaean names are indicated.
15.	Π Sepha. Ysopus	Sepha, Ysopus	*Hyssopus officinalis*, Hyssop.
16.	Π Solerata. (*read Scelerata*) Apium ris*us*.	Selerata, Aquilaria, Apium risus, Botracion (?)	*Ranunculus sceleratus*, Celery-leaved Buttercup; or *Levisticum officinale*, Koch. Lovage; or ? *Anthriscus sylvestris*, Wild Chervil.
17.	Π Silium merchsede	Selinu*m*, semen apii, Anglice Merchsede	*Apium graveolens* - Seed of Wild Celery.
18.	Π Semen Urtice		Seed of *Lamium* / *Urtica* ssp., Nettle seed.
19.	Acantium. Nettil sede		As above
20.	Π Semperviva (*sic*) Housleke	Semperviva, Barba Aaron	*Sempervivum tectorum* Houseleek
21.	Herba aaron Housleke		As above.
22.	Selfgrene Housleke	Anglice Synegrene	As above.
		Bray: Semen bulli, seme*n* grosse, Cepe, Oynounys or Oyninnet	
23.	Π Semen rose	Seme*n* Rose	Rose 'Seed' or Anthers
24.	Antera	Antera	As above.
25.	Sede of rose	Seed of Rose	As above.
		Bray: Semen Lini. Lynseed, Semen Saxifragii, Acinarticuli (?), Licospermatis	

Image, Folio and Line Numbers.	Betson Entry. [The alphabetical letters A-Z below are for reference only, and are not in Betson].	The Synonoma of John Bray: BL Sloane MS 282, with folio number and column.	Possible Modern Names, mainly Linnaean, and taken from Hunt (1989). Non-Linnaean names are indicated.
26.	Π Semen rapistri	Semen Rapistri, Armoinaca, Cherlok sede, Seme*n* Nasturciu*m*	*Raphanus raphanistrum*, Wild Radish, White Cherlock, or *?Lepidum sativum*, ?Garden-Cress Seed.
27.	Touncras sede	Toun cresse seed	As above.
28.	Senacio	Senacon	*Senecio vulgaris*, Groundsel; or *Cnicus benedictus*, Holy Thistle.
29.	Watercressis	Nasturciu*m* aquaticu*m*, Wate*r*cars	*Rorippa nasturtium-aquaticum*, Watercress.
30.	Seneciu*m*	Senico, Seniciu*m*	As above.
31.	Grounsaile *In margin:* gronswille	Groundeswylie	*Senecio vulgaris*, Groundsel; or *Cnicus benedictus*, Holy Thistle.
		Bray: Seme*n* sene, *t*he seed of a sene tree & hit ys lavatife. Senna	
Image 86 Left, Folio 81v, Col. B			
1.	Π Salvatelle been iv	Salvatille be*th* 4 (*sic*) veynes i*n* *the* handes	A vein in the feet and fingers
2.	wynes in the handis		wynes: veins.
3.	between the littil fin-	*Bray:* Bytwene *t*he litel finger & *t*he next fenge*r* & upo*n* the foote in *t*he same place.	
4.	ger and the fyng*er* next		
5.	hym		

189

Image, Folio and Line Numbers.	Betson Entry. [The alphabetical letters A-Z below are for reference only, and are not in Betson].	The Synonoma of John Bray: BL Sloane MS 282, with folio number and column.	Possible Modern Names, mainly Linnaean, and taken from Hunt (1989). Non-Linnaean names are indicated.
		Bray: Stercus Caprinus, *th*e donge of *th*e goote. Stercus Vaccar*um th*e donge of cowen. Stercus Ovium, *th*e donge of sheep. Stercus Columba*rum* the donge of colu*m*on (?) Stercus Anatis, *th*e donge of mawlards. Stercus Yrundinis, *th*e donge of a swalwe. [Fol. 173r. Col A] Stercus Muris, *th*e donge of a mows.	
6.	Π <u>Serpillum</u> pelege	Serpillum, Peletree	*Anacyclus pyrethrum,* Pellitory of Spain.
7.	Π Serpentaria	Serpenteria, Dragancia, Columbria, Cocodrilla,	*Polygonum bistorta,* Snake root, Bistort; (probably not *Dracunculus vulgaris,* Dragon Arum a Meditteranean plant).
8.	Nedir worte	Edderwort	*As above.*
9.	Π Scicida, *vide* nep	Scicida, Bryonia, Wild Nepe	*Bryonia dioca,* Bryony; or ?*Ecballium elaterium,* ?Squirting Cucumber.
10.	Π Simphonica	Simphonica, Caniculata, Iusquiamus,	*Hysocamus niger,* Henbane, for *Simphoniaca.*
11.	Hennebane	Hennebane	*As above.*
12.	Simphitum	Simphitu*m*, Anagall*is*, Anagallicu*m*, Consolida maior,	*Symphytum officinale,* Common Comfrey. See Hunt p.87.
13.	Conferey.	Conferye	*As above.*
		Sinapis,	*Mustard seed.*

Image, Folio and Line Numbers.	Betson Entry. [The alphabetical letters A-Z below are for reference only, and are not in Betson].	The Synonoma of John Bray: BL Sloane MS 282, with folio number and column.	Possible Modern Names, mainly Linnaean, and taken from Hunt (1989). Non-Linnaean names are indicated.
		Seneneysed	
14.	Π Synonum.	Sinonum, Petrosiliu agreste	*Sempervivum tectorum*, Houseleek; or *Smyrnium olusatrum*, Alexanders, Horse Parsley.
15.	Wilde Parsly sede	Wilde Persil sede	As above. See Hunt pp239-240 for variants.
16.	Π Sigillum Ste marie	Sigillum Ste marie	*Eryngium* esp., *E. maritinum*, Sea Holly.
17.	Seynt mary flour	Seynt marie floure	As above.
18.	Π Squilla see oynons	Squilla Cepa marina, Squilles	*Drimia maritima*, Squill. 'This poisonous Mediterranean plant should not be equated with edible onions.'EMED
19.	Π Squinatum esca camelorum	Squinantum, esca camelorum	*Cymbopogon schoenanthus*, Camel's Hay, Squinant.
20.	Camelismete	Camelis mete	As above.
21.	Π Sizinbeum baume, brookmyt [brook-mint]	Sisimbrium, Balsamita, Bawme	*Mentha sylvestris*, Horsemint; or *Mentha aquatica*, Water Mint.
22.	Π Strignum morel.	Strignum, Solatrum, Morell	*Solanum nigrum*, Black Nightshade.
23.	Π Spica celtica	Spica celtica,	*Valeriana celtica*, Celtic Spikenard; or *Ophioglossum vulgatum*, Adder's Tongue.
24.	Spikenard	Spicanardi	*Nardostachys jatamansi*, Spikenard;

Image, Folio and Line Numbers.	Betson Entry. [The alphabetical letters A-Z below are for reference only, and are not in Betson].	The Synonoma of John Bray: BL Sloane MS 282, with folio number and column.	Possible Modern Names, mainly Linnaean, and taken from Hunt (1989). Non-Linnaean names are indicated.
			or *?Cyperus longus*, Galingale.
25.	Π Sicomorus ficus	Sicomorus ficus	*Possibly the fruit of one of several trees: the Sycamore Fig, Ficus sycomorus; or the Common Fig, Ficus cariaca or the Mulberry tree Morus.*
26.	Fatua is at gode for them that ben love sike [love sick]	Ficus fatua, hit is good for hem *that* b*eth* love syke	*The fruit of the Sycamore Fig is insipid – 'fatua'. F. sycomorus is not hardy in Britain, But the common fig, Ficus carica, is. Both have similar leaves.*
27.	Π Stunci Stugni be*n* fisshis	Stincti, Stygni, *thei* b*eth* fishes as tench and water enetes.	Newts: *Lacerta agilis* ? Sand Newt ?
28.	Π Spinathia Spinach	Spinachia, Spinoche	*Spinarchia oleracea*, Spinach.
29.	Sistra, Dill, Agnetum	Sistra, Anetu*m*, Dille	*Anethum graveolens*, Dill.
30.	Π Sirnus (?) Betony	Sirnys, Betoyne	*Betonica officinalis*, Betony.
		Sileu*m*, semen Apii, Merch seed	
Image 86 right, Folio 82r, Col. A			
1.	Sisoleos siler mo*n*tanu*m*.	Siceleos Silerimontani, Seyrmo*n*tayne	*Laserpitum siler*, Sermountain.
2.	solirmountayn		As above.

Image 1: Thomas Betson, tonsured, and in the robes of a Syon Abbey deacon.

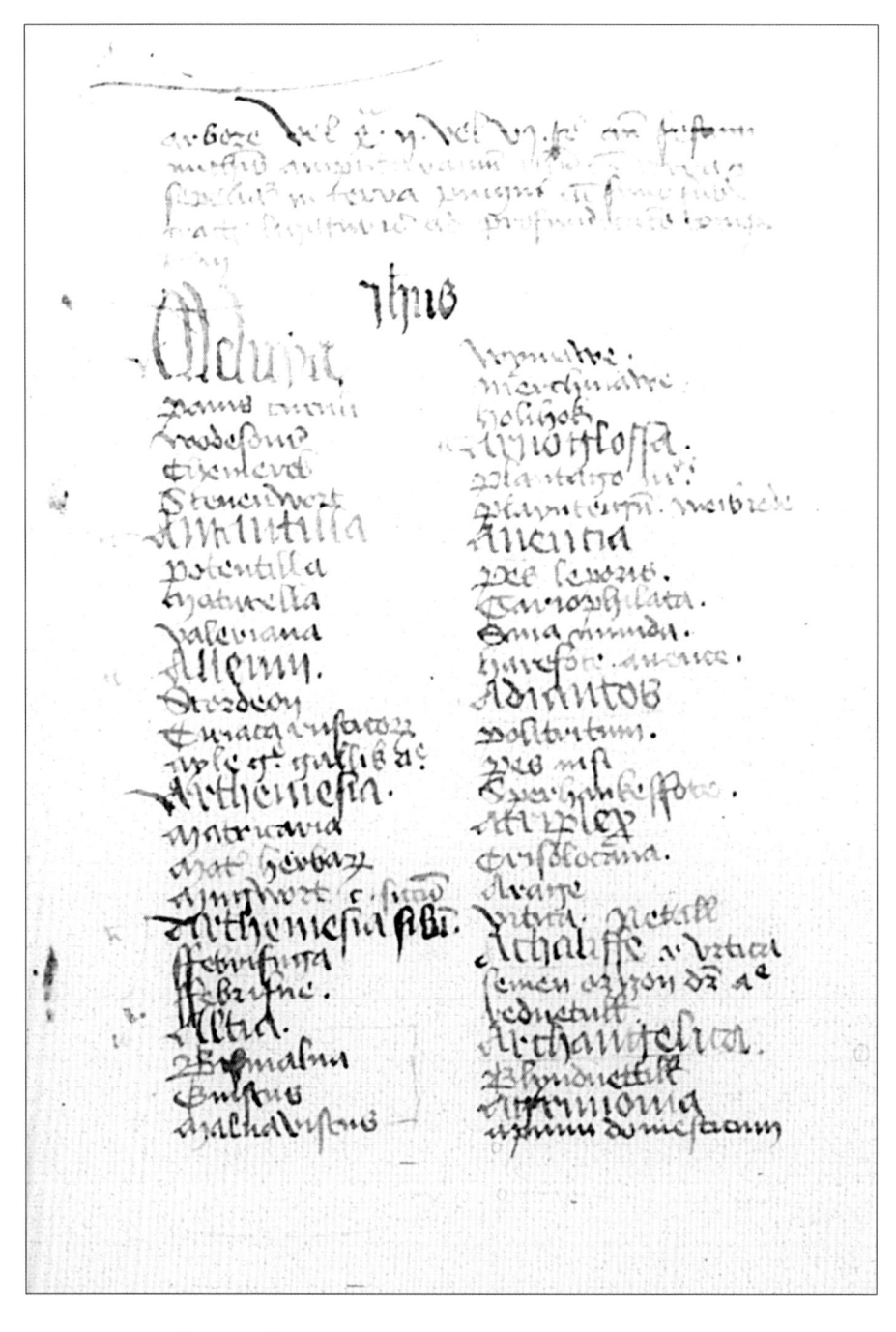

Image 2: St John's College MS 109 (E.6), Folio 70r. The beginning of the *Herbarium* (List of Plants) at 'Aleluia' (*Oxalis acetosella*, Wood Sorrel), and ending at 'apium domesticum', *Apium graveolens*, Wild Celery.

digestione materie morbi. In m[...]lla v[...]
put alia lapilli arenosi [et] tunc denotat y pri[...]
eius est calculus Et alij secundus est nigrum
[et] tunc ipse sunt p[er] talem v[...]a expulsio m[...]
[...]cruosi est [supra m]ort[...]

Explicit

Pro matrice take Rubarbe y[?]. tu[rbit?] — Sparsum
[...] zeos [?]. theodoricon y[?]. [?]amen y[?]
Sirisit. take in ti of oyle de olif and p[o]nde — Olei
of rose and haff a ponde in a glasse vessel — rosei
put it in a caldron full of wat[er] on the
fire and seethe it and pou hast pou oile of
rose gode and fi[n]e. Olei de violet olei
sambucinum olei mar[i]tim fiunt eodem modo
Sit fit. take pe white of egges and put — Olei
hem in a panne ou[er] the fire and styre he — mor[?]
w[ith] a staff till pei [waxen] rede. and take and
wryng oute pe oile. Take rede zelkis — p[ri]mofa[?]
and pe rotis of rede dockis. and do awey
the rend therof and mys[se] hem small as
jsup[?] and temp he to m[...] w[ith] vinegre
and make pl[a]s[ter] ag[ain]s[t] and lai it to pe morfu[...] — for any p[...]
v[n]m forth. Take peticonde confort pe — is gretter
rotis of wilde mako d[...]uence of eth[er] y[...]lles
my[?] and put he to mede [?] seth hem in ale
and hony and drink he feo[?] at morow and
at euen and pou shal be hole

Image 3: St John's College MS 109 (E.6), Folio 86r. End of the text on Urine, *De Urinalibus,* and beginning of Remedies, 'Pro matrice take Rubarbe'.

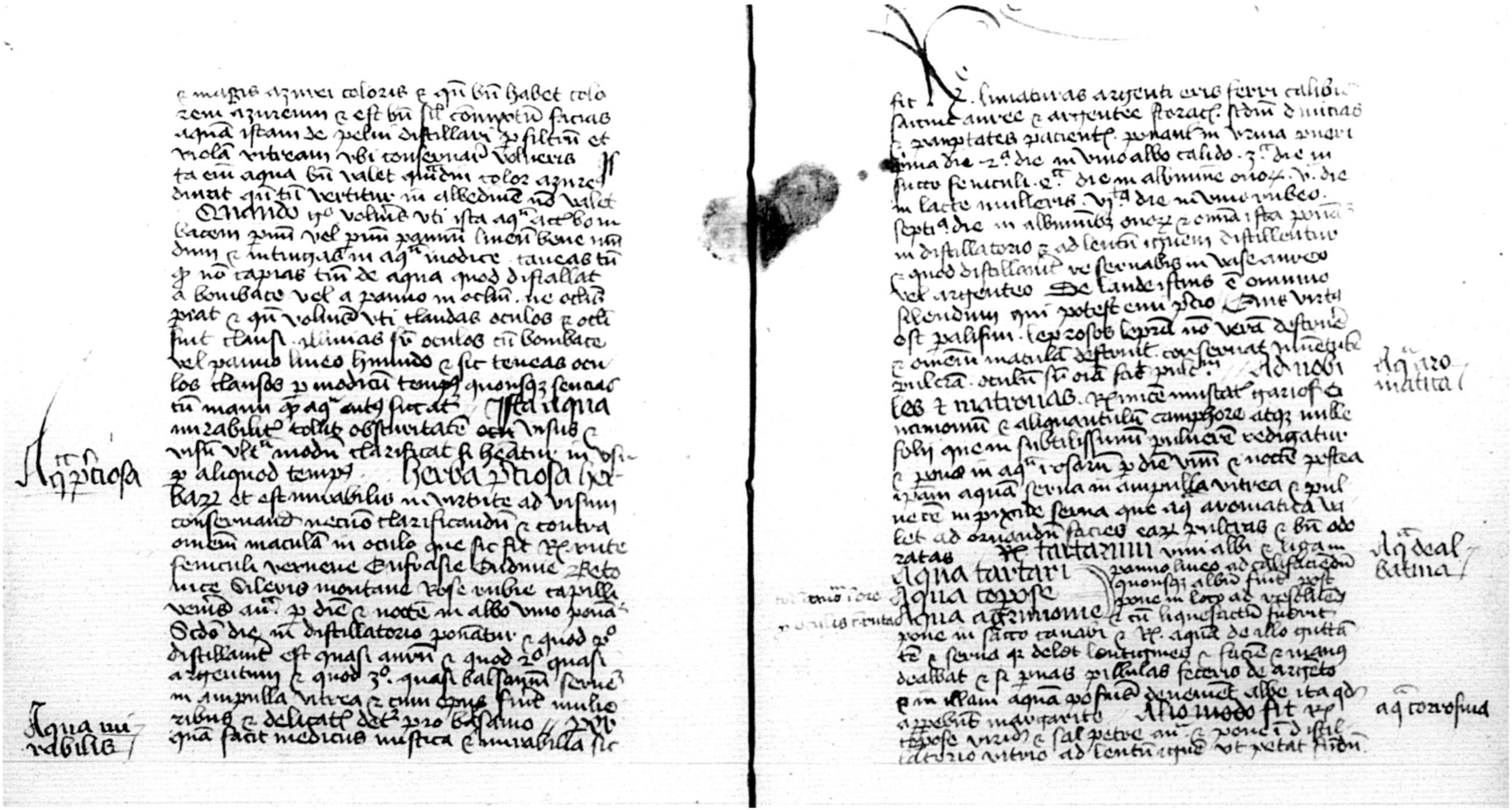

Image 4: Fingerprint, between folios 105v and 106r.
It is not known if this is the fingerprint of Thomas Betson.
Section on distilled essences – *Aqua Preciosa* and *Aromatica*.

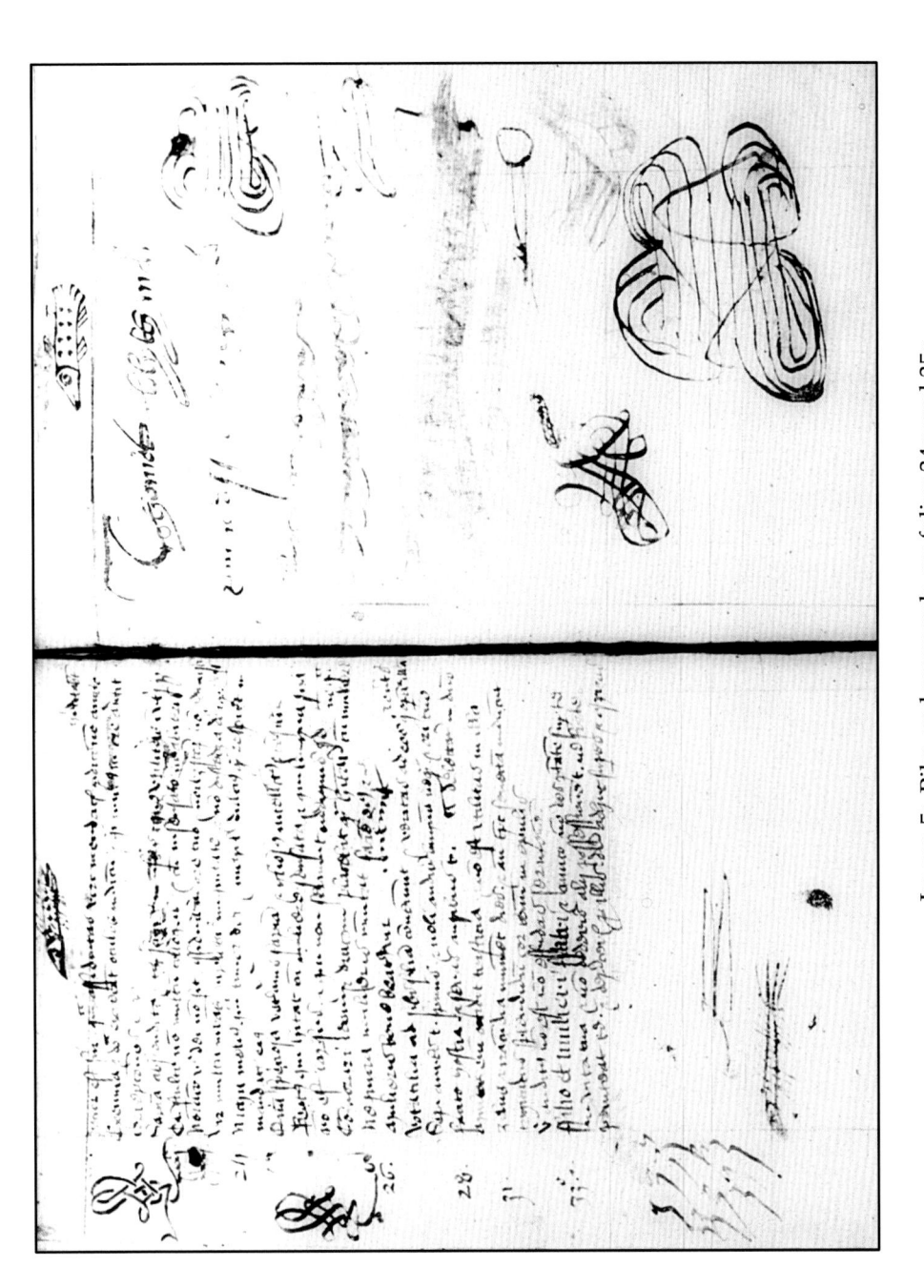

Image 5: Pike and penwork, on folios 34v and 35r. There were probably fishponds at Syon to provide fish for Fridays and other days of fasting.

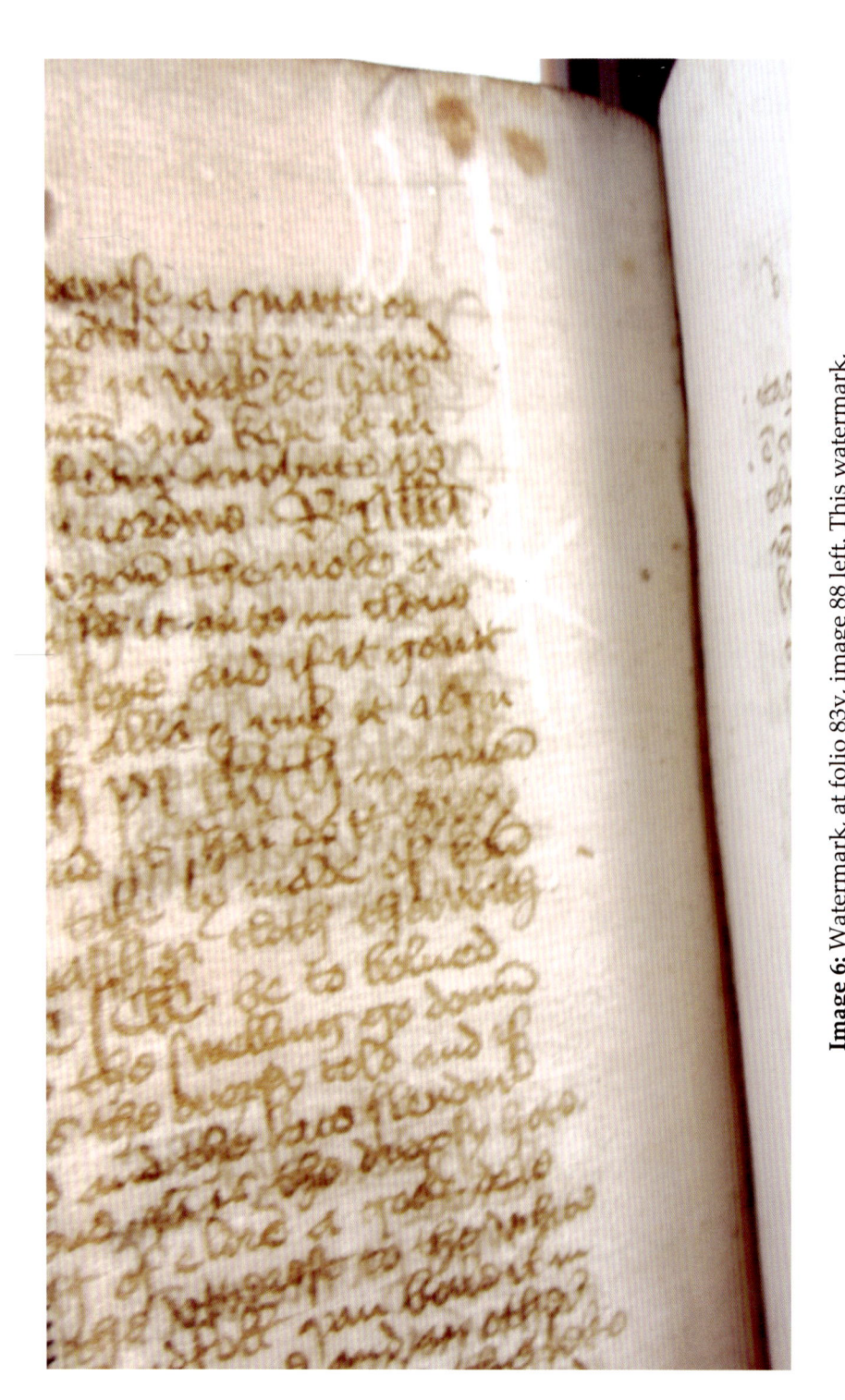

Image 6: Watermark, at folio 83v, image 88 left. This watermark, one of seven or perhaps eight identified, appears to show a single inverted cow's horn (to the left) with a stem ending in a star.

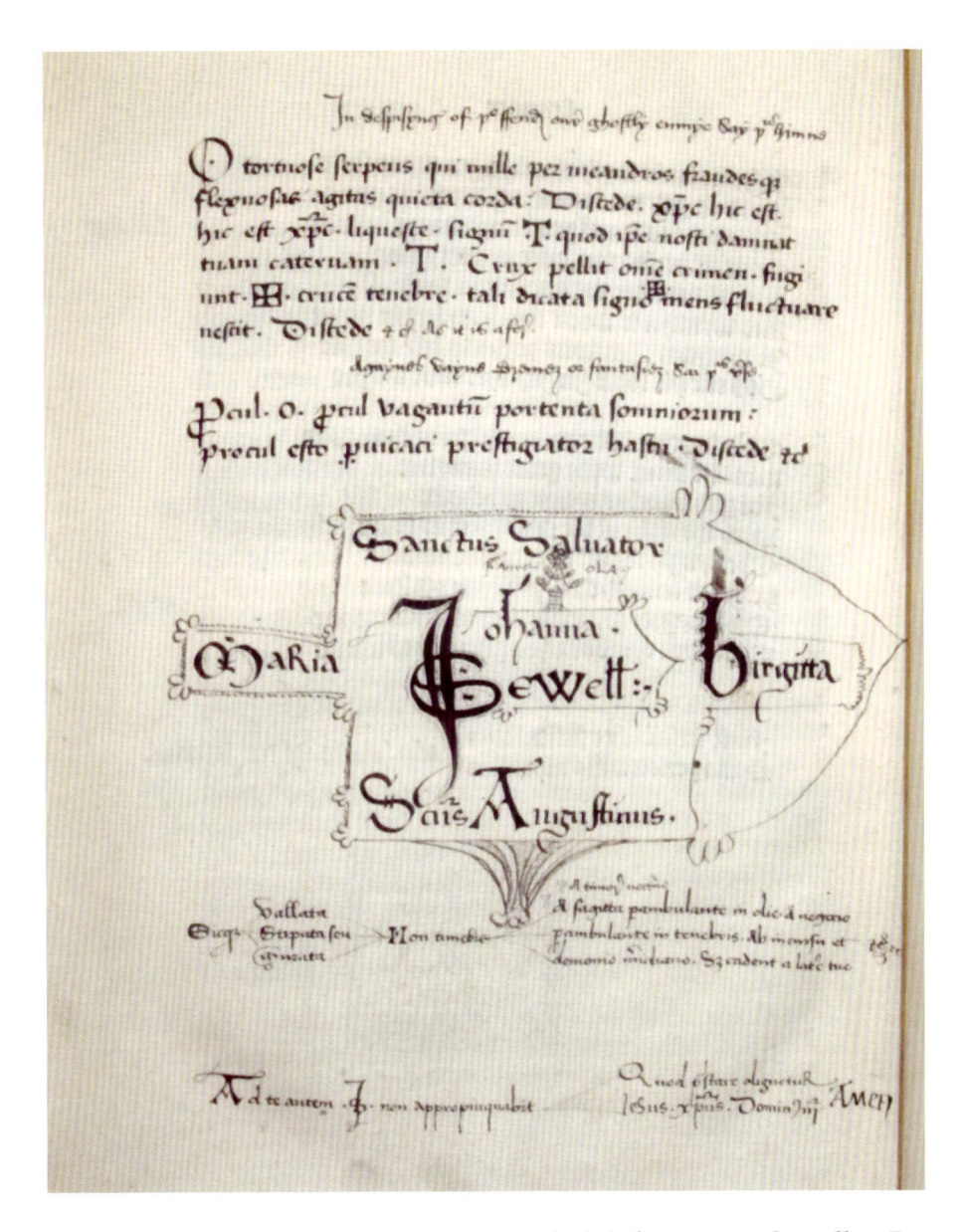

Image 7: Prayers written by James Grenehalgh for Joanna Sewell in Rosenbach Foundation H491, the *Scala Perfectionis* by William Hilton, folio 135v. See Appendix 5 for transcription and translation of the Latin.

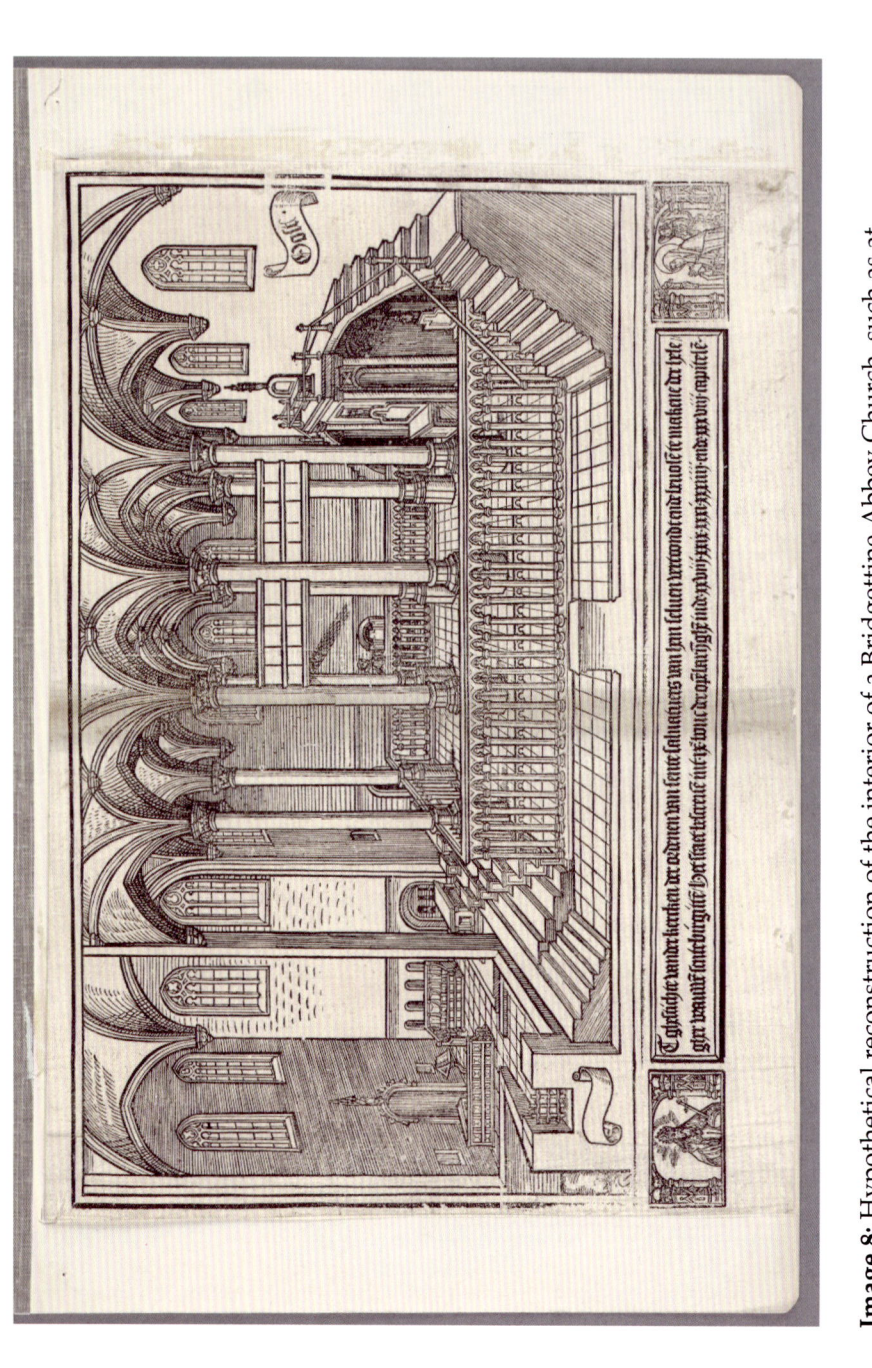

Image 8: Hypothetical reconstruction of the interior of a Bridgettine Abbey Church, such as at Syon Abbey, from a Dutch woodcut of 1500. (*National Library of Sweden, Stockholm*).

Image, Folio and Line Numbers.	Betson Entry. [The alphabetical letters A-Z below are for reference only, and are not in Betson].	The Synonoma of John Bray: BL Sloane MS 282, with folio number and column.	Possible Modern Names, mainly Linnaean, and taken from Hunt (1989). Non-Linnaean names are indicated.
3.	Π Sicla, Beta, Bleta	Sicla, Bleta, Betes	*?Beta vulgaris,* Beet
4.	Bletes.	Fol. 173R., Col B.	*?As above.*
5.	Π Siriarca. Malewis	Siriaca, Melochia, Malva, Malwes Stuptera, Alumen,, Zuccarium	*Althaea officinalis,* Marsh Mallow
6.	Π Sigia, Storax liquida	Sigia, Storax liquida	*A resin from the storax tree (Styrax officinalis), a kind of storax.* EMED
7.	Π Sinabrium	Sinabrum minium (?), vz fine (?) Vermilion	*Cinabrium in SB, p.43, Alphita, Mowat, p192 and footnote, as 'uzifur i. vermilion'.*
8.	Wuylow		*Salix* ssp, Willow
9.	Π Spodium Os elefan-	Spodium, os elephantis,	Ivory
10.	-tis vel ebur combustum	The bon of an elyfant, y brent or yvy brent	Burnt ivory
11.	Π Sponsi (sic) solis roden	Sponsa solis, Solsequium, cicoria, Incuba, Vericaria, Eleutropia, Anglice Rooden	*Calendula officinalis,* Pot Marigold; or *Lithospermon officinale,* Gromwell; or *Cichrium intybus,* Chicory.

Image, Folio and Line Numbers.	Betson Entry. [The alphabetical letters A-Z below are for reference only, and are not in Betson].	The Synonoma of John Bray: BL Sloane MS 282, with folio number and column.	Possible Modern Names, mainly Linnaean, and taken from Hunt (1989). Non-Linnaean names are indicated.
12.	Π Scordion harbell	Scordion, Allium agreste, Harebolle	Here *Hyacinthoides non-scriptus*, Bluebell / Wild Hyacinth; but also *Allium ursinum*, Ramsons, Wild Garlic, Crow Garlic.
13.	Π Scolopendria	Scolopendria, Ligna terrina,	*Asplenium scolopendrium*, Hart's Tongue Fern.
14.	Hertistong.	Hertestonge	As above.
		Storax rubia, confitta rubia	
15.	Π Scopa regia	Scopa regia, Herba perforate,	*Hypericum perforatum*, Saint John's Wort.
16.	Herba Johis cum ceteris [with the other (names)]	Bray: Herba Iohannis, Centum foramina, Ypicon, Fuga demonum, Seynt Ion ys wort.	
		Scrofularia, Scrobilia, Poma	
17.	Π Sulphur vivum.	Sulphur vivum, Tibarirum, Tipapirum	*Obsolete term for naturally occurring sulphur. Bray's alternative versions are ultimately a corruption of Dioscorides. See Alphita, Mowat p.186, 'Tybappari', 'Tybapirum', footnote 2, and p.32, 'Canibapirum', with footnote 19, for original Greek.*
		Sumac, Anagodan	

Image, Folio and Line Numbers.	Betson Entry. [The alphabetical letters A-Z below are for reference only, and are not in Betson].	The Synonoma of John Bray: BL Sloane MS 282, with folio number and column.	Possible Modern Names, mainly Linnaean, and taken from Hunt (1989). Non-Linnaean names are indicated.
18.	Sturtium	Sturtium, caulilus agrestis, caliculus agrestis, Brasica, Small Caule,	*Brassica oleracea,* Wild Cabbage; or *Saponaria officinalis,* Soapwort; or *Peucedanum ostruthium,* Master Wort; or *Crambe maritima,* Sea-Kale.
19.	Brasica smale caule		*Brassica oleracea,* Wild Cabbage.
20.	Π Succus prunella*rum*	Succus prunellarum, Acacia	*Prunus spinosa,* Sloe.
21.	Juse of sloue	Ith*e iuse of* the wide sloon	Sloe juice
		Spuma marina permis (?)	'Sea foam' ?
22.	Π Succus frume*n*ti	Succus frumenti	Starch
23.	Amydon	Amidon	*As above.*
24.	Π Sup*er*cillium veneris	Sup*er*cillium veneris	*Achillea millefolium,* Yarrow.
25.	Yarewe. Vent*er* apis ide*m*	Vent*er* apis, Millefoliu*m,* Yarwe	*As above.*
26.	Π Sandix Wodemad*ur*		*Isatis tinctoria,* Woad; or *Rubia tinctorum,* Madder. EMED has 'wild madder' as *Rubia peregrina,* or perhaps *Galium mollugo.*

Image, Folio and Line Numbers.	Betson Entry. [The alphabetical letters A-Z below are for reference only, and are not in Betson].	The Synonoma of John Bray: BL Sloane MS 282, with folio number and column.	Possible Modern Names, mainly Linnaean, and taken from Hunt (1989). Non-Linnaean names are indicated.
27.	Saliunca herba aspera est, alia calketrape, contra opilaciones		*Ulex europeaeus,* Gorse; or *Eryngium campestre,* Eryngo; or Valeriana celtica, *Celtic Spikenard.*
28.	Hamariscus Ameryndis	Tamaryndes, Oxi- [Fol. 173R., Col C.] -fencia, Dactulus acetosa,	Perhaps *Tamaris gallica,* Tamarisk
Image 86 right, Folio 82r, Col. B			
1.	[T] Π Tapsus moleyn	Tapsus barbastus, Flosmus, Ponfilion, fy Balinarie (?), Moleyne	*Vebascum thapsus,* Mullein.
2.	Π Tartarii Argoil	Tartari, Petra vini, Argoil	'The tartar produced by fermentation of wine, crude potassium bitartrate.' EMED
3.	Π Tarascon Scariole	Tarascon, Scariole	*Sonchus oleraceus,* Milk- or Sow-Thistle; or Lactuca serriola, 'Prickly Lettuce.'

Image, Folio and Line Numbers.	Betson Entry. [The alphabetical letters A-Z below are for reference only, and are not in Betson].	The Synonoma of John Bray: BL Sloane MS 282, with folio number and column.	Possible Modern Names, mainly Linnaean, and taken from Hunt (1989). Non-Linnaean names are indicated.
4.	*In right margin:* Tanacetum agreste pulvis eius desiccat vulnera et valet contra dissinteriam.	Tanasetu*m*, Tansye,	*Potentilla anserina,* Silverweed. *Hunt p249 also gives* Tansy, *Chrysanthemum vulgare at 'Tanasia'.*
5.	Π Tanacetum domes*ticum*		*Chrysanthemum vulgare,* Tansy; or *Potentilla anserina,* Silverweed.
6.	Terpentina	Terbentina,	*Pistacia terebinthus,* Terebinth, Turpentine.
7.	Terpentyne	Terbe*n*tyne	*As above.*
		Terra Hispania, Chimolea	*Chimolea est terra inuenta sub mola fabri ut uidetur per Rogerum capitulo de inflacione testiculorum. Alphita, Mowat p.38, and SAN, Mowat p 206*
8.	Π Terra Sarazenica	Terra sigillata, Terra Saracena	Potter's Clay
9.	Argentaria.	Argentaria	*As above.*
10.	Terra Sigulli Argilla	Terra sigulli, Argilla	*As above.*
11.	Potters cley	Tonkeres clay, or clay	*As above.*
		Triticum whete	

Image, Folio and Line Numbers.	Betson Entry. [The alphabetical letters A-Z below are for reference only, and are not in Betson].	The Synonoma of John Bray: BL Sloane MS 282, with folio number and column.	Possible Modern Names, mainly Linnaean, and taken from Hunt (1989). Non-Linnaean names are indicated.
12.	Tumbra Sandyugus (?)	Tumbria, Timbra, Satureia, Satiregia, Saverey	*Satureia hortensis*, Summer Savory; or *Satureia montana*, Winter Savory.
13.	Tibapirum.	Tibaripum, Cibapirum	Sulphur – see above Image 86 right, Folio 82r, Col. A, Line 17
14.	Sulphur vivum	Sulphur vivum	*A now obsolete term for naturally occurring sulphur.* EMED
		Bray: Trisogomis, Camedreos, Germandria, Quercula minor, Tymum, Tyme	
15.	Titimall plures sunt	Titimallus the beth many spices of the Walwort, Esula, anabulla, catapucia and other more.	*Euphorbia* spp., Spurge; or *Sempervivum tectorum*, Houseleek.
16.	Species earundem		'There are many species of them.'
17.	Walworte, esula		As above.
18.	Anabulla, catapucia		As above.
		Tysana, hit is decoction of water and Barlich	
19.	Laureola		(*Daphne laureola* or *Daphne mezereum*) Spurge Laurel, or Mezereon.

Image, Folio and Line Numbers.	Betson Entry. [The alphabetical letters A-Z below are for reference only, and are not in Betson].	The Synonoma of John Bray: BL Sloane MS 282, with folio number and column.	Possible Modern Names, mainly Linnaean, and taken from Hunt (1989). Non-Linnaean names are indicated.
20.	Tribulus ruby	Tribulus rinne*th(?)* rubeus, Ronce, Reed Brere	*Rubus* ssp., Bramble.
21.	Redebrere idem [red briar]		Red Brer: The dog rose (Rosa canina). *EMED. But here apparently Bramble*
22.	Toxima. Endyve	Toxima, Endive, Endiva	*Chicorium endiva,* Endive; or *Sonchus oleraceus* Sowthistle; or *Lactuca serriola,* 'Prickly Lettuce'.
23.	or Scariole.	or Scariole	
24.	Turiones. sumi-	Turiones, sumitates vitis su*nt, the* croppys of vynes whit or reed	*Vitis,* Vine shoots.
25.	-tates vitis, the top		
26.	of a vyne		
		Thus, Olibanum, Frankencence	
27.	Testiculus muris		*?Potentilla anserina,* Silverweed.
28.	Pim*e*rnella		*Anagallis arvensis,* Scarlet Pimpernell. *See Hunt p.207 for other possible identifications.*

Image, Folio and Line Numbers.	Betson Entry. [The alphabetical letters A-Z below are for reference only, and are not in Betson].	The Synonoma of John Bray: BL Sloane MS 282, with folio number and column.	Possible Modern Names, mainly Linnaean, and taken from Hunt (1989). Non-Linnaean names are indicated.
29.	Tormentilla *In margin* tem*perata* cum lacte ovino et diari*am* cedat.		*Potentilla erecta,* Common tormentill. Tr.: *mixed with sheep milk, it halts diahorroea.*
30.	Timbria, Bisworte		*Satureia hortensis,* Summer Savory; or *Satureia montana,* Winter savory.
31.	Sil*v*estris Pulegia *species* folia ha*bent*		*Origanum vulgare,* Marjoram; or *Mentha pulegium,* Pennyroyal; or *Thymus serpyllum,* Wild Thyme.
32.	longiora et plus subalbiora.		
33.	[U / V] Valeriana. Fu.	Valeriana, Feu, Amantilla, Potentilla, Zeduariu*m* agreste	*Valeriana phu* or *V. officinalis,* Valerian. *The latter is now more likely in Britain. Both kinds are mentioned as growing at Syon, along with dioca, montana, pyrenaica, sambucifolia and tripteris by Forrest 1831, p.194.*
34.	Valeriane	Valerian	As above.
Image 87 Left, Folio 82v, Col. A			
1.	Π Uve Acerbe	Uva mat*u*ra, rype grape Uva ac*er*ba, soure grape	'sour grapes'
2.	Soure grapes Uva passa	Uva passa	Raisins
3.	Π Reisy*n*s	Reysones **Fol. 173v., Col A**	Raisins

Image, Folio and Line Numbers.	Betson Entry. [The alphabetical letters A-Z below are for reference only, and are not in Betson].	The Synonoma of John Bray: BL Sloane MS 282, with folio number and column.	Possible Modern Names, mainly Linnaean, and taken from Hunt (1989). Non-Linnaean names are indicated.
4.	Π Vaccicinium	Vaccinum	*Vaccinium myrtillis*, Bilberry
5.	Morum nigrum.	Morum nigrum.	*As above.*
6.	Mirtilles. Hurtene	Myrtillis, Hoorten	*Vaccinium myrtillus*, Bilberry; or *Myrica gale*, Bog Myrtle.
7.	Π Venter apis	Venter apis, Supercilium veneris	*Achillea millefolium,* Yarrow
8.	Millefoile	Millefollium, Yarwe	*As above.*
9.	Π Uva Lupina	Uva lupina, Strignum, Morell	*Atropa bella-donna*, Deadly Nightshade, Great Morel; or *Solanum nigrum*, Black Nightshade, Petty Morel.
10.	Morell		*As above.*
11.	Π Verucaria	Verucaria, Cicoria, Incuba	*Calendula officinalis,* Garden Marigold.
12.	Rodenes	Roodes	*As above.*
		Bray: Vermes terrestres, Lubrici terrestres, Anglice Angultwyche, Wormes of *the* erthe *Various worms of which 'Angeltwiche' is attested in Mowat, Alphita, p. 87, under 'Isculi' and also footnote 12, and is (OED) precisely an 'angle twitcher....' They were used to consolidate 'nervos incisos'.*	
13.	Π <u>Vermicularis</u>	Vermicularis	*Sedum telephium,* Orpine *(V. maior);* or *Sedum acre,* Common Stonecrop *(V. minor).*

Image, Folio and Line Numbers.	Betson Entry. [The alphabetical letters A-Z below are for reference only, and are not in Betson].	The Synonoma of John Bray: BL Sloane MS 282, with folio number and column.	Possible Modern Names, mainly Linnaean, and taken from Hunt (1989). Non-Linnaean names are indicated.
14.	Crassula minor (sic)	Crassula maior	See above.
15.	Stonecrope	Stone crope	As above.
16.	Π Vervena In margin: Succus vervene, distemperatus cum lacte, nutrificit humores et valet ad rubeos (?) oculorum.	Vervena, Pisterion	*Vervena officinalis*, Vervain. *Pisterion is ultimately Dioscorides' Peristerion, SB, Mowat, p.33, where it is 'idem vervena'. See also Hunt p201, Persisterion.*
17.	Herba veneris	Herba veneris	As above
		Vernix, Bernix, Classia	
18.	Π Vespertilio	Vespertilio	A bat species.
19.	Reremous	A Reremous	Bat
20.		Vigellum, Popillus	*Agrostemma githago*, Corn Cockle, or *Lollium temulentum*. Both in Hunt at p262.
21.	Π Virga pastorum	Virga pastoris, Oseragi (?)	*Dipsacus fullonum*, Teasel.
22.	Wildetasill	Wildetasill	As above.
23.	Π Usifur vivum	Usifure vivum	Cinnabar
24.	Vermilion	Vermilum, Cinabrium, Vermelon.	As above.

Image, Folio and Line Numbers.	Betson Entry. [The alphabetical letters A-Z below are for reference only, and are not in Betson].	The Synonoma of John Bray: BL Sloane MS 282, with folio number and column.	Possible Modern Names, mainly Linnaean, and taken from Hunt (1989). Non-Linnaean names are indicated.
		Bray: Viola, Violaria, Violette, Viola alba, Wrachiell, Virtuosa. *Names for the violet. See Hunt p262 for variants of 'Wrachiell'.* Vitis agrestis, Labrusca, Vitecella, Wild Vine.	
25.	Π Vitriola. Herbarum	Vitriola, Herba muralis,	*Parietaria judiaca,* Pellitory of the Wall.
26.	Paritaria Perciados	Paritoria, Perciados Perco (?)	As above.
27.	Pitarye		As above.
28.	Π Vitriolum arment.	Vitriolum, Dragantum, Calcantum, Armen.	EMED: *Vitriol; iron sulphate, copper sulphate, or a mixture of the two: (a) used externally for its corrosive and astringent properties; (b) used as an emetic and cathartic; (c) used as a suppository. Also: Bleach.*
		Viscus quercinus, Wilde Cheyn, (= gui de chêne) or Mystelon of Oke	*Viscum album,* Mistletoe. *See Hunt p264 for these and other variants.*
29.	Π Umbilicus veneris	Umbilicus veneris, Cotiliden, , Cicube, Laria, Anglice Penywort.	*Umbilicus rupestris,* Pennywort.
30.	Pennyworte		As above.

Image, Folio and Line Numbers.	Betson Entry. [The alphabetical letters A-Z below are for reference only, and are not in Betson].	The Synonoma of John Bray: BL Sloane MS 282, with folio number and column.	Possible Modern Names, mainly Linnaean, and taken from Hunt (1989). Non-Linnaean names are indicated.
		Vulgago	*Asarum europaeum*, Asarabacca
31.	Azarabaccara	Azarabaccara, Gariofilus agrestis	*As above.*
32.	Agresas		*Not found. ?As above.*
Image 87 Left, Folio 82v, Col. B			
1.	Volubilis maior		*Lonicera periclymenum*, Honeysuckle, or *Convulvulus arvensis*, Bindweed.
2.	Edera arborea		*Hedera helix*, Ivy, *but perhaps here Honeysuckle – see Hunt p132 for wodebynd ivy under this name.*
3.	Caprifolium		*Lonicera periclymenum*, Woodbind, Honeysuckle.
4.	Π Volubilis minor	Volubilis minor	*Convulvulus arvensis*, Bindweed or *Glechoma hederacea*, Ground Ivy.
5.	Edera terrestris	Edera terrestris,	*Glechoma hederacea*, Ground Ivy.
6.	Heyhove	Heyhove Fol. 173v., Col B.	*As above.*
7.	Π Urtica mortua	Urtica mortua, Archangelica	*Lamium* spp., the dead nettles
8.	Blynde Netile	Blynd netel	*Lamium album*, White Dead Nettle; or *Lamium purpureum*, Red Dead Nettle.
9.	Π Urtica greca	Urtica Greca, Ronge Urteie, Lees Netel	
10.	Wildenettill	Wild Netel or deed netel	*?Urtica* spp.

Image, Folio and Line Numbers.	Betson Entry. [The alphabetical letters A-Z below are for reference only, and are not in Betson].	The Synonoma of John Bray: BL Sloane MS 282, with folio number and column.	Possible Modern Names, mainly Linnaean, and taken from Hunt (1989). Non-Linnaean names are indicated.
11.	Π Ungula caballina	Ungula caballina	*Here* Water Lily (*Nymphea*), *on account of the similarity in the shape of its leaves to horse hooves.*
12.	Et Radix lilii aquatici	Hit is the rote of Water Lilie, or elles of Menphie [Nenuphar]	Water Lily as above.
13.	vel radix nenuphar		*As above*
14.	Π Virga pastoris		*Dipsacus fullonum*, Teasel
15.	Wildetasill		*As above.*
16.	[X] Xantos interpretatur		*Almost identical to Mowat, Alphita, p. 193 'Xantos', which is described as 'cortex celsi'- presumably bark of the Mulberry Tree.*
17.	Rubeum inde ypoxanto		*As above.*
		Bray: Xilocassia, Cassia Lignea Cassia rubia et sicca	*These are all synonyms for* Cinnamomum cassia, Cassia Bastard Cinnamon. *See SB p44 - Xilocassia*
18.	Π Xillobalsamum	Xilobalsamum	Wood or bark of the Balsam tree (*Commiphora meccanensis* or *opobalsamum*). EMED.
19.	Lignum balsami	Lignum balsami	*As above*

205

Image, Folio and Line Numbers.	Betson Entry. [The alphabetical letters A-Z below are for reference only, and are not in Betson].	The Synonoma of John Bray: BL Sloane MS 282, with folio number and column.	Possible Modern Names, mainly Linnaean, and taken from Hunt (1989). Non-Linnaean names are indicated.
20.	Carpobalsa- mum id id *est* fru	*The* fruyt of *th*is ys y clypid carpobalsamum	As above. Mowat, Alphita, p.34, Carpobalsamum id est semen balsami. Hunt gives Teucrium Chamaedrys, 'Wall Germander' but 'fructus' does not seem right here.
21.	tus eius.		
22.	Xpīana h[abe]t folia ro-		Christiana Lathyrus ssp. Vetchling. or ?Senecio vulgaris, ?Groundsel.
23.	-tunda aliquantulum		
24.	spissa (?)		
25.	ut unum h*abe*t stipitem		
26.	magnum et multi p*a*rvi stipites		
		Ysopus, Ysope	
27.	**[Y]** Yp*e*ricon Perforata (sic)	Yp*e*ricon, Yercatou*m* Psillu*m*, Herba scti Iohis, Scopia regia, Seynt Ion Wort,	Hypericum perforatum, St John's Wort.
28.	Centum foramina		As above.
29.	Herba Iohannis		As above.

Image, Folio and Line Numbers.	Betson Entry. [The alphabetical letters A-Z below are for reference only, and are not in Betson].	The Synonoma of John Bray: BL Sloane MS 282, with folio number and column.	Possible Modern Names, mainly Linnaean, and taken from Hunt (1989). Non-Linnaean names are indicated.
30.	Π Ytea, wilow	Ytea, Salix, Wythie	*Salix viminalis*, Withy, Osier.
Image 87 Right, Folio 83r, Col. A			
1.	Π Yriana vitis agrestis	Yriana, Labrusca, Vitis agrestis,	*Sonchus* ssp. Sowthistle.
2.	Π Ypia maior	Yria maior, Morsus galline	*Stellaria Media*, Chickweed
3.	Chikenmete	Chyke mete	As above.
		Yris purpireum, flores gerit Yrios album. Gladiolus crocus or Spatula fetida Pupureus (?) Yris hath purpur flour. Yris hath a whit flour	
		Yposilia fabaria, Lemyk, Faverolle	*Veronica beccabunga*, Brooklime.
4.	Π Ypoquistodos	Ypoquistidos	Rose Gall
5.	Is a rounde appull	Beth ronde ball	
6.	growing aboute a brembill	Growing about a bremel	
7.	Π Ydromel is a watr	Ydromel is hony with water y soode	*Hydromel: A mixture of water and honey that becomes mead when fermented.*
8.	Drunk with hony.		
9.	Π Ygia. Netil sede	Ygia, Ozimum, netelseed	*Lamium / Urtica* ssp., Nettleseed.

Image, Folio and Line Numbers.	Betson Entry. [The alphabetical letters A-Z below are for reference only, and are not in Betson].	The Synonoma of John Bray: BL Sloane MS 282, with folio number and column.	Possible Modern Names, mainly Linnaean, and taken from Hunt (1989). Non-Linnaean names are indicated.
10.	Π Yposarcan is a dropsy of malencoly	Yposarcan is a dropesie that cometh of melancolye	*Modern medical terms: Hyposarca / Anasarca, meaning swelling of the flesh.*
11.	Π Ypomaratrium	Ypomaratrum	*Foeniculum vulgare,* Here Fennel Root & Fennel Seed.
12.	Wild fenell	Wilde Fenel	*As above.*
13.	[Z] Zacaton Persillum	Zachaton, Persilium Fol. 173v., Col C.	*Plantago indica,* Fleawort. *See Hunt Zaracon p.267; and Daems (Psillium) #368, p.228 where it is identified as Plantago afra.*
14.	Zodarium i. radix.	Zeduarium	*Curcuma zedoaria* Setwall, Zedoary, White Turmeric.
15.	Setwale	Sedewale	*As above.*
16.	Π Zima Fermentum	Zima Fermentum, Leveyne	Yeast.
17.	Leveyis		*As above ?*
18.	Π Zima is an apostum of flemus	Zimia is apostem Engendryd of flewme	'A pustule caused by phlegm.' EMED
		Bray: Zinzilion, Pentafilon, Anglice Fivelevedgras Zipule, crispule oynnones, Zinziber, Gynginer, Zuccura, Sugre, Zubus, Grece, Fatnesse.	
19.	Π Zyrungen Borage	Zyrungen, Borage	*Borago officinalis,* Borage.

Image, Folio and Line Numbers.	Betson Entry. [The alphabetical letters A-Z below are for reference only, and are not in Betson].	The Synonoma of John Bray: BL Sloane MS 282, with folio number and column.	Possible Modern Names, mainly Linnaean, and taken from Hunt (1989). Non-Linnaean names are indicated.
20.	Π Zyzania Kokkill	Zizzannia, Gith, Cokkle *Explicit Liber Synonum editus a Magistro JB.* (Johannes Bray)	*Agrostemma githago*, Corn Cockel.
21.	Π Zertia impetigo		EMED gives 'A pustular skin disease' for 'zerna'.
22.	Seripigo sive Serpiga		'A spreading skin eruption or disease, such as ringworm.'
23.	T inte*n*sa Impetigo ut su*perior*		Tr.: intense impetigo, as above.

Explicit Herbarium

THE SYON ABBEY HERBAL

II   THE REMEDIES

Table: Abbreviations for Apothecaries' Weights.

Weight	pound	ounce	dra(ch)m	scrupul	grain
Abbreviation:	℔, li	℥	ʒ	℈	gr.
Equivalents:	1 ℔, li	12 ℥	96 ʒ	288 ℈	5,760 gr.
		1 ℥	8 ʒ	24 ℈	480 gr.
			1 ʒ	3 ℈	60 gr.
				1 ℈	20 gr.
Metric Equivalents:	373 g	31.1 g	3.89 g	1.296 g	64.8 mg

Other Common Apothecaries' Abbreviations:

.lī	one pound	12 oz
.lī.h or .lī.dī (*half* and *dimidium*)	half pound	6 oz
qᵃrtº. or qᵃrtº. dī, '*quartroun*'	quarter pound	3 oz
qᵃrtº.h. or qᵃrtº. dī '*half quartroun*'	eighth of a pound	1½ oz.

β for the word '*semi*' meaning half of the preceding measure.

ʒ	a drachm	3 scrupuls
.ʒ.h or .ʒ.dī	half a drachm,	1½ scrupuls
.℈.j	a scrupul	20 wheatcorns, a '*pennyweight*'
.℈.h or .℈.dī	half a scrupul	10 wheatcorns
m.j	handful	
m.h or m.di	half handful	
ana	the same amount of each herb	

Source: *Medical Works of the 14ᵗʰ Century*, Henslow, page 131.

Note 1: the tentative Middle English, and modern English and Linnaean names of plants mentioned below are set out in full in Appendix 2.

Image 87 right – Folio 83r, Column B

1.	**For all maner**	*Similar in eVK2 under 'virgin wax'.*
2.	**of ache.** Re*cipe* ole de	*Olive oil.*
3.	olif & virgin wax	*Wax from new combs.*
4.	and Terbentyn. Melte	*Terebinth, Turpentine.*
5.	thies iij togidere *than*	
6.	take the juse of Rwe	*Rue*
7.	the juse of Bro*m*blossu*m*s	*Flowers of the broom.*
8.	and the juse of blem-	
9.	blis croppis, agode	*Top leaves of the Bramble.*
10.	quantite of thies juses	
11.	and put he*m* to *th*in oynt-	
12.	ment and lete it boil	
13.	but a litill and kepe	
14.	well this in an glas.	

in the right margin: **ffor the moder**   *Uterus, or Hysteria.*

15.	Re*cipe* Rosemary*n*	*Rosemary.*
16.	in poudur, and gif *the*	
17.	sike to drynk divers	
18.	tymes.	
19.	wheresoev*er* it be.	

in the right margin: **For an hors *that* is gallid.**   *Not in eVK2;* **gallid:** *chafed.*

20.	Re*cipe*. Take the sote in a
21.	fire stok or in a chym-
22.	ney and grynd it
23.	smal and cast it upo*n*
24.	the sore and bynde
25.	it fast, and every day
26.	do so onys till it sane.

in the right margin: **For the sauffleme**

27. Take Dragance

   saucefleume (n.): A skin ailment considered symptomatic of a type of leprosy. EMED.

28. whan he is moost / bry*m*mest and dry   **bry*m*mest:** *at its best.*
29. it in the su*n*, rote
30. and al, and grinde
31. it into poudre. *Th*an

Image 88 left, Folio 83v

1. take *the* wat*er* of the Rederose a quarte or

   Quarte: *two pints;* **Potell** *(two quarts): four pints or about 2.3 litres.*

2. a potell and put *th*is poudre *th*en in and
3. let it seth to gider till *th*e wat*er* be half
4. wastid *th*an take it down and kepe it in
5. a glasse and *with* a fedur anoynte *th*e
6. seke at eve*n* and at morowe.

in the left margin: **For a mole / in a lyne*n*cloth**   **Mole:** *stain.*

7. Re*cipe* Alle*lu*ia v*el* Wodesour rub it upon *th*e mole a   *Wood Sorrell.*
8. gode while *th*en wassh it oute in clen
9. water or in lye or in sope. And if it go not
10. a way take more of Allum and rub it as t*h*u
11. didist first.

in the left margin: **For a cloth *th*at is steined**

12. Wassh *th*i cloth in common
13. Ly, scalding hote and it shal do it awey   **ly:** *lye.*
14. and if it wole not, take ly made of ben   **ben ashis:** *bean ash.*
15. ashis warmed and wassh *th*i cloth ther*with*

in the left margin: **For to know *th*e cold dropsi fro *th*e hote.** *Not in eVK2.*

16. If the face of the seke be to bolned   **Bolned:** *To swell, become distended; EMED.*
17. and the necke and the swellings go down
18. to the leggis *th*an is the dropsy cold. And if
19. *th*e body be bolned and the face slenndur
20. and the leggis lene *th*an is the dropsy hote

214

21.	Re*cipe* yongspring of elder, a goode dele	*Take the first shoots of Elder.*
22.	and scrape away the utterest to the white	**utterest:** *outer.*
23.	till you have ii handful *th*an boile it in	
24.	a pottell of white wyne and an other	*four pints; about 2.3 litres.*
25.	of ale unto the half and make the seke	
26.	to drynk *there*of at eve*n* and at morrow,	
27.	and he shal pisse oute all *the* evell. **A Me-**	*Not in eVK2.*
28.	**dicyne for all man*ner* of sore eiyen:**	**sore eiyen:** *sore eyes.*
29.	take poudur of tutty[122] and poudur of Cala*m*int	

tutty: *a product obtained from smelting furnaces: Cadmium, oxide of zinc.*

30.	in like pr*o*porscio*un* and grend hem to gider w*ith*	
31.	fressh capou*n* gresse and make a plaistur	**capon gresse:** *chicken fat.*
32.	and ley to the sore eiyen.	

---

[122] '*Tutty*': *Medical Society MS136 folio 43v* - 'as they of Montpellier use it in the final stages of opthalmia' *Warren R. Dawson, A Leechbook, MacMillan, 1934, pp160-161,* his para no. 486, as an eye disease remedy.

De Urinalibus ('Concerning Urine Flasks')
(Image 88 right, folio 84r to Image 90 right, folio 86r, line 5)

This text, whose title means 'Concerning Urine Flasks' presents an interesting puzzle.[123] In the first place, urine flasks are nowhere else mentioned in this section of Betson's text. Second, the text appears at first glance to be the section on urines taken from '*Pro conservanda sanitate ... remediorum ... liber*' attributed to the Franciscan Priest-Cardinal, Johannes Vitalis (1260-1327), and first printed in 1531. However, the supposed Vitalis text, both in its original manuscript form and its later printed form, actually incorporates material already circulating earlier, in the twelfth century, and hence not by Vitalis.

M. Teresa Tavormina has identified Betson's text as in fact originating in two other widely circulating texts of the early Middle Ages, which she catagorises as *Urina Rufa* and *Colamentum sanguinis (Reddish Urine* and *Cleansing of the Blood)*. *Urina Rufa* is Betson's section from image 88 right, folio 84r, line 1, to image 90 left, folio 85v, line 1. *Colamentum sanguinis* runs on from image 90 left, folio 85v line 1 to the end of Betson's *De Urinalibus* text at image 90 right, folio 86r, line 5. The two texts both originated in a 12th-century uroscopy treatise that has been called by German scholars, for example Gundolf Keil, '*Der kurze Harntraktat*' (The Short Treatise on Urine).

The text is also listed, under its Incipit, as at Betson's Line 1 below (*Urina rufa significat salutem et bonam*), by Thorndike Kibre as .k 1610B), in eight examplars, of which four in the UK.[124] These have not been examined by us, but one or more may prove to be close to Betson's original source, since his text contains some questionable readings and omissions that might help identify related copies. M. Teresa Tavormina notes that in the known English and Anglo-Latin copies, the second source, *Colamentum sanguinis*, often ends, as in our text here in Betson with

---

[123] M. Teresa Tavormina has kindly provided this information on the origins of the text used by Betson. (Pers. Comm. August 2014, and her forthcoming in 2014 *"Uroscopy in Middle English: A Guide to the Texts and Manuscripts,"* in *Studies in Medieval and Renaissance History*, 3 ser., vol. 11.

[124] M. Teresa Tavormina has kindly provided 'a very partial list of other manuscripts in British libraries or of British origin containing the Latin texts of *Urina Rufa* and *Cleansing of Blood*' which includes Egerton 2852, 16^v-18^v (which begins and ends with similar wording to the Betson text); Royal 17 C.24, 1^r-4^r; Sloane 7, ff. 60^v-61^v; Sloane 1388, ff. 38^v-39^v; Ashmole 391, V, ff. 2vb-3va, Ashmole 789, f. 366^{ra-b}; Ashmole 1481, ff. 2^v-3^v, 42^{rv}; Bodley 648, 5^r-7^r; Bodley 591, ff. 33^r-34^v; Hatton 29, ff. 75^v-77^v and 78^r-79^v; Rawlinson D.1221, ff. 9^r-10^v; CUL Ii.6.17, ff. 42^r-47^r; Pepys 878, pp. 108-10; G&C 413/630, 32^r-34^v; TCC R.1.86, ff. 1^v-4^r; TCC O.9.31, 28^{rv}; Rosenbach Museum MS 1004/29; and the Dickson Wright MS (ed. Talbot 1961).

the wording, *'nisi fuerit per talem urinam expulsio materie venenose est signum mortale/mortis.'*

The attribution of the text to the *Harntraktat* solves an interesting bibliographical question, since there was no copy of Vitalis' *Pro conservanda sanitate* in the Syon *Registrum*, and none is listed in any of the current BL *Corpus* catalogues[125] as being present in Britain. Furthermore, the printed version of the imputed Vitalis text did not appear until 1531, and so again cannot have been used by Betson, who died in 1517.

On balance therefore, it seems that Betson had access to a Latin version of the *Harntraktat* rather than a copy of Vitalis, despite the latter's close similarity to Betson.[126] M. Teresa Tavormina also points out that there were printed versions of the text incorporated in the so-called Ketham *Fasciculus Medicinae* from 1481. The *Fasciculus* is also not in the Syon *Registrum* or indeed the BL *Corpus*, and so is unlikely to have been available a source for Betson. The textual relations among versions of these texts of the *Harntraktat* in the later Middle Ages have still to be worked out. There are a considerable number of treatises on urine listed in the Syon Abbey Library Catalogue, and it may be that one of these will eventually provide a source.[127]

---

[125] SHARPE, Professor R., Editor, (1990-2013). *Corpus of British Medieval Library Catalogues*.

[126] The 1531 printed text used by Vitalis, from which Betson deviates only slightly, can be accessed at: http://reader.digitale-sammlungen.de/en/fs1/object/display/bSB_10149531_00022.html

[127] Edited by Vincent Gillespie (2001).

Image 88 right, Folio 84r

De Urinalibus

1. //Urina rufa significat salutem et bonam
2. dispositionem corporis humani. //Urina
3. subrufa sanitatem bonam significat non omnino
4. ita perfecte sicut rufa. //Urina citrina quando
5. est cum substantia mediocre et quando circulus est eiusdem
6. color est laudabilis. Et etiam subcitrina licet   *subcitrina*: pale yellow.
7. non ita perfecta sicut citrina. //Urina ru-
8. bea sicut rosa significat febrem effemeram et si
9. continue mingatur significat febrem continuam.
       continue mingatur : continuous urination.
10. //Urina rubea sicut sanguis in vit° significat fe-   read as *vitro*: glass.
11. brem ex nimio sanguine et tunc statim debet
12. fieri minutio nisi luna fuerit in signo geminorum   *minutio* : blood-letting.
13. //Urina viridis quando mingitur post rubeam
14. significat adustionem et est mortalis//
        Some Vitalis 1531 text missing in Betson, including:
        'Similiter, urina nigra post rubeam est mortalis'.
15. Urina rubea a claritate omnino remota declinationem
16. morbi significat // Urina rubea permixta ali-
17. quantulum nigredine epatis calefactionem significat
18. //Urina pallida significat defectionem stomachi
19. Et impedimentum secunde digestionis. // Urina
20. Alba sicut aqua fontis significat cruditatem hu-
21. morum et in acutis febribus est mortalis. //Urina
22. lactea et cum spissa substantia et si accidit in muli-
23. eribus non est ita perculosum sicut in viris propter
24. indispocitiones matricis tamen in acutis febribus est
25. mortalis. //Urina lactea superior et inferior
26. obumbrata circa mediam regionem clara
27. ydropsim significat. Item: urina in ydropico ru-
28. fa vel subrufa mortem significat. //Urina
29. karapos significat multitudinem humorum   *karapos*: 'the colour of camel hair'.
30. corruptorum sicut accidit in flemmatico ydro-
        phlegmatic, dropsical, gouty persons.

31.   pico, padagro et sic de aliis. //Urina nigra
      padagro: read podagro, gouty person.

Image 89 left, Folio 84v

1.   ex <u>calore</u> naturali extincto tunc est mortalis
2.   et potest esse propter expulsionem materie venenose
3.   que expellitur per vias urinales et tunc significat
4.   salutem. In quartana semper est mortalis et mala.
5.   //Urina lucida sicut cornu significat indispositiones
      lucida sicut cornu: as transparent as (yellow) horn.
6.   splenis et indispositiones quartane. //Urina cro-   **quartan**: perhaps malarial.
      Vitalis 1531 has '**dispositiones quarternae**'
7.   cea cum spissa substantia fetida et spumosa ictericiam   **ictericia**: jaundice.
8.   Significat. //Urina rufa vel subrufa infer-
9.   ius habens resolutiones rotundas vel albas significat superius
10. aliquantulum pinguis febrem eticam significat. //Urina
      'Rufa or subrufa urine with round or white sediments below,
      somewhat fatty above, signifies hectic fever.'
11. in fundo vasis usque ad medietatem clara
12. postea vero spissa, gravidinem pectoris significat. //U-
13. rina spumosa clara et quasi subrubea dolo-
14. rem in dextero bracchio magis quam in sinistro
15. significat. //Urina alba et spumosa significat majorem
16. dolorem in sinistro latere quam in dextro. Frigidius est
17. enim sinistrum latus quam dextram. //Urina tenuis
      Several lines of Vitalis 1531 edition reversed.
18. aceto similis fleuma significat. ~~Urina tenuis~~
      Betson's crossing out. Vitalis 1531:
      'Urina tenuis, pallida et clara, acetosum phlegma significat.'
19. Si circulus urine nullo quiescente tremulus
20. apparuerit decursum flegmatis aliorumque humorum
21. a capite per collum et per posteriora ad inferiora
22. significat. //Urina spissa et plumbea circa me-
23. diam regionem nigram paralisim significat. //Urina
24. spissa et plumbia (sic) circa mediam regionem. Ut supra.
25. //Urina spissa et lactea et pauca et crassa
26. inferius cum squamis, lapidem demonstrat.

27. //Urina sine squamis spissa et lactea et pauca
28. fluxtum ventris significat. //Urina spissa et lactea
29. et multa guttam in superioribus partibus significat vel
30. inferioribus membris. //Urina inferius   *1531: vel membris corporis.*
31. pallida in viris dolorem renum, in mulieribus

Image 89 right, Folio 85r.

1. vero vitium matricis significat. // Urina in qua frusta   *frusta: piece.*
    Sloane 2852 & 1531 versions both have 'frustula' meaning 'a small piece'.
2. apparent, si pauca sint si pauca sint *(repeated)* et turbida,
    Vitalis 1531 version: 'sit', agreeing with 'pauca..urina', singular,
    and not with 'frustula' plural.
3. vene [venae] rupturam circa renes et vesicam significat. //U-
4. rina in qua sanies apparet in fundo vasis con-   **sanies**: *bloody matter, pus.*
5. tiguam renum et vesice putredinem vel apostema
6. significat. Etsi in tota urina sanies apparet totius
7. corporis putritudinem significat. //Urina in qua
8. frusta apparent parva et lata vesice excorationem
9. significat. // Urina athomosa per multum tempus
    Urina athomosa: *Vitalis 1531: 'arenosa' – 'sandy' or 'gritty' as 'gravel'.*
10. lapidem in renibus significat. //Urina alba sine
11. febre in viris et in mulieribus aliquando dolorem renum
12. aliud aliquando impregnationem mulierum significat. //Urina
13. pregnancium si unum mensem vel duo vel tres ha-
14. buerint debet esse multum clara et alba, yposta-
15. stasim debet habere in fundo. Si vero quatuor menses
16. habuerint urinae debet esse serena et ypostasis alba   **ypostasis**: *deposit.*
17. et grossa in fundo. Solet imago in vase u-
18. rinali tamquam in speculo apperere. Si urina illa
19. sit mulieris, conceptionem factam significat. Et
20. si ymago iudicantis appareat in urinam pacientis
21. febres interpoellatas vel epaticam egritudinem
22. prolixitatem morbi significat. //Urina spumosa
23. ventositatem stomachi in mulieribus vel ardo
24. rem in umbilico usque ad guttur & sitim significat.
    *1531 version: '**ab** umbilico';   'heat from the navel to the throat.'*
25. // Urina vero virginis quasi subcitrina debet

26.	esse. Un*de* urina lucida livida *(sic)* et nimis serena
	Vitalis 1531version: Unde urina livida nimis, virginem.
27.	virgine*m* declarat constant*am*. // Urina
28.	turbida in qua seme*n* apparuerit in fundo vasi*s*,
29.	muliere*m* recente*m* cu*m* viro sig*nifica*t. Mulieres
	Betson's text omits three lines of the Vitalis 1531 version here.
30.	menstruatae faciunt urinam sanguineam.
31.	Et si iste sangui*s* sit coagulatus in muliere

Image 90 left, Folio 85v.

1.	apparebit pregnans donec dissolvatur. OMNIS[128]
2.	urina est colamentum sanguinis et e*st* duarum
3.	rerum p*ro*prie significativa. Aut eni*m* sig*nifica*t passione*m*
4.	epatis et venarum aut vesice et renum. Aliarum re-
5.	rum est improprie significativa. Sed in uri*n*a
6.	consideranda sunt diversa *scilicet* sub*stanti*a colores
7.	regiones et contenta. Aliud *[blank space]* [129] causa sed*iminis* *of sediment.*
8.	cum enim in humano corpore quatuor quali-
9.	tates scilicet caliditas frigiditas siccitas et
10.	humiditas sint cause sub*stanti*e et coloris. Calidi-
11.	tas e*st* ca*usa* coloris rubei frigiditas albi, siccitas
12.	e*st* causa tenuitatis et humiditas spissae.
13.	//Urina in quatuor p*ar*tes dividitur. Sup*er*ior
	Vitalis 1531 version: Urina autem plures in partes dividitur.
14.	est circulus 2ᵃ corpus aieris, 3ᵃ p*er*foratio.
15.	4ᵗᵘˢ fundus. P*er* circulum capitis et cerebri. P*er*
16.	corpus aieri*s* spirit*ua*liu*m* membrorum et stoma-
17.	chi p*er* p*er*foratione*m* epatis et splenis. P*er* fundu*m*
18.	renu*m* et matricis et inferiorum membrorum
19.	accidencia iudicamus. // Urina h*abe*n*t* 3 regiones *scilicet*

---

[128] M. Teresa Tavormina suggests that the capitals here for 'OMNIS' may suggest the use of a different text, since MS Ashmolean 391, for example, also ends at 'dissolvatur', the last word of line 1 above. *Pers. Comm. Aug. 2014.*

[129] 'Omission of logically necessary material here also occurs in Ashmolean 391, though not in Fasciculus medicinae or Bodley 648; the blank space suggests that Betson recognized there was a problem.' M. Teresa Tavormina, *Pers. Comm. Aug 2014.*

20. infim*am* mediam et sup*re*mam. Infima incipit
21. a fundo urinalis et durat per spatiu*m* duorum digi-
22. torum. Media regia incipit ubi terminatur infi-
23. ma et durat usque ad circulum qui circulus e*st*
24. in supprema. Et qu*ando* in ista regione suppr*e*ma
25. e*st* spuma sig*nifica*t ventositate*m* ebullientem
26. in viis urinalibus vel inflationem vel aliud
27. vitium pulmonis. Circulus v*ero* grossus sig*nifica*t
    Betson here omits two sentences found in the Vitalis 1531 version.
28. nimia*m* replecionem in capite et dolore*m*. In
29. regione media queda*m* nebula e*st* in sanis
30. malu*m* signu*m* e*st*. Sec in febricitantibus significat

Image 90 right, Folio 86r.
1. digestionen materie morbi. In infima regione
2. sunt aliquando lapilli arenosi et tunc denotat quod pac-
3. ciens est calculosus. Et aliquando sedimen est nigrum
4. et tu*nc* nisi fuerit p*er* tale*m* urina*m* expulsio mat*er*ie
5. venenose, est signum mortis.   Explicit.[130]

In right margin **Laxativu**m

6. **Pro matrice** take Rubarbe[131] ii.d*ram*; turbit   *matrix: uterus*
7. ii.dram; Ireos i dram; Theodoricum ii dram; Scamoniu*m* ii dram.
    Ireos: *Yellow flag.* **Theodoricum**: *'A purgative medicament; EMED; Scammony.*

in the right margin: **Oleu**m **Rosarum** *(Tr: Oil of Roses).*
8. Sic fit: take iii. li*bra* of oyle de olif, ane pounde
9. of Rosis and half a ponde in a glasse vessil.
10. Put *them* in a cawdroun full of wat*er* aun the   *aun: on.*
11. fire, and stry it. And *th*an hast *th*ou oile of   *stry: stir.*

---

[130] 'Like Ashmolean 391, and other Anglo-Latin copies, the concluding '*De modis iudicandi*' text found in Vitalis and in Fasciculus medicinae is not given by Betson.' T. Taormina *Pers. Comm. Aug. 2014.*

[131] See folio 81, col A, line 10 and SB, Mowat, p.36: '*Reubarbarum radix quaedam est, quae affertur de barbaria.*' (Tr.: '*a certain root which is imported from barbaria*'). It is sometimes unclear if Rhubarb or Iubarbe (Sempervivum tectorum, Houseleek) is meant. Here the association with laxatives suggests Rhubarb, but the amounts seems rather small, ¼ and ½ oz.

12.	Rosis, gode and fine. Oleu*m* de Violet, oleu*m*	
13.	Sambucinum, oleum Martinu*m*, fiunt de eodem modo.	
	Oil of Elder, oil of Myrtle.	

In the right margin: **Oleu*m* Ovoru*m***   *Tr.: oil of eggs.*

14.	<u>Sic Fit</u>: take of the white of eyren and put	
15.	hem in a panne over the fire and styre hem	
16.	*with* a sklise till *th*ey wax rede and take and	**sklise**: *spatula* EMED.
17.	wryng out *th*e oile.	

In the right margin: **Pro Morfea**   *Tr.: a skin disease.*

18.	<u>Take rede yelkis</u>	
19.	and *th*e rotis of rede dockis and do awey	
	rede yelkis: *red egg yolks* EMED; **rede dockis**: *'Red Dock'*	
20.	*th*e skyn *there*of and myse he*m* smale as	**Myse**: *mince,* EMED.
21.	gynger and temp*er* he*m* to gidere w*i*th vinagre	
22.	and make *there*of a plaist*u*r and lei it to *th*e morfu	

in the right margin: **For a ma*n* *that* is bresten *with*inforth.**   *Perhaps 'ruptured.'*

23.	Take petico*n*sou*d*e, Confery, *th*e	**Withinforth**: *inside.*
24.	rotis of wilde Brakis, Aveunce of ech ylike	
	Daisy, Comfrey[132]*, Fern, Avens.*	
25.	mych and put he*m* to gid*u*r & seth he*m* in ale	
26.	and hony and drink the licour at morn and	
27.	at even, an*d* *th*ou shal be hole.	

Image 34 Right, Folio 30r:
This single sheet, though early in the MS, may not be in Betson's hand.[133]

1.	**Urina habet signa vi**	*(but list shows eight signs).*
2.	P*er* collorem, p*er* spumam, p*er* sub*s*t*a*nti*a*m, p*er* quantitate*m*	
3.	p*er* odorem, per circulum, p*er* ypostasim , p*er* consistencia	
	ypostasis: *the lower part of the urine sample, in which sediment settles.*	

---

[132] The use of Comfrey an ingredient for internal use is now banned in many countries as too dangerous, because of its association with liver failure.

[133] The authors are grateful to Dr Winston Black, Emily Reiner and T. Tavormina for their invaluable help in transcribing this difficult hand, and in identifying its sources. Tavormina also points out that the forms of *v, d,* and *e* are different from Betson's, and possibly the forms of other letters as well.

4. **Urina Rubea**
5. In Thysi, in Ydropisi, in Appoplexia, in Epilencia,
6. in Periplimonia, in Paralisi, in Colica, indifferenter significat mortem.
   Periplimonia: abscesses on the lungs.
7. **Urina Mulieris**[134]
8. Virginis est lucida et serena. Corupte est turbida,
9. et sperma viri apparet in fundo vasis. Menstruate
10. aparet sanguinea. Pregnantis in primo mense, 2º et 3º,
11. nebulas habet minutas inferius. Est grossa et
12. lucida et ypostasim habet albam et urina est nimis
13. clara. In 4º mense serena est et viridem habet
14. colorem & ypostasim albam.
15. Urina habens animum iocundum est aurei coloris
    animum iocundum: 'happy spirit' from Ps-Albertus Magnus, De secretis mulierum. The lines here seem to be curtailed. Albertus says: 'Si vero fuerit aurei coloris, clara et ponderosa, continet animi iucundi signum, id est appetitum, et hoc est verum in non corruptis...."
16. clara et ponderosa
17. Pulvis silicis nigre bene provocat urinam ut expertum
18. a quampluribus.
    Pulvis silicis nigre: powdered black flint. British Library, Harley 2340 and Stockholm, Royal Library 10.90 contain a similar preparation for gout (and for treating hawks). For Betson recipe see: Image 109 Left, Folio 104v, line 27. Black flint is common in Southern England.

19. **Emigraniea**   *Migraine.*
20. Medicina probatur (?) ad tollendum emigram *[illegible]*
21. Recipe bene magnam cepe *(sic)* et proferando detrahatur partes
22. iacentes iuxta *[illegible]* et assetur perfecte super car-
23. bones, et quando perfecte assatus est, extrahatur et infundatur
24. oleum de oliva et iterum assatur, et postquam fuerit cale-
25. factum applicatur oleum cum cepe ad partem illam capitis contrariam
26. partem capitis in qua est emigrania, iacendo super cepe per
27. duas horas vel per unam ad minus.

---

[134] Monica Green (2011, p179) cites a similar version of lines 7-13, collated from two other MS: BL Sloane 1621; Bethesda (MD); National Library of Medicine NLM E8. Sloane is dated to '16th century' though the text itself seems to be early 12th century, according to Green (p190).

Omitted:
Image 91 Left, Folio 86v, Line 1: Tract*us* de disposicione ho*min*is.
Image 93 Left, Folio 88v, Line 10: Explicit de disposicione ho*min*is.

Betson has included here a general section on the influence of the planets on the human character. We have omitted it on the basis that it has no direct relevance to the herbal, though the astrological implications for health would not have been lost on readers at the time.

Betson's source appears to be similar to Bodleian Digby MS 29, Item 32, ff194b – 196, *Tractatus Brevis sed Perutilis de Constellacionibus,* which begins, as Betson, *'Sciendum quod si quis nascitur in aliqua hora diei'.* Betson's text also has strong similarities to the Middle English treatise *The book of physiognomy* which appears in at least three surviving manuscripts: Cambridge University Library Ll.4.14, ff 156b-159b (1400-50); University College, London, Anglice 6, f 48b (1450-1500); and Colombia University Library, Plimpton 260 ff 14a – 31b (1400-1425). See also *Reading Faces: Translation of a Latin text and translation and edition of a Middle English text concerning physiognomy, by Marjan Grinwis.* (Web document from: igitur-archive.library.uu.nl/student-theses.)

Image 93 Left, Folio 88v, from Line 11.

In right margin: **Pro siatica Passione**   *Tr. : For the pain of sciatica.*
11.   Take colde Uryn a quantite and alsmykill   *Not in eVK2.*
         alsmykill: *as much as, the same amount of .*
12.   dreggis of ale, and seth he*m* in a clene vessill
13.   and steme hem well and put to the*m* a quanti-
         steme: *to boil,seethe or simmer. EMED.*
14.   *t*e of whete bran and alsmikill comyn salt,
15.   cromys of soure brede *an ounce*, and boile he*m* tille
16.   *t*hei be thyk and *t*hen plaist*ur* hem. ----

In the right margin: **Powdur Holand**
         Powder of Holland is not in EMED; The OED has 'a medicinal powder taken for the treatment of abdominal pain' dated to 1534. eVK2 kas a 'Powder of Holland' remedy – but not this one.
                    -----*Recipe* Carawey,
17.   Fenell, Spykenard, Anice, Synamome, Galang*ur*
18.   of alkon d ʒ, a nounce Gromell, a nounce Lico-
         alkon: *of each one. half a drachm each of Caraway, Fennel, Spikenard, Aniseed, Cinnamon, Galanga; one ounce of Gromwell and Liquorice, one ounce of Groundsel (?).*

19.	res, ʒ j, Senecium, sicut de omnibus, and make all	Senecium as the others.
20.	in powdur and it is a singuler poudur for the	
21.	colek and the ston.	

In right margin: **Pro Pestilencia**   Tr.: For the Plague - Not in eVK2.

            Take the juse of Feverfue,

22.	Matfelon, Modirwort, Goldis, Scabiose, Dogefe-
23.	nell, Avance, Dandelion and put all thies to-

            Common Centaury, or Feverfew, Knapweed, or Silverweed, Motherwort, Corn Marigold, or ?Bindweed, Scabiose, ?Stinking Camomile, Avens, Dandelion.

24.	gidere with Triacle and temper hem with white
25.	wyn or els stale ale and gif the pacient vj
26.	or vij ~~tymes~~ sponefull to drynk. **Pro eodem**
27.	Take juse of Madeworte, Gouldis, Avance.

            Perhaps *Motherwort, Corn Marigold, Avens.*

28.	Tryacle mellid with whyte wyn is gode also.

Image 93 right, Folio 89r.

1.	**Medicina contra difficultates:**	Not in eTK.
2.	**Anelitus et grossum flegma.**	

       (Tr.: A Medicine for difficulties: breathlessness and heavy flegm).

3.	Recipe Minte, Absinthei ʒ. ii, Zinziber, Cinamon	
4.	ana anª ʒ. j. & β., , Galange ʒ. ij, Zeddoar, Maratri	
5.	ana anª ʒ. j. & β., Anisi ʒ. iij, Liquirico ʒ. iiij, Zuccarum	

       two drachms of Mint and Wormwood, one and a half drachms of Ginger and Cinnamon; two drachms of Galangal; one and a half drachms of White Turmeric and Fennel,; three drachms of Aniseed; four drachms of Liquorice; one ounce of Sugar.

6.	ʒ .j, misceantur et fiat pulvis. Utatur mane et	
7.	cero cum servicia calida.	with hot beer.

	For al manere of fevers	Not in eVK2.
8.	Acc(ipe) borage ij handfull, of Ysope, Hertistong	
	Borage, Hyssop, Harts tongue.	
9.	of ech demi handfull, of Letuse iij godehand-	*Letuse: Lettuce var.*
10.	full, of Anneys sedis obolus brokun grete &	*Aniseed.*
	obolus: *half-penny-weight*	
11.	bounden in a faire cloth. Boile ye thiese in	
12.	rennyng water and with the licour streyned of	

226

13.   almond*is that* suffisen make *the* Almond
14.   mylk to drynk. And thi*s* drynk mad ple-
15.   saunte *with* lof Sugur and used plenteuosely
16.   shale mekyll ease.   Amen God grante.

In right margin: **A tisane for *the* stomak**

17.   Take rotis of Fenell, Alisa*und*r*e*, P*a*rsyly and
18.   Smalach, a godehandfull, well and clen, was-
        Fennel, Alexanders, Parsley, Wild Celery.
19.   he*n* and wel stanpid in a morter & seth
20.   hem in a pottel of wat*er* to *the* half and do
21.   *ther*to a litill hony and clens it and dri*n*k it
22.   at even and at moroun, ix sponfull at oone*s*.   *at oones*: at one go.

In right margin: **Contra omnem Tussim**   *Tr: for every cough.*

23.   Re*cipe* Liquirice ℥ j.   zz quart*er semi*, se*men* Coriandri,
        zz: Ginger, Zinziber.
24.   Carewey, Silur Montanum, Galanger an*a* ℥ j.
        One ounce of Liquorice; 1/8 ounce Ginger;
        One ounce each of Coriander seed, Caraway, Marjoram, Galingale.

In right margin: **A Medicine for Felou*n***
        Feloun: *'Some kind of suppurative sore; perhaps, a carbuncle of virulent type'. EMED.*
25.   Take Scabiose & Matfelon, the juse of
        Scabwort and Knapweed varieties.
26.   thie*s* two, then take vynagre and hony,
27.   and the white of an egge and floure
28.   of whete, and make a plaist*er*.

For *the* jaundis:
29.   Take penyworte and dry   *Not in eVK2.*
30.   him in the su*n* & bete into pouudre & farce
31.   him and put *there*to v p*er*ties of ludworte
        ludworte: *a rare name; see Appendix 1 below for possible identifications from EMED.*
32.   and an gode qua*n*tite of yvery and lete   *ivory.*

Image 94 left, Folio 89v

1. the seke receyve it at even*ing* last and at
2. morn*ing* fastyng. -----

in left margin: **For to make White Sope**   Not in eVK2.

                     ----Take ij busshel of   **Busshel:** *about 80lbs, 36kgs each.*

3. bene ashes or of wode and sift hem clene
4. in a faire flou*r* wi*th* a busshel of quyk
5. lyme and medle hem to gidere. *th*an do
6. hem in a masshfatte *with* an hole in the

         masshfatte: *'a vat for boiling malt and water in the first stage of brewing.'* EMED.

7. botom and ley on that hole a dissh wi*th*
8. small holis and a pyn of tre in the ne*th*er
9. hole. Fyll up *th*at fat *with* faire wati*r*
10. and lete it stonde xxiiij houris *th*en lete
11. it ren softly oute aboute the pyn and
12. wha*n th*ou hast y gaderid thy lye do it
13. in a vessil on the fire. and do *th*erin two
14. or iij olde rotins shone for *th*at wole make   **rotins shone:** *rotten shoes.*
15. it grey and lete it seth to gidere iiij^{our}
16. houris *th*an put *th*erto a pottel or iij. q*u*arter of
17. mete oyle and a pottell or more of Bay   **mete oyle:** *vegetable oil.* EMED.
18. salt, and lete it boyle well to gidire and
19. stere it to gider *with* a sklis. Thanne forto   **sklis:** *spatula.*
20. wiete whan it is well, tak a litill
21. of *th*at skyme *with* thy sklis in *th*i lift hand

         'Then, in order to know when it is ready,
         take a little of the skim with thy slice in thy left hand.'

22. and *with th*i ~~lift~~ right fyngir, rolle it
23. in thin hand & if it will roll it is well,
24. and if it do not, do in more salt. *Th*anne
25. wi*th th*i skymin cast it in ca*k*es and lete it
26. stonde till it be colde. -----

228

In left margin: **For to make Blak Sope**

	----Take j. parte	
27.	of wode askis or pruse askis and two	*pruse askis*: Spruce Tree ashes.
28.	p*ar*ties of quyk lyme and iij p*ar*ties of comon	Not in eVK2.
29.	asshis and dep*arte* he*m* in vj p*ar*ties and put	
30.	he*m* in vj vessils w*ith* holes in *the* botome	

Image 94 Right, Folio 90r

1.	and ley a wasse of stree on ich hole and	
	wasse of stree: bundle of straw. EMED gives 'wase'.	
2.	put hote wat*er* in the first vessil, and *th*at lye	
3.	poure into an o*the*r wessill and so fro*m* vessill	
4.	to vessill till *th*ou have alldo & so *th*ou shalt	
5.	have lye *tha*t wole defoule a wollen cloth.	**Lye** *that will clean a woollen cloth.*
6.	Re*cipe* t*he*n vj galons of *th*at ly and j. galon	
7.	of ole de olyve and boile hem togidere	
8.	vj. houres and *th*en ley a litill on a tiliston*e*	*Tile stone.*
9.	til it be colde, and if it be blak ynough	
10.	it is well. *Th*en put it in barrels, & if it	
11.	be not blak ynough boile it to it be well	
12.	and on*ce* more prove on a tiliston*e* as it is befor*e*.	

in right margin: **de albo sapone**: *('Re white soap')*

13.	Take of the same lye on*e* p*ar*te and vj.	
14.	p*ar*ties of talough and o*n* p*ar*te of co*mm*on sal*t*	*Talough*: tallow, grease or fat.
15.	and boile hem to gidere till it be white	
16.	& thik and assaye it on a tilistone til it	
17.	be colde. *Th*an rubbe it in the palme of the	
18.	hande and if it smell grecy or be fatty	
19.	boile forth til it be white & not grecye	
20.	nor smelling of talowe. *Th*en cast it in	
21.	moldis and dresse it as *th*ou wole have it.	

in right margin: **Oyle of Tartary**

22.	Re*cipe* j. li. of Tartar made of lies of	
23.	wyne. Put hem in an erden pot wel anelid	*anelid*: oiled and fired.

229

24.	and fire him strongly untill he turnid into	
25.	salt *th*an lete him be sette in a moist place	
26.	till he relent into oyle.	*turns back into oil.*

For all man*er*
27.	**of evels in a mannys body.** *R*e*cipe* Sca-	
28.	biose, Primp*er*nell, Turmentil & Detayn, Wor-	
29.	mode, Fumitor and Goldis make a water of	
	Scabwort, Scarlet Pimpernel; Dittany (?), Wormwood, Common Fumitory, Corn Marigold, or ?Bindweed.	
30.	all *th*iese and dri*n*k it.	

Image 95 Left, Folio 90v
1.	Mat*er* herbar*um*, Mugworte, Mod*ur*worte id*em*	
	All three are Artemisia vulgaris, Mugwort.	
2.	Ypocras seith it is hote and dry in the	
3.	thride degree. This helpith to conceyve childe	
4.	and clensith the womb and makith a wo-	
5.	man to have her flour*is*. And it destroy-	*her flouris: her periods.*
6.	Eth the emerodis *th*at growen in the fun-	*emerodis: haemmoroids.*
7.	dament, and on this man*er*: First he shalbe	
8.	garsed, aftur take powdur of Mugwort and strew	*garsed: cut, scarified.*
9.	on the pappis. Also and a chide be dede	*and: if a child be dead.*
10.	in his modurs womb, take Mugwort and	
11.	stamp it smale and ley it to *the* wombe al	
12.	colde and she shal have delyverance w*ith*	
13.	outen p*er*ell. Also it is gode for the stone	
14.	and the gravel in *the* reynes. Also and a	*reynes: kidneys; and: if*
15.	man bere it upon him ther shal no ve-	
16.	the yalow evell for to drink it w*ith* wyne.	*Yalow evell: jaundice.*
17.	nomose beste dere hym and it is gode for	*dere: hurt, wound, frighten. EMED.*
18.	And it confortith the stomake & makith	
19.	wome*n* of gode colour. -----	

in left margin: **Planteyn**

----*Th*e **juse of Planteyn**

20.	mergid w*ith* hony and venegre and Poud*er*

21.	of Alows helith the cancur in the mouth	*Alows*: Aloes.
22.	and floyng into the gomes. Also take iij	*floyng*: *flowing*.
23.	rotes of Plantayn & stamp & temp hem with wa-	
24.	ter & gif him to drynk that hath the fe-	
25.	vere tercian & he shal be sane Also	
26.	stamp it and let use it to gider and temper	
27.	hem with vynagre and make a plaistre	
28.	and ley it to the right side of a man	
29.	that hath the yelowsought and use it	**yelowsought**: *'yellow jaundice'*. EMED.
30.	till he be hole. -----	

In left margin: **Henbane**   *No illness is specified. Perhaps used as a painkiller.*

-----Take and seth it

Image 95 Right, Folio 91r

1.	in water and with it wassh the templis of	
2.	the seke and his fete also hote as he may	
3.	suffir and make a plaister of the sedis	
4.	beten to powder temperd with vinagre and wo-	
5.	man's mylk, and ley it to the templis.	

In right margin: **Warenyce Madur.**   Madder.

6.	Seth it in water and wassh thi hede therin	
7.	and it shal make the redehere. Also take	
8.	the greteist that thou maist fynd, and shave	
9.	it withouten, and anoynt it & strew theron	
10.	powdur of Scamony and bynde a threde a	?Scammony.
11.	boute the ende and lete a woman put it in	
12.	to hir private when she seith tyme, and drawe	
13.	oute and she shal have delyverance.	

In right margin: no/va **Ysope No**^{va}

14.	Ysope is hote and drye inthe thride degre	Hyssop.
15.	and as Ypocras seith, if a man use to drink	
16.	it fastyng, it make him of gode coloure	
17.	and to have god sight & sleith wormys	

18.	in the womb, and it is gode for the stomak	
19.	and the lev*er* and the longis, and it is gode	
20.	for a woman *that* travalith of childe: lete h*er*	
21.	drink it w*ith* leuk wat*er* and she shal have	
22.	delyv*er*ance anoon. And it is gode for dropsy	
23.	and othre many thyng*es*.	

In right margin: **Letise** *Lettuce.*

24.	Is colde & mo-
25.	ist in the ij. Degree. It purgith the stomak
26.	and softeneth the womb, and makith a ma*n*
27.	to slepe well & make a woma*n* have grete
28.	plente of mylk.

In right margin: **Cressis** *Cress.*

29.	Is hote and drye	
30.	in the iij^de degree. The sede wole dure v.	**dure:** *will last five years*
31.	yere. Take *the* sede and brisse it in	
32.	a morter and gif the seke to drynk iij daie*s*	

Image 96 Left, Folio 91v

1.	ev*er*y day a pen*n*y weight *with* rede wyn*e*	
2.	leukwarm and he shall be stanchid or	
3.	el*s* dy. Also it is gode for the palsy. Take	
4.	the sede and seth it in wyn*e* and do it in	
5.	a pokett and bynd it to his side, there	
6.	as the sore is. Also it is gode for a mannys	
7.	fundement that go*s* oute, and is tak*n*	**fundement:** *anus.*
8.	of colde. It must be put in and take the	
9.	pow*er* of the sede and put in the fundeme*n*t.	
10.	Anoynte *the* lendis *with* hony & same (?)	
11.	poud*er* above and poud*er* of Commyn & Colofyn.	*Cumin; Pine Tree gum.*
12.	Take *the* juse of rewe and comy*n* made	
13.	in poud*ur* and mell he*m* togid*er* and wete	**wete cotim:** *wet cotton.*
14.	cotim *the*rin and ley the blerid eiyen. Also	
15.	for a ma*n that* hath dro*n*kun venom, gif him	

16.	Rew to drink *with* wyn and he shal be hole.	Rue.
17.	Also for a wom*an that is with* dede child, gif	
18.	hir to drynk the same and she shal be deli-	
19.	verid. Also it is gode for the dropsy & ti-	
20.	sik, and it distroieth lechery & wormys i*n the*	
21.	body. Also take Rwe & Fenell and stamp	Rue & Fennel
22.	hem w*ith* hony and ev*er*ose and it is a p*re*ciose	?Eyebright.
23.	wat*er* for the sore eiyen. Also *the* juse of	
24.	Rwe stanchissh blode of *the* nose whan it	
25.	is pourid into *the* nose thrilis. Also who	
26.	so etis ev*er*y day fastyying xx levis of Rewe	Leaves of Rue.
27.	and iij figgis and a litill salt that day	
28.	schal no venym greve hym *th*of he were	though he were poisoned.
29.	poysond. Also take Rew, Com*on* Pepp*er*mi*n*t	
30.	of echon that p*ro*p*or*cioun by weight and	

Image 96 Right, Folio 92r

1.	grynde hem well togidere and melle he*m*	
2.	with hony and vinagre and that is a p*re*ciose	
3.	oyntment for the breest and for the vaynes	

In right margin: **Scabius**   For Scabius see Appendix 1.

4.	is cold and moist in the ij. degree.	
5.	Stamp it and seth it w*ith* white wyn and *it*	
6.	is a gode drynk for the lyv*er* and for to *de*stroy	
7.	wykid humors in the stomak and drink it	
8.	*with* Ev*er*ose ich day fastyng & then schalt yew	?Eyebright.
9.	have impostim breking. Writh in (?) the pow-	impostim: abscess.

In the right margin: **Wermode**

10.	*d*ur of it and of Centory and Betony of ich y-	Common Centaury, Betony.
11.	like p*ro*portion sleyth the wormys gifen in	
12.	metis and drynkis. Also for *the* mylte *that*	mylte: spleen.
13.	is harde and swollen of colde mat*er*, seth it i*n*	
14.	wyn*e* and lete the seke drynk *ther*of and *it* shal	
15.	hele and make a plaist*ur* and ley it to *the* sore.	

16.	Also stamp Wermote and temper it *with*	Wormwood.
17.	vynagre and some brede tostid, and of	
18.	juse of Myn*tes* and Weybrede, and fry he*m*	**Weybrede**: *Plantain.*
19.	well to gidur and make a plaistur and	
20.	ley to the mouth of the stomak and *that*	
21.	shal stanche brakying and castyng. Gif it	
22.	in wyne soden cold for the dropsy. And	
23.	the juse put in the ere distroieth wormes.	
24.	Also ley it to *the* byting of a wode hounde	**wode hounde**: *a mad dog.*
25.	wi*th* hony, Rewe and salt and it shal draw	
26.	oute *the* venym and sase the akyng, and	**sase the akyng**: *cease aching.*
27.	do awey the ranclyng afar (?) and hele it up.	**ranclyng**: *suppuration.*
28.	Is hote and dry in the iij^{de} degree. ----	

In the right margin: **Centory**   *Common Centaury.*

---- It is
29.	gode for cenose *that* is sprent. Seth it in wa*ter*	**cenose**: *sprained sinews.*
30.	and wassh *the* ioyn*tes* and cenose in the wa*ter*	
31.	stampe the erbe and fry it *with* oile olif	
32.	and make a plais*ter* and ley it *there*to. Also	

Image 97 Left, Folio 92v
1.	a lectuary made of Centaury and hony, well
2.	thikked, and *that* is gode for the stomak and
3.	shall man have gode talent to mete.

In left margin: **Betayn / hot dry 2**   *Betony.*

4.	Stillid, it shal make a man of fair and
5.	gode colou*r* and it is a noble drynk for the
6.	stomak & he shal have no dropsy *that* day *that*
7.	he drynk nor shall be dronkyn nor have
8.	the fe*ver* tercian.[135] ----------

---

[135] The use of Betony against drunkenness can be traced in Britain from at least the 12th century 'Physicians of the Myddfai' up to the 19th century. (Christina Stapely, pers. comm).

In left margin: **Verven hot dry 2º**

                -----Mengid *with* planteyn an*a* ℥

        Plaintain (and either Betony or Vervain) one ounce of each.

9.   wole make a goode breth and do away
10. the stynch of the mouth and it is gode
11. for the tercian and quarteyn w*ith* iij. rot*es*   **tercian and quarteyn**: *i.e. fevers.*
12. and iij troppis dro*n*k w*ith* wyne white.

In left margin: **Violet**

                   Colde

13. and moist in the seconde degre. Take it,   *(i.e. the Violet).*
14. myr*rh* and Safron. Make a plaist*er* of hem and ley
15. to thy sore eiyen that swollen and it aba-
16. tyth the swelling and doth away the ake.

In left margin: **Smalach / merch**   *Wild Celery, Lovage.*

17. Cold and moist in the iij*r*d degree. It co*n*-
18. fortis the stomak and sleyth wormes in
19. the womb. Take Smawlach and Rew sede,
20. pepur and salt, and temp*er* he*m* to gidur
21. whe*n* *th*ei ar grondis w*ith* viniagre. And that
22. drynk doth awey all colde humors of *the*
23. Stomak. Hote and dry 2nd g*re*. ------

In left margin: **Camomyll**   *Sweet Camomile.*

                   --------- It *[read 'if' ?]* stillid   **stillid**: *distilled.*

24. and dronkon w*ith* wyn, is gode for the
25. stone & *the* bled*er* and gravell in the reyns.   *in the kidneys.*
26. Also it helpith women of div*er*se sekenesse
27. and makith hem gode stomakis, and is gode
28. for the hede ake and bren*n*yng ague.   *'burning ague' EMED, c.1400.*

In left margin: **Netill**   *Nettle.*

29. If a woman have *the* maris that is

       maris: *a disturbance or disorder of the uterus.* (EMED);
       frete: *to rub or chafe. EMED.*

30. full of wikid humoris lete her frete
31. hir with the levis thereof and drinke

Image 97 Right, Folio 93r
1.   w*ith* wyn and she shal be well *thereafter.*

In right margin: **Sauge**   Sage
                    Hote
2.   and dry. It is gode for cenose for to wash   *Sinews.*
3.   *ther*in. Moreov*er* stamp it & ley it to a wonde
4.   full of blode, and it wole drawe oute the
5.   blode and hele the wou*n*nde cleane. Also drynk
6.   sauge w*ith* wyn a litill warm and it
7.   shal sease the ake undir the sidis and of the
8.   wombe and of the stomak. ------

In right margin: **Parslye**
                    ----- Is hote and
9.   moist in the iij degre and multiplieth man-
10. *n*ys blode and doth awey the tisik and it   **tisik**: *wasting of lungs etc.*
11. helpith for the fe*ver ter*cian and the dropsy
12. and confortith the hert and the stomak and
13. is gode for potage. ------

In right margin: **Fenell**
                    ---------Is hote and dry
14. in the secunde degre. It confortith the sto-
15. make and clensith *the* lyver and the long*es*
16. and stanschith *the* fev*er*, and sethe it in wat*er*
17. and ther*with* wassh *th*in hede and it wele
18. stanch *the* hedehak. ---------

In right margin: **Cenerfole**   *Honeysuckle - as cheverfoil. EMED.*
                    -------Is a man*er* of Wode-
19. bynd and berith a fewe white flow*ers*   *Woodbind, as above.*
20. almost like a Lily. It is hote and dry in *the*

236

21.	secunnde degre. Stamp it and temp it *with* hony	
22.	and it is gode for the kancer in *the* mouth	
23.	and drink it with wyn, and it doth awey	
24.	the gnawing of the womb. Also seith it	
25.	in wa*ter* and wassh *th*i hede *there*in and it he-	
26.	lith a sekenes callid *the* vertigine. V*er*tigo la*ter*alis.[136]	
27.	Also frie it in oile and shepis talow and	
28.	*th*at is a gode plaister for swelling of vyniys	
	of vyniys and of iontis: *of veins and joints*.	
29.	and of iou*n*tis *th*at is takn of cold. Also fry	
30.	it *with* wax and ~~berbr~~ borus grese and it	**borus grese**: *boar's grease*.

Image 98 Left, Folio 93v

In left margin: **Mynt**

1.	is gode for al ma*ner* swelling of lymys and	
2.	muctose (?) *th*at ben synsprong (?). Is hote in	*neither found*.
3.	*th*e seconde degre it restreineth braking	**braking**: *vomiting*
4.	and it is gode for the lyver. And if a wo-	
5.	man drynk it w*ith* watur it shal cause	
6.	hir to have gode delyverance. And it	**it**: *eaten with salt*.
7.	w*ith* salt, is gode for bityng of an hond &	*for a dog-bite*.
8.	shal draw oute the venym. Rose is cold and	
9.	dry in the iind degree. Stamp him smal and	
10.	ley it to a brennyng sore and it shale	
11.	sease *th*e aking and the brennyng. Also he	
12.	is gode for the fe*ver* in the stomak. Lete	
13.	a woma*n* drynk it w*ith* wyn and it shal re-	
14.	streyn bleding of the maris. Also roseole	
	maris: *uterus*. EMED. **Roseole**: *Rose oil*.	
15.	is principall thing for prikyng of senows	**senows**: *sinews*.
16.	and wa*ter* of he*m* gode for yyen. *Th*e oile is gode	**yyen**: *eyes*.
17.	for the hed ake, for to anoynt the te*m*ples.	
18.	*Th*e rote is gode to draw oute we*n* or tre	**wen or tre**: *swellings or splinters*.
19.	in mannys fote. ------	

---

[136] Vertigo does appear in English until 1538 (OED).

	-----**Lilye** Cold and dry in the	
20.	thrid degre. *The* levys sothu*n* in wa*t*er is a gode	
21.	plaistur for senewe shortned etc. -------	

	----------**Millefoly** and Ya-	*Yarrow.*
22.	row is all on*e*. It is hote and dry i*n* 3º gra.	
23.	It is gode to stau*n*ch the flux and it hel-	
24.	pith the tothake wha*n* it is chewid fas-	
25.	tyng *etc.* ------	

	-------**Synonu*m*** is gode for hem that hav lost	
26.	her spech in her sekenesse. Temp yt w*ith*	
27.	water & lete *th*e seke drynk it. Also if a ma*n*	
28.	have eten raw mete lete him ete an	
29.	oyno*n* and it shal disavow the maladye	
30.	therof. Also if a man be costif, fry he*m*	***costif:*** *constipated*
31.	and fressh grese togidur, and ley hem	

Image 98 Right, Folio 94r

1. to his navill als hote as he mai suffur.

In right margin: **Garlik /. h.d.4º g.**
   Tr: Presumably *'hot and dry in the fourth degree.'*

2. Stampe it and temper it w*ith* salt, and it
3. is gode for the *to*the ak. Also stampe
4. it *with* buttu*r* and seth it in white wy*ne*
5. and it shal make him *that* is stokun in the
   stokun: *To stab or pierce someone; thrust with a weapon.* EMED.
6. breest forto delyve*re* glet and filth.   ***glet:*** *phlegm, mucus.* EMED.

In right margin: **Pro ydropisi bo*na* medi*c*ina *et* probata**
   Not found in eTK or eVK2 (2014).

Re*cipe* Rede

7. Mynt, Rede Fenel rote, Ysope, P*a*rcly, cu*m* radi-
8. ce, et Sauge in mai*ora* quantitate q*uam* om*n*ia
   Mint ssp., Red Fennel, Hyssop, Parsley with its root, Sage.
9. alia & pistentur in sourdough et cu*m* fuerit suf-
10. ficien*ter* pistata imponatur in una olla terrea

11.   plena cervisie dissicate quando fuerit extracta
12.   a ferno *(read: furno)* et obturat*ur* os olle per diem et noctem
        ***a ferno**: from the oven.*
13.   et tu*nc* mane et vesp*ere* det*ur* egro.

In right margin: **pille pestilen*cie***   *Tr.: pills for the plague.*

14.   Re*cipe* Aloes cicotrini abluti ʒ iiij , Mirri, Crocei, an*a* ʒ ij
        Other texts read 'Aloes epatici' – see eTK1317 L & M.
        See also Herbarium image 76 left, Folio 71v, Col. B, lines 23-26 for Aloes variants.
15.   Ligni Aloes, Spicenardi, Cinamom an*a* ʒ i.
16.   Fiat pulvis et distemp*era* cu*m* Aq*ua* de Fumo Terre
17.   et fac pillul*as*.
        Four drachms of Aloes (?), two drachms each of Myrrh, Crocus; one drachm each of
        Agarwood, Spikenard(or Valerian) and Cinnamon; distillation of Common Fumitory.

In right margin: **P*ro* calore epatis**   *Not found in eTK.*
        Re*cipe* Aque Endivie, Rose salti
18.   an*a* ʒ, Rosarum Sandal*orum*, Spodii, accipe an*a* ʒ sem, c*am*-
19.   phore .℈. 4 s, aceti ℈. ij. In istis intinge pa*n*-   *aceti: of vinegar.*
        One ounce one drachm each of Water of Chicory (?) and Roses;
        half a drachm each of Roses, Sandalwood, Ivory,
        and half a scrupul of Camphor Laurel. Of vinegar 2 (?)
20.   nu*m* de scarleto et supponatur epati. -------.
        ***pannum de scarleto**: a piece of scarlet material*

In right margin: **Contra Usturas**   *Tr.: for burns.*
        -----Recipe folia
21.   Lilii cu*m* acete soluta et decocta. Usturas sanat.   *Not found in eTK.*

In right margin: **For eke and scab**   *eke: dry scab (OED).*
22.   Take oile de Bay and Mercury mortified
        oile de bay: *oil from the Baytree, Laurus nobilis. EMED;*
        Mercury mortified: *'sublimed to clearness and splendor, and sold by Apothecaries.'*
23.   with fasting spattill and anoynte *th*i hands
        fasting spattill: *'the spittle of one observing a fast or eating sparingly.' EMED.*

In left margin: **To cle*n*s a wo*n*de**
24.   wi*th*in, and the solis of *th*y fete. Take
25.   juse of Sali*n*e and te*m*p it with hony & plaist*ur*
26.   it to the wonde. Tak of Pynp*er*nell the

> *Saline*: *perhaps a vulnerary mixture of vinegar and salt (Mowat, Alphita,pp.132-33.*
> *Osalinum and Oxalmon).*   **Pynpernell**: *Scarlet Pimpernel.*

27. rote and stamp it w*ith* hony and ley it to
28. *th*e sore and it shal gete oute ire*n* or wode
29. of *th*e wonde. ------

In right margin: **To hele a wo*n*de**

-----Take powd*ur* of Centaury

Image 99 Left, Folio 94v

1. and lay on the wonde and wassh it w*ith* white
2. wyne or w*ith* stale of a man childe.

In left margin: **Ut acetu*m* cito fiat**.   *Tr.: To make vinegar quickly.*   *Not found in eTK.*

3. R*ecipe* vas terrenum et imple bono vino cu*m*
4. fabis assatis vel pane ~~us~~ calidius ~~et~~ pistata
5. et obstrue os diligen*ter* et pone in caldario
6. pleno aqua et bulliat.

In left margin: **Ut se*r*vicia no*n* ace*r*bat.**   *Tr:.to prevent beer from going sour.*

R*ecipe* ova cruda et

7. impone et si sit male saporis impone ova

Not found in eTK. ***Ova assata dura***: *eggs roasted (e.g. in ashes) till hard.*

8. assata dura. **Pro vino albo discolerato:**   *for discoloured white wine.*
9. pone in dolio un*am* libr*am* vel plus de a-
10. romatico et si si*t* corruptu*m* impone unu*m*
11. sacculu*m* p*arvulum* plenu*m* de testibus ovorum.
12. **Ut panis non putrescat**: pone pulverem
13. Baccarum Lauri *[space]* pastor   *powdered Bay Tree berries.*

In left margin: **Ut acetu*m* convertatur in Vinum**   *Tr.: to change vinegar into wine.*

Accipe seme*n* Porri   **Porri**: *Leek seed.*

14. et impone et p*er*mitte stare p*er* duos vel tres
15. dies. **Ut Rose serventur:** fac vini ca-   *Not found in eTK.*

16. dum de quercum et impleatur Rosis et obturatur

vini cadum de quercum: *an oakwood wine barrel.*

17. et post suspende in aqua currente.

18. **Ut talpas capias:** pone unam cepam super foramen   *Not found in eTK.*
      Tr.:To catch moles.
19. et exibit. **Ut fructus serventur per annum**:   *Not found in eTK.*
20. ponatur fructus cum foliis eiusdem arboris
21. in vaso aliquo bene obturato a vento. **Ut fere**   *fere*: wild animals.
22. **te sequantur**: porta tecum ignem et impone
23. de Assafetida. ---------

In left margin: **Ut Litere appareant in cultello**

      ------Recipe Vitriolum vel alum glas
24. Sal Armoniacum, Ysalgar ana et bulliantur.
      Assafetida, ?sulfuric acid, potash alum, ammonium chloride, red arsenic.
25. in aceto usque ad tertiam partem, et cum eo scribe.
26. **Ut Littere sint auree:** Recipe salem, acetum,   *auree*: gilded.
27. Vitriolum et distilla, prima aqua abiecta.
28. **Ut littere legantur in nocte et non in**
29. **die**: Recipe fel canis, succum Sambuci, glas
      Dog bile, Elder juice, white and yolk of an egg, and make ink.
30. et albumen ovi et fac encaustum. **Ad eva-**
31. **cuendam vermes a brasio**: impone Abro-
      Ad evacuendam vermes a brasio: to rid malt of worms.

Image 99 Right, Folio 95r

1. tanum, idem Sothernwod. **UT Serpentes manu**
2. **capias sine dampno**: unge manum tuam
3. cum succo Herbe Sancti Johannis Baptisti et non nocebis.   St John's Wort.
4. **UT ovum induratur**: Accipe unum (*insert*: ovum) vacuum,
5. et imple cum albumine ovorum et exsicca in so-
6. le et induresset ut vitrum. --------

In right margin: **Pro Pestilencia**   *Not found in eVK2.*

      ------Take ij parties
7. of Tansey and one of Solseqiuy and drynk
      Tansy, Garden Marigold.
8. the juse within xiiij houris. For the my-
9. gryme take the gall of a bull or of a   *mygryme*: migraine.
10. nox, and ry mele and hony, and plaister   gall of an ox and rye meal.
11. hem to thy temple so thei tuche not thi nee.   touch not thine eye.

In right margin: **For to breke *the* ston**

12.   ꝑ Use to ete unsett Lekis, optima medicina.
      unsett Lekis: *Leeks that have not yet been transplanted.*

In left margin: **For *the* flux:**

13.   poud*er* of Pep*per*m*int* & rostid yelkis of egg*es*.
14.   ꝑ For the colyk drynk the juse of Dita*n*y.
15.   ꝑ **For a sore**, make a plaister of Smalach,   *Wild Celery.*
16.   Ditaigne, a white of a negge, whete mele.   *Ditany.*
17.   ꝑ For to kepe a sore fro*m* spreding, anoy*n*t
18.   the sore w*ith* juse of Avence. **For him**   *Avens.*
19.   *that* **may not brouke drynke or ete,** *th*e   **brouke**: *retain food. EMED.*
20.   poud*ur* of clowis. For agueilis (?) cut   *Cloves*
21.   *th*em til *th*ei blede and brisse Garlek
22.   and do *ther*to. **For *the* flux:** Ete rere   *eat raw eggs.*
23.   eggis with juse of Millefoly. For   *Yarrow.*
24.   **to pourge *the* breste of yvel hume*rs*:**
25.   Take Fenell rote, P*ar*cily rote, Rede Mynte,
26.   Ysope, Centaury, Licores and seth he*m* in
      Fennel, Parsley root, Mint spp., Hyssop, Common Centaury, Liquorice.
27.   white wyn or in water fro*m* a galo*n* to a
28.   quarte. **For stynk of *the* mouth**
29.   seth the rote of Quinfoile in wat*er* till it *[be rede]*.   *Creeping Cinquefoil.*

Image 100 Left, Folio 95v

Above main text:
1.   Cent*au*rea bibit*ur* cum aq*ua* calida,   *Not in eTK.*
2.   provocat appetitum et sitim tollit.
     Tr.: **Centaury** *is drunk with hot water,*
     it stimulates the appetite, and takes away thirst.

Main text continues:
3.   be rede and put *that* licou*r* in thy mouth; also
4.   ꝑ Macis soden in wyn. For hym *that* pissis   **Macis**: *outer covering of the nutmeg.*
5.   ꝑ blode drink the juse of Husleke. **For him** *that*   *Houseleek.*
6.   **may not pisse**, drink juse of Mugwort and

7.	⁊ of P*arc*elly rotise. **Succus minte & decoctio**	
8.	**Ysopi** causant mulierem concipere.----	
	Mugwort, Parsley root, Juice of Mint, Hyssop.	

In left margin: **Contra Casum Capillorum**   *Tr.: Against hair loss.*

	------Lava fre-	
9.	quentur in lexiva facta de Vervena et Absinthi*o*	
	lexiva: *soap or lye made from Vervain and Absinth.*	
10.	⁊ **Contra Idropisim** de utraque causa	*Not in eTK.*
11.	Accipe radicem Petrocillini, Alexandrie, Lappa-	
12.	cii accuti, radicem Sambuci, radicem Ebuli, et	
13.	folia savine, et buliant*ur* in vino et aqua	
	Parsley root, Alexanders, Dock, Elder root, Dwarf Elder root, ? Juniper leaves.	
14.	et biba*tur* mane et cero. *To be drunk morning and evening('sero'; late).*	

15.	**Contra dolorem pedum**	*Not in eTK.*
16.	valet succus Urtice cum sepo arietum	***sepo arietum***: *fat of a ram*
17.	fricentur cum sale et aceto vel oleo. **Contra**	*against cramp.*
18.	**Spasmum:** valet bibere Salgea*m* et oleu*m* Rute.	*Sage and Rue.*
19.	⁊ Succus Apii et Plantaginis restringunt	*Juice of Wild Celery and Plantain.*
20.	⁊ sanguine*m* nasus. Succus Feniculi cu*m*	*juice of Fennel.*
21.	vino albo potatus valet contra tussim.	
22.	Succus absinthii cum aq*ua* mixtus ponat*ur* in ore et	*Juice of Wormwood*
23.	⁊ restaurat loquela*m*. Ut mulier cito	***loquelam***: *speech*
24.	concipiat: decocio*nem* Nepte bibite p*er* 3 dies.	*Catmint*
	Catmint was also an abortifacient.	
25.	⁊ Unge facie*m* et manus cu*m* succo Malve contra	*Juice of Hollyhock*
26.	morsu*m* apium vel vasparum. Succus Rute cu*m*	*Juice of Rue*
27.	⁊ butiro va*let* co*ntra* spasmum **Ad dentes dealbandas:**	
28.	farinam ordei, sal, mel et acetum: misce, et f*rice*tur.	
29.	⁊ **Pro eis qui non possunt retinere urinam**:	
30.	fac pulverem de ungulis porcinis et bibe.	*powdered pigs' trotters*
31.	⁊ **Ad Cancru*m***: pulvis Tormentille impositus	*powdered Tormentill*
32.	⁊ ubicumque fuerit, sanat. **Contra morsum venenosum:**	
33.	tere Rutam et Solsequium et bibe succu*m* et apponatur s*u*bstanti*a*	
	Rue and Garden Marigold	

Image 100 Right, Folio 96r

BL MS Sloane 521 at folio. numbered (227 / 204 / 7v), line 15, in John Bray's own remedies begins here, with small variants in the text, as far as image 101 left, folio 96v.

1. **For *the* hede ake:** Take (?) and Verven and   *Bray has 'Cepe' as missing word.*
2. Betagny or Wormode and Mo*d*erwort. **W**asshe *the* seke
     Vervain, Betony, Wormwood and Honeysuckle.
3. hede and then make a plaist*ur* above the molde   ***molde:*** *crown of head.*
4. in this man*er*: take the same herbis when
5. *t*hei are sodun and wring *then* p*ur* and grynde
6. small in a mortar and temp hem with
7. the same lico*r* ageyn and do *there*to whete
8. bran forto holde in the lico*r* and make a
9. garland of a kercheve and bynde the seke
10. hote as he may suffur it and bynd the hede
11. w*i*th a volup*er* and sithen w*i*th a kap above,   ***voluper:*** *head bandage;* ***sithen:*** *after.*
12. and do this but thre tymes, and he shal be
13. hale. ----

In right margin: **For clensi*n*g of *the* hede**

       ------Take Pillatory of Spayn and chewe   *Pellitory of the Wall.*
14. the rote v. daies, a gode qua*n*tite, and it
15. shal purge the hede and do awey the aking
16. and festen the tethe in the gomys. **For**
17. ***the* vanite of *the* hede**: Take juse of Wal-   ***vanite:*** *light-headedness.*
18. warte, salt, hony and incence and boile   ***Walwarte:*** *Pellitory-of-the-Wall.*
19. *them* to gidere overe the fire and *thur*with anoy*n*t
20. thy*n* hede and *the* templis. ----

              -----**For ill hery*n*g**:
21. take grene assh plantes, ley hem on a
22. brandiren and bren hem and kepe *the* wat*er*
23. *that* cometh oute of the endis or els chys   ***chys gres:*** *cheese grease.*
24. gres, and *the* juse endes of lekys w*ith* fasyngs
25. a shelfull, and a shelful of hony, and melt
26. *that* to gidere & boile he*m* a litill & do hem
27. in a fiole of glas and do *ther*of in the hole   ***fiole of glas:*** *a glass vial.*
28. of the ere and he shal be hole but ley
29. *the* seke on *that* side *that* he is defe & put *the*

244

Image 101 Left, Folio 96v

1. medycine on *the* tothir and he schal be hole
2. wi*th*in ix daies. And take woole of a blak shepe

In left margin: Aliud   *Tr.: Another (remedy).*

3. and wombpull it (?) and wi*th*it *therein* & stopp   *(stop the ear with it).*
4. **For *the* same**: take grece of an ele and   *ele: eel.*
5. juse of Sengren of athir ilik and mell tham
    of athir ilik: same amounts of both.
    Sengren: Houseleek, Sempervivum tectorum.
6. togidur and bolie *them* a litill and do it wel
7. in the hole ere of *the* seke, as it is before seid.
    Betson's text ceases following Sloane 521 at folio (228/205/208v) line 11. This may be the meaning of the Π sign immediately below at line 8, where Betson switches to another source.
8. **Π A medicyne for wormes** *th*at etene
    Lines 8-30, and next folio 97r, line 1 are also in Sloane 3285, Folio 93v Lines 1-25
9. *the* liddis *(illustration of eye)*: take salt and bre*n*n it wi*th* a
10. clote and temp it wi*th* hony and wi*th* a fedr   *clote: Burdock; fedr: feather.*
11. Π anoynt the ee*n* lyddis. **A medycyne**   *Cf. Sloane 521, Folio 236/233/36, line 6.*
12. **for the web** in the *(illustration of eye)*: Take Everrose a
    ? Everose: ?Perhaps Euphrasia officinalis, Euphrasy, Eyebright.
13. gode quantite and temp it well and take
14. oute the juse and wring thorow a clouth
15. and take borisse grece and capon's grece and
    boar's grease and chicken fat.
16. gece grece, and melle thaim to gidere and   *gece grece: goose grease.*
17. put in a brason panne and ster hem wel   *brason: made of brass.*
18. togidere wi*th* a rounde staf. And boile it
19. well and lete it kele and *than* do it in a   *kele: cool.*
20. boist and whan *the* seke goth to bed do a li-   *boist: box.*
21. π tl in his sore iyen. **For hym *that* ha*th***
22. **lost his spech in his sekenesse**, take
23. juse of Sauge or Primerose, and do it in   *Sage or Primrose.*
24. π his mouth and he shal speke. **For a ma*n***
25. ***that* spitt*is* blode**: take juse of Betayn   *Betony.*
26. and temp it *with* got*is* milk and late *the*
27. seke drynk *ther*of iij tymes v daies. Ite*m* tak

28.	Smalach, Mynt, Rwe and Betayn and boile	*Wild Celery, Mint, Rue and Betony.*
29.	hem wel in gote*s* milk and late *the* seke	
30.	sope it hote. -----	

In left margin: **Purgam:**   *Tr.: A purge.*

                      -----Take Laureal and make   *Spurge Laurel.*

Image 101 Right, Folio 97r

1.	poudir therof and temp it with hony, of a*ther*
2.	ylike moch, and gif *the* seke. For hym *that*
	of ather ylike moch: the same amount of both.
	Lines 2 onwards are repeated, with variations in text and order in Sloane 3285 Fol 93r to 95v.
3.	hath **no talent to mete**, take Centory *no talent to mete: no appetite.*
	Centory: *Common Centaury.*
4.	and seth it wel in stale ale, & whe*n* it is wel
5.	sodun do it in a mort*ur* and temp it small, and
6.	do *tha*t age*n* into *the* pot and seth it well. And *then*
7.	streyn it, and *tha*n take ij. p*ar*ties of *tha*t licour
8.	and *the* thrid p*ar*te of hony, but boile it and
9.	skome it and mell he*m* well to gid*er* and gif
10.	the seke to drynk iij. sponefull ilk day fasting
11.	till he be hole. **For alle evyls in a ma*n*s**
12.	~~body~~ **stomake**: Re*cipe* Ache sede, Lyne sede and *Smallage or Parsley, Linseed.*
13.	Comyn of ilkon ilik, and temp *tham* wel togidur *Cumin.*
14.	and gif *the* seke w*i*th hote wate*r* to drynk. For
15.	him *that* has *the* **perilose kogh**: Take Rue and
	perilose kogh: *? consumption, EMED. In Henslow – Ms* **Sloane 2584.**
16.	Sauge, Comyn & powdur of Pep*er* and seth
	Rue, Sage, Cumin, powder of Pepper.
17.	*th*em to gidre in hony and make a letuary,
18.	and use *ther*of a sponfull at eveyn and ano*ther*
19.	at morn. **For grynding and akyng**
20.	**in *the* womb**: Re*cipe* a Vyne lef & stamp
21.	it and temp*er* it w*i*th stale ale and lete *the* seke
22.	drynk *ther*of a sponfull at onys and Pilliole *Pennyroyal.*
23.	and bynd it to hys navill as hote as he may
	Betson picks up Bray Sloane 521 again at folio (229/206/9), line 8.

24.	suffur. Idem Re*cipe* Rwe and stamp it *with* salt	
25.	and temp it *with* ale or *with* wa*ter* and gife *the*	
26.	seke to drynk. **For a man that has evel**	
27.	**in his bak**: Take Ach & Egrimony and sta*mp*	*Agrimony*
28.	hem wel togider and do *ther*to bore grece &	
29.	asill & fry *them* well and make a plais*ter* & lay	*Asill: vinegar*
30.	itto as hote as he may suffry to the sore	
31.	side. **For *the* flix:** take Hencresse and	

flix: flux – diahorrea. **Hencresse**: *Shepherd's Purse.*
This remedy from image 101 right, folio 97r, line 31 above, to image 102 left, folio 97v, line 11 below, also occurs with some variations, in Sloane 3285 at folio 2, lines 12-22.

Image 102 Left, Folio 97v

1.	croppis of Wodebynde and stamp *them* and	*Honeysuckle.*
2.	temp *th*am *with* warm rede wyn and gif	
3.	*the* seke drynk and lete him ete iij daies	
4.	ilk day frost v. lek*es with th*arf brede that	

frost: first; **tharf brede**: *unleavened bread.*

5.	is hote and drynk but rede wyn warn	*warn: read:'warm'.*
6.	and lete him sit un a stole *with* a segge	*a 'segge stool' or 'commode'.*
7.	and make *ther*under a litle chare cole fire	
8.	and lete him be closid *with* a cloth don	
9.	to the erth *that the* hete may passe up into	
10.	the fundement and lete him sit theron as	
11.	yern as he may sitt, to he be hote. **For**	*yern: willing.*
12.	**the stone, a gode medycyn:** Recipe Gromel	*Gromel: Common Gromwell.*
13.	and pale rede Nettill, Violet & Ach and	*Ach: Smallage or Parsley.*
14.	bray them in a stone mortell and cheris	*bray: pound, crush.*
15.	tons kirnels and bray *them* in a brasyn	*cherrystone kernels.*
16.	mortar and put *them* in a pot of erth and	
17.	do *ther*to white wyn and lete hem seth	
18.	over *the* fire and so lete hem stande in	
19.	the same vessill and gif *the* seke to dry*n*k	
20.	lewk warm and *that* shal make him hole.	
21.	**For a man *that* mai not well pisse:**	

Lines 21-24 are also in Sloane 3285 at folio 3, Lines 23-27.

22.	Take Rewe, Gromell and P*er*cel, and stamp he*m*	*Rue, Gromwell, Parsley.*

247

23.	and mell *tham* wi*th* wyn and gif *the* seke to	
24.	drynk warm. ---	
	Betson's text here ceases to follow Sloane Ms 521.	
	-----For hym that hath a	
25.	**skaldid pyntill**: Take lyncloth that	
	skaldid pyntill: an inflamed penis.	
26.	is wasshen cle*ne* and bryn it and make *ther*of	
27.	poud*ur,* and take oyle of eggis and anoint	
28.	the sore and put *the* poud*ur* in the holis wha*n*	
29.	*the*i be anoyntid. ------	
	-------//**Laxativum**: Take Malues and Mer-	Hollyhock.
30.	cury and seth wi*th* a mese of pork and	Mercury: ?Dog's Mercury.

Image 102 Right, Folio 98r

1.	make therof potage and lete the seke ete	
2.	hem and drynk whyte wine and *that* shal	
3.	make hi*m* soluble. **For fete** that ben swol-	***soluble***: *unconstipated. EMED.*
	Lines 30 to 3 above also occur in Dawson (page 72, para 186)	
	and Sloane 521 at folio 271 /208/11, Line 16.	
4.	len wi*th* travell: Take Mugwort and stamp it	Wormwood.
5.	and do *ther*to boris grece and fry	boar's grease.
6.	*th*em togid*ur* and make a plaist*ur ther*of and	
7.	ley thereto. **For the syngles**, a good med-	shingles.
	Sloane 521 at Folio 231 /208/11 r, Line 25, verbatim.	
8.	ycin. It is a malady and it is rede in	
9.	maner of wild firen and it is wondre perilose	
10.	for if it but lepe a man he shall be dede sikir	*lepe a man*: perhaps 'encircle' .
11.	ly. And *there*fore take dof drite that is moist	dove droppings.
12.	and barly meal of au*ther* half a ponde	*auther: of both*
13.	and stamp hem wel togidre and so lay it	
	Sloane 521 adds 'half a pint of good vinegar.' Folio 231 /208/11v, Lines 8-9.	
14.	colde unto *the* sore and ley wort*is* levis a-	
15.	bof to holde in the lico*r* and bynd a cloth	
16.	above all aboute him and let it ly iij	
17.	daies unremevid and on *the* thrid day,	
18.	if it be nede, refressh wi*th* new and at *the* most	

19.   he shall be hole within iii plaisturs

20.   **For the Morphew, whyte or blak**: Take ℥.j.   *one ounce of verdigris*

    *Morphew: 'a skin disease characterized by leprous or scurfy eruptions; **blak ~**, a morphea arising from the humor melancholy and characterized by dark scabs; **white ~**, a morphea arising from the humor phlegm; also, leprosy.' EMED.*

21.   of Vertgrece, another of White Brimstone   *Vertgrece: verdigris.*

    Betson, Lines 21-30: in both Sloane 521 and BL Sloane 3285, folio 94, lines 32 to 38 (Remedy Collection A).

22.   and make them both in poudur as small as
23.   you may and take ij shepe hedis that ar fat
24.   and clef the headis and take out the braynes   *clef: separate, cleave.*
25.   and wassh hem clene and seth hem til thei be
26.   tendur and then take down thi vessill and lete it
27.   kele, and gedure the grece and tempur it   *gedure: work the grease.*
28.   with the powdur and make an oyntment
29.   thereof but let it negh no fire for it shulde   *negh: near.*
30.   be wrought colde. **For the gulsough**:   *gulsough: jaundice.*
31.   Take Worduode and seth it in water and   *Wormwood.*

Image 103 Left, Folio 98v

1.   wessh wel the seke therin twise or thrise and
2.   gif the seke to drynk Evory shavyns in wyn.   *Evory : ivory shavings in wine.*
3.   **For a norissh that wolde have milk**:   *norissh: a wet-nurse.*
4.   Take Verveyn and drynk with wyn or
5.   Fenell and ete Letuce and buttur and drink
6.   wyn with Fenell sede, or take Cristall and brek   *crystallized quartz.*
7.   it and make poudur therof and drynk it with milk.
8.   **For to wite whether a mann shal lif or dy**
9.   **that hath the menesoun.** Take a peny   *menesoun: dysentery.*
10.   weight of Touncresse sede and gif the seke

    Touncresse: *Garden cress, Lepidium sativum. EMED.*

11.   to ete and gif him to drink rede wyn or
12.   watur and do thus iij. daies and if he staunch
13.   he may lif with help and if he do not he is
14.   but dede. **For a shepe louse crepen**
15.   **into a man's hede or beestis**: Take juse of
16.   Wormode or of Rewe or juse of Sothernwode &   *Wormwood, Rue, Southernwood.*

17.	do it into *th*in her.	*Rub into thine hair*

Betson ceases to follow Sloane 521 at folio (233/210/12), line 4, perhaps indicated by // below.

//For *the* ake of *the* hede:

18.	Take Rew and Fenell and seth hem wel	
19.	to gider in wat*er* and wassh *the* seke hede	
20.	and *ther*of make a plaastur as it is before.	
21.	//**For yyen *th*at ar goundy**: Take Arne-	*goundy*: gummed-up eyes.
22.	ment and hony and white of ane ege	

Arnement: Vitriol. Iron sulphate, copper sulphate, or a mixture of the two. EMED.

23.	and temp*er* th*em* wel togider and anoynt	
24.	the sor*en* yyen when he goth to bed. **For**	
25.	**to make a faire white face**: Take	
26.	fressh bore grese and the white of an	
27.	eye and mell *th*am well togidur w*ith* *the* poud*ur*	*eye*: egg.
28.	of Bays and anoynt *th*i face *ther*with al about.	

Betson ceases to follow Sloane 521 at Folio 235/212/12, Line 6, as perhaps indicated by // below.

29.	//**A noyntment for sore yyen proved**:	
30.	Take vynagir and put it in a clene basin	
31.	and the juse of Slos and plain Aloen and	*slos*: sloes; **aloen**: aloes.

Image 103 Right, Folio 99r

1.	mell *th*am well togid*ur* and cov*er* thy vessell	
2.	and so lete it stande iij daies and iij nyght*es* &	
3.	*th*en do it into a box and do *ther*of into *the* sore yyen.	
4.	Item take a jordan pot much usid & put out	*jordan pot*: a chamber pot. EMED.
5.	all *the* watur and take *the* creme of mylk and	
6.	ley it in a bason & cov*er* the creme w*ith* *the* seid	
7.	pot a day or more & ley of *that* on *the* liddes	
8.	*th*at ben rede & *th*ei shal be hole. **For *the* web**	

Similar to lines 8-13 in Sloane 3285 at fol 5v, lines 4-7.

9.	**in *the* iye**: Take *the* gall of an hare and hony	
10.	purid, of au*ther* ilik, and mell *th*am well togid*ur*	

of au*ther* ilik: *the same amount of both.*

11.	and w*ith* a fedur ley it on *the* sore yy*en* and it
12.	shall breke it w*ith*in iij nyghtes and sane *th*i

250

13. sight. **For a manis molde that is donn**:
    Lines 13-19 also in Sloane 3285 fol.7 lines 1-6.
    molde: *crown of the head, perhaps the fontanelle.*
14. Re*cipe* a gode quantite of levis of Egrimonye &   *Agrimony.*
15. wassh hem and grynde and do *ther*to a gode
16. quantite of lif hony and lat hem fry wel
17. to gid*er* and lat shave the hede as far as
18. *th*e plaist*ur* shal ly, and ley *th*e plaist*ur* on as hote
19. as *th*ou may suff*ur*. ------

In the right margin: **Nosto pr*o*batum**

        -----**For mygryme in *th*e**   *migraine*
20. **hede and for dropsy in the hede and**
21. **for *th*e fevere in *th*e hede & for *th*e ake**
22. **in *th*e hede:** Take iij. penyweight of *th*e
23. rote of Pellitary of Spayn and half a pe-   *Pellitory of the Wall.*
24. nyweight of Spikenard and grynde it to   *Spikenard, or Valerian .*
25. gid*er* and boile *th*em in gode vinaigre and take
26. a gode sponfull of hony and fill a sauserful
27. of Mustard and mell *th*am well to gid*er*
28. and lete *th*e pacient use *ther*of half a spo*n*full
29. at onys, and hold it in his mouth as long
30. as he may say ij credis and *th*en spit it oute
31. into a vessel and eft take a no*th*ur and do

Image 104 Left, Folio 99v

1. *th*us x tymes or xij., agode while af*ter th*ou hast
2. ety*u*n at none, and a litill before evyn x. ty-
3. mes or xij. and algate*s* spite it oute into a ves-   **algates**: *always.*
4. sill, a basun is best. And wha*n th*ou shal go to
5. bed wassh *th*i mouth clene and drynk a dra*u*gh*t*
6. a*n*d ~~god~~ go to *th*i bed and use thre iij dayes,
7. and take oute *th*e foule glet, and heve it up
   gleu: *'viscous medicinal preparations made from vegetable matter'. EMED.*
8. *with* a stik, for it wole rope as it wer*e* birdes
   See BL MS Sloane 3825, f3., lines 14-22, for a similar remedy.
9. lyme. *Th*is medycyn is provid. **For *th*am *th*at be**

251

10.	**poysond**: Take a penyweight *tha*t is calde	
11.	Simphony and temp*er* it *with* woma*n*'s urine and	
	Symphony: henbane, (Hysocamus niger) ?.	
12.	gif it *the* seke to drynk. **For all gouts**: R*ecipe*	
13.	Take an ole and poule him and opyn him	**ole**: *owl;* **poule**: *pluck.*
	Similar in Dawson p206, para 655, Henslow MS A, Line 15, p19,	
	and Sloane 3285 fol3v, lines 14-32. Also in Culpeper (Last Legacy) as late as 1671.	
14.	as *th*ou wolde ete him, and salt him wel and	
15.	do him in an erthyn pot, and ley a bord	
16.	*ther*on and set it into a litle hoven where me*n*	
17.	set in dogh. And wha*n* me*n* draw forth, lok if *th*i	
18.	oule be ynough for to make poud*ur*, and if	
19.	it be not, lat it stand still to it be ynough,	
20.	and *th*en bet it to powd*ur* and temp*er* it *with*	
21.	bore grese, and anoynt *the* seke by the fire.	
22.	**For swelling of a ma*n*'s yerde**: Take	
	*See also BL Sloane MS 3285, f29r, lines 21-23, where '**yerde**' (penis) is replaced by 'pintel.'*	
23.	lekys *with* all *the* fasynge*s* and wessh *th*am and	
	***fasynges**: the small rootlets at the base of leeks.*	
24.	stamp *th*em and fry *th*em in bore grese and make	
25.	a plaist*ur* and lay aboute *the* yerde.	

Betson picks up the Sloane 521 text again here, at Fol 236/213/16, Line 14, but transposing the entries at Line 26 and 6 below.

For all

26.	**maner swellyng of leggis or of fete**:	
27.	Take welcresse and shrede it small and	*common water cress.*
28.	do it in an erthyn pot and do *ther*to wyn	
29.	dregges and whete bran and wethur talow	
	***Wethur talow**: fat from a wether (a castrated ram).*	
30.	of ilkon ilike by weight and seth *th*em	
31.	well to gidd*ur* to *th*ei be right thyk and take	

Image 104 Right, Folio 100r

1. a lyn cloth and bynd it aboute *the* swelling as
2. hote as *the* seke may suff*ur* it & so lete it be still
3. a nyght & a day unremevyd and wha*n* thou ta-
4. kis it awey ley *ther*to fressh as hote as he may

5.   suffre it, & *th*at shal swage *th*e swellyng and
6.   cease the ake. **For ake in a mannys lendis**:
        lendis: loins and lower body.
7.   Take *th*e rote of Smalach and clene it & wash   *Wild Celery.*
8.   sta*m*p and temp*er* it *with* stale ale and boile it
9.   wel to gid*er* & strene it and gif *th*e seke to drink
10.   at eve*n* hote, at morow cold. **For strokis *th*at**
11.   **ar blo and not brokin**: Take *th*e juse of
        strokis that ar blo: bruises that are blue, and have not broken the skin.
12.   Wormode and hony and ~~medldke~~ mede wax &
13.   bore grese and poud*ur* of Comyn, of ilkow ilik   *each one the same.*
14.   by weight, and fry hem all to gid*er* and make
15.   a plaist*ur* and ley it to *th*e sore and *th*is shal do
16.   awey the blaknesse. **For *th*e jaundis and**
17.   **golsough**: Re*cipe* harde spaynes sope and a litle
        Betson picks up BL MS Sloane 521 at Folio 239/216/19, line 2.
        Golsough: Variant of 'yelowsought' See image 95 left, folio 90v, line 28,
        'yellow jaundice.' EMED.
18.   ale in a cup and rub *th*i sope ayen *th*e cup boto*m*
19.   to *th*i ale be white and shave *th*ereover every,   *every: ivory.*
20.   and lete *th*e seke drink. -------
        Betson omits two short remedies in Sloane 521, then continues the text:

        ------- **For wymen**
21.   **pappis *th*at aken and be rancled**: Re*cipe*   *rancle: to fester, swell. EMED.*
22.   Groundeswall and Dayse *th*at is Pety Cousell   *Groundsel and Daisy.*
23.   a delle Grounswall and the iij[de] pte Daise and   *a delle: one part.*
24.   wassh the*m* and stamp the*m* and drynke the*m* *with*
25.   stale ale first and last. -------

In the right margin: **pro*n*ostica*t*io vite et mor*t*is vuln*er*ati**
        Tr.: to predict the life or death of a wounded person.

        ----- <u>Re*cipe* Moushere</u>   *Mouse Ear Hawkweed.*
26.   *a*nd stamp it small and *(read: 'with')* stale ale and gif
27.   him to drynk and if he cast it, he shal be   *cast: vomit.*
28.   dede & if he kepe he shal lyve. ------
        The English text Lines26-28 reflects the Latin of Mowat, Alphita, p.144, for
        Pilocella, (Mouse Ear Hawkweed): " bibita a vulnerato, si evomuerit morietur, si non, vivet."
        Betson resumes Sloane 521 at folio (240/217/20) Line 19.

In the right margin: **Alia de non vulnerato sed egrotato**

    Tr.: Another (method) to predict for someone not wounded, but sick.

          -----R*eci*pe Urine

29. of him *t*hat is seke, and kast it on a Rede Ne-
30. till at ones whan he hath pist, and come
31. agen at *t*he morow and if *t*he Netill be not
32. dede, it is a token of lif. And if it be dede, he

Image 105 Left, Folio 100v

1. shal dy. -----

    Betson omits several Sloane 521 remedies, but resumes below lines 1-3.

    -----For the kanc*u*r in a Woma*n*'s pappis:

2. Take *t*he penn*s* of *t*he white gose, and *t*he juse   **penn*s***: *feathers.*
3. of Cellidony and bray *t*hem well to gider and   *Greater Celandine; pound, crush.*
4. ley *t*her*o*f to *t*he sore pappe. **To make *t*hem**
5. **swete *t*hat is seke**: Take dry Cummyn and   ***swete***: *sweat*

    See similar at BL MS Sloane 3285, folio 23v, lines 23-24, and folio 24r, lines 1-5.

6. make poud*u*r *t*her*o*f and mell it *w*ith oile de Olif
7. and *w*ith bore grece and fry *t*hem to gider
8. well and *t*hen facene *t*hem and do it in boistis

    ***f*acene**: *shape* **boistis**: *boxes or vials, EMED.*

9. and anoynt *t*he seke agen a chercole fire
10. und*er* *t*he fete and *t*he armys and do him a
11. bade and hill him warm. **For *t*he colik**:

    bade and hill him: *bathe and cover him.*

12. R*eci*pe Lauriall and powd*u*r it and do hony *t*her*t*o   *Spurge Laurel.*
13. nd ete *t*her*o*f a sponefull or two. **For teth**
14. *t*h*a*t **roggen**: R*eci*pe horsmere and a*n*oynt thi toth

    roggen: *shake;* **horsmere**: *horsedung. EMED.*

    See similar at BL MS Sloane 3285, Folio 39v, lines 21-23.

15. and *t*hi cheke. *T*his is proved. **To sle wor-**
16. **mys in *t*he teth**: Take *t*he rote of Henbane
17. and kerve a small shyve *t*her*o*f and ley it to
18. *t*he teth iij. nyght*i*s. **For *t*he stomake en-**
19. **glemed**: R*eci*pe a sauc*e*rfull of clarified hony

    englemed: *perhaps affected by phlegm.*

20. and a sauc*e*rfull of gode venegre and half a

254

21.	saucerfull of Mustard and xx or xxx Pep*er*	
22.	Corny*es* stampid in a mortar and vj. Sauge	
23.	levys, hakkid small, and meng all togider	**meng**: *to mix or mingle.* EMED .
24.	& seth it not but a little in a clene vessel,	
25.	and *th*en take a gode sponfull of *th*at same	
26.	lic*or* in *th*i mouth as hote as *th*ou may suff*ur*	
27.	it, first at morn when *th*ou art fastyng,	
28.	and travers it well in *th*i mouth and in	
29.	thy throte, to it benygh and colde, and *th*en	
	to it benygh and cold: *until it is almost cold.*	
30.	spitte it oute and do *th*us iiij. or v. tymes	

Image 105 Right, Folio 101r

1.	to gidere and aft*er* if *the* nede, and loke wel *that*	
2.	noun passe *th*i throte. **To make a gode**	Not*a*
3.	**stomake:** Re*cipe* a handfull of Redemynt and	
4.	a handfull of Comyn and sta*mp* them to gider a litle	
5.	and *th*erwith cro*mm*ys of sow*er* brede and temp*er*	
6.	*th*at up *with* fyne vynag*er* or alegre so *th*at it	
	Alegre: *Soured ale, malt vinegar.* EMED.	
7.	be thyk and make a plaist*er* ther*of* and *th*en do it	
8.	in a pokket of lyn*en* cloth and chauf it at *the*	
9.	fire to it be hote and *th*en bynd it to *the* sto-	
10.	make as hote as *th*ou may suffre and when	
11.	it kelis and dryeth, chauf it ag*en* at *the* fire.	
12.	and moist it ag*en with* vynagre and use *th*is oft.	Explic*it*
13.	**Forto make oyle Rosett**	
	See similar at BL Sloane MS 3285, folio 6, lines 4-18.	
14.	Take half a pounde of Rosys *that* er gederid	
15.	erly whilis *the* dewe lasts and be full spredd,	
16.	and put of *the* croppes and clipp*en* them *with* a pair	
17.	of sher*es* on small pec*es*, and do hem into a	
18.	glass vessill & put *ther*to oile de Olif of *the* gre-	
19.	nest. And mell *th*am well to gid*er* in the vessill,	
20.	and stop well *th*i wessill and hing it ag*en*	
21.	*the* sonn xx dayes, and *th*en draw it thorew	
22.	a kanvas, and put it into *the* vessel of glas	

23.	and kest awey the groundis of the rosis, and	
24.	stop well thi vessell that thermay none ever	
25.	come oute. And everilkday on the mornyng,	
26.	when thou shalt heng forth thi pot bifore	
27.	it be wrought, take a spater of tre and stur	*spater of tre: wooden spatula.*
28.	it well, and stop agen during xx. daies.	**Alio modo**
29.	Recipe of Roses and of oyle of ather ilike and	*Tr.: by another method.*
30.	shrede hem & do hem to gider in a vessell	

Image 106 Left, Folio 101v.

1. of glas, and heng it in a vessill full of water
2. up to the nek during ij. monethis, & ech dai
3. stere it ounys and stop it ayen. And streyn it
4. aftur thorow a canwas, and do awei the grondes
5. of the Rosis, and put it in a vessill of glas,
6. for this is colder of kynd then the other. A pre-
7. cious water **to draw awey perle or**
8. **haw** whether it be and to clarifi [*eyes –sketch*]
   > *perle or haw: morbid growth in the eye. EMED.*
   > *Also: London, British Library, Harley 2378.*
9. Recipe: rede roses Smalage and Rwe, Verveyn
10. and Maidenhere, Eufrace, Endiss, Sengren, Hil-
11. wort, Rede Fenell, Celidon, of ilkon half a quart
    > *1½ ounces each of Red Roses, Smalage, Rue, Vervain, Maidenhair fern, Eyebright, ?Endive*
    > *Sowthistle, or Corn Sowthistle, Houseleek, Pennyroyal, or Wild Thyme,*
    > *Red Fennel, Greater Celandine.*
12. and wassh hem and ley hem in gode white win
13. a day and a nyght. And aftur still hem in the first
14. watur the which wole be like golde, the secunde
15. as silver, the thrid as bawm and kepe that well,
    > *Similar recipe to above lines 6-17 in Med. Soc. of London MS 136, para 988.*
16. for it is worth bawm for all maner of mala-
17. dies for sore yyenn. ----   *sore yyenn: sore eyes*

In right margin: **pro pestilenciam optima medicina**   Similar in eVK at .k 0951K
> *Tr.: an excellent medicine for the plague.*
-----Take Fetherfuge and

18.	Matfelon, Mugwort, Solsecul, Scabious and	
19.	Maythes, of ilkon ilike & wassh and stamp	

Feverfew or the Lesser Centaury, Knapweed, or Silverweed, (Hunt), Mugwort,
Garden Marigold; Scabwort or Knapweed; Stinking Camomile or similar plant.

20.	hem with stale ale and gif the seke to drink	
21.	vj. sponfull at ons. // **For to make**	
22.	**oile of Rwe**: Take a perte oile de olif and	*a parte: one part.*
23.	the fourte perte of wyn and put therto agode	
24.	quantite of Rwe and seth hem all togider	
25.	to the wyn be wasted and wryng it than tho-	
26.	rough a kanvas. **Unguentum geneste**: Take	*Tr.: Ointment of Broom.*
27.	floures of Brome and Wodwis and stamp	

Broom, Dyer's Greenweed.

28.	them to gider with may buttur and lete them	
29.	stande all a nyght, and on the morow melt	*a nyght: one night.*
30.	hem in a pan, and purifie it thorow a kan-	
31.	vas. This oyntment is gode for almaner colde sores or colde goute.	

Image 106 Right, Folio 102r,

1.	**Pro omni vitio oculorum & experta**: Recipe Feniculi	*Not in eTK.*
2.	Vervene, Rose, Cellidonie, Rute, Agrimonie, Pim-	
3.	pernelle, Sanamunde, Filaginis, Eufrasie, Caprifolii,	
4.	Betonice, de virgis coruli suspensis, foliis propa-	*hung from Hazel rods.*
5.	gine vitis terantur in mortario et aspergatur vinum al-	
6.	bum tunc imponetur de pulvere lapidis Calaminaris	
7.	tritici, Aloes Epatice, Camphore, ana, et distillentur len-	
8.	te igne.	

Fennel, Vervain, Roses, Rue, Greater Celandine, Agrimony, Scarlet Pimpernel,
Herb Bennet, Avens, ?Cudweed; Eyebright Honeysuckle, Betony, Calamine or Zinc Carbonate,
Aloes, Liverwort Camphor Laurel.

In right margin: **AQUA EUFRASIE**		*Not in eTK.*
9.	Aqua Eufrasie sic fit: extrahatur aqua	
10.	de foliis eufrasie singularia et specialia sunt	*Eyebright.*
11.	aqua huius lacrimas de causa calida constringere,	
12.	et intercipere palpebras de calida causa tumescen-	*Palpebras: eyelids.*
13.	tes, et cancrum curare visum impeditum de fri-	

14.	gida ca*usa* clarificare, maculas de frigida ca*usa*	.
15.	constringere.	

In right margin: **Aqua rosarum contra febrilem calorem:** *Not in eTK.*
                Extrahitur eodem modo.

16.	Singularia et specialia huius aquae sunt factae in unc	
17.	tione circa frontem et tempora et venas pulsa-	
18.	tiles, volas manuum et pedum, calorem febrilem	**volas**: *palms of the hand.*
19.	reprimere et alterare facta inunctione cir-	
20.	ca venes cerebru*m* confortat*ur*. Spiritus a*ni*males	
21.	augmentare accepta p*er* os in ca*usa* calida fluxum	
22.	ventris int*er*cipere.	

In right margin: **Aqua viole laxativa** *Not in eTK.*
                //Eod*e*m modo fit et eosdem

23.	habet effectus sed in hoc est differentia, quia
24.	illa constringit*ur*, ista de Violis relaxat. Se-

In right margin: **Aqua fabarum mundificata:**

25.	quitur de aquis mu*n*dificativis facei et p*ri*mo	
	Lines 25-29 are very similar to the BB, folio263v, col. A, lines 21-24.	
26.	de aqua fabarum quae sic fit: extrahatur aqu*a* de flo-	*Not found in eTK.*
27.	ibus fabarum ut de aliis aquis dictu*m* est. Et cu*m* ista	*Purified bean water.*
28.	aqua delineat*ur* facies et collum et manus. Sp*e*cialia	
29.	huius aque su*n*t membra dealbare, cutem atte-	
30.	nuare, et colericas maculas removere. Iterum	**colericas maculas**: *bilious spots.*
31.	pulverizata muscata conficiant*ur* cu*m* aqua	*Nutmeg or Woodruff.*

Image 107 Left, Folio 102v.

1.	p*re*dicta et fiant pillule et desiccentur in umbra et	
2.	cu*m* opris fuerit, facta fumigatione cu*m* aqua	**opris**: *for 'opus' (Latham).*
3.	decocionis palei Ordei et Avene distemperentur	
	palei Ordei: *barley chaff.* **Avene**: *oats.*	
4.	due pillule cu*m* p*re*dicta aqua et facies deliniatur	
5.	et peple*tur* per totam noctem et in crastino lavetur	**pepletur**: *is covered.*
6.	cu*m* colatura furfuris vel lotura fabarum et post	
	with sifted husks of grain, or water in which beans have been washed (?).	

258

7.   cu*m* aqua simplici istud fortius (?) habet faciem
8.   dealbatam, cutem attenuatam, maculas pannos
9.   lentigines de ca*usa* calida dissolvere et abstergere.

In left margin **Aqu*a* alia mundificativa co*ntra* morpheam**
    Tr.: A cleansing water against skin disease.
10.   Accipe flores et folia Gerse et Dragancie et   *Not found in eTK.*
11.   Brionie et extrahatur aqua et deliniatur facies, collum
    ?white lead, Dragonwort, White Bryony.
12.   et manus. Singularia et specialia huius aque
13.   sunt faciem dealbare que est ex melancolia de-
14.   nigrata maculas pannos lentigines ex fr*igida*   **lentigo**: *spot on skin.*
15.   causa abstergere et morpheam.

In left margin **De mundificati*vis***   *Tr: On Cleansing (Waters).*
        …..// Sequitur
16.   de aquis mu*n*dificativis spiritualium. Extrahatur
    (membra) **spiritualia**: *cleansing the thorax, lungs and heart.*
17.   aqua de foliis Ysopi, Satureie levistici et flo-
18.   rum Yvees, Prassii, Enulicampane, florum trifolii
19.   quod dicitur Mellilotum, illi*us* q*uia* multos flores fe*cit*
    Hyssop, Lovage , ?Ivy flowers, White Horehound, Scabwort, Melilot.
20.   ad qu*a*n*titatem* Nucis Gallice isti enim du*m* sugguntur
    Nucis Gallice: *walnut;*   **dum sugguntur**: *when they are sipped.*
21.   h*a*bent in se quasi ~~humores~~ mel vel zuccarriam.
22.   Singularia et specialia huius aque su*n*t flemati-
23.   cos humores circa spiritualia dissolvere et consu-
24.   mere, sputum attenuare et de facili expellere.

In left margin **Co*ntra* calorem spiritualium:**   **spiritualium**: *thorax, heart, lungs.*
25.   Extrahatur aqua de foliis Plantaginis, Quinque-
26.   nerviae, Torme*n*tille et Rose. Singularia et specia-
    Greater and Lesser Plantain, Common Tormentill and Roses.
27.   lia huius aque sunt si recipiatur in potu cu*m* cali-
28.   do vino, calorem spiritualium reprimit & alt*er*at ulcera
29.   facta de causa calida consolidat. Extrahatur
in left margin: Aqua de / floribus Sambuci   *Elderflower.*

30. eodem modo. Singularia huius aque su*n*t si
31. recipiatur p*er* os flemmaticos humores existe*n*-
32. tes in stomacho et intestinis dissolvere et p*er*

Image 107 Right, Folio 103r
1. ventrem expellentur, unde cibus factus de floribus
2. Sambuci, et virtutem habet laxandi fleumaticos
3. humores vel colera*m* citrina*m* vel vitellina*m* vel   *vitellina*: yellow. EMED.
4. de fleumate salso vel vitreo vel dulci et cetera.

In right margin **Aqua Ardens**
5. Fit hoc modo: recipe vini nigri vetustissimi
6. quantum op*o*rtet sulphuri utriusque auripig-
7. menti an*a* ℥ viii, calcis vive lib. j, olei co*mmun*is
8. vetustissim*um* ℥ vi. Hec omnia coque in vino tam
   eight ounces each of sulphur and orpiment, one pound of quicklime,
   and six ounces of very old common oil.
9. diu quousque ad duas partes co*n*suma*tur* tu*n*c extrahi-
10. tur p*er* embotum sicut extrahitur aqua rosis alius <u>tum</u>.
    per embotum: by means of a funnel.
11. Modus faciendum ea*m* cu*m* proprietatibus scripta
12. est alibi. ------

In right margin: **Aqua vite Perfectissima**
    -------// Pro corpore humano
13. et passionibus frigidis: Recipe Camphore ʒ ii,
14. Candi ℥ j, Mente, Salvie, Ysopi, utriusque Sci-   *one ounce*
15. cados an*a* *manipulum semis*, Tartari Albi, Picis navallis,
    two drachms of camphor laurel, one ounce of candy; **manipulus sem:** *half a handful each of*
    mint, sage Hyssop; **Pyx navallis:** *'ship tar.'*
16. Gummi Arabici, Colofonie, Terebentine, Olei Oliva*rum*
17. an*a* ℥ *sem.* salis co*mmun*is, salis gemme, an*a* ʒ ii masticis,
    half an ounce of salt; two drachms of mastic. For list of ingredients see below line 27.
18. Mellis Euforbii, Asellii Serapini, Opoponacis oli-
19. Bani, Storacis, Cynamomi, Gariofilorum, Gariofi-
20. late, Nucis Musca*tarum* an*a* ʒ ii Piretri, Alexan-
    two drachms of these ingredients: see list below line 27.

21.	dri, Caparis, Squinanti, Spodii, Pip*eris* Longi an*a*

two drachms of these ingredients: see list below line 27.

22.	℥ sem*is* Zedoar, ʒ ii, Muscu*m* bonu*m* parum, et etiam mo-

half an ounce of Turmeric, two drachms of good musk.

23.	dicu*m* ossis de corde cervi, C*ar*pobalsami cassie
24.	ligni Aloes, Anacardi, Ambre orie*n*talis
25.	an*a* ʒ ii que su*n*t terenda terantur et gummi

of each two drachms See list of ingredients below line 27.

26.	in bono vino odorifero dissolvantur, et ponantur
27.	ad predicta, et distillentur. ------

Camphor Laurel, sugar candy, Mint, Sage, Hyssop, ?White Bryony, Houseleek, potassium tartrate, ship tar, Gum Arabic, Pine resin, Turpentine, Olive oil, common salt, Rock salt, mastix gum, Spurge Honey ?, ?Marjoram vinegar, Opoponax, Sweet or Bisabol Myrrh; Styrax officinalis, Cinnamon, Cloves, Avens, Nutmeg, Pellitory of the wall, Alexanders, fruit of the Caper Bush; Squinant, ground Ivory; black Pepper; Turmeric (?); musk, bone (or cartilage) in the ventricle of a stag's heart; Wall Germander (?), Agarwood, cashew nut, Amber?

In right margin: **Aqu*a* vite p*er*fecta lenioris compositionis**

Tr.: An Aqua Vitae of lighter composition.

------Recipe radices Sax-

28.	ifrage, Petrocilli, Feniculi, Ysopi, Timi, Pule-
29.	gii Regalis, Rosmarini de m*on*tibus an*a* ʒ iiii
30.	et lava in aqua pura et tere modicu*m* in mor-
31.	tario ana Galange, Piperis Nigri, Gariofilorum,
32.	Zinziberis, Nucis muscat, macis quibubiis Spicenardi

Image 108 Left, Folio 103v

1.	croci de omnibus videlicet quartam partem ʒ et fac	

Four drachms of each of Saxifrage roots, Parsley, Fennel, Hyssop, Thyme, Pennyroyal, Rosemary. A quarter of an ounce of each of English Galingale; Black Pepper, Cloves, Ginger, Nutmeg, Mace, Spikenard, Saffron.

2.	pulverem de speciebus et misce si*militer* pulveres	
3.	specieru*m* et herbas tritas in una lagena vini	*lagena: flask of wine.*
4.	boni rubei, quia tantu*m* sufficit et no*n* minus, et dis-	
5.	tilla qu*ando* sunt b*en*e mixta in distallatorio vitreo	
6.	et in vase vitr*e*o reserva cu*m* fuerit distillatum.	
7.	// Ista aq*ua*, s*ecun*du*m* quosdam, reputatur ita bona	
8.	sicut alia in mu*n*do. Effectus istius aque est	

9.	maxime contra omnes frigidas passiones in	
10.	corpore humano et debet sumi per os recipientis,	
11.	ieiunio stomacho, ad quantitatem unius cocliaris.	*cocliare: spoonful.*
12.	Valet enim in dolore capitis antiquo ex frigida	
13.	causa. Ex ea capite non purgato retardat ca-	
14.	niciem. Omnem scabiem curat si quolibet mane	*caniciem: grey hairs.*
15.	cum ea lavetur. Memoriam specialiter iuvat si de	
16.	ea petetur seu capud *[read: caput]* ex ea ungatur si distemperetur	
17.	cum modico tiriace, et recipiatur, ieiunio stomacho,	
18.	bis vel ter interpositis diebus curat perfecte.	
19.	Valet in appoplexia similiter administrata.	
20.	Valet contra paralisim et tremorem membrorum.	
21.	Contra vero paralisim lingue bibat predicto modo	
22.	et teneat peciolam ex aqua predicta linita super lin-	*linita: anointed*
23.	guam non tantum semel, sed bis vel ter, donec sanetur.	
24.	// Contra tortuositatem faciei ex verberatione	*ex verberatione: from a beating.*
25.	subita ungat faciem ex ea et bibat predicto	*Not found in eTK.*
26.	modo et sanabitur. Contra melancoliam et tristi-	*tristicia: sadness.*
27.	tiam quolibet: mane unum cocliare, ieiunio	*cocliare: spoonful.*
28.	stomacho, lacrimas mirabiliter sistet. // Et	
29.	mirabilis est omni gutte oculorum. // Valet	
30.	surdidati, potata et iniecta in aurem bomba-	
31.	ce missa. Valet contra dolorem dentium.	
32.	//Valet dentibus corumptis bibita, et lini-	
33.	ta, hanelitum fetidum emendat. Valet in asmate,	

Image 108 Right, Folio 104r

1. potata cum decoccione Ficuum et Liquiricie. // Valet
2. doloribus stomachi fleumaticis ventosis et me-
3. lancoliis. //Valet in opilacione epatis et splenis et
4. renum super omnem materiam. // Valet in colerica
5. frigida bibita et clisterizata. Nerves contractus
6. sanat. Omnem dolorem et omnem guttam ex frigida
7. causa curat. Ydropicum ex frigida causa in potu
8. frequentata curat si ex ea sumatur ter totidie
9. et quantitatem dimidio teste ovi // Omnem quar-

262

10. tana*m* adiunctis sibi debitis herbarum, florum, specierum
11. et radicu*m* cito sanat. Datur etiam ante accessione*m* **accessio:** *onset of fever.*
12. liberat. // Valet subtilitati ex fr*igi*da ca*usa* dissen-
13. teria*m* et lienteria*m* curat. Valet arteticis, sciaticis,
    'is of use for dysentery and the flux…gout and sciatica.'
14. in fr*igi*da ca*usa* potetur purgatione co*n*venienti p*er*-
15. missa. Vuln*eri*bus multu*m* valet si cu*m* ea laventur.
16. Cancru*m*, fistula*m*, Noli-me-tangere, omnes si-
    'Noli me tangere est aposteme venenosum faciei'. SB Mowat, p.31.
    (Tr.: **Noli me tangere** *is a poisonous swelling of the face).*
17. miles passiones curat. Venenum expellit.
18. P*er*cussus a m*er*curio vel malicia mercurii accepta
19. de eo et oleo lat*er*nio an*a* bibat, et loca lesa irri-
    oleo laternio: *with oil that has gone off.* **loca lesa:** *the injured places.*
20. get. / Vinum corruptum et acetum reparat et ad
21. pristinam bona*m* reducit, si de ea adponatur. It*em*//
22. Valet difficie*n*tib*us* appetitum cu*m* Salvia, Cerfolio,
23. Petrocilio et Pip*ere* // Item contra fluxu*m* ventris
    Sage, Honeysuckle, Parsley, Black Pepper.
24. et men(s)truorum et plagis putridis, et emoroidis
25. fluentibus constrinigendis. // Item valet pro pus-
26. tulis fleumata salsa et lentiginibus *[duarum?]* dolentibus.
    fleumata salsa: *phlegm mixed with choler, salt phlegm. EMED.*
    lentigo: *spot on skin.*
27. Item: Valet pro faciebus leprorum. Item car-
28. nes et pisces in sua naturali bonitate con-
29. servat // Item si camphora modico temp*o*ris
30. spatio in hac aqua reservetur, remanerit aqua
31. clara sicut prius et retinet in se virtute ca*m*
32. phore ad delendum maculam oculo*rum* et ista aq*ua*
33. camphorata infundatur s*uper* aq*ua*m commune coagu-

Image 109 Left, Folio 104v
1. latur ad modum lactis albissimi. Item: valet
2. contr*a* tortuositate*m* faciei ex obumbratione solis
3. facta si ex ea facies ungatur //Item ista dissolu-
4. it aurum calcinatum in aq*uam* convertendum corp*o*ra
    aurum calcinatum: *an ingredient for potable gold. EMED.*

5. leprosorum et transmutandum ea ad veram sani-
6. tatem ex egritudine lepre. Item ista ponat*ur*
7. loco Balsami secure et si balsamus esset coniunctus
8. cu*m* ea melior esset quoniam tunc h*ab*eret omnes vir-
9. *[tu]*tes balsami, et sine ipso non. Omnes istas vir-
10. tutes habet quelibet aq*ua* vite, et plures alias.

In left margin: **Aqua ardens non ledens**   **non ledens:** *not harmful.*

    aqua ardens *may have been methanol, a different distillate to aqua vitae.*

11. Fit etiam isto modo: Recipe ollam et imple eam   *Not in eTK.*
12. semiplene vino rubeo *[inserted above: et sale]* et coop*er*i eam et fac bullire
13. et cu*m* fuerit bullitum discooperi et appone candelam
14. ardentem fumo et ardet. -----

In left margin: **Aqua ardens et ledens**   **ledens:** *harmful.*

    Lines 15-19 below are almost identical to Mirfield's Breviarium, folio 262r, col. A, line 48.
    But the other 'Aqua Ardens' texts in Betson differ greatly from those of Mirfield.

                       ------Eodem modo fit sic*ut*

15. aqua ardens non ledens sed in loco salis debemus
16. imponere pulverem Sulphuri, vini et Colofonie et debet
    Sulphur, wine, Pine resin.
17. distillari modo p*re*dicto et ista ardet omnem rem.

In left margin: **Aqua ardens no*n* lede*n*s**

18. Re*cipe* Tartari albi sulphuris// ledendo
19. vini Colofonie accipe salis tosti ad maiore*m* quantita-
    sal tostus*: heated or melted common salt.*
20. te*m* vini rubei ad medietatem vasis distallatur
21. igne lentissimo. Si linias pannum ex hac, arde-   **linias pannum:** *smear a cloth.*
22. bit sine p*er*ditione sue [*suae*] substantie et si aliq*uis* h*ab*eat
23. capud flemmaticu*m* potet de liquore isto et
24. consumetur illud fleuma sine dampno cerebri
25. et valet ad consumptionem flemmatis, pa*ra*lisis
26. litargie, et ad gutta*m* potatur. ----   **litargie:** *lethargy, coma.*

    Lines 30-37 below are very similar to BB Folio 266r, col. A, lines 50-54.

In left margin: **Aqua silicis**   *Tr.: Flint Water.*

                        ------//Hoc modo debetur

27. fieri: Recipe silices nigras et frange in p*ar*vas
28. pecias et calefac diu inter prunas, quousque   **prunas:** *live coals.*

29. fuerint albe et pone postea in distillatorio
30. et asperge super cilices *(sic)* dum sint calide aliquantulum
31. aceti, et magnum fac ignem in circuitu et fac
32. distillare et ardet sicut aqua ardens et valet
33. contra guttam frigidam. **Aqua que dicitur**

Image 109 Right, Folio 105r

1. **Lac Virginis**: Recipe ℥ iiii salis petre   *Four ounces.*
2. et unam unciam spume vitri et dissolve ea in aqua
     spuma nitri / vitri: sodium carbonate, washing soda.
3. calida. Post distilla per filtrum. Deinde recipe vi ℥
4. Litargiris et dissolve in aceto albo fortissimo,
     Six ounces of Litarge (?lead monoxide; ?litharge of silver). EMED.
5. quia melius est quam acetum rubeum, si poterit reperiri,
6. et distilla per filtrum et misce has duas aquas
7. simul et vertentur ad modum lactis et ideo vocatur
8. lac virginis // Ista aqua valet ad cutem subti-
9. liandam et pulcram reddit faciem et lucidam et valet
10. omnibus apostematibus et virge virili et cancro
11. et contra salsum fleuma et guttam rosaceam et contra
     salsum fleuma: *'phlegm mixed with choler, salt phlegm.' EMED.*
     guttam rosarum *or* ***gutta rosacea*** *, swelling, redness of the face. EMED.*
12. plures alias infirmitates. -----

In right margin: **Aquamellis**

                              ----// Recipe mel bonum
13. et fac inde aquam. Primam aquam serva per se et etiam
14. secundam. Si prima aqua fuerit alba, omne nigrum
     Similar for Aquamel in Ashmole 1447 (18) p.216.

In left margin: valet ad capillos restaurandos, et [eos crescere et ?] facit, et destruit
                    vermes capillos corrodentes.

15. dealbescit et alia ~~nigra~~ aqua nigrescit et palescit.

In right margin: **Aqua aurea et viridis**

16. Aqua que erit aurea super nigrum et viridis
17. super album. Recipe arsenicum, sanguinem vitri et cu-
18. peros, per equales porcionces. Resolvantur in aqua aceti

19. et tunc distilla in vase vitreo que erit aurea super
20. nigrum, et viridis super album. //....

In right margin: **Aqua m***irabilis* (?)

......Ad visum clari-
21. ficandum: et si uno tempore vis facere unam fio-
22. lam vitream plenam, continentem decem coclearia magna:
    fiola vitrea: glass vial. ***cocliareria***: *spoonfuls.*
23. Recipe unam patellam eneam bene mundatam et in
    patellam eneam: *a brass or copper plate.*
24. fundo pone de pulvere calcis vivi ad quantitatem
25. unius coclearis et dimidii vel duorum ad maximum,   **cocliaris**: *spoonful.*
26. et infundas de aqua clara xi coclearia vel xii.
27. Postea unam petram salis armonici ad quan-   *ammonium chloride.EMED.*
28. titatem magne nucis. Et fincens illam petram   read: fingens – *moulding.*
29. bene cum manu in medio cum aqua et pulvere
30. calcis vive [sic] quousque aqua incipiat habere colorem
31. azureum, et quanto magis resolvitur de sa-
32. le armoniaco, tanto magis erit clarior

Image 110 Left, Folio 105v

1. et magis azurei coloris et quando bene habet colo-
2. rem azureum et est bene simul commixtum, facias
3. aquam istam de pelvi distillari per filtrum et   **pelvis**: *large basin.*
4. violam vitream ubi conservare volueris. Is-
5. ta enim aqua bene valet quamdiu color azureus
6. durat quando tamen vertitur in albedinem, non valet.
7. Quando ergo volueris uti ista aqua, accipe bom-   **bombax**: *cotton.*
8. bacem parvum vel parvum pannum lineum bene mun-
9. dum et intingas in aquas modice. Caveas tamen
10. quod non capias tantum de aqua quod distallat
11. a bombace vel a panno in oculum, ne oculus
12. periat et quo volueris uti, claudas oculos et oculi
13. sint clausie, illinias super oculos cum bombace   **illinias**: *anoint*
14. vel panno lineo humido et sic teneas ocu-
15. los clausos per modicum tempus quousque sentias
16. cum manu quod aqua intus (?) siccatur. Ista Aqua

17. mirabili*er* tollit obscuritate*m* ~~oeu~~ visus
18. visu*m* ultra modu*m* clarificat si h*a*beatur in usu
19. *p*er aliquod tempu*s*. …

In left margin: **Aqua Preciosa**

                              …..// Herba *p*reciosa her-
20. barum et est mirabilis in virtute ad visum

> *eTK.k 1324I has similar remedy, from the Tractatus mirabilium aquarum*
> *(De preciosa aqua ad oculos) by Petrus Hispanus, beginning:*
> *'Recipe feniculi, ruthe, verbene, euffragie, endive' as line 23 below.*

21. conservandum nec*n*o*n* clarificandum et contr*a*
22. omnem maculam in oculo, que sic fit: recipe Rute,
23. Feniculi, Vervene, Eufrasie, Endivie, Beto-
24. nice, Sileris Montane, Rose Rubie, Capilli
25. Ven*e*ris, an*a* p*e*r di*em* et nocte*m,* in albo vino ponat*ur.*

> *Rue, Fennel; Vervain, Eyebright; ? Sowthistle, Betony, ?Sweet Marjoram,*
> *Red Roses, Maidenhair Fern.*

26. Sec*un*do die in distillatorio ponatur et quod *p*rimo
27. distillaverit est quasi auru*m* et quod 2° quasi
28. argentum et quod 3° quasi Balsamu*m.* Servet*ur*
29. in ampulla vitrea et cu*m* opus fuerit mulie-
30. ribus et delicatis, det*ur* pro balsamo. // Per
31. qua*m* facit medicus mistica et mirabilia. Sic

Image 110 Right, Folio 106r

> *This section lines 1- 13 loosely follows Sloane 1754, folio 27v, lines 12 – 25.*
> *It is also similar to an Incipit in eTK with five examples - k 0021B.*

In left margin: **Aqua mirabilis:**

1. fit: Recipe limaturas argenti, eris, ferri, calibis   *limaturas: scrapings of silver.*
2. *[illegible]* auree et argentee storacis, sec*undum* divitias
3. et pauperitates patientis. Ponant in urina pueri
4. prima die; 2ᵃ die in vino albo calido; 3ᵗᵃ die in
5. succo Feniculi; 4ᵃ die in albumine ovorum; vᵃ die
6. in lacte mulieris; vi*ᵗᵃ* die in vino rubeo;
7. septi*m*a die in albuminibus ovorum et omnia ista pona*ntur*
8. in distillatorio et ad lentum ignem distellentur
9. et quod distillaverit, reservabis in vase aureo

10. vel argenteo. De laude istius *est* omnino
11. silendum qui potest emi *pretio*. Eius virt*us*
12. est p*ar*alisim, leprosos, lepra*m* no*n* vera*m* destruere
13. et om*n*em maculam destruit. Conservat iuventutem
14. pulcra*m*, oculum sup*er* om*n*ia facit pulc*rum*.

In right margin: **Aqua Aromatica:**

15. les et matronas: Recipe Nucem Muscatam, Gariofilos, Ci-
16. -namomu*m* at aliquantulu*m* Camphore atque Mille-

   Nutmeg, Cloves, or Asarabacca, Cinnamon, Camphor Laurel, Yarrow.
   A different version of this is at BB, folio262r, col. B, line 47.

17. folii que in subtillissimu*m* pulvere*m* rediga*tur*
18. et pone in aqua rosaru*m* per diem unum et nocte*m*. Postea
19. ipsam aquam serva in ampulla vitrea et pulv-
20. ere*m* in pixide serva. Que aqua aromatica va-
21. let ad ornandum facies ea*rum* pulchras et b*ene* odo-
22. -ratas.

In right margin: **Aqua dealbativa:**

In left margin in closely written note: contra *[illegible]* in ore / p*ro* oculis r*ecipe* ruta.

   Recipe Tartarum vini albi et liga in

23. **Aqua Tartari:**   panno lineo ad califaciendum
24. **Aqua Copo*r*ose:**   quousque albu*m* fuerit. Post,
25. **Aqua Agrimonie:**   pone in loco ad resoluendum
26. et cu*m* liquefactu*m* fuerit
27. pone in sacco canabi et r*ecipe* aquam de illo gutta*n*-

   sacco canabi: take the liquid dripping through a hemp sack.

28. te*m* et serva quia delet lentigines, et facie*m* et manus   *lentigo: spot on skin.*
29. dealbat et si p*ar*vas pillulas feceris de arge*n*to
30. et in illam aqua*m* devenient albe ita quod
31. apparebu*n*t margarite. -----

In right margin: **Aqua corrosiva**

                -----Alio modo fit: Recipe
32. copo*r*ose viridis et sal petre, an*a* et pone in distil-
33. latorio vitrio ad lentum igne*m* ut petat fu*n*du*m*.

Image 111 Left, folio 106v.

1. Post repone igne et distilla et quod distillaverit
2. est aqua corrosiva na*m* sup*er* o*m*nia optime corrodit
3. ferrum. -----

In left margin: **Aqua de floribus malve**   *Marsh Mallow.*

    ----Extrahatur ut de aliis herbis

4. Specialia istius ~~herbe~~ aque est alterare et laxare
5. in causa calida et idem facit aquam florum Viole.   *Violet.*

In right margin **Aqua Nenufaris est flos Ungule Caballine:**

6. Aqua Nenufaris est flos Ungule Cabal-   *White or Yellow Water Lily.*
7. line. Sed duplex e*st* Ungula Caballina maior et
8. minor. Maior croceos habet flores, m*i*nor vero
9. albos, et albis v*er*o floribus extrahatur aqua ut p*r*edictum est.
10. Valet contr*a* dolorem capitis ex calore solis, et valet
11. ad facies matronarum b*ene* refrigerandu*m*. De radici-
12. b*us* euisdem herbe fiant rotule et pona*n*tur in lixivio   *lixivium: lye, soap.*
13. et dimittant*ur* diu residere ablut*i*o istius lixivi
14. Capillos prolongat et multiplicat, alterat et cla-
15. rificat. // Aqua de foliis Caprifolii, Pim-
16. pernelle et Filaginis eodem modo extrahitur

    Honeysuckle, Pimpernel, Cudweed.

17. sicut de aliis herbis sup*er*ius dictum est. Eius
18. virtus est contra p*a*ralisim lingue et loquelam   *restores loss of speech.*
19. deperdita*m mi*rabiliter restaurat. //Aqua Plan-
20. taginis, Vervene et Morelle eodem extrahit*ur*

    Great Plantain, Vervain, Deadly or Black Nighshade.

21. sicut de aliis herbis. Eius virtus est ad oculos
22. rubicundos et inflatos. // **Aqua de virgul***is*   *virga corulii: Hazel rods.*
23. **corulii** extrahatur in distillatorio sicut de herbis.
24. Et eius virtus contr*a* oculos fissos vulnera-
25. tos et p*er*cussos. // **Aqua Terbentine** sic f*it*:   *Terbentine: Turpentine Water.*
26. Recipe Terbintinam et pone in cucurbita vitria cu*m*   *A glass cucurbit, with alembic.*
27. suo alembico b*ene* conglutinato, et distilla aq*uam*
28. p*ri*mo lento igne, postea acriori. Hanc aq*uam*,
29. si sup*er* aqua*m* vel vinum posueris et attenderis,

269

30.	ardet sup*er* ipsam similiter scintilla aut cocclear*e*	*cocliare: spoon.*
31.	unc*titur* illa aqua et si ipsam sup*er* sulphur ignitum	
32.	proieceris, dat flamma*m* horribilem et est p*r*incipa*lis*	

Image 111 Right, Folio 107r

1.	aqua ignis greci et valet sup*er* om*n*ia medicamina
2.	in passione splenis et epatis et guttis ex frigida causa
3.	et est mirabilis efficax et exp*er*ta.----

In right margin: **Aq*ua* cu*m* q*ua* possis scriber*e* i*n* calibe.**

----- Sic fit: Re*cipe*

4.	una*m* uncia*m* de sal petre, et una*m* unciam de
5.	vit*r*io romano id est cop*er*os viride et pulveriza
6.	be*ne* ista duo minutim et ponas in alembico
7.	ad distillandu*m*, et distilla eum sicut distillat*ur* aqua
8.	ardens et cu*m* ista aq*ua* sit distillata, scribe q*ui*cq*ui*d volueris
9.	in calibe et optime app*ar*ebit litt*er*a. -----

In right margin: **Aqua nobilis quam Rex Edwardus III[us] utebat*ur***

------Aq*ua*

10.	Nobilis *pro* om*n*i vit*io* oculo*rum* qua quide*m* aqua
11.	Do*mi*n*u*s Rex Edward*us* tertius utebat*ur per* conciliu*m* ma-
12.	gistri W*illel*mi de Tynchewik[137] *et* alio*rum* medico*rum*
13.	p*er*fectissimo*rum*. Re*cipe* Feniculi, Rute, Eufrasie, V*er*-
14.	vene, Turmentille, Betonice, Rose Rubee, Rostri
15.	Porcini, Gallit*r*ici, Morsus Galline, Pimp*er*nelle
16.	Rubie, Cellidonie, Filaginis, Pionie, Foliorum Vitis,
17.	Apii agrimonie, Caprifolii an*a*. Prima die trita

Fennel, Rue, Eyebright, Vervain, Common Tormentill, Betony, Red Roses, Sowthistle; Darnel, Chickweed, Scarlet Pimpernel, Greater Celandine, Cudweed, Peony, Vine leaves; **Apium agrimonie**: *perhaps for* **Apium agreste** *– Sanicle, Chervil or Smallage; Honeysuckle.*

18.	ponant*ur* in vino albo; 2º die in urina pueri
19.	masculi et virginis; 3º die in lacte mulieris;

---

[137] William of Tynechewik is not among the four doctors to Edward III listed in Gask (1926). There was, however, a Nicholas Tingewick (c.1291-1339), who was Royal Physician to Edward I and also employed by Edward II but in non-medical capacities. See C H Talbot and E A Hammond (1965), and WAY, A., (1857) – the latter cited by Getz (2010).

20.	quarto die in melle bono. Et tunc postea distil-	
21.	lentur in aqua. Bene custodias in vase vitrio quia est	
22.	aqua aquarum nobilissima pro omni causa et omni vi-	
23.	tio oculorum. -----	

In right margin **Aqua Preciosa**

-----Aqua preciosa pro oculis

24.	qui apparent pulcri et clari et tamen sunt ceci:	*caeci*: blind.
25.	Recipe Apii, Feniculi Rubii, Vervene, Betonice,	
26.	Agrimonie, Quinque Folii, Pimpernelle, Eufrasie,	
27.	Salgie, Celidonie, ana ʒ iij lava bene omnes	

*Three ounces each of Smallage; Red Fennel; Vervain, Betony,
Pimpernel, Eyebright, Greater Celandine, Sage, Creeping Cinquefoil.*

28.	istas herbas. Et postea tere in mortario et	
29.	quando sunt bene trita, impone in una patella	
30.	enea et capeas de pulvere xv grana piperis	*enea*: brazen.
31.	bene mundata totam, et unam pinctam boni	*unam pinctam*: one pint.
32.	vini albi et tria coclearia mellis boni et quinque	*cocliaria*: spoonfuls.

Image 112 Left, Folio 107v.

1.	coclearia de urina pueri masculi innocentis et	
2.	misce hec omnia simul cum herbis et postea facias	
3.	omnia ista bullire cum herbis parum. Et postea co-	
4.	la totum per unum pannum lineum mundum. Et ser-	*cola totum*: strain.
5.	va post in uno vase vitreo obturato et quando	
6.	volueris uti ista aqua misce de ista in oculo in-	
7.	firmi cum una pluma. Et si ista aqua desicca-	
8.	verit in vase adde ei vinum album et tempera	
9.	simul. Ista aqua est multum bona pro omnibus vi-	
10.	tiis oculorum et infirmitatibus, et facit hominem	
11.	videre infra xv dies, si umquam erit sanus.	
12.	Sine dubio. Ista aqua est sepius experta a quodam	
13.	magno practico. // **Aqua tollit rubidi-**	

In left margin: **Aqua**

14.	**nem faciei**: Recipe Alumen de roche ʒ. ii., alu-
15.	men glaciei ʒ. j. et fac pulverem et cum ij libris
16.	rosarum ponas in stillatorio et fac aquam. Cum ista

17. aqua unge faciem no*n* tangendo oculos.
18. Aqua Tanasie agrestis extrahatur p*er* alem-
    Tanacetum agreste: *Alphita, Mowat,p. 181, 'pulvis eius desiccat vulnera et valet contra dissinteriam. Anglice gosegres'. Silverweed (Potentilla anserina). EMED.*
19. bicum ut alie aque herbarum. Specialia huius
20. aque sunt cutem attenuare si de aqua lavet*ur*
    cutem attenuare: *to shrink the skin.*
21. et pustulas rubeas in facie delere si cu*m* ea
22. lavent*ur*. ----

In left margin: **Ardens**

                  -----// Aqua Ardens alio modo
23. fit quam supra. // Accipe sextarium unum vini ru-
    sextarium unum: *one pint.*
24. bicundissimi et vetustissimi et ponatur in
25. distillatorio et ponatur utriusque sulphuris
26. ʒ iiii; utriusque auripigme*n*ti; et aluminis, salis
    Four ounces each of Sulphur; **Auripigmentum**: *Orpiment; Arsenic sulphide;* **aluminis**: *Alum.*
27. Armoniace, Tartaris, salis co*mmun*is, mirre et olei
28. co*mmun*is vetustissimi an*a* ʒ ii. Hec omni*a* ponantur
    Two ounces each of Sal Armoniac, Tartar, common salt, Myrrh and common oil.
29. in distillatorio et distillentur et si ponat*ur* in aq*ua*, ardebit
30. et no*n* extinguetur. // Nota quod virtutes aque
31. ardentis sint Lxxiii. Sec*un*du*m* ph*i*los*oph*os ardet sine   *Lxxiii: 'numbering 73'.*

Image 112 Right, Folio 108r.

    *From * 'Valet' below to image 113 right, folio 109r, line 8, the text follows (with some variations), BL Sloane 1754 (English, c. AD 1300, from St Augustine's Canterbury), folio 19v, line 3 to fol 20v. See Ó Conchubair (1988).*

1. dampnacione subiecti redolet sap*it*. *Valet ad
2. omnes infirmitates et passiones et dolores et
3. langores que proveniunt ex fr*igida caus*a. Valet et
4. ad tusses, sed contr*a* humores frigidos reuma-
5. tizantes a cerebro ad pectus cu*m* Diadraganto

6.   et Penidion cum Storace calido vel cum Marubio

       Diadraganto: *(Diadragagantum) electuary based on gum Tragacanth, (Getz 2010, p325),*
       Astracantha gummifera; **Penidion**: *Diapenidion, electuary based on barley sugar, (Getz);*
       cum Storace calido: *Storax, the fragrant gumtree Styrax officinalis;*
       Marubio Albo: *Marrubium vulgare, White Horehound.*

7.   albo. Valet contra scinanciam idest contra humo-

       scinanciam: *or squinanciam, inflammation of the throat.*

8.   res descendentes ad guttur cum [illegible] vel
9.   cum allumine canis. // Valet contra corizas

       Diamoron: *juice of Black Mulberries and honey;* **allumine canis**: *a form of alum;*
       coriza: *catarrh, cold, runny nose.*

10.   et humores descendentes ad nares, cum succo
11.   Edere Terrestris. Valet contra fetorem narium

       Edere Terrestris: *Juice of Ground Ivy*

12.   cum Castoreo vel Euforbio. // Valet contra feto-

       Castoreo: *either extract from the testicles of a beaver, or more likely Castor oil; see*
       Image 78 right, folio 74r, col. A, line 15. **Euforbio**: *Euphorbium,* Spurge.

13.   rem oris sive sit vitio stomachi sive capitis
14.   cum nuce muscatta et gariofilata. Valet ad   *Nutmeg and Avens.*
15.   variolas in facie cum aqua rosarum. // Valet
16.   ad pustulas leprosorum ut non appereant exterius
17.   cum succo Fumiterre et Lappacii Acuti et aceto.   *Fumitory, 'Red Dock'.*
18.   // Valet ad cutem subtilandam. Sordes et immun-
19.   dicias tollit cum forti lixivio et melle et farina   **lixivio**: *with lye.*
20.   cicerum. Confortat ad pustulas faciei cum li-   **cicerum**: *as common food.*
21.   targiro et oleo. Confortat ad guttam rosa-   **Litagiro**: *litharge, lead monoxide.*
22.   ceam cum sulphure et argento vivo et sanguine
23.   recenti. Confortat ad morpheam albam cum
24.   coperosa. Confortat ad venenum acceptum cum
25.   cibis et potibus, cum tiriaca et nucibus. // Confor-
26.   tat ad venenum * et serpentum cum succo porei //

       * the sense demands insertion of 'vermium' as in Sloane 1754 – 'poison of worms and
       serpents'. **Succo porei**: *juice of leek (porri).*

27.   Confortat ad morsuram canis rabidi cum
28.   urina. Valet ad omne vitium intestinorum cum
29.   Ligno Aloes vel cum Musco vel cum Menta

       Agarwood musk, mint.

30.   Et eodem vitium membrorum interiorum. // Valet ad

31. yliaca*m* passione*m* et det*ur* cu*m* Diaconithon   *Yliaca passio: Violent vomiting.*
In right margin: Diacathicum

        Diaconithon / Diacathicum: *Perhaps read either '****Diacatholicon****' – a purge or universal remedy, or* **Diacitoniton**, *a preserve from the pulp of quinces. Sloane MS 521 corrupt here.*

32. Valet ad dolore*m* et inflatione*m* testiculo*rum*.

Image 113 Left, Folio 108v

1.   cum uvis passis et cinimo. // Valet ad lumbri-   *raisins and cinnamon.*
2.   cos interficiendum cu*m* centinodia. // Valet ad conf
        ad lumbricos interficiendum: *for killing worms;*
        centinodia: *Knotgrass.*
3.   ortandum stomachum cu*m* Zedoaris. Valet ad apos*t*-   *White Turmeric.*
4.   ema stomachi cu*m* Oculo Xpi. //Valet ad p*e*ripli-   *inflammation of the lungs.*
        Oculus Xpi *(Christi): identity of plant unclear.*
5.   moniam cu*m* Scabiosa. // Valet ad opilacione*m*   *Scabwort.*
6.   epatis cu*m* Mentasto et Origano // Valet ad a-   *Mint, Marjoram.*
7.   postema epatis cu*m* Absinthio et salvia. // Valet   *Wormwood, Sage.*
8.   ad sincopim cu*m* osse de corde cervi et dia-
        sincopis: *a heart disease.*
        cu*m* osse de corde cervi: *bone (or cartilage) in the ventricle of a stag's heart.*
        Diamargariton: *an electuary based on pearls.*
9.   margariton. // Valet ad litargia*m* cu*m* Ruta et ac-   **litargie:** *lethargy, coma.*
10. eto. // Valet thisicis cum Camphora. // Valet   **thisicis:** *those with TB.*
        Rue, Camphor Laurel.
11. ad emoroidos cu*m* sanguinaria. // Valet ad
        sanguinaria: *Shepherd's Purse.*
12. dissenteria*m*.// Valet ad diaria*m*. Confortat ad
13. pleureticos sive sit ex epilacione sive ex aliquo
14. alio malo cu*m* Scabiosa et Scariola. Valet ad   *Scabwort, Sowthistle.*
15. duas species ydropsis ex c*aus*a frigida sed no*n*
16. ad alias ex c*aus*a c*a*li*d*a. // Valet ad stranguriam.
        stranguria: *painful discharge of urine.*
17. // Valet ad diabete*m*. Valet ad m*i*nge*n*tes dif-   *those urinating with difficulty.*
18. ficulter cu*m* P*a*ritaria et Peucedano. // Valet ad emoroidas cu*m* apio
        Pellitory of the Wall, Hog's Fennel, Lesser Celandine, (Pilewort).
19. emoroida*rum* // Valet ad i*m*moderatu*m* fluxu*m* menstruoru*m* cu*m* Plan-
20. tagine. Valet ad sufficatione*m* matricis
21. cu*m* Oleo Rosa*rum* inferius apposito. Valet ad
22. excoriatione*m* matricis et apostema eiusdem
23. // Valet ad podagram . Valet ad sciaticam et

24.	dolore*m* ancharum. Valet ad p*a*ralisim si fu*erit*	**ancharum**: *of the hips.*
25.	p*a*rticularis. Valet ad rep*a*randum memoriam,	
26.	fantasticam cellulam confortando// Item yma-	
27.	ginariam, tollit pusillanimitate*m* et impeditu*m*	
28.	lingue. //Valet ad cancrum gingiva*rum* et oris	
29.	si in ore teneatur. //Valet ad commotione*m* et	
30.	dolore*m* dentium, et confortat et confirmat	
31.	dentes. Valet ad cancrum in virga et alibi.	
32.	Valet ad carbunculum, hoc est rupto apostemate	

Image 113 Right, Folio 109r

1.	*At top of text in another hand:* Noverint universi.	
2.	Valet ad fistulam, ipsam mortificat facta	
3.	Prius incisione debita. Valet ad omne vulnus	
4.	putridum, ipsum mu*n*dificat et sanat// Valet ad	
5.	quartana*m*: si in potu accipiatur, infra tres	*quartan fever*
6.	accessus liberabit*ur* patiens. //Valet tertio-	
7.	nariis; no*n* detur cotididianariis nec in acutis	
8.	febribus // Confert ad venenu*m* scorpionis,	

Extract from Sloane 1754 ends here at its folio 20v, line 1.

9.	acceptus in cibis et potibus etc, Amen.

In right margin: **Aqua calamis calamaris** (?)

*Read perhaps: aqua **calami**: 'reed water' from the sweet smelling Acorus Calamus ?*

10.	Extrahatur p*er* alembicu*m* sicut alie
11.	aque de herbis. Sp*e*ciale istius aq*ue* est faciem deal*b*are
12.	si exlavet*ur*//

In right margin: **Aqua mirande virtutis**

Que s*i*milit*er* valet in calidis

13.	panibu*s* sicut aque vite in frigidis scilicet in acutis	
14.	et p*er*acutis effemeribus calidis oculorum et doloribus	*ephemeral fevers.*
15.	capitis ex ca*u*sis calidis ad fastigiu*m* stomachi	

fastigium stomachi: *upper part of the stomach.*

16.	ad lupu*m* et fistula*m*, ad dolorem lateris, ad cale-
17.	faccione*m* virge ex coitu, et omnem passionem

18.	circa hec membra et si*m*ilia ex *causa* calida, summ*um*	
19.	et exp*ertum* remedium est. Et post p*artum* mulieris	
20.	valet multu*m*. Intingat unum pannum in istam	
21.	aquam et ponat ad vulva*m*. Ponatur in die sup*er*	
22.	locum passionis cero. Vel si fuit in stomaco	*read:* **sero** *late*
23.	inferius imittant*ur* p*er* clisterae*m*. Si in virga *per* si-	
24.	ringam aut exponatur sup*er* dextrum latus pan*n*us	
25.	madefactus in ea ter in die, tamen cave*ndum* sic fit.	
26.	Re*cipe* florum Sambuci, florum Ungule Cabal-	
27.	line an*a* li j., se*min*is Lactuce, se*min*is Portulace	
28.	an*a* li iii. Folio*rum* Solatri ʒ. i. debent aute*m* re-	

> one pound each of the flowers of Elder and Greater Burdock; three pounds each of Lettuce seed, Green/Golden Purslane seed; one drachm of the leaves of, Deadly Nightshade or of Black Nightshade.

29.	cipi viridia et ad meliore*m* *p*erfectione*m*. Fiat in	
30.	vasis novis et eodem modo distilletur septies.	
31.	et in vase vitreo profundo in terra reservetur.	
32.	Hec aqua maxime habet sanguine*m* depuratu*m*.	*Perhaps 'purifies the blood.'*

Image 114 Left, Folio 109v

1.	Hec in sole cum calefacit in m*er*idie facit volare	
2.	vasa vitrea, vel lignea levia, vel testes	
3.	ovorum vel ymagines. Item quicquid in ea	
4.	intinctus fuerit, ab igne no*n* ledetur, ymmo	**non ledetur:** *will not be harmed.*
5.	ab igne resilit, si intus p*ro*iciatur. Si de hac	
6.	aq*ua* una scutella in aiere aspersarie fundatur	
7.	nube*m* magna*m* et densa*m* facit subito et ca-	
8.	lore*m* solis magno tempore mitigat. Men-	
9.	struum sedat, provocat sudore*m*, p*ro*hibet dolo-	
10.	rem capitis ex calida causa ut ex febribus	
11.	vel solis adustione, et plures alias virtutes	
12.	maximas habet. Aqua que dealbat	
13.	mulieres, fit de Oleo Tartari et Litargiro et	
14.	Camphora et Cerusa: an*a* cu*m* succo vitis idest Bironie	

> '*Oil of Tartar*' *lead monoxide, Camphor Laurel, White Lead, White Bryony.*

15.	**Explicit de Aquis**

16.	**Incipit de Oleis**	
17.	**Oleum Rosar*um* sic fit**: R*ecipe* flores	*Not found in eTK.*
18.	Rosa*rum* viridiu*m* et repleatur fiola de floribus	
19.	Oleo sic quod pro j. li. olei apponatur ii. li. rosarum.	
20.	Et obturetur vas et exponatur soli *per* xx^ti	
21.	dies et singulis diebus moveatur, semel post deco-	
22.	ccione*m* colet*ur per* pannu*m* lineu*m* et hec oleum super	
23.	aquam fr*igi*dam ponatur et movet*ur* corulo excoriato	

    movetur corulo excoriato: stirred with a stripped hazel stick.

24.	et it*er*um ponatur sup*er* alia*m* aqua*m* et ita decies
25.	moveatur. Ex ista lavatura adquirit fri-
26.	giditate*m* et minore*m* siccitate*m* unde magis
27.	infrigidat atque humectat.// Item ponatur
28.	in fiola vitrea et reponatur soli ~~absq~~ usque aque
29.	humidiate*m* que intravit per pores consu*m*pta

Image 114 Right, Folio 110r

1.	sit, in frigida alia regione ubi, ex lento habito
2.	calore aieris, non potest dequoqui, pona*tur*
3.	in vas plenu*m* aque et bulliat *per* duos dies
4.	vel tres vel ad tertia*m* parte*m* consumpt*ionis*.
5.	Et si non habeas oleu*m* olivaru*m* fac oleu*m* de nucib*us*
6.	recentibus excoriates. Et cu*m* illo oleo re*serva*, et excor-
7.	ientur nuces vetuste, et infrigentur (?) *per* duos
8.	dies in aqua frigida. Deinde ex*tra*hatur oleu*m*
9.	ut lac nucum recentium possit dari febricitatibus
10.	continue in frigid regione sicut amigdala*rum*
11.	in calida. Singularia et specialia istius
12.	olei sunt si fiat inuncio febricib*us* continua
13.	vel interponita (?) circa fronte*m* et volas et manuu*m*

    forehead, palms of the hands and soles of the feet,

14.	et pedu*m* et circa venas pulsatiles, dolorem re-
15.	primit, calorem alterat, sompnum inducit. Sed hec
16.	non d*ebet* dari in die cretico. //....

    in die cretico: not to be given on a 'critical' day.

In right margin **Oleum rosarum**

....Alio Modo et

17. bene *R*ecipe li sem. ros*arum* coll*ectarum* c*um* rore et plene expa*n*sar*um*
     one and a half pounds of roses, picked with the dew, and fully open.
18. et scinde folia in parvas p*ar*tes. Abiecta albedine
19. folio*rum* et pone in vase vitreo et appone eis olieu*m*
20. olive viridis ℨ i vel plus, si necesse fuerit   *one ounce of olive oil.*
21. et misce b*ene* si*mul* in vase vitreo et obtura b*ene*
22. vas et pende erga solem p*er* xx^{ti} dies et tu*nc* exprime
     pende erga solem: *hang in the sun.*
23. p*er* unum pannu*m* lineu*m* fortem et iterum impone
24. in vase vitreo, et proice feces qui sunt in panno,   **proice feces:** *discard the residue.*
25. et videas quod vas sit b*ene* obturatum ita quod aier
26. no*n* possit intrare et omni die in aurora quando vis
27. exponere vas ad solem a*n*tequa*m* oleum sit exp*re*ssum
28. de rosis, move b*ene* simul rosas cu*m* oleo cu*m* una spatula
29. et si pendeat p*er* duas menses in aq*ua* fridida *(sic)* ad
30. os, esset melius ad infrigidandu*m* calore*m* febrile*m* et ce*tera*.
     ad os: *presumably with cold water up to the <u>mouth</u> of the glass container*

In right margin **Oleum Ovorum**   *Tr.: Oil of eggs.*

31. // Sic fit: *Recipe* vitella o*vorum* cruda et pone
     vitella ovorum cruda: *raw egg yolks.*   *Not found in eTK.*
32. in urinali vitreo et os eius claude cu*m* coop*er*culo

Image 115 Left, Folio 110v

1. et argilla cum luto magisterii ne respirare
    luto magisterii: *cement to seal the pot.*
2. valeat et in fimo fige duo ligna et desup*er*   ***fimum:*** *dungheap.*
3. ista ligna pone unum lignu*m* p*er* tra*n*sversum
4. ut sit modum furcarum et ibi pende dictu*m*   ***furca:*** *fork.*
5. ~~lignum~~ urinale p*er* filum in medio et pone in
6. circuitu et desup*er* satis de fimo prope urinale
7. ita ta*men* quod fimus urinale no*n* tangat. Et stet
8. ibi p*er* 40 dies et vitella valde putrescent
9. et cave a fetore. Postea distilla inde oleum
10. P*er* alembicum et est mire virtutis. Dicit

11. eius doctor quod posuit in crucibulo valde mo-
12. dicum et cum eo parum bombacis et accendit illud
13. et linnum duravit ibi circa 3ᵉˢ eddomedas,
14. nec oleum fuit diminutum. Sic fit: in die-

In left margin: **Oleum leprosorum**　　　　　　　　　　　　　Not found in eTK.

15. bus canicularibus accipiatur serpens vivus in
16. vase vitreo et apponatur oleum violarum bonum et
17. electum et vas bene obturetur et exponatur
18. soli per 40 dies, post coletur quolibet mane acc-
19. ipiatur leprosus, ieiunio stomacho, offam unam　　***offam***: *a morsel.*
20. de mica panis calidi in oleo predicto made-　　***mica panis***: *breadcrumbs.*
21. factus (?). Eodem potest fieri unguentum ad leprosos utile.
22. Oleum Violarum est constrictivum per antifysum. (?)

In left margin: **Oleum/Violarum**　　　　　　　　　　　　　Not found in eTK.

23. Specialia huius olei sunt si eadem sit mixta cum
24. succo mercurialis per clister mittatur in acutis　　***clyster***: *pipe for enemas.*
25. continuis (?) et interpolatis, suaviter remollit intestina
26. et etiam superfluitates expellit. ------

In left margin: **Oleum Benedictum**

Bray has a mineral oil of the same name, while Trease (1959, p50) suggests it may have been an Oleum Nardinum Benedictum, after Arnoldus Villanova.

　　　　　　　　　　--------Oleum Benedictum

27. valet in causa frigida et optimum. Et inter cetera, si pis-
28. catores unxerint retia sua, multitudinem piscium
29. congregabunt. // Infra tres unciones

In left margin: **Unum Oleum de frumento et Iunipero**　　　Not found in eTK.

30. [illegible] mulierum et puerorum curat et sanat et plures [alia].
31. Oleum Iuniperi extrahitur a semine Iuniperi

Image 115 Right, Folio 111r.

1. sicut oleum lauri a bacca lauri. Singular-
　　lines 2-5 are marked with an image of a feather pen in the right margin.
2. ia istius olei sunt frigidas causas reprimere fac-

3.   ta in unccione ab umbelico usque ad muliebria
4.   et super renes matricem frigidam confortare et eius hu-
5.   midatem desiccare, et eam conceptui preparare.

In right margin: **Oleum Pulegii**   *Oil of Pennyroyal*

6.   // Recipe summitates Pulegii cum floribus et
        Pulegii: Pennyroyal.   *Not found in eTK.*
7.   foliis Puloigii Regalis et decoquatur in oleo in
8.   duplici vase. Istud enim oleum reprimit
9.   frigidas causas sed specialiter et singulater facta inuncci
10.   one circa regionem matricis. Habet etiam confor-
11.   tare eam et frigidos humores desiccare et eam
12.   habilem conceptui reddere.// Oleum ederatum

In right margin: **Oleum ederatum**
        Oleum ederatum: presumably ivy steeped in oil.   *Not found in eTK.*
13.   frigidum est et valet contra dolorem capitis ex
14.   febrili calore vel ex alia causa per contra fer-
15.   vorem stomachi et intestinorum et contra fervorem
16.   matricis. Conficitur sic: Edere terantur et in vino
17.   vel oleo predicto inde coquantur.
18.   **Oleum Urticarum**: contra dolorem dorsi et tremorem (?) in pedibus.
19.   **Oleum Pulegii** recuperat membra debilitata, prout et ad omnes dolores.
20.   **Oleum de sinapio** valet in paralisi et contra emigraneam ex frigida causa
        Oleum de sinapio: Perhaps 'Oleum (seminum) Sinapis Volatile', Mustard (seed) Oil.
        None of the above found in eTK.

21.   **Explicit.**   **Incipit**

22.   **Unguentum contra Guttam**. Recipe unum   *Not found in eTK.*
23.   canem antiquum et pinguem valde in Autumpno
24.   inter festum assumpcionis et nativitatis Beate Marie, et ex-
        between August 15th and September 8th – perhaps the 'Dog Days'
25.   corea eum et tolle intestina cum capite et pedibus
26.   sed non apponas aliquid aquam ad illum quando extrahis
27.   intestina tunc recipias ~~intestina~~ ranas in
28.   magna quantitate ad illum, et impone eas vivas

29. in ventre predicti canis. Si non poteris, capias
30. tot quot poteris habere, tunc capias predictum
31. canem et affer super unum verure, et quando vides   *verus (n.): a spit.*

Image 116 Left, Folio 111v

1. quod stillat materia aquosa ab eo, abicias illam
   in left margin: Expertum est
2. materiam sed quando incipit stillare pinguedo ~~alba~~
3. bona et pulcra serva illam pinguedinem bene
4. in uno vase. Et cum illo unguento unge gut-
5. tam ubicumque fuerit, et infra breve curabitur
6. patiens. **NOTANDUM EST QUOD** quia (?) iste   *In left margin:* Nota.
   The following section bears a strong resemblance to the BB, folio 271b
7. est modus generalis faciendi unguenta de quibus-
8. cumque herbis volueris, quando volueris, ad tuam causam
9. valere. // Primo herbas ponas in olla et ad sum-
10. mum impleatur aqua. Post, coopereatur os olle cum panno
11. lineo et sigilletur cum argilla, ne fumus exeat.
12. Et apponatur igni usque ad consumptionem aque.
13. Et iterum impleatur olla aqua et iterum bulliant tritis
14. tamen herbis ante secundam decocionem deinde pon-
15. antur herbe ille cum tota deccocione in panno lineo
16. forti et exprimatur succus, et succo illo utere
17. in unguentis faciendis, quod si volueris servare,
18. confice cum cera et reservetur in pixide. Un-
19. guentum pro scabie: Recipe unguenti albi

In left margin: **Unguentum pro Scabie.**

20. sulphuris communis melius est *[illegible]* vivi si reperiatur,
21. argenti vivi viridis greci ana, et misce bene simul
22. et fac unguentum et valet bene pro scabie et vermis *[illegible – capitis ?]*.

In left margin: **Unguentum provocans menstrua**

23. Unguentum quod suppositum pectore pro-
24. vocat vomitum, super umbelicum movet ventrem,
25. super pectinem movet menstrua. Recipe olei
26. ʒ. i. terebentine, ʒ. i. fellis tauri, quod sufficit.

One ounce turpentine, one drachm bull gall.

In left margin: **Unguentum provocans vomitum.**

27. Unguentum quod si manus inunguantur, semper
28. vomitus, si plante pedis, fluxus ventris [provocatur]:
29. Recipe Elebori Albi et Nigri, Hermodactili, Iusq-
30. uami, aceti, Sempervive, Brionie ana ; conficiantur
31. cum veteri auxungia et cum restringere volueris,

> *White or False Hellebore; Black Hellebore; Ramsons, Henbane,* **aceti***: vinegar, Houseleek; White Bryony;* ***cum veteri auxungia****: with old grease.*

32. laventur manus et pedes et & ungantur de populeoni.[138]

> ***populeoni****: Henslow p52, (MS A, p289) has 'Popiliol' as an ointment, with Henbane, but also poplar leaves, omitted by Betson's source, but which presumably gave it its name. Similar in Sloane MS 521 (98/264/291), line 9.*

Image 116 Right, Folio 112r

In right margin: **Unguentum pro Spasmo**

1. Unguentum pro Spasmo de replecione. Recipe
2. urinam et dequoquatur usque sit nigra et spissa
3. quasi unguentum. -----

In right margin:: **Unguentum contra pediculos**

    -----// Extingue argentum vi-
4. vumcum auxungia porcina et succo Absinthii
5. et exinde unge cingulum et cingatur iuxta carnem.

In right margin **Unguentum Alabastri preciosum contra omnem dolorem in quacumque parte corporis.**

6. Unguentum Alabastri nimis carum
7. sed preciosum tamen est. Recipe ~~cunas~~ xl cimas rubei
8. teneras et pista eas ad modum salse ex alia parte
9. habeatis lagenas duas boni vini albi et pona-
10.   ***duas lagenas vini****: two flagons of wine, of about one gallon each*
11. tis simul in olla, et cum eis plenum pugillum Rute   *a handfull of Rue.*
12. et ℥ . iiij. florum Camoilulle [*read: camomille*] sicce et viridis

> ***Camoilulle****: presumably Chamaemelum nobile, Sweet Camomile., of which four ounces.*

---

[138] For recipe see OGDEN, M. S. (1938) *Liber de Diversis Medicinis*, (p109, note 61/ 15,19, 33). OUP.

13.	et de lapide alabastri li. sem, Seminis Feniculi ℥ sem
	half a pound of alabaster, and half an ounce of Fennel seed.
14.	olei Ros*arum* li unum et cera ℥ j, et hec omnia
	one pound of oil of Roses, and one ounce of wax.
15.	pistentur antequam in p*re*dicto vino; pona*n*tur p*ra*eter
16.	flores Camomille, et ceram. Et postea ponatur
17.	olla sup*er* lentu*m* igne*m* cu*m* p*re*dict*is* rebus, et bulliat,
18.	donec vinum totum co*n*sumet*ur* ita quod videat*ur*
19.	frigere. Et postea habeatis albumina ovo*rum* et i*n*
20.	olla cu*m* predictis commisceat*ur* donec be*ne* firmetur,
21.	deinde habeas pannum lineum et tota ista colatura
22.	ponatur in pa*n*no et coletur. Et optime inde exit
23.	preciosu*m* ungu*en*tu*m* alabastri. Et de isto Un-
24.	guento ungatis tempora et fronte*m* usque ad super-
25.	silia, et cu*m* sola unctione liberabit istos panni-
26.	culos qui apparent in oc*u*lis granum milii. // Et
	granum milii: *a grain of millet, though sometimes asserted to be the French 'Grémil', English 'Gromwell'. Presumably here meaning small flecks in the eye.*
27.	vere ubicu*m*que est dolor in capite vel in
28.	corp*or*e seu pede vel in quacu*m*que parte pectoris
29.	fuit, vel corp*or*is. Et si pacie*n*s unxerit se, libe-
30.	rabitur statim ab ipso dolore. // Et cu*m* invenie-
31.	bamus mulieres habentem *(sic)* dolorem vel tortionem,
32.	donabamus eis ad comedendu*m*, ac si esset electuarium
33.	et statim liberabant*ur* et si*mi*liter cu*m* inveniebamus

Image 117 Left, Folio 112v.

1.	mulieres *(at top of page:* vel viros*)* habentes stomachum dolentem, facie-
2.	bam*us* ungere eos sup*er* stomachum, manus
3.	et pedes et renes, et statim requiescebant a
4.	laboribus suis. Et si*mi*liter valet potenter ad
5.	omn*em* emigraneam dolore*m* et ad omnem o-
6.	culo*rum* egritudinem unctione facta i*n* fronte,
7.	timp*or*ibus [*read:* temporibus] et superciliis.
8.	Emplaustr*um* co*n*tra dolorem nervo*rum*, probatum.
	'probatum' in lighter ink and in margin.

9.   Emplaust*rum* ex*per*tum cont*ra* nerv*orum* dolor*em*
10.   vel ven*arum* vel gutta*m* alicui[u]s membri. R*ecipe*
11.   succus *(sic)* apii, farine ordei, olei co*mmun*is vel nucum
12.   et butirum et vinum quod sufficit. // Ista om*n*ia
13.   fricentur ita calidum su*per* locum et cooperiat*ur*
14.   cu*m* pannis bene. Istud probatum est sepe a M*a*gistro/a. c. b.

            a **Magistro/a. c. b.**: *an unknown person, perhapsy a physician.*

In left margin: **Emplast*rum* prop*ter* digestio*n*em sto*ma*chi**

15.   R*ecipe*: Absinthii, Mente, Ortholane, an*a* ma*nipulum*,
16.   unum cimini,Thuris, an*a* ℥ β Deinde panis

            half an ounce each of Cumin; Parsnip; or Skirret, incense.

17.   frumenti be*ne* fermen*ta*tus, ad ignem be*ne* assatur,
18.   et postea terant*ur* in mortario et cum aceto
19.   forti ut sit spissum, diste*m*peret*ur*, tu*n*c ponatur
20.   in bursa panni linei factus triangularis sic

            illustration in right margin of a dripping triangular linen pocket, suspended from a bracket.

21.   et post pona*tur* in aceto forti calido et sic tepidum.
22.   Ponat*ur* stomacho cu*m* frigidu*m* fuerit, iterum sic
23.   calefac ad igne*m*. // Emplastrum
24.   cont*ra* subv*er*sione*m* stomachi: R*ecipe* Mente, Absin-

            cont*ra* subv*er*sionem stomachi: *for an upset stomach.*

25.   thei, an*a* ma*n*ipulum j, cimini, ros*arum* an[a] ℥ j, masticis
26.   olibani an[a] ~~manipulum~~ ℥ β, panis tosti, et aceti qu*ar*ti

            a handful each of Mint and Wormwood var., one ounce each of Cunin and roses;
            half an ounce of putty of Franincense. One quart of vinegar.

27.   j fiat empl*astru*m su*per* stomachum et os eius.

      Potio pro Pestilicencia

28.   R*ecipe* Febrifuge Maioris, Iasie *(inserted above:* Matfelon) maioris, Artheme-
29.   sie, Dens Leonis, Solsequii, Scabiose, Amarusce,

            ?Feverfew ?Knapweed var., or, Silverweed, (Hunt), Mugwort, Dandelion, Garden Marigold;
            for Scabiose see Appendix 2; Stinking Camomile.

Image 117 Right, Folio 113r.

1.   an*a* lava be*ne* et tere si*mu*l om*n*es istas herbas in mor-
2.   tario et distemp*er*a cu*m* servicia, be*ne* dissicata, et da

            perhaps the mixture was washed, dried, and then enough beer added to make it drinkable.

3.	pacienti ad bibendum vj coclearia uno tempore	*cocliare: spoonful.*
4.	et si tempestive sumat, destruit corrupt*i*onem	*tempestive: timely.*
5.	et sanabit recipie*n*tem. --------	

In right margin **Potio ad o*m*nes plagas**　　　　　　　　　　*Tr.: a drink for all wounds.*

　　　　　　　　　　-----// Potio proba-
6.　　tissima que om*n*es plagas sanat sine appo-
7.　　sic*i*one alicu*ius* emplastri vel unguenti et sine
8.　　o*m*ni tenta, *per*fectissime sanat. R*ecipe* Sanicle,　*without use of a probe.*
9.　　Millefolii, Bugule Nigre an*a*, tere in mor-
　　　　　Sanicle, Yarrow, Bugle Nigra (Turner: 'it is a blacke herbe').
10.　　tario et cu*m* vino sufficienti distemp*er*a et vul-　　**No*ta* bene**
11.　　nerato bis vel ter dabis omni die ad bibe*n*du*m*
12.　　donec sanet*ur*. Et nota quod Bugula tenet
13.　　plaga*m* ap*ertam*, Millefolium purgat, Sanicla sanat, et cetera,

In right margin: **Potio ad plagas sanandas**　　　　　　　*a drink to heal wounds.*
14.　　sine instrumento sirurgico, et sine fer-
15.　　re, et sine ligno, et sin*e* tenta, et exit p*er* plaga*m*
16.　　et sanat per mensem vel aliqua*n*tulu*m* et aliqua*n*tulu*m*
17.　　minus. **Plaga que no*n* sanaret*ur* forsitan *per* me-**
18.　　**diu*m* annu*m* per op*er*acionem cirurgie:**　R*ecipe* [*illegible*]
19.　　de Tanaseti, seminis Canabi. Consulo quod humo-
20.　　sitas canabi quando fructus in ea maturus est
　　　　　Feverfew or Silverweed, ?Hemp Agrimony.
21.　　colligat*ur*, et per totu*m* annum servetur, et de ea granis
22.　　utere in dicta pocione folio*rum* Callis rubee, Pi-
23.　　loselle, Buglosse, an*a* mani*puluum* dimidium et Semine Ca-
　　　　　Red Cabbage, Mouse-ear Hawkweed, half a handful of Bugloss;
　　　　　one ounce of ?Hemp Agrimony.
24.　　nabi ℥ j. Pista om*n*ia p*re*dicta simul in mor-
25.　　tario et distemp*er*a cu*m* optimo vino albo oderi-
26.　　fero et no*n* oportet decoqui. Et usui reserva et
　　　　　non opertus decoqui *– boil down with lid on.*
27.　　mane et cero (*read:* sero) tria coclearia p*ro*pria (?) et maxi*me*
　　　　　mane et cero: *morning and evening, three 'shells' - spoonfuls.*
28.　　si est paciens vulneratus sine febre, longe

29. ~~post~~ ante com*m*estione*m* et longe post, et pone
30. sup*er* vulnus folium Caulis Rubee[139], removendo
31. illud bis in die, et liga cu*m* panno et ca-
32. nabino.   **Canabino**: *presumably* **Canabino filo**: *a cloth secured by a hempen thread.*

Image 118 Left, Folio 113v.

in left margin: **Pocio ad fistulam**   *Not found in eTK.*

1. Pocio ad fistulam: R*ecipe* Gariofilat*um* , Agrimo-
2. nia, Filaginem, p*er* equales portiones terantur
   Avens, Agrimony, ?Cudweed.
3. optime sicut esset salsiame*n*tu*m* et coquatur in
4. bono vino optimo albo valde diu, sicut essent
5. carnes. Tu*n*c ita apponat*ur* vinu*m* quod *[text damaged – 'herbe' ?]* re-
6. tineant vi*m* sua*m*. Postea colent*ur* *[text damaged]* utatur paciens
7. singulis diebus p*er* tres eddomedas, vel p*er* unum
8. mensem, vel p*er* duos menses donec sit cura-
9. tus. Et no*n* bibat aliu*m* potu*m*. Quida*m* curatus
10. fuit cu*m* hac pocione, qui habuit fistulam
11. sub testiculis *per* quam exivit parum de urina
12. et lavare solebat fistulam ter vel quater in die
13. et apposuit emplast*rum* de herbis ~~re tu~~ illis tritis
14. frigidis su*per* fistula*m* illa*m*.

15. **Compositiones Sirupo*rum*.**
16. Compositio sirupi constrictivi et frigidi:
17. R*ecipe* iiii ℥ florum Rosarum siccarum et coque in iiij li
    four ounces of dried roses, boiled in four pounds of clear water
18. aque clare et coque ad consumptione*m* tertie partis
19. vel usque Rose vada*n*t ad fundu*m* vasis. Post hoc
20. cola p*er* pannum et p*er*mitte frigessere. Post hec
21. capias albumine*m* unius ovi vel duo*rum* et malexa *(read **malaxa**)*
    malexa: *DMLBS gives 'malaxare' "to soften, esp. with hand, to knead."*

---

[139] *Guy de Chauliac, in his Surgery cites this use of cabbage leaves as a 'Teutonic' practice. See:* ZIMMERMAN & VEITH *Great Ideas in the History of Surgery,* Norman Publishing, 1993, p203

22. bene et tunc pone in predicto vas cum rosis super ig-
23. nem et misce bene simul quousque sit aliquantulum
24. calidum et tunc non moveas plus, et sic illud albuminen
25. attrahit ad se omnes superfluitates et natabit
26. superius et tunc permitte bullire quousque sit satis
27. coctus. Quod sic cognosces: pone unam guttam super
28. unguem et si stet, satis est. ~~Et~~ si fluat, non est. Et si sit,
29. bene cola tunc per pannum lineum. Et serva in vase
30. vitreato, quod optimus reputatur sirupus.

Image 118 Right, Folio 114r.

1. **De Floribus Violarum** potest fieri sirupus. Sed quia   *Violarum: of violets.*
2. iste sirupus est laxativus, ideo flores non debent
3. bullire nisi usque descendant ad fundum. Eodem
4. modo debent fieri sicut superius precedens. Et valet
5. pro *[text damaged]* febre terciana et etiam pro febre calida.
6. *[text damaged]* Facit pacientem bene dormire et cetera. Pro febre cotidi-
7. ana potest iste sirupus dari pro medicina primo
8. mane et ultimo in sero.
9. **Suppositoria et Pessaria Compositiones clisterarum**
10. **Entractus De Gratia Dei Series**

> In this context, "Gratia dei" must be the common entrete (salve or plaster) as "gratia dei," which has a variety of recipes but usually includes wax, volatile resins, herbs, and a good deal of heating and boiling down. [140] See also EMED –' Gratia Dei þat is ane enplaster' c.1440.

11. Recipe terebintine li β bene depurata, li 4 nove   *Depurata: refined.*
12. cere, ʒ iiii mastici, ʒ β de herbis, Recipe Beto-
13. nice, Vervene, Pimpernell, ana maniulum j herbe

> half a pound of turpentine, four pounds of new wax, four ounces of putty,
> half an ounce of herbs (?); a handful each of Betony, Vervain, Scarlet Pimpernel.

14. vero pistentur, deinde coquantur in lagena bo-
15. ni vini albi usque ad consumptiones medie
16. partis. Postea coletur vinum ab herbis, post po-
17. natur resina in vino deinde cera deinde mastix,
18. semper agitentur et fortiter, ne adhereant fundo,

---

[140] M. Teresa Tavormina, Pers. Comm. Sept. 2014.

19. et bulliat lento igne. Dein*de* deponatur ab igne
20. dein*de* ponatur terrebentina et frigidare p*er*-
21. mitte, et tolla*tur* quod sup*er*nataverit. Et herbe de*b*ent
22. collegi circa festum Joh*ann*is Bapt*iste* S*a*ncti. // Et d*icitur* quod
    (Eve of) The Feast of St John the Baptist: June 23rd.
23. iste entractus habet omnes virtutes quas h*abet*
24. alius entractus eiusdem no*min*is et ultra hoc curat
25. gallos transfixos (?) p*er* mediu*m* cerebri.   *Not found.*

26. **Pulvis Laxativus et co*n*fortans**
27. Re*cipe* Cinamo*mi* ℥ ij, Esule ʒ iij, Anisi masticis an*a*
28. ʒ β, Liquoricie ℥ β, Zuccarie, ℥ β, mittatur in cibis.
    two ounces of Cinnamon, two drachms of Dwarf Elder or Spurge; half a drachm of Aniseed putty (?), half an ounce of Liquorice, half an ounce of sugar.
29. Π Pulvis Pullegii Regalis cu*m* melle potui da-
30. Π tus compescit tussim.// Pulvis Pullegii Monta*ni*   *Pennyroyal, Wild Thyme.*

Image 119 Left, Folio 114v.

1. potui datus valet ad malos humores. // Pulvis
2. Rosarum potui datus vel commestus vel asp*er*sus,   *Powdered Roses.*
3. sanat putridas gingivas. // Pulvis Salgie   *Powdered Sage.*
4. bibitus vel commestus prestat paralitisis *(read: paraliticis).* // Pul-
5. vis Lattuce se*min*is cu*m* lacte datus provocat   *Powdered Lettuce seed.*
6. sompnu*m.* // Pulvis Se*min*is Plantaginis in vul-   *Powdered Plantain seed.*
7. neribus asp*er*sus mirifice sanat. // Pulvis

In left margin: **Pulvis et Tiriaca de Boys**

8. qui a quibusdam vocatur Tiriaca de Boys: Re*cipe*
    *Tiriaca: 'treacle' – a medicine or antidote. '**Boys**' is probably from French 'boire' – to drink. Both Henslow (42/11) and Dawson (p222, para 704) have varieties of this recipe under 'Boyre'.*
9. una*m* libra*m* de radicibus Turme*n*tille, de radicibus
10. Philipendule, Anisi mu*n*dati, de Bais no*n* mu*n*datis,
11. De Apio, de grano solis, de Carui, Zinzibere, de Sax-
12. ifraga Montana, de Betonica, de Cinamomo,
13. de omnibus an*a* videlicet ii quarter, de Liquricia duo q*uartroun.*
    Common Tormentill, Dropwort, Aniseed, Bay Tree Berry, Smallage, Gromwell, Caraway; Ginger; Saxifrage Montana: perhaps Satureia montana, Winter Savery, (also called

       'Saturegia' at Mowat, Alphita p. 158), Betony, Cinnamon, Liquorice; two quartroun of each:
       six ounces.

14.   mundent*ur* et pulverizent*ur* et valet cont*ra* vene-
15.   num et confert stomacho et iuvat cont*ra* carnes
16.   crudas commestas et tollit malos humores inf*ra*
17.   corpus existentes et pl*ur*ibus aliis infirmitatibus
18.   infra corp*us* subvenit.
19.   **Compositiones Confectionu*m***
20.   Ad Faciendum Zinziberum viride: Re*cipe* zinziberii
21.   optimi electi li β et infundatur in lixivia satis

       Lixivia: *'a solution obtained by leaching, as lye.'*

22.   de cin*er*ibus clavelatis vel alia forti lixivia p*er* 3s

       cineribus clavelatis: *(also **clavetalis** etc) - the lees of wine, dried and roasted.*

23.   die aut quatuor, aut diutius, si necesse fuerit,
24.   quousque omnes radices sint molles. Postea ex-
25.   trahatur et ponantur *(sic)* sup*er* pannu*m* lineu*m* mu*n*du*m*
26.   et succu*m*, ut liquoris infusi p*er* panni siccitate*m*
27.   valeat exhauriri. Et sic iaceant quousque fuerint
28.   be*n*e siccata. Postea infundant*ur* cu*m* aceto fortissimo
29.   per 2as dies vel cum zuccaria liqu*e*facta per ta*n*tum
30.   tempus sicut iaceba*n*t in laxivia et iteru*m* desic *[-centur]*

       The following four lines are written illegibly at bottom of page, and perhaps not in Betson's hand:

31.   Re*cipe* j partem salis petri et aliam sulphuri vive
32.   et molle sup*er* marmoreum et *potatur* urina   *in right margin:* **secretum**
33.   super ortu lune et veneris, et erit bonum
34.   *[Line illegible]*

Image 119 Right, Folio 115r.

1.   *[desic-]*centur ut p*re*dictum est et deponatur cortices facte
2.   p*re*missis. Re*cipe* li j zucc*ari* et dissolva*tur* cu*m* aqua ad ig-
3.   nem modicu*m* et clarificetur et coletur p*er* pannu*m* lineum
4.   et mu*n*du*m*. Potest e*s*se eadem zuccara sup*erius* liqu*e*fact*a*
5.   cu*m* aq*u*a no*n* *[?]* tu*n*c clarificatur, deinde coquatur ad
6.   spissitudinem debita*m*, et tu*n*c ponatur Z*i*nziber in olla vitre-
7.   ata, fundens predicta*m* zuccara*m* desup*er* tum (?) dummodo sit
8.   calid*us* et sic stent simu*l* p*er* eddomebdam antequam inde

9.	aliquis sumat. **Ad Faciendum Co*n*servat*ionem*
10.	**Ros*arum*:** Re*cipe* flores ros*arum* viridium antequem expandantur
11.	et abscisse albedine*m*, Bene terantur cu*m* zuccara et ponantur
12.	in vase vitreo et bene miscea*n*tur et movea*n*tur cotidie
13.	et sic s*er*vatur p*er* triennium. Proporcio rosarum et zuccarae debet
14.	esse in tribus vel in quatuor libra zuccare vel plus,
15.	li i. de Rosis et adhuc quida*m* quando faciunt conservat*ionem*
16.	ad 2as ponunt 4^or de zucc*ara*. // Pomum Am-
17.	bre pro divitibus: Re*cipe* Lapdani ʒ β., Storacis, Calaminte
18.	ʒ j, Ligni Aloes, Macis Nucis Muscate, Gariofili,
19.	an*a* ʒ ii, Camphore, Musca an*a* scrupli j, Amb*er*

> *half an ounce of ?Gum Rockrose, one ounce of Styrax officinalis and Calamint spp., two drachms of Aloe wood, Mace from the Nutmeg; Cloves; one scruple of Camphor Laurel and four drams of amber.*

20.	ʒ. iiii, conficitur sic: lapdanu*m* resolutum in aqua
21.	calida pone mortario et pistetur cu*m* pistello donec
22.	sit b*en*e resolutum, tu*nc* adde Storace*m*, Calaminte.
23.	Ad ult*imum* adde pulv*er*em predicta*rum* specie*rum* et inunctis
24.	manibus cu*m* oleo muscilino. Adde ambra*m* ad ult*imum*

> **oleo muscilino:** *oil of musk*

25.	ad camphoram et miscitur. // Pomu*m* Ambre
26.	quod val*et* contr*a* reuma capit*is* et tussim et maxi*me*
27.	pro illis qui de regionibus frigidis su*n*t. Re*cipe* Masticis
28.	Olibani, Storacis, Calami*n*te, Camphore, Lapdani, Dauci
29.	an*a* ʒ j., Ligni Aloes ʒ j., fiat pomum Ambre

> *One ounce of putty made from Frankincense, Wild Carrot, or Wild Parsnip and the other ingredients, as above, lines 19-22. One drachm of Aloes wood.*

30.	et decoquatur ad ignem. Et paciens fumegium recipiat et partibus
31.	in manu sua et teneat ad nares. Valet multum antiquis hominibus
32.	quia habent confortari viscera.
33.	Explicit Explicuit

Image 120 Left, Folio115v

1.	**For the Mygryme**.	*Migraine*
2.	Take *the* rote of Flour Delice viz Gladiole [*above*: and tak the jus *ther*of]	

> *Yellow flag. Hunt gives also Gladden and other Iris varieties under Fleur- de-Lis (p283).*

3.   & take *the* jusse *ther*of & put *ther*to alsmuch vy-
4.   nagre & as moch of womma*n*is mylk & squyrte
5.   it w*ith* a squyrte into the nose thrylys   *nose thrylys: nostrils.*
6.   on the seke side, & lete *the* pacient ly
7.   a litle whil on *the* same side.
8.   <u>Bona decoct*io*</u> for all disesis in the body:
9.   Take Centory, Horhond, Yssope et Nepte et
           Common Centaury, White Horehound, Hyssop Catmint, Pennyroyal.
10.   Piliol Rial et decoquantur usque dimedia*m*, mane et sero.
           (Tr.: 'boiled down to one half remaining, morning and evening'.)
11.   **For a birser or eny ach**
           Birser: not in EMED, but from context and recipe probably 'bruise' or similar.
12.   Take ma*num* 2ᵒˢ de Sothernewode et j q*u*artroun albi
           Sothernewode: *Artemesia abrotanum, Southern Wormwood.*
13.   vini et bulli in s*imu*l usque di*midium*. Postea acc*ipe* deneratus (?)
14.   de olio olivarum et ponat*ur* ad p*re*dictum et i*terum*
15.   bulliant*ur* donec densantur modo emplastr*um*
16.   et mu*n*dificat*ur* et strenatur et ungat*ur* [illegible]
17.   vel tale morbidum cont*ra* ignem et sanab*itur.*

In right margin: **A preparative tofore evacuac*ion* of fleume**
18.   Take the rotis of Fennell, the rotis of Percelly, of erthe
19.   half an handfull, the rote of Radissh a quartron   *Fennel, Parsley and Radish.*
20.   of an handfull. Bray hem togedur & seth hem   *bray: pound, crush.*
21.   up in vynagre, & *then* streyn he*m* up, & take *then* two
22.   p*ar*tyes of *the* vynagre & *the* p*ar*te of puryd hony &   *puryd: purified. EMED.*
23.   boile hem up togider, till it be sumwhat stiff. Take
24.   *then* v. sponefull of this, and asmoch of clene   *asmoch: as much.*
25.   well wat*er* & cast hem to gider & warm it by the
26.   morow a day and use thereof thre dayes or thou
           or thou reseyve: before you take the laxative.

Image 120 Right, Folio 116r.
1.   reseyve the laxatif of turbit or eny other laxative.   *Turpeth.*
2.   For fleume a*ccipe* x. sponefull at oouns in a cupp.
In right margin: **Pro p*ur*gatione / fleumatis**.

3. Re*cipe* Turbit, *Zinziber*, *Zuccarram*, an*a* et de isto pulvere detur plus
   The same amount of Turpeth, Ginger and Sugar.
4. vel minus, secundum tenorem virtutis et exigentis
5. mat*ere* cum vino vel cervisia vel sero lactis,
6. et dicit Avicenna quod pulvis iste p*ur*gat fleuma grossum,
7. non calefaciens nec arsuram intestinorum faciens,
8. quoniam turbit proprie respuat fleuma in ore stomachi,
9. et si per se detur, purgat fleuma subtile. Et si detur
10. cu*m* Zinziber et zucc*arra* purgat fl*eum*am grossam.
11. Tria tantummodo sunt signa ad accipi-
12. endum laxativam, viz Cancer, Scorpio et Pisces,
13. si sunt vacuas ab aliis planetis, quam in Luna et
14. no*n* sunt radices ~~solis~~ co*n*iunctio*n*is nec oppositionis   *astrological terms.*
15. viz p*er* xxxiiii horas an*te* co*n*iunctionem solis et lune
16. et p*er* xxxiiii horas post co*n*iunctio*n*em, et consimiliter
17. de oppositione. **Oportet Dare Laxativa**
18. post digestiam in signo mobili Luna no*n* existente
19. in signo imminanti ut patet in almenacis…

In right margin: **Purgant coleram**
                                                  …Su*n*t
20. Mirabo*lanum* citrinum, Nux vo*m*ica, Scamonea, Aloes, Se*men* Pepli
21. Ell*eborus* Al*bus*, Res*u*ris (?), Catap*u*cia, Tapsia. Sunt Epi*timum*

In right margin: **Purgant melancoliam:**
22. Polip*odium*, Lap*is* Arm*enicus*, Lap*is* Lazuli, Centauria, Sene,
23. Hermo*dactili*, Mirabolani indi , Succo Radicis Cameactis.

In right margin: **Purgant fleu*m*a**
24. Succus Turionis, Fili*cis*, Sunt Camepi*theos*, Aloe,
25. Turbit, Cuscute, Kebuli, Bellirici, Coconid*ium*, Polipo-
26. dium, Agaricus, Coloq*uinthida*, Titimallus….

In right margin: **Purgant San*g*uinem** :
                                                    …Sunt: Cassi-
27. a fistula, Tamarindi / Tamaria, Pulegia Rial, Cete*ral*.

The above named plants are much abbreviated. Some are repeated as separate purges for the four humours. *?Belleric, Bastard Myrobalan ? ,'Poison Nut';* *?***Scinno,** *Aloes; Sun Spurge, White or False Hellebore, ?Rhubarb, ?Caper Spurge; 'deadly carrot or Mullein, Thyme Dodder, Male Fern, ?Azurite,Lapis Lazuli, Common Centaury, Ramsons, ?Bastard Myrobalan, ?Nidi , Dwarf Elder, Vine shoots, Male Fern, Germander Speedwell, Aloes, Turpeth, Common Dodder; ? Bastard Myrobalan, Bay Tree, Male Fern, Field Mushroom, White Bryony, Caper Spurge, Pods of the Cassia Fistula, Tamarind, Pennyroyal, White Turmeric.*

Image 121 Left, Folio 116v

At top of page:

1.	Est Aries muniendo bonus, sic Libra, Sagitta	*muniendo*: protecting
2.	Sic et Aquarius est nec non Pisces *[illegible]*	
3.	Politricum, Adiantos, Capillus Veneris, Centauria, Mirabolani	
4.	Emblici, {space} Epatica, Cimbaria	

Maidenhair fern, Common Centaury, Bastard Myrobalan, ?Wood Sage, Pennywort.

In left margin: **Pro colica passione**

5. Recipe poudur oland with ale fastyng and it shal ese.

6. **Item for the Migryme probatum.** *migraine*

7. Recipe Sanguinem Draconis, terram sigillatam,
8. Et Bolum Armenicum et misceantur et subtiliantur
   Resin from Dragon Tree, clay, Armenian bole.
9. cum albumine ovi et applicetur parti dolenti.

10. **For to make here grow** *here*: hair.
11. Recipe a quantite of bees[141] dried in an hoven
12. And a quantite of browne breed, of the cromes *cromes*: breadcrumbs .
13. And another quantite of unsett Leke of this
    unsett leke: not yet transplanted leeks (EMED)
14. iuse and meng hem with the ~~of~~ oyle *[illegible]* *meng*: mix. EMED.
15. and anoynt the bare *(part)* and here shal grow. *here*: hair shall grow.

In the left margin: **Item pro colica**

16. Recipe the inward pith bi twix the kirnell of
17. Wallnottes and to the quanite of xxx or xl that
18. ben not corrupt and bray hem to poud(er) and drynk *Bray*: pound, crush.

---

[141] A similar recipe was still being cited in Britain, in print, as late as 1753, in 'The Compleat Housewife or Accomplish'd Gentleman's Companion' by Eliza Smith; there were also American editions.

19.	it with ale or Malmesy or Tire *[wine]* or els the juse
	Tire: *a sweet wine probably imported from Tyre in Syria. EMED.*
20.	of Tyme with ale and [illegible]
21.	*[illegible – probably Rewe. See EMED, Tire (3c) for use of Tyre wine with Rue.]*

Image 121 Left, Folio 116v, Lines 21-36, to Image 122 Left, Folio 117v, Line17.

The text follows with an almanac in Latin with forecasts for each month according to the weather (windy or thundery), with the suitable times for blood-letting, and foods to be eaten or avoided. The handwriting is at times unlike that of Betson and very difficult to read. This is a commonly occurring format, and it has little by the way of herbs. We have therefore decided to omit this section. Extracts from English Chronicles follow the forecasts; these are also not included here. Remedies continue below.

Image 124 Left, Folio 119v

20.	**For to dissolve flewm**	
21.	Take a handfull of Isop & lete it stande in stale ale j quarte,	Hyssop.
22.	iij or iiij houris, & then boyle it & skomme it clene & do therto	
23.	white sugur, as moch as ye lust, & drynk therof hote two or	
24.	iij gode draghtis when ye go to your bed, with powdur of	
25.	Gyngur as moch as it plesith you. And use to wassh	Ginger.
26.	your fete every nyght with hote water wher in the dust	
27.	of Hey & Malewis & Smalage is boyled yn. And thys done,	
	Hay, Mallows and Wild Celery.	
28.	oftyn wele resome your flewm and warantise & open your brest.	
	resome your flewm: *bring up your phlegm;* **warantise**: *protect.*	
29.	**Nota**	
30.	Take Malewis, Holyhoks, Violetts, Mercury Bletis of ech	
	Mallows, Hollyhock, Violets; **Mercury Bletis**: *'various plants of the family Chenopodiaceæ' (OED.). This group (now renamed) includes Goosefoot, and Good King Henry – which was also called Mercury Goosefoot.*	
31.	an handfull, of Blynde Netyl, [illegible], Archangell,	
	Lamium album and Lamium purpureum. Hunt p.33 and EMED.	
32.	Hertwort of ech demi handfull, of Whete Brenne	**Hertwort**: *violet.*
33.	an handfull. Seth all thies in Tamiyse water	
	Tamiyse Water: *Thames or Tamarind water –*	
	see note, Image 124 right, folio 120r, line 8 below.	
34.	or other rynnyng water from a galon to a pynte.	

Presumably: 'Reduce by boiling from a gallon to a pint.' ?

Image 124 Right, Folio 120r

1. *Th*en strayn the wat*er* fro*m* the herbes & fry the residew
2. *with* butt*er* a litle salted, for an plast*or* to ~~the bely~~ be layd
3. to the bely hote of a gode largenesse and or ye lay
4. the plaist*ur* to the bely, *[illegible]* your bely *with* the oyle warme.
5.   **For mylk of Almond*es***
6. Take Borage, Spynage, Violet*tes*, of ech an handfull,
7. of Pe*r*sely the third of an handfull, Goldys, Stychworte:
   Borage, Violets, Spinach, Corn Marigold, Stitchwort.
8. of ech half an handfull seth all in a galon of Thamys wat*er*
   Thamys wat*er: *'water of tamarindes, a decoction made from this fruit ?' EMED;* **or** *possibly 'Thames water'. See Sloane MS. 73. lf. 214 (Halliw.) , c.1450. ' Put therto tweyne galones of clene Temese water that is taken at an ebbe.'*
9. unto half a pynte, and in myddys of this
10. decocion cast in half a unce of the grosse powder
11. of Sene, *with* a spoonful of Anys sede, grossly braised, *Senna and Aniseed.*
12. and *with th*is wat*er* strayned, make yo*ur* mylke of
13. almondis blanchid. Dulcorate *with* a litle sugre & **Dulcorate:** *sweeten.*
14. take it as a drynk undir ij draughtes one after
15. the other, warme. *[illegible]*
16. of Endyff or Sowthistyll, j handfull; of Eupatray d*imidium* manus li
    Sowthistle, Wild Sage.
17. and seth hem as is writyn afore.
18.   **For a suppository**
19. Take hony, Alow, an*a* egges, poud*ur* of Colyander, and poud*ur*
20. of Bayeberys, and poud*er* of Alexander sede, and poudur of Sene,
21. and poudur of Gyng*er* & put all thies to gider in a little herthen
22. pott and set it on the fyre tyll it be styff and drye.
23. *[illegible]* poudur for a lax in ea opulacionis ep*atis*
    Opulacion: *obstruction. Used of liver and of the spleen.*
24. Re*cipe* Galang*er*, Piperis Long*us*, Gariofilati, Cardom*onis* Maioris, Se*men*
    Aneti,
25. Carui, an*a* ʒ. j, nuces muscate, ʒ β., Bacc*e* Lauri excorticate
26. ʒ 4 au*tem* mu*n*dati, ʒ j folio*rum*, Semen Clatt ʒ j , pulv*eris*
    one drachm each of Galingale, Pepper, Cloves, water cress var., (but context and genitive form may suggest the spice Cardomom), Aniseed, Caraway; half a drachm of nutmeg; four drachms

        of peeled Bay Treel (berries ?) ; one ounce of the leaves (?); one ounce of Burdock seed; Clatt:
        the common burdock (Arctium lappa) EMED; half an ounce of Liquorice.

27.   Liqu*o*ricie ʒ β . Fiat pulvis subtilis.
28.   Take two times in the week of this poudur a gode sponful
29.   in y*our* potage and w*a*te litle. For it disterbeth digestion and by
30.   co*n*tinua*n*ce causith opilacio*un* wit*h* co*n*stipacio*un*, and use this
31.   poud*u*r sp*e*cially when ye be constipate. T*he* which well
32.   usid shalbe a fynale conclusion and remedy for y*our* dissess*es*.

Images 125 and 126, left and right, (folios 120v 121r, 121v, 122r) and image 127 left, folio 122v left, are blank. Image 127 right, folio 123r, lines 1-17, image 129 left, folio 124v and, image 132, right, inserted horizontally above the music, on endpages, are illegible and unlike Betson's handwriting.

Image 128 Right, Folio 124r.
1.   **A sirope for all dissesis in the stomake**
2.   Take ffrumetye and bray it & wrynge out the juse &   *pound,crush.*
3.   put it in a clene vessell on the fire, and atte fyrst
4.   Wamble. Put of the scomme and thanne take it of the fyre.
          Wamble: *seething or bubbling up, when brought to boiling-point. OED.*
          Put of the scome: *remove the scum…take it off the fire.*
5.   And take as moche of hony clarified and put t*her*to.
6.   And lete him boyle to the honey be dissolvyd. T*hi*s is
7.   a sov*er*eyn medycyne for the *[illegible]* or fever and disseses in
8.   the stomake what some ev*er* they be and are
9.   Primo
10.   *R*ecipe jj of the leves of Sene & seth hem in white wyne
11.   And strene hem and put to hem suger & drynk it loukwarm.
12.   & use claret wine wit*h* water of Wormode.   Wormwood.
13.   Ieiuna, vigila, modicu*m* bibe, sepe labore
14.   Te calidu*m* serva, si vis expellare flegma.

The *Regimen Sanitatis Salernitanum* has a similar text: 'Jejuna, vigila, caleas dape, valde labora, Inspira calidum, modicum bibe, comprime flatum: Haec bene tu serva si vis depellere rheuma.'

Image 131, Left: inserted into the space inside the capital letter P, on endpage:

ANNO DOMINI. / 1500 / peribit omnis caro per ignem.

Tr.: In the year of the Lord 1500, all flesh shall perish by fire.

APPENDICES

Appendix 1: The Modern Linnaean Names of Betson's Plants and Ingredients.

Tentative Modern Technical Names for Plants and Ingredients in the Remedy Sections of the Syon Abbey Herbal.

This Section does not include entriesthe *Herbarium* section, where the tentative equivalents are given in the text in column 4.

Note: This list is for internal reference to the text, and has no medical or any other practical applications. The modern identifications below are tentative. The Latin names have been included, for ease of reference, in the same cases as in the text – e.g. the first entry is in the genitive, *Absinthei*, and not the nominative *Absintheum*.

Absinthei: Artemisia absinthium, Wormwood.
Acetum: vinegar.
Ach, Ache sede: Celery-like plants, such as Smallage or Parsley, *Apium graveolens* etc.
Adiantos: *Adiantum capillus-veneris*, Maidenhair fern.
Agaricus: *Agaricus campestris*, Field Mushroom.
Agrimoina, Agrimoine, Agrimonie: *Agrimonia eupatoria*, Agrimony.
Alexander sede, Alexandre, Alisandir, Alisaundre: *Smyrnium olusatrum*, Alexanders, Horse Parsley.
Alkon: ?*Alkanna tinctoria*, Alkanet.
Alleluia: *Oxalis acetosella*, Wood Sorrell.
Allumine canis: a form of alum.
Aloes, Aloes Epatica, Aloen: *Aloë* L ssp. Aloes.
Alum glas: potash alum.
Amarusce: *Anthemis cotula*, Stinking Camomile.
Anacarde: *Anacardium occidentale*, cashew nut.
Anice: *Pimpinella anisum*, Aniseed.
Apii, Apio, Apium agreste: *Apium graveolens,* Smallage.
Apium agrimonie: perhaps for ***Apium agreste*** – Smallage.
Apium emoroidarum: *Ficaria verna*, Lesser Celandine, Pilewort.
Archangell: *Lamium album* or *Lamium purpureum*. White or Red Dead Nettle.
Arnement: Vitriol. Iron sulphate, copper sulphate, or a mixture of the two.
Arthemesie: *Artemisia vulgaris*, Mugwort.
Aselli serapini: perhaps 'Marjoram vinegar'?
Assafetida: *Ferula assa-foetida*, Assafetida.
Aurum calamentum: calamine, zinc ore (Latham).
Avence: *Geum urbanum*, Avens.

Bacce lauri excorticate: *Laurus nobilis*, peeled Bay Tree berries.
Bais: *Laurus nobilis*, Bay tree berries.
Bayeberys: *Laurus nobilis*, Bay tree berries.
Ben ashis: bean ash.
Betayn , Betoinice, Betonice, Betonie, Betony: *Betonica officinalis*, Betony.
Bironie: *Bryonia dioica*, White Bryony.
Blemblis croppis: *Rubus fructicosus*, (top leaves of the) Bramble.
Blynde Netill: *Lamium album* or *Lamium purpureum*. White or Red Dead Nettle.
Bolum Armenicum: A red astringent earth, Armenian bole.
Borage: *Borago officinalis*, Borage.

Borus grese: boar's grease.
Brakis: an unspecified variety of fern.
Brionie: *Bryonia dioica*, White Bryony.
Brome, Bromblossums: *Cytisus scoparius*, Flowers of the broom.
Buglosse: *Anchusa arvensis*, Bugloss.
Bugule Nigre: *Ajuga reptans*, Bugle . (Turner: 'it is a blacke herbe').
Bursa Pastoris: *Capsella bursa-pastoris*, Shepherd's Purse.

Calami (aqua): 'reed water' from fragrant *Acorus Calamus* ?
Calaminte: *Calamintha sylvatica* or *C. officinalis*, Wood Calamint or Common Calamint.
Camepiteos ?: *Veronica chamaedrys*, Germander Speedwell.
Camoilulle, Camomyll: *Chamaemelum nobile*, Sweet Camomile.
Camphore: *Camphora laurus* (Dryobalanops aromatica) Camphor Laurel.
Canabi (seminis): perhaps seed of *Eupatarium cannabinum*, Hemp Agrimony, or Cannabis sativa.
Canabino: perhaps **Canabino filo:** a cloth secured by a hempen thread.
Candi: Sugar candy.
Caparis: *Capparis spinosa*, the Caper Bush.
Capillus Veneris: *Adiantum capillus-veneris*, Maidenhair fern.
Capon gresse: Chicken fat.
Caprifolii: *Lonicera caprifolium*, Honeysuckle.
Caraway, Carewey: *Carum carvi*, Caraway.
Cardomonis Maioris: *Elleteria Cardamomum*, Cardamom.
Carpobalsami : 'shrubs of the genus Commiphora' (EMED), Myrrh.
Carui: *Carum carvi*, Caraway.
Cassiasist: Pods of the *Cassia Fistula*, Drumstick tree.
Cassie: ' the tree cassia fistula' (EMED).
Catapucia: Euphorbia lathyris**,** Caper Spurge.
Caulis rubee: *Brassica oleracea var. capitata f. rubra*, red cabbage.
Celidon, Celidonie, Cellidone, Cellidonie, Cellidony: *Chelidonium majus*, Greater Celandine.
Cenerfole: *Lonicera caprifolium*, Honeysuckle.
Centauri, Centaurie, Centaury: *Centaurium erythraea, Rafn.*, Common Centaury.
Centinodia: *Persicaria aviculare*, Knotgrass.
Centory: *Centaurium erythraea, Rafn*. Common Centaury.
Cerfolio: *Lonicera caprifolium*,Honeysuckle.
Cerusa: White Lead, Hydrocerussite.
Ceteral ?: *Curcuma zedoaria*, Setwall, Zedoary, White Turmeric.
Cimbaria: *Cymbalaria murali*, Pennywort
Cimini: *Cuminum cyminum*, Cumin.
Cinamom, Cinamomum, Cinamon, Cinamonus: *Cinnamomum zeylanicum*, Cinnamon.
Clowis: *Syzygium aromaticum – formerly Eugenia caryophillata,* Cloves.
Colofonie, Colofyn: Pine resin, Colophony.
Coloquinthida ?: *Bryonia dioica*, White Bryony ?
Colyander: *Coriandrum sativum*,Coriander.
Commyn, Comyn: *Cuminum cyminum*, Cumin.
Coconidium: *Laurus nobilis*, Laurel.
Confery: *Symphytum officinalis*, Comfrey.
Coriandri: *Coriandrum sativum*, Coriander.
Cressis: cress.
Cristall: crystallized quartz, rock crystal, or some material resembling crystal.
Cucscute: *Cuscuta epithymum*, Common Dodder.

Cynamomis: *Cinnamomum zeylanicum*, Cinnamon.

Dandelion, Danndelion: *Taraxacum vulgare*, Dandelion.
Daucus: *Daucus carota*, Wild Carrot, or *Pastinaca sativa*, Wild Parsnip.
Dayse: *Bellis perennis*, Daisy.
Dens Leonis: *Taraxacum vulgare*, Dandelion.
Diaconithon: Perhaps read '**Diacatholicon**' – a purge or universal remedy.
Diadraganto: (Diadragagantum) electuary based on gum Tragacanth, *Astracantha gummifera*.
Diamargariton: an electuary based on pearls.
Ditany, Ditaigne: *Dictamnus albus*, Ditany.
Dof drite: dove droppings.
Dogefenel: Perhaps *Anthemis cotula*, Stinking Camomile.
Dragancie: *Dracunculus vulgaris*, Dragonwort.

Ebuli (radicem): *Sambucus ebulus*, Danewort, Dwarf Elder.
Edere Terrestris: probably *Glechoma hederacea*, Ground Ivy .
Egrimonye, Egrimony: *Agrimonia eupatoria*, Agrimony.
Elebori Nigri: *Helleborus niger*, Black Hellebore.
Ellborus Albus: ? *Veratrum album*, White or False Hellebore.
Emblici: *Terminalia bellerica*, Belleric, Bastard Myrobalan.
Endiss: perhaps Endive - sowthistle (*Sonchus oleraceus*) or corn sowthistle (*Sonchus arvensis*).
Sengren: *Sempervivum tectorum*, Houseleek.
Endivie, Endyff (or Southistyll): *Sonchus var*. Sowthistle.
Enulicampani: *Inula helenium*, Elecampane, Horseheal, Scabwort.
Epaturi: (Eupatorium ?): *Teucrium scordonia*, Wood Sage ?
Epitimum ?: *Cuscuta epithymum*, Thyme Dodder.
Esule: Henslow has *Sambucus Ebulus*, Dwarf Elder, but perhaps also *Euphorbia ssp.*, Spurge.
Euforbii: *Euphorbia var.*, Spurge.
Eufrace: *Euphrasia officinalis*, Eyebright.
Eupatray: *Salvia verbenaca*, Wild sage, ambrose. ? or *Teucrium scorodonia* Wood Germander
Everose: perhaps *Euphrasia officinalis*, Eyebright.
Evory: Ivory.

Fasynges: the small rootlets at the base of leeks.
Febrifuge Maior: *Tanacetum parthenium*, Feverfew ?
Fenell, Fennell: *Foeniculum vulgare*, Fennel.
Feniculi Rubii: *Foeniculum vulgare 'Rubrum*, Red Fennel.
Fetherfuge, Feverfue: *Centaurium erythraea*, Common Centaury, or *Tanacetum parthenium*, Feverfew.
Filaginem: *Filago germanica*, Cudweed.
Filicis: *Dryopteris filis-mas*, Male Fern.
Flour Delice viz Gladiole: *Iris Pseudacorus*, Yellow flag. Hunt gives Gladden and other Iris varieties.
Foliorum Vitis: Vine leaves.
Fumiterre (cum succo), Fumitor: juice of *Fumaria officinalis*, Common Fumitory.

Galange, Galanger:, Galangur: ?*Alpinia officinalis*, Hance. Galangal – ginger. Or: *Cyperus longus*,
    Galingale, 'English Galingale', or *Cyperus rotundus* or *C. longus*, Rush or Galingale.
Gallitrici: *Lolium temulentum*, Clary or Darnel.
Gariofilata, Gariofilati, Gariofilatum: *Geum urbanum*, Avens.
Gariofili, Gariofilorum, Gariofilum: *Syzygium aromaticum*, Cloves.
Gece grece: Goose grease.

Gerse: white lead ?
Gladiole: *Iris Pseudacorus*, Yellow flag. Hunt gives Gladden and other Iris varieties.
Goldis, Goldys, Gouldis: *Glebionis segetum*, Corn Marigold. or ?*Convolvulus arvensis*, ?Bindweed.
(de) Grano solis: *Lithospermum officinale*, Common Gromwell.
Gromel: *Lithospermum officinale*, Common Gromwell.
Groundeswall, Groundsele: *Senecio vulgaris*, Groundsel.
Gum Arabic: A natural gum from either *Senegalia (Acacia) senegal* or *Vachellia (Acacia) seyal*.

Hencresse: *Capsella bursa pastoris*, Shepherd's Purse.
Herbe Sancti Johannis Baptiste: *Hypericum perforatum*, St John's Wort.
Hertistongue: *Asplenium scolopendrium*, Harts tongue.
Hertwort: *Viola* ssp., Violet.
Hervmodactili: *Allium ursinum*, Ramsons.
Hey: Hay.
Hilwort: Mentha pulegium, Pennyroyal. or Wild Thyme, *Thymus serpyllum*.
Hogges grece: Bacon fat.
Holyhoks: *Althaea officinalis*, Hollyhock
Horhond: *Marrubium vulgare*, White Horehound.
Houndesfennel: Perhaps *Anthemis cotula*, Stinking Camomile.
Husleke: *sempervivum tectorum* Houseleek.

Iasie maioris: (Iacea), *Centaurea nigra*, Knapweed.
Iusquami: *Hysocamus niger*, Henbane.

Kebuci bellin: *Terminalia bellerica*, Belleric, Bastard Myrobalan.

Lactuce: *Lactuca sativa*, Lettuce.
Lapdani: probably *Cistus ladanifer*, Gum Rockrose, rather than *Laudanum*.
Lapis calammaris: Calamine or Zinc Carbonate.
Lapis Armenicus / Armoniacus: probably Azurite.
Lapis Lazuli: Lapis Lazuli.
Lappacii accuti: *Rumex aquaticus / sanguineus*, Dock, esp. Red-Veined Dock.
Laungdebef : *Anchusa arvensis*, Bugloss.
Laureal, Lauriall: *Daphne laureola*, the spurge laurel.
Letise, Letuse: lettuce: *Lactuca sativa*, Lettuce.
Licores: *Glycyrrhiza glabra*, Liquorice.
Ligni, Lignum Aloes: probably *Aquilaria agallocha* or aloe-wood
Liquiric , Liquoricie, Liquricia: *Glycyrrhiza glabra*, Liquorice.
Litagiro: litharge, lead monoxide.
Lixivia: 'a solution obtained by leaching, as lye.'
Ludworte: (a) ?the dwarf elder (*Sambucus ebulus*). (b) ?the common, or wall, pellitory
  (*Parietaria officinalis*). (c) ?buck's horn plantain (*Plantago coronopus*).
Ly: lye.
Lyne sede: *Linum usitatissimum*, Linseed (Flax).

Macis Nucis Muscate: *Myristica fragrans*, Mace from the Nutmeg – the membrane around the nut.
Madeworte: not identified, perhaps *Leonurus cardiaca*, Motherwort.
Madur: *Rubia tinctorum*, Madder.
Maidenhere: *Adiantum capillus-veneris*, Maidenhair fern.
Malevis, Malewis , Malowis, Malues, Malve: *Althaea officinalis*, Marsh mallow.

Maratri: *Foeniculum vulgare*, Fennel.
Martinum: ?*Myrtus communis*, Common Myrtle.
Marubio Albo: *Marrubium vulgare*, White Horehound.
Masticis: mastix gum.
Maslin: mixed corn and wheat.
Masticum Olibani: a sealant made from Frankincense.
Mater herbarum: *Artemisia vulgaris*, Mugwort.
Matfelon: *Centaurea nigra*, Knapweed, matfellon. also, *Centaurea scabiosa*, Greater Knapweed.
  ? *Centaurea jacea*, Lesser Knapweed or ?*Potentilla anserina*, Silverweed.
Maythes: *Anthemis cotula*, Stinking camomile, or similar plant.
Mellilotum: *Melilotus officinalis*, Melilot, Sweet Clover, or *Trifolium pratense*, Red Clover.
Menta: a mint variety.
Mentastum: read 'mentastrum', a mint species.
Merch: *Levisticum officinale*, Lovage.
Mercury Bletis: 'various plants of the family *Chenopodiaceæ*' (OED.). This group (now renamed)
  includes Goosefoot, and Good King Henry – which was also called Mercury Goosefoot.
Micis: Mace.
Millefolii, Millefoly: *Achillea millefolium*, Yarrow.

Milii (granum): a grain of millet, though sometimes asserted to be the French 'Grémil', English
'Gromwell'. Presumably meaning here small flecks in the eye.
Minte: *Mentha*,'Garden Mint' or ssp..
Mirabolanum ? *Terminalia bellerica*, Belleric, Bastard Myrobalan ?
Mirre: perhaps *Commiphora myrrha*, Holmes, Myrrh.
Modirwort, Modurwort: Unidentified: Hunt (p295) gives 14 possibilities; EMED adds others, q.v.
  Betson (image 95 left, Fflio 90v, line 1) identifies it with *Artemisia vulgaris*, Mugwort.
Morelle: *Atropa belladonna* or *Solanum nigrum*, Deadly or Black Nighshade.
Morsus Galline: *Stellaria media*, Chickweed.
Moushere: *Pilosella officinarum*, Mouse Ear Hawkweed.
Mugwort: *Artemisia vulgaris*, Mugwort.
Musca: Musk.
Muscatta: (=Nux muscata), *Myristica fragrans*, Nutmeg.
Muscata (Herba): *Galium odoratum*, Wood-ruff; or *Myristica fragrans* 'nutmeg' – Nux muscata.
Mynte: Mint ssp..

Nenufarus: *Nymphea alba / lutea*, White or Yellow Water Lily.
Nepte: *Nepeta cataria*, Catmint, Catnip.
Nucem Muscatam, Nuces Muscate: *Myristica fragrans*, Nutmeg.
Nucis Gallice: *Juglans regia,* Walnut
Nux Vomica: *Strychnos nux-vomica*, 'Poison Nut'.

Oculus Xpi (Christi): identity unclear. See Hunt p189.
Oile de Bay: *Laurus Nobilis*, Oil from Bay Tree.
Oile de Olif, Ole de olif: *Oliva europeae*, Olive Oil.
Oleo Tartari: 'Oil of Tartar'.
Oleum de sinapio: Perhaps '*Oleum (seminum) Sinapis Volatile*', Mustard (seed) Oil.
Oleum ederatum: presumably ivy steeped in oil, or oil from ivy.
Opoponal Olibani: Perhaps *Opoponax*, Sweet or Bisabol Myrrh.
Origano: *Origanum vulgare*, Marjoram.
Ortholane: *Pastinaca sative*, Parsnip, or *Sium sisarum*, Skirret.

Ossis de corde cervini: bone (or cartilage) in the ventricle of a stag's heart.

Palei [read: **paleae**] **Ordei:** barley chaff
Parcelly rote, parcily rote, Parcly cum radice, Parsely sede, Parslye, Parsyly:
    Petroselinum crispum, Parsley, 'with its root'.
Paritaria: *Parietaria officinalis / diffusa*, Pellitory of the Wall.
Pellitary of Spayn: *Parietaria officinalis / diffusa*, Pellitory of the Wall.
Pepli (Semen): *Euphorbia helioscopia*, Sun Spurge.
Penidion: Diapenidion, electuary based on barley sugar, (Getz 2010, p325).
Percel, **Percelly, Persely**: *Petroselinum crispum*, Parsley.
Peticonsoude: Consolida minor, *Bellis perennis*, Daisy.
Petrocilio, Petrosillum (radicem): *Petroselinum crispum*, Parsley root.
Pety Cousell: *Bellis perennis*, Daisy.
Peucedano: *Peucedanum officinale*, Hog's Fennel.
Philopendule: *Filipendula vulgaris*, Dropwort.
Piliol Rial, Pilliole: *Mentha pulegium*, Pennyroyal.
Piloselle: *Pilosella officinarum*,Mouse-ear Hawkweed.
Pimpernell, Pimpernelle: *Scarlet Pimpernel*, Pimpinella saxifraga.
Pionie: *Paeonia mascula or officinalis*, Peony.
Piper: *Piper nigrum*, Black Pepper.
Piperis Longus: ?*Piper nigrum*, Black Pepper.
Pipris Nigri: *Piper nigrum*, Black Pepper.
Piretri: *Parietaria officinalis*, Pellitory of the wall. EMED
Pitar: *Parietaria officinalis*, Pellitory of the wall.
Plantaginis, Plantago, Planteyn: *Plantago* spp., Plantain.
Polipodi: ? *Polypodium ssp.*, Male Fern, Polypody.
Politricum: *Adiantum capillus-veneris*, Maidenhair fern.
Populeoni: In various other MSS; Henslow p52 (MS A, p289) has 'Popiliol' as an ointment containing Henbane, but also poplar leaves - omitted by Betson's source.
Porrus: *Allium* spp., Leek.
Portulace: *Portulaca oleracea*, Green/Golden Purslane.
Prassium: *Marrubium vulgare*, White Horehound.
Primerose: *Primula vulgaris*, Primrose.
Primpernell, Primpernelle Rubie: *Anagallis arvensis*, Scarlet Pimpernel.
Pulegia Rial, Pulegii Regalis: *Mentha pulegium*, Pennyroyal.
Pullegii Montan (Pulvis): *Thymus polytrichus*, Wild Thyme.
Pullegii Regalis, (Pulvis): *Mentha pulegium*, Pennyroyal.
Pulvis Baccarum Lauri: *Laurus nobilis*, powdered Laurel berries,
Pulvis silicis nigre: powdered black flint.
Pynpernell: *Pimpinella saxifrage*, Scarlet Pimpernel.
Pyx navalis: 'ship tar'.

Quibubiis: *Piperaceae*, pepper.
Quinfoile, Quinque Folii: *Potentilla reptans*, Creeping Cinquefoil.
Quinquenerviae: *Plantago* spp., Plantain.

Radissh: ?*Raphanus raphanistrum*, Wild Radish.
Rede Dockis: *Rumex aquaticus*, 'Red Dock'.
Rede Fenell: *Foeniculum vulgare rubrum*, red fennel.
Rede Netill: *Lamium purpureum*, Red Deadnettle.

Resuris? : *Rheum raponticum*, Rhubarb.
Rew, Rewe: *Ruta Graveolens*, Rue.
Rose Rubee: red roses.
Rosemaryn: *Rosmarinus officinalis*, Rosemary.
Rostrum Porcini: *Sonchus var.*, Sowthistle.
Rosys: Rose spp.
Rute, Rwe: *Ruta graveolens*, Rue.

Sal Armoniacum: ammonium chloride.
Sal gemme: rock salt.
Salgie (Pulvis), Salvia: *Salvia spp.* , Sage, or *Teucrium scordonia*, Wood Sage.
Sambucus: *Sambucus niger*, Elderflower.
Sanamunde: *Geum urbanum*, Herb Bennet, Avens.
Sanguinaria: *Capsella bursa-pastoris*, Shepherd's Purse.
Sanguinem Draconis: *Dracaena draco*, resin from Dragon Tree.
Sanicle, Saniclye: *Sanicula europaea*, Sanicle.
Satureie Levistici: *Levisticum officinale*, Lovage.
Sauge: *Salvia officinalis*, Sage or *Teucrium scordonia*, Wood Sage.
S**avine (folia)**: perhaps leaves of *Juniperus Sabina*.
Saxifrage Montana: perhaps for *Satureia montana*, Winter Savery – also called 'Saturegia'.
Saxifrage: *Saxifrage* ssp., Saxifrage.
Scabiose, Scabious, Scabius: *Inula helenium*, Scabwort; or *Centaurea iacea / scabiosa*, Knapweed var.; or else a 'Scabious' variety (*Knautia arvensis* or *Scabiosa columbaria*). S*e*e Hunt p231
Scamonia: Perhaps *Convolvulus scammonia*, Scammony.
Scariola: a *Sonchus* species, Sow thistle.
Scicados: *Sempervivum tectorum*, Houseleek.
Semen Aneti: *Pimpinella anisum*, Anise, Aniseed.
Semen Clatt: Perhaps **Clote** – *Arctium lappa*, Greater Burdock.
Semen Hermodactilis: *Colchicum autumnale*, Meadow Saffron**.**
Sempervive: *Sempervivum tectorum*, Houseleek.
Sene, Poudur of: powdered Senna – 'The powdered leaves or pods of senna, a plant of the genus
    Cassia, esp. the Alexandrian senna (*C. acutifolia*) or Tinnevelly senna (*C. augustifolia*).'
Senecium: *Senecio vulgaris*, Groundsel.
Sengren: *Sempervivum tectorum*, Houseleek.
Sepo arietum: Goat fat.
Siler Montanum: *Maiorana hortensis*, Moench. Sweet Marjoram.
Silfhole: *Stellaria media*, Chickweed.
Siluris Montane: *Maiorana hortensis*, Moench. Sweet Marjoram.
Slos: *Prunus spinosa*, sloes.
Smalach, Smalage: *Apium graveolens*, Wild Celery.
Solatri: *Atropa belladonna*, Deadly Nightshade, or *Solanum nigrum*, Black Nightshade.
Solsecul, Solsequiy: *Calendula officinalis*, Garden Marigold.
Sothernwode: *Artemesia abrotanum,* Southernwood.
Southistil, Southistyll (Endyff): Plant having small yellow flowers and seeds like a dandelion. perh. sowthistle (*Sonchus oleraceus*) or corn sowthistle (*Sonchus arvensis*).
Spikenard, Spkykenard: 'aromatic plant of the *Valerianaceae* family, esp. *Nardostachys jatamansi*. OR *Valeriana officinalis*, Valerian.'
Spodium: 'A powder derived from ashes of ivory.'
Spynach, Spynage: a variety of *Spinarchia oleracea*, Spinach.
Squinantum: *Juncus odoratus*, Sweet Rush.

Storax: vanilla-scented resin from the tree *Styrax officinalis*.
Stychworte: *Stellaria holostea*, Stitchwort.
Succus Sambuci: juice of *Sambucus nigra*, Elder.
Synamome: *Cinnamomum zeylanicum*, Cinnamon ?
Synonum: *Petroselinum crispum*, Parsley.

Tamarind / Tamaria: *Tamarindus indica*, Tamarind.
Tamiyse Water: Thames or perhaps Tamarind water.
Tanacetum agreste: *Potentilla anserin* , Silverweed.
Tansey: *Chrysanthemum vulgare*, Tansy.
Tapsia: *Thapsia garganica*, 'deadly carrot (from West Mediterranean) or *Verbascum thapsus*, Mullein.
Terbentine, Terbentyn, Terebintine: *Pistacia terebinthus*, Terebinth, Turpentine.
Terra Sigillata: A kind of clay.
Thuris: incense.
Timi: *Thymus serpyllum*, Thyme.
Tire: a sweet wine probably imported from Tyre in Syria.
Titmali: *Euphorbia lathyris*,Caper Spurge.
Tormentille: *Potentilla Erecta*, (Common Tormentill).
Touncresse: *Thapsia garganica* , Garden cress,.
Turbit: *Ipomoea turpethum*, the root of Turpeth. (From India and China.)
Turionis (succus): *Vitis*, Vine shoots.
Turmentille: *Potentilla erecta*, Common Tormentill.
Ungule Caballine: *Arctium lappa*, Greater Burdock or *Nymphea spp*. White or Yellow Water Lily.
Unsett Lekis: Leeks that have not yet been transplanted.

Vertgrece: verdigris.
Vervain, Vervene: *Verbena officinalis*, Vervain.
Vetusti auxungia: with old grease.
Vitriolum: ?sulfuric acid.

Walwarte: *Parietaria officinalis* / *diffusa*, Pellitory of the Wall or *Euphorbia esula* – Leafy Spurge.
Warenyce: *Rubia tinctorum*, Madder.
Welcresse: (*Rorippa nasturtium aquaticum*), or *Nasturtium officinale*, common water cress.
Wermode, Wermote: *Artemisia pontica*, Wormwood.
Weybrede: *Plantago spp*. Plantain.
Whete Brenne: Wheat Bran.
Wodebynd: *Lonicera caprifolium*, Honeysuckle.
Wodesour: *Oxalis acetosella*,Wood Sorrell.
Wodwis: *Genista tinctoria* , Dyer's Greenweed.
Worduode, Wormode, Wormode: probably *Artemisia absinthium* (rather than *A. pontica*, Wormwood).

Yarrow, Yeraw: *Achillea millefolium*,Yarrow.
Yongspring of elder: the first shoots of Elder.
Ysalgar: 'realgar' or 'risalgar' a kind of red arsenic.
Ysope, Yssope: *Hyssopus officinalis*, Hyssop.
Yvees: *Hedera helix*, Ivy flowers ?

Zeddoar: *Curcuma zedoaria*, White Turmeric.
Zinzber, Zinzib, Zinziber , Zinzibero: *Zinziber officinale*, Ginger.
Zuccarie, Zuccarra, Zuccarum: sugar.

Appendix 2: List of Illnesses and Conditions from Betson

The mediaeval names of illnesses and conditions, with their diagnosis and treatment, are unlikely to coincide with modern medical views. This table is for statistical purposes only, and to indicate those conditions which Betson chose to include in his Herbal.

Aches (7): *All manner of*: Image 87 right – Folio 83r, Column B.
All mener of evylls in a mannes body: Image 94 right, Folio 90r, Line 27; *side, womb and stomach*: Image 97 right, Folio 93r, Line 8; *contra omnes dolores*: Image 116 right, Folio 112r, Lines 6-24; *in quacumque parte….. corporis*, Image 116 right, Folio 112r Lines 27-31; Image 120 left, Folio115v, Lines 1-10 & 11-17.

Allopecia (4): *Contra casum capillorum* (hair loss), Image 100 left, Folio 95v, Line 7 Image 109 right, Folio 105r, Line 15; Image 110 right, Folio 106r, Line 14; *and dried bees*: Image 121 left, Folio 116v, Lines 11-16.

Apostem (12): *Adustio*: Image 88 right, Folio 84r, Line 13; Image 89 left, Folio 84v, Line 9; In herbarium Image 87, Right, Folio 83r, Col. A, Line 8; Image 89 right, Folio 85r, Line 5; Image 109 right, Folio 105r, Line 10; Image 113 Left, Folio 108v, Lines 3 & 22; *Wen*: Image 98 left, Folio 93v, Line 18; 'Apostemata': Image 89 right, Folio 85r, Line 5 & Image 109 right, Folio 105r, Line 10 & Image 113 Left, Folio 108v, Lines 6 & 22 & 32.

Appetite (4): *loss of*: Image 97 left, Folio 92v, Lines 1-3; Image 100 left, Folio 95v, Line 2; Image 101 right, Folio 97r, Line 3-11; Image 108 right, folio 104r, 22-23.

Apoplexy (1): Image 108 left, folio 103v, Line 19.

Arms, Pains in (2): Image 89 left, Folio 84v, Line 16 dolorem in dext[ro] bracchio majorem quam in sinistro; Line 17 majorem dolorem in sinistr[o] latere q*uam* in dextro.

Asthma (1): Image 93 right, Folio 89r. Line 1 (Anelitus et grossum flegma).

Backache (2): Image 101 right, Folio 97r, Lines 26-31; Image 115 right, Folio 111r, Line 18.

Bad Breath (3): Image 99 right, Folio 95r, Line 29; Image 108 left, folio 103v, Line 33; Image 112 right, Folio 108r, Lines 12-13.

Bathing (4): *abstines*: Image 121 left, Folio 116v, Line 27; Image 121 right, Folio 117r, Line 18; Image 121 right, Folio 117r, Line 31; *pro balneo* Image 129 Left, Folio 124v, Line 21.

Bladder (2): Image 97 left, Folio 92v, Line 30; *vesice excorationem:* Image 89 right, Folio 85r, Line 8.

Bloodletting (5): Image 88 right, Folio 84r, Line 12; *good months for*: Image 114 Right, Folio 110r, Line 12 & Image 121 right, Folio 117r, Line 13; & Image 121 left, Folio 116v, Line 23 onwards, & Image 121 right, Folio 117r Line 1 onwards.

Brain (1): *gallos transfixos per medium cerebri* : Image 118 right, Folio 114r, Line 25, (meaning unclear).

Bruising (2): Image 104 left, Folio 99v, Lines 10-16; Image 108 left, folio 103v, Lines 24-27.

Burns (1): Image 98 right, Folio 94r, Lines 20-21.

'Calida causa' (2) : Image 106 right, Folio 102r, Line11; Image 114 Left, Folio 109v Line 10;

Calculus (1): Image 90 right, Folio 86r. Line 3.

Cancer (5): 'cancur in the mouth and floyng into the gomes', Image 95 left, Folio 90v, Line 21 & Image 97 right, Folio 93r, Line 22; Image 100 left, Folio 95v, Line 31; cancrum gingiv*arum* et oris: Image 113 Left, Folio 108v, Lines 28-29; *Cancrum in virga*: Probably prostate cancer: Image 113 Left, Folio 108v, Line 31.

Catarrh (1) (*Coriza*): Image 112 right, Folio 108r Lines 9-12

Chest Pains (5): *Gravidines pectoris* Image 89 left, Folio 84v, Line 12; Image 96 right, Folio 92r, Line 3; Image 99 right, Folio 95r, Line 24; *colerica frigida:* Image 108 right, folio 104r, Lines 4-5; Image 112 right, Folio 108r, Lines 4-5.

'Colera' (2): Image 120 right, Folio 116r, Line 21 onwards; Coleria: Image 129 Left, Folio 124v, Line 21.

Conception and Pregnancy (9): *Pregnancy, Periods and urine:* Image 34 Right, Folio 30r; *impregationem mulierum*, Image 89, Folio 85r 12 right, & *Urine in pregnancy – in the period one to four months*: Folio 85r 12; Image 89 right, Folio 85r 13 -19; *Conception*: Image 95 left, Folio 90v, Line 3; Image 100 left, Folio 95v, Lines 23-24; Image 100 left,

Folio 95v, Line 8; Image 115 right, Folio 111r, Lines 1-5; Image 115 right, Folio 111r, Lines 10-12.

Constipation (4): Image 98 left, Folio 93v, Line 30; Image 102 left, Folio 97v, Lines 29-30; Image 118 right, Folio 114r, Lines 26-30; suppository: Image 124 right, Folio 120r, Lines 19-22, & 23-32.

Coriza (Catarrh) (1): Image 112 right, Folio 108r, Line 9.

Cosmetics (8): white face - Image 102 right, Folio 98r, Lines 25-29; *faciem dealbare* Image 113 Right, Folio 109r, Lines 11-12; *cleansing*: Image 106 right, Folio 102r, Lines 21-30 & Image 107 left, Folio 102v, Lines 1-10; *Lac virginis*: Image 109 right, Folio 105r, Lines 1-10; *Aqua aromatica ad nobiles et matronas*: Image 110 right, Folio 106r, Lines 14-15; *ad facies matronarum bene refrigerandum* : Image 110 right, Folio 106r, Line 11. Image 114 Left, Folio 109v, Line 13 onwards.

Coughs (4): Image 93 right, Folio 89r, Line 25. Image 100 left, Folio 95v, Line 21; 'perilous': Image 101 right, Folio 97r, Lines 15-19; Image 112 right, Folio 108r, Line 4.

Cramps (2): Image 100 left, Folio 95v, Line 18; Image 116 right, Folio 112r, Lines 1-3.

Deafness (2) ill of hearing, Image 100 left, Folio 95v, Line 21 onwards; Image 108 left, folio 103v, Lines 29-30.

Death, Signs of, (3) *signum mortale*, Image 90 right, Folio 86r. Line 5; *Urina nigra....in quartana semper est mortalis*, Image 89 left, Folio 84v, Line 4; vomiting and nettles: Image 104 left, Folio 99v, Lines 25-32.

Delivery and Childbirth (3) Image 95 right, Folio 91r, Lines 11-13; Image 98 left, Folio 93v, Lines 4-6; *post partum mulieris*: Image 113 Right, Folio 109r, Line 19.

'Diabetes' (1): Image 113 Left, Folio 108v, Line 17.

Dropsy (13): *Cold and Hot*: Image 88 left, Folio 83v, Lines 17-22; Image 95 right, Folio 91r, Line 22; *Ydropsis, in phlegmatic, dropsical and gouty persons*: Image 88 right, Folio 84r, Line 30; Image 96 left, Folio 91v, Line 19; Image 113 Left, Folio 108v, Line 15; Image 97 left, Folio 92v, Line 7; Image 97 right, Folio 93r, Line 11; Image 98 right, Folio 94r, Line 6; Image 100 left, Folio 95v, Lines 10-14 & Lines 11-21; Image 103 right, Folio 99r, Line 20; Image 108 right, folio 104r, Lines 7-9; Image 113 Left, Folio 108v, Lines 14-16.

Drunkeness (1): Image 97 left, Folio 92v, Line 7.

Dysentry (11): *Fluctum ventris*, Image 89 left, Folio 84v, Line 28; Image 98 left, Folio 93v, Line 23; Image 99 right, Folio 95r, Line 14; Image 99 right, Folio 95r, Line 23; *flix*: Image 102 left, Folio 97v, Lines 1-11; Image 102 right, Folio 98r, Lines 8-14; *calida fluxus ventris:* Image 106 right, Folio 102r, Lines 19-20; Image 108 right, folio 104r, 12-13; flux: Image 108 right, folio 104r, Line 23; *Diariam*: Image 113 Left, Folio 108v, Line 12; Image 116 Left, Folio 111v, Line 32.

Ears (1): *Lice in*: Image 102 right, Folio 98r, Lines 10-14.

Eyes (24): *A Medicyne for all manner of sore eiyen*, Image 88 left, Folio 83v, Lines 29-34; Image 96 left, Folio 91v, Line 23; Image 97 left, Folio 92v, Line 18; Image 98 left, Folio 93v, Line 16; *worms in the eyelids*: Image 100 left, Folio 95v, Lines 10-11; *web*: Image 101 left, Folio 96v, Line 12; *'goundy'*: Image 102 right, Folio 98r, 17-24; Image 102 right, Folio 98r, Line 29 onwards; Image 103 right, Folio 99r, Lines 8-13; *Peral or Haw*: Image 105 right, Folio 101r, Lines 6-17; *pro omni vitio oculorum*: Image 106 right, Folio 102r, Lines 1-7 & 8-14; Image 108 left, folio 103v, Lines 26-29; Image 109 right, Folio 105r Lines 1-19 & 19-31; Image 110 right, Folio 106r, Lines 1-13; Image 111, left, folio 106v, 19-22 & 22-25; Image 111 right, Folio 107r, Lines 9-23 & 23 onwards; *oculos vulneratos et putridos*: Image 113 Right, Folio 109r, Lines 3-4; Image 113 Right, Folio 109r, Line 14; Image 115 right, Folio 111r, Line 19; Image 117 left, Folio 112v, Lines 4-7; in Herbarium: Image 87 Left, Folio 82v, Col. A, Line 16.

Feet (4): *Pain in*: Image 100 left, Folio 95v, Lines 15-17; *swollen with travel*: Image 102 right, Folio 98r, Lines 3-7; *swelling*: Image 104 left, Folio 99v, Line 26 onwards; *tumours in*: Image 115 right, Folio 111r, Line 18.

Fevers (21)
    Non-specific (10): *passing and continuous and from surfeit of blood (febris effemera, continua; ex nimio sanguine)*: Image 88 right, Folio 84r, Lines 7-9; *Febris etica*: Image 89 left, Folio 84v, Line 10; *All fevers*, Image 93 right, Folio 89r., Line 8; Image 97 right, Folio 93r, Line 16; *in the stomach*: Image 98 left, Folio 93v, Lines 11-12; *in the head*: Image 103 right, Folio 99r, Line 21; Image 115 right, Folio 111r, Lines 12-17; In Herbarium: Image 75 Left, Folio 70v, Col. A, Line 1.
    Fever, Tertian (5): Image 95 left, Folio 90v, Lines 24-25 and Image 97 left, Folio 92v, Line 9; Image 97 right, Folio 93r, Line 11; *calorem febrile reprimere*: Image 106 right, Folio 102r, Lines 14-18; Image 113 Right, Folio 109r, Lines 6-7.
    Fever, quartan (6): Image 89 left, Folio 84v, Line 6; *Fever, tertian and quartan*: Image 97 left, Folio 92v, Line 13; *Febres interpellatas*: Image 89 right, Folio 85r, Line 21; *'burning ague'*: Image 97 left, Folio 92v, line 33; Image 108 right, folio 104r, Lines 9-10; *infra tres accessiones liberabitur*: Image 113 Right, Folio 109r, Lines 6-7.

Fistula (4): Image 113 Right, Folio 109r, Line 1; Image 113 Right, Folio 109r, Line 16; Image 118 left, Folio 113v, Lines 1-10; (perhaps not Betson) Image 129 Left, Folio 124v, Lines 12-20.

Flemma, Flegma: See Phlegm.

'Frigida Causa' (6): Image 106 right, Folio 102r, Line 13; Image 108 right, folio 104r, Line 6-7; Image 108 right, folio 104r, Line 7; Image 108 right, folio 104r, Line 12 & 14; Image 111 right, Folio 107r, Line 2; Image 112 right, Folio 108r, Line 3.

Genitals, male (7): **Image 102 left, Folio 97v, Lines 24-29;** *swelling*: **Image 104 left,** Folio 99v, Lines 22-25; *virge virili*: Image 109 right, Folio 105r, Line 10; *ad dolorem et inflationem testiculorum*: Image 112 right, Folio 108r, Line 32; *ad calefacionem virge ex coitu*: Image 113 Right, Folio 109r, Lines 16-17 & Line 23 onwards; *fistula sub testiculis*: Image 118 left, Folio 113v, Line 10-15. *Cancrum in virga*: Probably prostate cancer: Image 113 Left, Folio 108v, Line 31.

Gout (9): *guttam in superioribus partibus*, Image 89 left, Folio 84v, Line 29; *baked owl*: Image 104 left, Folio 99v, Lines 13-21; Image 105 right, Folio 101r, Lines 24-31; Image 109 left, folio 104v Lines 29, & 29-37; Image 111 right, Folio 107r, Lines 1-3; Image 113 Left, Folio 108v, Line 23; *unum canem antiquum*: Image 115 right, Folio 111r Line 22 onwards; Image 117 left, Folio 112v, Lines 9-14.

Haemorrhoids (5): Image 90 right, Folio 86r, Line 6; Image 96 left, Folio 91v, Lines 6-7; Image 108 right, folio 104r, Lines 24-25; Image 113 Left, Folio 108v, Line 11; *apis emoroidarum*: Image 113 Left, Folio 108v, Lines 18-19.

Head, crown of (1) Image 103 right, Folio 99r, Lines 13-19.

Headache (14) Image 97 left, Folio 92v, Line 33; Image 97 right, Folio 93r, Line 18; Image 100 left, Folio 95v, 1-16; Image 102 right, Folio 98r, Lines 17-21; Image 103 right, Folio 99r, Line 21; *in dolore capitis antique*: Image 108 left, folio 103v, Line 12; *from sun*: Image 111, left hand, folio 106v, Line 10 & Image 114 Left, Folio 109v, Line 11; Image 113 Right, Folio 109r Line 15; Image 114 Left, Folio 109v, Line 9; Image 115 right, Folio 111r, Line 13.

Heart (*syncopis* of) (1) : Image 113 Left, Folio 108v, Lines 8-9.

'Humours' (14): in Herbarium: Image 87 Left, Folio 82v, Col. A, Line 17; Image 89 left, Folio 84v, Line 20; Image 96 right, Folio 92r, Line 7; Image 96 right, Folio 92r, Line 26; Image 97 left, Folio 92v, Lines 26 & 36; Image 107 left, Folio 102v, Line 24; Image 112 right, Folio 108r, Line 4; Image 115 right, Folio 111r, Line 11; Image 121 left, Folio 116v, Line 28; Image 121 right, Folio 117r, Line 23; Image 129 Left, Folio 124v, Line 21; *'malos humores'* Image 119 left, Folio 114v, Line 1 & 19

'Humiditas' (1) Image 90 left, Folio 85v, Line 10 & 12; Image 114 Left, Folio 109v, Lines 17-19.

Impostim / Apostem (12): *Adustio*: Image 88 right, Folio 84r, Line 13; Image 89 left, Folio 84v, Line 9; In herbarium Image 87, Right, Folio 83r, Col. A, Line 8; Image 89 right, Folio 85r, Line 5; Image 109 right, Folio 105r, Line 10; Image 113 Left, Folio 108v, Lines 3 & 22; *Wen*: Image 98 left, Folio 93v, Line 18; 'Apostemata': Image 89 right, Folio 85r, Line 5 & Image 109 right, Folio 105r, Line 10 & Image 113 Left, Folio 108v, Lines 6 & 22 & 32.

Intestines (4): Image 112 right, Folio 108r, Lines 28-30; Image 121 right, Folio 117r, Line 25; Image 115 right, Folio 111r, Line 15; *confortari viscera*: Image 119 right, Folio 115r, Lines 1-32.

Jaundice (5): *Ictericia*, Image 89 left, Folio 84v; *Yalow evell*: Image 95 left, Folio 90v, Line 17 ; *Yelowsought:*Image 95 left, Folio 90v, Line 29; Image 102 right, Folio 98r, Line 30 onwards; Image 104 left, Folio 99v, Lines 16-20.

Kidneys (5) *in viris dolorem renum* Image 88 right, Folio 84r, Line 31; 11 *dolorem renum in mulieribus:* Image 89 left, Folio 84v, Line 31; Image 89 right, Folio 85r, Line 11; *Vene [venae] rupturam circa renes et vesicam* Image 89 right, Folio 85r, Line 3; *opilacio:* Image 108 right, folio 104r, Line 3.

Lactation (2): Image 95 right, Folio 91r, Line 26; Image 102 right, Folio 98r, Lines 3-7.

Laxatives: *see Constipation.*

Lechery (1): Image 96 left, Folio 91v, Line 20.

Leprosy: see Skin Diseases below

Lice (2) pediculos: Image 116 right, Folio 112r, Lines 3-5; *Lice in eyebrows*: Image 116 right, Folio 112r, Lines 24-27.

Liver (8): *Heating of - calefactio epatis)* Image 88 right, Folio 84r, Line 16; Image 89 left, Folio 84v, Line 7; Image 98 right, Folio 94r , Lines 17-19; *Disease of the Liver - hepaticam aegritudinem:* Image 89 right, Folio 85r, Line 21; *opilacio:* Image 108 right, folio 104r, Line 3; Image 111 right, Folio 107r, Lines 1-3; Image 113 Left, Folio 108v, Lines 6-7; Image 124 right, Folio 120r, Lines 23-32.

Loins (1): Image 104 left, Folio 99v, Lines 6-10.

Lungs (3): *'Tisik'*, Image 97 right, Folio 93r, Line 10 & Image 113 Left, Folio 108v, Lines 9-10; *ad pleureticos*: Image 113 Left, Folio 108v.

Mad dog bites (2): Image 89 left, Folio 84v, Lines 24-27; Image 112 right, Folio 108r, Lines 27-28.

Memory (2): Image 108 left, folio 103v, Line 15; Image 113 Left, Folio 108v Line 25.

Migraine (6): Image 34 Right, Folio 30r, Image 99 right, Folio 95r, Lines 9-12; Image 103 right, Folio 99r, Line 19; Image 115 right, Folio 111r, line 20; Image 120 left, Folio115v, Line 1-7; Image 121 left, Folio 116v, Lines 7-10.

Navel (2): *Pain in*: Image 89 right, Folio 85r, Line 24; *super umbelicum movet ventrem*: Image 116 Left, Folio 111v, Line 27.

Nipples (2): *inflammation of*: Image 104 left, Folio 99v, Lines 20-25; *kancur*: Image 105 left, Folio 100v, Lines 1-4.

Nosebleeds (2) Image 96 left, Folio 91v, Line 24; Image 100 left, Folio 95v, Lines 19-20.

Palsy (4): Image 96 left, Folio 91v, Line 3; Image 108 left, folio 103v, Line 20-23; Image 113 Left, Folio 108v, Line 24; Image 119 left, Folio 114v, Lines 3-4.

Paralysis (5): *nigram paralisim*, Image 89 left, Folio 84v, Line 23; *Letargie*: Image 109 left, folio 104v & Lines 28-29; Image 113 Left, Folio 108v, Lines 9-10; *mustard*: Image 115 right, Folio 111r, Line 20.

Passions, cold (3) Image 107 right, folio 103r, Lines 12-32 & Image 108 left, folio 103v, Lines 1-11; *spleen and liver*: Image 111 right, Folio 107r, Line 2.

'Phlegm' (Flemma, Flegma) (10): *decursum flegmatis* Image 89 left, Folio 84v, Lines 20-21; *a capite per collum et per posteriora ad inferior*; *Flemma*: Image 89 left, Folio 84v Line 18; Image 107 left, Folio 102v, Lines 23-35 & Image 107 right, folio 103r, Lines 1-12; Image 109 left, folio 104v, Lines 24-28; Image 109 right, Folio 105r, Line 11; Image 120 right, Folio 116r, 18-26; Image 120 right, Folio 116r, Lines 3-11; Image 122 left, Folio 117v, Lines 20-28; Image 128 right, Folio 124r, Lines 10-14.

Plague, (*Pesticilencia*)(5) Image 93 left, Folio 88v, Line 21; *pills for*: Image 98 right, Folio 94r, Lines 13-17; Image 99 right, Folio 95r, Lines 6-9; Image 105 right, Folio 101r, 17-21; *drink for*: Image 117 left, Folio 112v, Line 30 onwards.

Poison (5): *Drinking*: Image 96 left, Folio 91v, Line 15; Image 96 left, Folio 91v, Lines 25-28; *poison*: Image 104 left, Folio 99v, Lines 9-12; *venenum expellit*: Image 108 right, folio 104r, Line 17; Image 119 left, Folio 114v, Line 16.

Purges (2): Image 101 left, Folio 96v, Line 30 onwards; Image 122 left, Folio 117v, Lines 12-18.

Sciatica (4): Image 93 left, Folio 88v, Line 12, Image 108 right, folio 104r, Line 13; Image 113 Left, Folio 108v, Line 23 & *pain in hips*, Line 24.

Shingles (2) Image 102 right, Folio 98r, Lines 8-19; *Cingles (perhaps not by Betson)*: Image 127 right, Folio 123r, Lines 9-17.

Skin Diseases and Leprosy (15): *Sauffleme*: Image 87 right – Folio 83r, Column B, Line 25; *Scab*: Image 98 right, Folio 94r, Lines 22-24; *morphew*: Image 102 right, Folio 98r, Lines 20-30; *morphea*: Image 107 left, Folio 102v, Lines 10-22; *'Cancrum, fistulam, Noli-me-tangere'* : Image 108 right, folio 104r, Line 16; *Leprosa*: Image 108 right, folio 104r, Line 27; *leprosy*: Image 109 left, folio 104v, Lines 3-6; & Image 112 right, Folio 108r, Lines 16-17 & 18-24 & *Oleum Leprosorum*: Image 121 right, Folio 117r, Line 21; *sunburn*: Image 109 left, folio 104v, Lines 1-3; *variolas in facie:* Image 112 right, Folio 108r, Lines 14-15; *ad lupum*: Image 113 Right, Folio 109r, Line 16; *'scabie'*; Image 116 Left, Folio 111v, Lines 21-24; *contra scrophulas*: Image 86 right, Folio 82r, Col. B, Line 1.

Sleep (4) Image 95 right, Folio 91r, Line 27; *provocat*: Image 119 left, Folio 114v, Lines 4-6; Image 122 left, Folio 117v, Lines 1-2; In Herbarium: Image 75 Left, Folio 70v, Col. A, Line 1.

Sores (4): *brennyng*: Image 98 left, Folio 93v, Lines 8-11; *Felon*: Image 93 right, Folio 89r, Line 27; Image 99 right, Folio 95r, Lines 16-19; *cold*: Image 105 right, Folio 101r, Lines 24-31.

Speech, Loss of (5): (perhaps meaning either ' loss of voice' or Aphasia after a stroke): Image 98 left, Folio 93v, Lines 25-26; Image 100 left, Folio 95v, 22-23 ; Image 100 left, Folio 95v, Lines 21-24; *palisim lingue et loquelam*: Image 111, left hand, folio 106v, Lines 15-19; Image 113 Left, Folio 108v, Lines 27-28.

Spitting Blood (1): Image 101 left, Folio 96v, Lines 25-30.

Spleen (4): *Indispositiones splenis*, Image 89 left, Folio 84v, Lines 5-6; *'hard and swollen'*: Image 89 left, Folio 84v, Lines 13-14, *opilacio:* Image 108 right, folio 104r, Line 3; Image 111 right, Folio 107r, Lines 1-3.

'Sinews' (6): *Sprains*: Image 89 left, Folio 84v, Lines 24-27; Image 97 right, Folio 93r, Line 2; Image 98 left, Folio 93v, Line 15; Image 98 left, Folio 93v, Lines 20-21; *Nerves contractos*: Image 108 right, folio 104r, Lines 5-6; *'nerves'* Image 117 left, Folio 112v, Lines 9-10.

Stillbirth (2): Image 90 right, Folio 86r, Line 6, Image 96 left, Folio 91v, Line 17.

Stomach and digestive problems (21): *ventositatem stomachi in mulieribus*: Image 89 left, Folio 84v, Line 7; Image 97 left, Folio 92v, Lines 22 & 28; *'gnawing of the womb'*: Image 97 right, Folio 93r, Line 24; *All the evells in a man's stomach*: Image 101 right, Folio 97r, Lines 11-15; *grynding and akyng in the womb:* Image 101 right, Folio 97r, ines 19-26; *englemed*: Image 105 left, Folio 100v, Line 17 onwards; *a good stomach*: Image 105 right, Folio 101r, line 1-12 ; Image 108 right, folio 104r, Lines 1-3; Image 113 Left, Folio 108v Lines 2 & 3; Image 113 Right, Folio 109r, Line 16; *in men and women*: Image 117 left, Folio 112v, Lines 1-4; *digestion*: Image 117 left, Folio 112v, Lines 15-25 & 26-29; *Colik*: Image 99 right, Folio 95r, Line 15 & Image 105 left, Folio 100v, Lines 11-13 & Image 121 left, Folio 116v, Lines 17-22; Image 128 right, Folio 124r, Lines 1-9.

Stone (6): *gravel in the reynes*: Image 95 left, Folio 90v, Lines 13-14 ; Image 97 left, Folio 92v, Line 30; *lapidem in renibus*: Image 89 right, Folio 85r. Line 10; *to break the stone*: Image 99 right, Folio 95r, Line 13; Image 102 left, Folio 97v, Lines 12-20; Image 129 Left, Folio 124v, Lines 24-29.

Sweating (3): *to induce*: Image 105 left, Folio 100v, Lines 5-11; Image 114 Left, Folio 109v, Line 10; pro *sudario*: Image 129 Left, Folio 124v, Line 21.

Throat (3): *Pain in*: Image 89 right, Folio 85r, Line 24; Image 108 right, folio 104r, Lines 6-7; Image 112 right, Folio 108r, Lines 7-8.

Teeth and Gums (7): Image 98 left, Folio 93v, Line 24; Image 100 left, Folio 95v, Line 27; *loose teeth*: Image 105 left, Folio 100v, Lines 13-17; *Scinanciam* : Image 108 left, folio 103v, Line 31; *commotionem.. dentium*: Image 113 Left, Folio 108v, 29-31; *putridas gingivas (rotted gums)*: Image 119 left, Folio 114v, Lines 2-3; In herbarium Image 84, Right, Folio 80r, Col. B, Line 14.

Urine (10): *Pregnancy, Periods:* Image 34 Right, Folio 30r; Image 89 right, Folio 85r, Line 23 *Urina vero virginis*: Image 89 right, Folio 85r, Line 24; *mulierem recentem cum viro* Image 89 right, Folio 85r Line 29; *ventositatem ebullientem in viis urinalibus*, Image

90 left, Folio 85v; 22-23; *blood in*: Image 100 left, Folio 95v, Line 5; *retention of*: Image 100 left, Folio 95v, Line 6; Image 100 left, Folio 95v, Line 29; Image 102 left, Folio 97v, Lines 21-24; *ad stranguriam*: Image 113 Left, Folio 108v, Line 16 & 17-18. See also *De urinalibus*, ff84r to 86r for more detailed treatment of urine by colour, consistency etc.

Uterus (9): *in mulieribus…vitium matricis*: Image 89 right, Folio 85r. Line 1 *maris*: Image 97 left, Folio 92v, Line 35; *bleeding*: Image 98 left, Folio 93v, Lines 12-14; Image 113 Left, Folio 108v, Lines 19 & 20 & 21; *menstruum sedat*: Image 114 Left, Folio 109v Line 9; *matricem….ab umbelico usque ad muliebria*: Image 115 right, Folio 111r, Lines 1-5 & 6-10; *Super pectinem (pubic bone) movet menstrua*: Image 116 Left, Folio 111v, Line 28; *Menstruation, and urine*: Image 89 right, Folio 85r, Line 30; *Flouris*: Image 95 left, Folio 90v.

Veins (6): *Vene [venae] rupturam circa renes et vesicam* Image 89 right, Folio 85r, Line 3; *venum et vesice putredine vel apostem*: Image 89 right, Folio 85r, Line 5; *Oyntment for*, Image 96 right, Folio 92r, Line 3; *gravel in the*, Image 97 left, Folio 92v, Line 30; Image 97 right, Folio 93r, Line 28; *venas pulsatiles dolore* : Image 114 Right, Folio 110r, Line 14.

Venomous bites (6): *Deterring bites*: Image 95 left, Folio 90v, Lines 15-16; Image 98 left, Folio 93v, Lines 7-8; *ut serpentes capias*: Image 99 right, Folio 95r, Lines 1-3; *bees and wasp stings*: Image 100 left, Folio 95v, Lines 25-26; Image 112 right, Folio 108r, Lines 25-26; *ad venenum scorpionis*: Image 113 Right, Folio 109r, Line 8.

Vertigo (2): Image 97 right, Folio 93r, Line 26; *vanite of the hede*: Image 100 left, Folio 95v, Lines 17-21.

Vomiting (4): Image 89 left, Folio 84v, Line 21; Image 112 right, Folio 108r, Line 31; *provocat vomitum*: Image 116 Left, Folio 111v, Lines 25-27; Image 116 Left, Folio 111v, Line 31.

Worms (8): Image 95 right, Folio 91r, Line 17, Image 96 left, Folio 91v, Line 20; Image 89 left, Folio 84v, Line 11; *in the ear*: Image 89 left, Folio 84v, line 23; Image 97 left, Folio 92v, Line 22; *worms in the teeth*: Image 105 left, Folio 100v, Lines 13-17; *worms in the hair:* Image 109 right, Folio 105r, after Line 15; Image 113 Left, Folio 108v, Line 1; '*pro vermis capitis*': Image 116 Left, Folio 111v, Line 24.

Wounds (6): Image 97 right, Folio 93r, Line 2; *stabbing*: Image 98 right, Folio 94r, Lines 3-6; Image 98 right, Folio 94r, Line 24 onwards; *plagis putridis*: Image 108 right, folio 104r, Lines 24-25; Image 117 left, Folio 112v, Lines 5-17 & *Plaga que non sanaretur* 17-32; Image 119 left, Folio 114v, Lines 6-7.

Appendix 3: Plants at Syon, Sheen and 'aboute London' listed by William Turner, Physician to Protector Somerset from c.1547 to 1551.

Marie Addyman.

Introduction

Sometime between his return from the continent following the death of Henry VIII in 1547, and his departure for the West Country in 1551, William Turner (c.1508-1568) acted as physician to Edward Seymour, Duke of Somerset and Protector of the realm under Henry's son, now Edward VI. Turner refers to having a house at Kew at this time, and from there he could serve as an active member of Somerset's household, moving with him as required between the ducal properties on either side of the Thames at Syon House (the former Syon Abbey) and Shene, as well as to the ducal house in London itself (on the site of the present Somerset House).

From Syon Turner completed his second book on herbs – his first in English – in 1549. This was *The Names of Herbes*, in which he noted several plants growing mainly at Syon, but also at 'Shene', Richmond, and 'aboute London'. In later years Turner continued to refer to the plants he had found at these properties and vicinities. Part 1 of his *Herball*, published in 1551, contains a cluster of further references. There were a few further additions in Part 2, published in 1562 and incorporated with Part 1 and a new Part 3 into the tri-part *Herball* published in 1568, the year of his death.

The record Turner provides of plants in and around Somerset's properties cannot be taken as exhaustive, but within its limits it shows some illuminating variety. It includes: some common English natives for which a vernacular name already existed (e.g., *Filipendula vulgaris* [dropwort]); plants which he had seen abroad but encountered in England only at Syon or Sheen (e.g., *Cistus salvifolius*; *Artemisia pontica*, which he himself had brought from Germany and planted at Syon); a reference to a plant he had in his own garden at Kew (*Sonchus oleraceus* [smooth sow thistle]); and an indication of both plants and knowledge exchanged with those who would be classed as Somerset's and/or Edward VI's servants (*Armorica rusticana* [horseradish]) grown in the gardens of the royal apothecaries, Rich and Morgan.

Turner may have found still growing at Syon plants which had been generally in the monastic medical repertoire. These may have included *Paeonia mascula* and *P. officinalis*, which occur in Betson and Bray as *Glicida, Pionia*; and *Veratrum album*, the plant referred to at this time as 'white hellebore', or in Bray as *Elleborus albus*; *Adarasta*; 'clovetong'. The existence of remedies in both Betson and Turner for white hellebore acts as a reminder of the continuity of medical belief and practice over the late mediaeval and early modern period, since this plant was used within the framework of humoral medicine to induce sneezing and to act with other herbs as a purge by inducing vomiting: Betson states: *purgant choleram*).[142]

One plant listed by Turner which casts a light back onto at least some possible continuity of plants between pre- and post-Dissolution Syon is the pomegranate tree. Betson, who together with Bray used the then common English term 'Pomme garnet', listed pomegranates in his *Herbarium*, though not among his remedies. However, his entry does not incontestably prove that pomegranates were at Syon in the period around 1500 to 1517, since Betson was probably copying a source similar to BL Sloane MS 282 or the *Sinonoma Bartholomaei*, both of which mention *Malum punicum* and *Malum granatum*, the then common names Latin for pomegranates.

Nevertheless, it seems likely that if a pomegranate tree did exist at Syon in the mid-sixteenth century, its planting there belongs probably to the more settled monastic period, rather than to the turbulent times preceding Turner's incumbency under Somerset.It could, for instance, have been the gift of Catherine of Aragon, who was in England from 1501 to 1533, and whose emblem was this fruit. If so, this would make the tree anywhere between 16 and 48 years old when Turner first observed it in 1549.

If there can be only a limited success in showing which plants grew at Syon in both Betson's time and Turner's, it is equally difficult to show for what innovations Turner was responsible. There is one plant he specifically noted that he had brought from Germany to Syon (*Artemisia pontica*), but otherwise there are mainly speculations which have hardened into a rather dubious "tradition". So, for instance, the 1962 edition of *A History of the County of Middlesex* (vol.3, pp.97-100) records that '[Dr William] Turner is said to have planted the mulberry tree by the east front [of Syon House]' – the first mulberry to be planted in England, according to other writers – and moreover that 'The laying out of the formal gardens within the wall around the house is traditionally attributed' to him. But mulberries had been introduced to England by the Romans and they were sufficiently prevalent throughout the Middle Ages and the early modern period, via seedlings and deliberate replanting, for them to be reasonably common in the great gardens of the sixteenth century. Turner himself noted that he had seen them in 'diverse' gardens in England. As for the idea that he was responsible for the layout of Somerset's garden, while it is true that he would have seen some impressive gardens while abroad in the 1540s and also that he cultivated a garden for himself whenever and wherever he could, it is doubtful he had the expertise to create what was in effect a

---

[142] Image 120 right, folio 116r, line 21.

royal garden, compared to the professional gardeners Somerset could call on. But if the Duke wanted to include specifically in his design an up-to-date physic garden, or a garden of rarities, then his best candidate for providing it was the apothecary Hugh Morgan. Morgan had multiple contacts among the merchant importers, and lived on site. His own garden was admired by many including Turner, who praised him for his extensive knowledge.

Turner and Morgan could of course have conferred. In which case, instead of a dubious attribution to a lone genius (Turner) Somerset's creation reflected the current tendency of wealthy and influential Renaissance princes in France, Italy and Germany to harness a team of experts for a given princely project. And indeed, when Turner completed his first book in English on plants and dedicated *The Names of Herbes* to Somerset in 1549, Edward Seymour was at the height of his power. Turner's list of the Duke's titles records this fact, by following customary procedures in 16th century dedicatory preambles. These formalities also meant that the writer could bask in his august patron's glory, particularly when in this instance Turner could say that he was addressing his letter 'from your graces house at Syon'.

> 'To the mooste noble & mighty Prince Edward by the grace of God Duke of Summerset, Erle of Hertford, viscount beuchamp, lord Semour uncle unto the Kynges highnesse of Englande, governour of his moste royall person and Protectour of al his realms dominions and subiectes, lieuetenaunt generall of al his maiesties armies boeth by lande and sea, Treasurer and Erlmarshal of Engande, governoure of the Iles of Guernsey and Jersey, Knyght of the garter, William Turner his servaunte wisheth prosperitie boeth of bodie and Soule.......From your graces house at Syon / Anno Dom. M.CCCCCxlviij [1548, old style, 1549 modern style] / Martii xv.'

By the time Turner came to dedicate Part 1 of his *Herball* to him in 1551, the Duke had survived being deposed as Protector in 1549, imprisoned, and then released from the Tower in 1550. Turner however maintained his links to Syon and Shene. He remained in Somerset's service throughout this period, and he records preaching in April 1551 in the church at 'Thistleworth' – that is, Isleworth, and immediately next to Syon Park. Somerset eventually lost his head in January 1552, and the Seymour family relinquished the property at Syon. Horticultural fashions over the following centuries would inflict great changes on the Syon House gardens. As the eighteenth-century landscape movement gathered force, culminating in the work of Capability Brown at Syon, Somerset's innovative triangular terrace by the south-east side of the house was swept away along with other features, and along, no doubt, with many plants.

There certainly are species growing at Syon today which Turner noted four-and-a-half centuries ago and these have been noted on the list below, following the records kept by the present Head Gardener. But it is not possible to state categorically that they represent an unbroken continuity or deliberate planting, apart from the continuing presence of the sixteenth-century mulberry tree. Some are wild flowers in the surrounding meadows and countryside which one would expect to see: *Hypericum maculatum* [St John's wort]; *Trapogon pratensis* [goatsbeard]; *Filipendula vulgaris* [meadowsweet] towards the Thames; *Picris hieriacoides* (hawksweed – if this was indeed what Turner saw), and the occasional occurrence of *Orobanche rapum-genistae* [greater broomrape]. Some plants, such as *Acanthus mollis*, have been common features of English gardens for centuries. Two are deliberate modern re-plantings: *Cistus salvifolis* and *Cupressus sempervirens*. In some cases the genus, but not the species noted by Turner, is represented: *Artemisia*; *Euphorbia*. Finally, on the whole, as will be seen from the list below, the plants found at the present at Syon do not include those Turner recorded at Shene and 'aboute London'.

Turner's plant lists

A. *The Names of Herbes* (1549)

83   **Acanthus** [*Acanthus mollis*].
'in the greatest plentie that I euer sawe it, I did see it in my Lorde Protectours graces gardine at Syon'.
WT name: 'Branke ursin'.
Common English name: bear's breeches.
2014: at Syon.

86   **Alysson Plinii** [*Sherardia arvensis* L.].
'Alyscon Plinii is a rare herbe whiche I coulde neuer see but once in Englande and that was a litle from Syon'.
WT name: 'purple goosgrase'.
Common English name: field madder.
2014: not at Syon.

89   **Ascyron** [*Hypericum maculatum*].
'... is not very common in England, howe be it I sawe it thys last yere in Syon parck'.
WT name: 'square saint Johans grasse'; 'great saynt Johans grasse'.
Common English name: imperforate St John's wort.
Not listed by Forrest (1831), pp163-164.
2014: in the meadows at Syon.

91   **Barba hirci** [*Trapogon pratensis*].
        '... groweth in the fieldes aboute London plentuously'.
        WT name: 'gotes bearde'.
        Common English name: goatsbeard.
        2014: in the meadows at Syon.

92   Betonica Pauli aeginete [*Veronica officinalis*].
        'it groweth... in a parke besyde London'.
        WT name: 'Paul's Betony'; 'wood penyryal'.
        Common English name: heath speedwell.
        2014: at Syon.

92   **Blitum [*Chenopodium sp? Blitum virgatum*?].**
        'I neuer saw it in England but in my lords gardine'.
        WT name: 'Blete'.
        Common English name: none/unclear.
        2014: *Genus* at Syon; *species* unclear.
        Listed as occurring only in France, Germany and Scandinavia by Fitter (1974).

93   **Calamintha** [*Calamintha ascendens*].
        '[one kind] groweth muche aboute Syon in Englande'.
        WT name: 'bush calamint', 'hore calamynt'.
        Common English name: none.
        2014: not at Syon.

97   **Cisthus** [*Cistus salvifolius*].
        'one kinde of cisthus growth in my lordes gardine in Syon'.
        WT name: cittsage'; 'bushsage'.
        Common English name: none.
        2014: at Syon.

99   **Coronopus** [*Plantago coronopus*].
        'it groweth much about Shene aboue London'.
        WT name: 'Crowfote weybreade'; 'Herbe Iue'.
        Common English name: buckshorn plantain.
        2014: not at Syon.

100   **Cupressus [*Cupressus sempervirens*].**
'…growe in great plentie in my lordes graces gardine at Syon'.
WT name: 'cypresse tree'.
Common English name: cypress.
2014: at Syon.

102   **Ephemerum non lethale** [*Convallaria majalis*].
'Ephemerū…groweth… not in England that I euer could see, sauinge in my Lordes gardine in Syon'.
WT name: 'May Lilies'.
Common English name: lily of the valley.
2014: at Syon.

108   **Hyacinthus verus** [*Hyacinthoides non-scriptus*].
'The cōmune Hyacinthus is muche in England abouet Syon and Shene…Some use the rootes for glue'.
WT names: 'crowtoes'; 'Crawtees'.
Common English name: bluebell.
2014: at Syon.

108   **Lotus syluestris** [*Melilotus italica*].
'Thys herbe groweth nowe in Syon gardine'.
WT name: 'Melilote'; 'wylde lote'.
Common English name: mellilot.
2014: not at Syon.

113   **Lysimachia** [*Lysimachia vulgaris*].
'it growth by the Temes side beside Shene'.
WT name: 'yealow Lousstryfe'; 'herbe Wylowe'.
Common English name: yellow loosestrife.
2014: at Syon.

114   **Malus punica** [*Punica granatum*].
'there are certayne in my Lordes gardine in Syon, but their fruite cometh neuer unto perfection'.
WT name: 'Pomgranat Tree'.
Common English name: pomegranate.
2014: not at Syon.

116   **Narcissus** [*Narcissus poeticus*].
'one with a white floure…groweth plentuously in my Lordes gardine in Syon'.

WT name: 'Whyte daffadyl'; 'whyte Laus tibi'.
Common English name: narcissus.
2014: not at Syon.

117   **Oenanthe** [*Filipendula vulgaris*]
'..groweth in great plentie beside Syon & Shene in the middowes'.
WT name: 'filipendula'.
Common English name: dropwort.
2014: at Syon.

118   **Ornithogalum** [*Ornithogalum umbellatum*].
'I never saw it in Englande, sauyng onely in Shene, herde by the Temmes side'.
WT name: 'dogleke'; 'dogges onyons'.
Common English name: common star of Bethlehem.
2014: at Syon.

119   **Panicum** [*Setaria italica*].
'I have not seene it in Englande, saving in my Lordes gardine at Syon'.
WT name: 'Panike'.
Common English name: none; probably a form of millet.
2014: not at Syon.

121   **Pinus.**
'…one fayre one in Richmund'.
WT name: 'pyne tree'.
Common English name: pine.
2014: several species at Syon.

127   **Satyrion** [*Spiranthes spiralis*].
'a certurne ryghte kynde… groweth besyde Syon'.
WT name: 'Lady traces' (*i.e.* 'tresses')
Common English name; Autumn lady's tresses.
2014: not at Syon.

130   **Sison** [*Sison amomum*].
'ther groweth a kynde of this beside Shene'.
WT name: 'wylde Perseley'.
Common English name: stone parsley.
2014: not at Syon.

130		**Solanum vesicarium** [*Physalis alkakengi*].

'Thys herbe groweth much in my Lordes gardine at Syon'.
WT name: 'Alkaceng' 'wynter cheries'.
Common English name: Cape gooseberry.
2014: at Syon.

131   **Spartum frutex** [*Retama monosperma*].
'Spartium or Spartum is… founde… in my Lordes gardine at Shene'.
WT name: 'French Broume'.
Common English name: bridal broom.
2014: this species not at Syon; others present.

132   **Symphytum** [*Prunella vulgaris*].
'this herbe groweth about Syon, seven miles above London'.
WT name: 'unsavery Margeru[m]'.
Common English name: self-heal.
2014: at Syon.

132   **Thlaspi** [*Armorica Rusticana*].
'…groweth plentuously beside Syon'.
WT name: 'Boures mustard', 'dyshmustard', 'treacle mustard'.
Common English name: horse radish.
2014: at Syon.

134   **Veratrum** [*Veratrum album*].
'This kinde groweth in Syon Parcke in Englande'.
WT name: 'Nesewurt or whyte Nesewurt'.
Common English name: false hellebore.
2014: not at Syon.

[Addendum to *Names*] 'Names of newe founde Herbes, wherof is no mention in any olde auncient wryter'

136   **Bipennella Italica** [*Sanguisorba officinalis*].
'It groweth much about Syon and Shene'.
WT name: 'Burnet'.
Common English name: great burnet.
2014: at Syon.
Ray (1947), p. 238, has reservations about this identification.

139   **Saxifragia** [*Silaum silaus*]
       'Thys groweth by the Temmes side about Shene'.
       WT name: 'saxifrage'.
       Common English name: pepper saxifrage.
       2014: not at Syon.

B. *A New Herball* Part 1 (1551)

The plants in all three parts of *A New Herball* are set out on the model of Dioscorides' *Materia medica*, with one plant per chapter. Eight of the plants Turner refers to in *H*1 as being at either Syon or Sheen or 'aboute London' had been previously listed in *Names*. These chapter headings are:

35   **Of brank ursine** [*Acanthus sp.*]: 'plentuously in my lordes gardyne at Syon'.
79   **Of great Saint Johnes wurte** [*Hypericum maculatum*]: 'in Syon parke'.
89   **Of bukkes bearde** [*Trapogon pratensis*]: 'about London'.
94   **Of Paulis Betony** [*Veronica officinalis*]: 'in Syon gardyn and in dyuerse woddes not far from Syon'.
97   **Of blites** [*Chenopodium sp.*]: 'in my Lordes gardyne at Shene'.
109   **Of Calmynte** [*Calamintha ascendens*]: 'aboute Syon'.
144   **Of Cistus** [*Cistus salvifolius*]: 'in my lordes garden at Syon'.
162   **Of herbe Iue** [*Plantago sp.*]: 'about Shene in the highway'.
176   **Of the Cypres tre** [*Cupressus sempervirens*]: 'the female groweth right plentuously in the gardin of Syon'.

The new entries are:
29   **Of wormwode** [*Artemisia sp.; Artemisia pontica*].
       'Wormwood pontyke groweth…only in my lordes gardyne at Syon, & that I brought out of Germany'.
       WT name: 'pontike wormwode'.
       Common English name: old man.
       2014: various species of *Artemisia* at Syon.

55   **Of Ami** [*Ammi maius*].
       '… in my lordes gardyne at Syone in England'.
       WT name: 'Ammi'.
       Common English name: (form of) wild carrot.
       2014: not at Syon.

64 **Of camomyle** [*Anthemis nobilis*].
'uiii [8] myle aboue London, it growth in the wylde felde, in rychmonde grene, in brantfurde grene, and in mooste plenty of al, in hunsley hethe'.
WT name: 'camomyle'.
Common English name: camomile.
2014: at Syon.

137 **Of Cicerbita** [*Sonchus oleraceus*].
'...in the gardine of the barbican in London and I haue it in my garden at Kew'.
WT name: 'sowthystel'.
Common English name: smooth sow thistle.
2014: at Syon.

185 **Of Lauriel or lowry** [*Daphne laureola*].
'Thys herbe groweth...at Sion'.
WT name: 'Dapnoides'; 'lauriel'; 'lowry'; 'lorell'.
Common English name: spurge laurel.
2014: not at Syon.

C. *A New* Herball Part 2 (1562)

Two of the plants Turner refers to in part 2 of the New Herball as being at either Syon or Sheen or 'aboute London' had been previously listed in *Names*. These chapter headings are:

328 **Of treacle mustard called Thlaspi** [*Armorica Rusticana*].
'in moste plentye aboute Sion. In London it growth in maister Riches gardin/ and maister Morganes also'.
Common English name: horse radish.
2014: not at Syon.

330 **Of the kindes of Tithymales or kinds of Spourges** [*Euphorbia sp.*].
'in Sion parke aboute London'.
WT name: 'the male called Chariacias/ of other Comeles/ of other Cobius or Amigdeloides'.
Common English name: spurge.
2014: *Euphorbia characias* at Syon.

The new entries are:
51 **Of Hawke wede** [*Picris hieriacoides; Crepis* sp?]

'…in the medowe a lytle from Shene'.
WT name: 'greate hawkweed'; 'yealow sucory'.
Common English name: hawksbeard; smooth hawksbeard.
2014: at Syon.
Chapman (1995), n.61, p.611, points out that Turner's illustration is of *Crepis capillaris*.

166 **Of Orobanche** [*Orobanche rapum-genistae*].
'…in the South countre a lytl from Shene, in the broum closes. But it hath no name there'.
WT name: 'Orobanche'; 'chokefitche'; 'stragletare'.
Common English name: greater broomrape.
2014: occasional at Syon.

191 **Of bothe the kyndes of Peonye** [*Paeonia officinalis; P.mascula*].
WT records Galen's recommendation to hang 'the roote of Peoni' round the neck of a child suffering from "the falling sickness" (epilepsy), and says he did this with great success 'at Syon in my lord of Summersettes house'.
WT name: 'peoni'.
Common English name: peony.
2014: not at Syon.

314 **Of French or Spanish brome** [*Spartium junceum*].
'…at Shene in the gardine'.
WT name: 'Spanish brome'.
Common English name: Spanish broom.
2014: at Syon.

318 **Thystelles** [? *Carduus acanthoides*]
'The one… called in Greek acantha leuke [and] Spina Alba… groweth…beside Syon in England'.
WT name: 'whyte thystel'
Common English name: none.
2014: other *Carduus* spp. at Syon.
Chapman (1995), n. 291, p.625 points out that Turner conflates several 'thystelles', leaving unclear the species referred to here. There is no illustration to aid identification.

Texts, references, and further reading

A. TURNER TEXTS

i. *The Names of Herbes*. Quotations from *Names* are taken from J. Britten, B.D Haydon & W.T. Stearn's facsimile edition, *William Turner, Libellus de Re Herbaria Novus, 1538 & The Names of Herbs, 1548* (The Ray Society, London, 1965). It should be noted that the editors in their introductory essay did not comment on the dating of the work. The date Turner gave, March 15th, 1548, reflects 'old-style' dating when the year was reckoned as beginning on March 25th. In modern dating, the year of publication therefore is 1549.

The text of *Names*, with some OCR errors can be seen at:
http://www.archive.org/stream/namesherbes01britgoog/namesherbes01britgoog_djvu.txt

ii. *A New Herball*, Part 1. Facsimile edition, edited by G. Chapman & M. Tweddle (The Mid-Northumberland Arts Group & Carcanet Press, Ashington and Manchester, 1989).

iii. *A New Herball*, Parts 2 and 3. Facsimile edition, edited by G. Chapman, F. McCombie & M. Wesencraft (CUP, Cambridge etc, 1995).

Page references are to the facsimile texts in the modern editions. Quotations retain Turner's various spellings for the same word ('saynt'/ 'saint' etc), his eclectic use of capitals, and the standard 16th century use of 'u' for 'v' ('euer') and 'y' for 'i' ('whyte').

B. REFERENCES AND FURTHER READING

i. R. Fitter, A. Fitter & M. Blamey, *Wild Flowers of Britain and Northern Europe* (1st pub, 1974; Harper Collins, London etc, 1993). This has been used to check the modern common English names applied to English native plants. Some plants, coming from the continent, have proved harder or impossible to identify from Turner's descriptions; others have no common English name.

ii.R. Forrest, *Alphabetical Catalogue of the Plants of Syon Garden 1831*. (A&R Spottiswoode, London 1831). Comparison with Forrest's list is instructive, as indicating plants Forrest either omitted, could not find, or included as growing at Syon when he was writing.

iii. G. Grigson, *The Englishman's Flora* (1st pub. 1955; fac. ed., J.M. Dent and Sons, London etc, 1987). This gives commentaries on many old English vernacular names, including occasional details from Turner (e.g., making glue from bluebell sap), and is worth consulting for any of the entries below.

iv. For more information on Turner and his presence at Syon see:
iv.a. M. Addyman, *William Turner: the Father of English Botany* (Northumberland County Council, Morpeth: 2008)
iv.b. M. Addyman, *Physic and Philosophy: William Turner's Botanical Medicine* (forthcoming)
iv.c. C. Raven, *Early Naturalists from Neckham to Ray* (CUP, Cambridge: 1947)

v. For information on Protector Somerset, see:
W.K. Jordan, *Edward VI: The Threshold of Power* (Harvard UP, Cambridge, Mass.: 1970).

Thanks to Topher Martyn, Head Gardener at Syon, for providing notes which make it possible to show which of the London plants Turner referred to in 1549 can be seen in and around Syon today. Thanks also to John Adams for helpful discussions on pomegranates and mulberries.

Marie Addyman. August, 2014

Texts, references, and further reading

a. TURNER TEXTS

    i.   *The Names of Herbes*. Quotations from *Names* are taken from J. Britten, B.D Haydon & W.T. Stearn's facsimile edition, *William Turner, Libellus de Re Herbaria Novus, 1538 & The Names of Herbs, 1548* (The Ray Society, London, 1965). It should be noted that the editors in their introductory essay did not comment on the dating of the work. The date Turner gave, March 15th, 1548, reflects 'old-style' dating when the year was reckoned as beginning on March 25th. In modern dating, the year of publication therefore is 1549.

The text of *Names*, with some OCR errors can be seen at:
http://www.archive.org/stream/namesherbes01britgoog/namesherbes01britgoog_djvu.txt

ii. *A New Herball*, Part 1. Facsimile edition, edited by G. Chapman & M. Tweddle (The Mid-Northumberland Arts Group & Carcanet Press, Ashington and Manchester, 1989).

iii. *A New Herball*, Parts 2 and 3. Facsimile edition, edited by G. Chapman, F. McCombie & M. Wesencraft (CUP, Cambridge etc, 1995).

Page references are to the facsimile texts in the modern editions. Quotations retain Turner's various spellings for the same word ('saynt'/ 'saint' etc), his eclectic use of capitals, and the standard 16th century use of 'u' for 'v' ('euer') and 'y' for 'i' ('whyte').

b. **References and Further Reading**

i. R. Fitter, A. Fitter & M. Blamey, *Wild Flowers of Britain and Northern Europe* (1st pub, 1974; Harper Collins, London etc, 1993). This has been used to check the modern common English names applied to English native plants. Some plants, coming from the continent, have proved harder or impossible to identify from Turner's descriptions; others have no common English name.

ii. R. Forrest, *Alphabetical Catalogue of the Plants of Syon Garden 1831*. (A&R Spottiswoode, London 1831). Comparison with Forrest's list is instructive, as indicating plants Forrest either omitted, could not find, or included as still growing at Syon.

iii. G. Grigson, *The Englishman's Flora* (1st pub. 1955; fac. ed., J.M. Dent and Sons, London etc, 1987). This gives commentaries on many old English vernacular names, including occasional details from Turner (e.g., making glue from bluebell sap), and is worth consulting for any of the entries below.

iv. For more information on Turner and his presence at Syon see:
iv.a. M. Addyman, *William Turner: the Father of English Botany* (Northumberland County Council, Morpeth: 2008)
iv.b. M. Addyman, *Physic and Philosophy: William Turner's Botanical Medicine* (forthcoming)
iv.c. C. Raven, *Early Naturalists from Neckham to Ray* (CUP, Cambridge: 1947)

v. For information on Protector Somerset, see:
W.K. Jordan, *Edward VI: The Threshold of Power* (Harvard UP, Cambridge, Mass.: 1970).

**Appendix 4: Text of folio 135v in Rosenbach Foundation H491,
the Scala Perfectionis, written by James Grenehalgh, Brother at Sheen Carthusian
Priory (1414-1539) for Joanna Sewell, Sister at Syon Abbey.**

The Latin Text is taken in part from the hymn *Cultor Dei Memento* by Prudentius
(d. around AD 413), and from Psalm 90 (Septuagint numbering).

*

In despsisyng of *th*e Fend, oure ghostly enmye, Say *th*is himne:

O tortuose serpens qui mille per meandros fraudes*que*
[O crooked serpent, that with a thouand twisted and winding deceits]
flexuosas, agitas quieta corda. Discede. Christus hic est.
[distrubs the quietness of hearts, Depart. Christ is here.]
Hic est Christus. Liquesce. Signum. T. quod ipse nosci damnat
[Here is Christ. Melt away. The sign of the cross, which you well know, damns]
tuam catervam. T. crux pellit omne crimen. Fugi
[thy horde (of devils). The cross drives out all guilt. Darkness]
-unt. + Crucem tenebre. Tali dicata signo. +. Mens fluctuare
[flees the cross. Blest with this sign of the cross, the mind]
Nescit. Discede & cetera. As it is afore.
[does not waver. Depart, etc]

Agaynes vayne dremes or fantaisies sai *th*is verse:

Procul. O. Procul vagantum portenta somniorum
[Away, away, the omens of vain dreams]
Procul esto pervicaci prestigiator hastu. Discede & cetera.
[Away, you deceiver, with your endless guile. Depart, etc]

*

Appendix 4, Rosenbach Foundation H491, the Scala Perfectionis, f.135v, continued:

Around and within a drawing of a Church:

Sanctus Salvator
Aureola[143]

Maria　　　　　　　　Johanna Sewell　　　　　　　　Birgitta

Sanctus Augustinus

	Vallata		A timore nocturno,
Sicque	Stipata seu	Non timebis	A sagitta per ambulante in die. A negocio
	Murata		Perambulante in tenebris. Ab incursu, et et cetera
			Demonis meridiano.
			Sed cadent a latere tuo

Translation (using Douay Reims, Psalm 90):

			Of the terror of the night.
	Fortified		Of the arrow that flieth in the day, of the business
So that	Enclosed or	Thou shalt not be afraid	That walketh about in the dark. Of invasion, or
	Walled up		Of the noonday devil.
			(A thousand) shall fall at thy side,

Ad te autem [JS monogram] non appropinquabit. Quod prestare dignetur
　　　　　　　　　　　　　　　　JeSus Christus Dominus Noster. AMEN.

But it shall not come nigh thee [JS]. Which be pleased to grant,
　　　　　　　　　　　　JeSus Christ, Our Lord. AMEN.

---

[143] Perhaps an internal reference to Hilton's *Scala Perfectionis* fol. lxi, 'Thyse thre werkes..shull haue specyall mede whyche they callen aureole.' The three works are martyrdom, preaching and virginity. The Hilton text goes on to praise the enclosing of anchorites, whose reward in heaven may be greater than that of priests.

Appendix 5: Text From Joseph Strutt, *Bibliographical Dictionary* (1785), plate iv, and text, page 28. To accompany the copy of the Image itself.

"Plate IV: This singular curiosity is already spoken of in the fourth chapter of this Essay (*pp17-19. Strutt had bought the plate at a sale in 1784*); there is the greatest reason to believe it was engraved in England, and the plate itself bears every mark of great antiquity. It had a hole at the top quite through it, by which it appears to have been fastened by a nail to the wall, perhaps of some religious place, and to this circumstance, it is not improbable, we owe its preservation. The scratches and other defacements which it has sustained from the hand of time, could not be removed without danger of destroying the originality of the engraved work, and for that reason it was conceived to be much better to let them remain as they are, than to run any hazard that was not absolutely necessary. The plate is in my own possession.[144]

The prayers contained upon the plate are, as my readers may readily see, in Latin; but as this work may fall into the hands of some persons unacquainted with the old manuscript forms of letters, which are here closely imitated, I have transcribed them (some few words excepted, which are by no means intelligible to me.)"

ORATIO DE OMNIBUS SANCTIS

Gaude mater salvatoris
Felix fide flos decoris
Mundique solacium
Nunc letare celi choris
Ju hoc festo et langoris
Nostri sis remedium.

Gaude Michael *in* hac die
Gabriel Raphaelque Messie
Angelorum ordines
Nos precamu*r* nobis pie
Sitis cause melodie
Supra celi cardines.

Gaude Petre cum sodali
Paulo Xto speciali
Luceus orbis climata
Et caterva (*celestia ?*) generali
Vestri sita loco tali
Nos cum eis adiuva.

Gaude Thoma, spes Anglorum
Et Georgi tutor horum
Cum Edwardo nobili
Tu *Laurenti* regem lorum
Ut *tuamur poli* chorum
Cum favore Stephani.

---

[144] Current whereabouts unknown.

Gaude ventre conservatus
O Baptista mire natus
Sacer degens seculo
P*a*triarchis sociatus
Et p*r*ophetis viae *(vite ?)* flatus
Ffac finire jubilo,

Gaude presul on Martine
Nicholai hugo line
Posse nobis gratiam
Erkenwalde que Birine
Iam cum tuis Augustine
Da supremo gloriam

Gaude Virgo Katerina
Margaretta, Magdalena
Cum Brigitta Birgida et
Anna ffides & Xristina
Nos servando…… *divina*
Gens celorum jubila
Amen. Letamini in D*o*m*i*no &c
Et G*lo*ria, *o*m*n*es.

Concede quibus o*m*nipotens Deus, ut intercessio sancte Dei genetricis Marie sancta*rum* q*ue* o*m*nium celestiu*m* virtutum & beato*rum* patriarcha*rum*, propheta*rum*, ap*o*sto*l*o*rum*, evangelista*rum*, martyro*rum*, c*o*nfessorum atque virginu*m* & et o*mnium* electo*rum* tuo*rum* nos ubiq*ue* letificet ut du*m* eo*rum* merita recolem*us* proemia *(senciamus?)*, per eundem Xristu*m* dominum nostrum Amen.

'The words printed in italics are such as are very difficult to decipher; and I am by no means certain, that the true meaning is given to them. In the seventh prayer, there are two words which I cannot explain.'

SELECT BIBLIOGRAPHY

Select Bibliography

ADAMS, J. S., (2012). A Bibliography of Syon Abbey to the Dissolution in 1539, with some Sources for the Early History of Syon House to 1600. http://syonabbeysociety.wordpress.com/sara-bibliography/

ADMAN, A. Fredriksson (1997). *Vadstena klosters bibliotek: en analys av förvärv och bestånd*. Uppsala.

ALLEN, D. C. (1941), *The star-crossed Renaissance: the quarrel about astrology and its influence in Englan* . Duke University Press.

ANAGNOSTOU, Sabine, EGMOND, Florike, & FRIEDRICH, Christoph, (2011). *A Passion for Plants: materia medica and botany in scientific networks from the 16th to the 18th centuries*. Quellen und Studien zur Geschicte der Pharmazie. Wissenschaftliche Verlaggesellschaft, mbH, Stuttgart, Germany.

ANDERSON, Frank J. (1997) *An Illustrated History of Herbals* Columbia University Press .

ANDERSSON, E., (2011). *Responsiones Vadstenenses: Perspectives on the Birgittine Rule in Two Texts from Vadstena and Syon Abbey*. Acta Universitatis Stockholmiensis, Studia Latina Stockholmiensia LV, Stockholms Universitet. Stockholm, Sweden.

ANDERSSON, R. (1994) *Predikosamlingar i Vadstena klosterbibliotek*. Upsala, Sweden.

ANDERSSON-SCHMITT, Margarete, & HEDLUND, Monica (10 Volumes 1989 -) *Mittelalterliche Handschriften Der Universitatsbibliothek Uppsala*. Almqvist & Wiksell International, Stockholm.

ANDRÉ JACQUES, (1985). *Les Noms de Plantes dans la Rome Antique*. Les Belles Lettres. Paris, France.

ARBER, A. 1938. *Herbals, Their Origin and Evolution,* University Press, Cambridge.

ARRIZABALAGA, Jon. (1998). *The Articella in the Early Press, 1476-1534*. Cambridge Wellcome Unit for the History of Medicine & CSIC Barcelona, Department of History of Science.

AUNGIER, (1840). *History of Syon Monastery*, J. Nichols and Son, London.

AVICENNA, *Canon of Medicine*, Ed. O. Cameron Gruner, AMS Press, New York, 1929.

BAADER, Gerhard (1985). *Mediaeval Adaptations of Byzantine Medicine* in The Dumbarton Oaks Papers, Number thirty-eight, 1984, Symposium on Byzantine Medicine. John Scarborough, Editor. Dumbarton Oaks Research Library and Collection, Washington DC.

BAINBRIDGE , Virginia R. (2004). '*Reynolds, Richard [St Richard Reynolds]* . Oxford Electronic Dictionary of National Biography, Oxford University Press.

BARKER, Juliet (2005). *Agincourt*. Little, Brown.

BARRATT, Alexandra (2001).*The knowing of woman's kind in childing : a Middle English version of material derived from the Trotula and other sources*. Cheltenham: European Schoolbooks.

BARTHOLOMAEUS ANGLICUS, (1975 and 1988). *On the Properties of Things, John Trevisa's Translation of Bartholomaeus Anglicus De Proprietatibus Rerum, a Critical Text*, eds. M. C. Seymour, et al., vols. 1 and 2 (1975); vol. 3 (1988).

BATESON, Mary (1898). *Catalogue of the Library of Sion Monastery, Isleworth*. CUP.

BAYARD, Tania (1985). *Sweet Herbs and Sundry Flowers; Medieval Gardens and the Gardens of the Cloisters.* New York: The Metropolitan Museum of Art, David R. Godine Publisher.

BECK, R. T., (1974). *The cutting edge: early history of the surgeons of London*. London.

BECKETT W. N. M., (2009). *Thomas Betson. Oxford Electronic Dictionary of National Biography*, Oxford University Press.

BECKETT, Neil (1993). *St Bridget, Henry V and Syon Abbey*. In *Studies in St. Birgitta and the Brigittine Order, Volume2, pp125-150, Analecta Cartusiana 35:19, Spiritualität Heute und Gestern, Band 19.* HOGG, James, Editor. Institut Für Anglistik und Amerikanistik, Universität Salzburg, Austria.

BELL, David N. (1992). *Corpus of British Medieval Library Catalogues*, Volume 3 (1992). *The Libraries of the Cistercians, Gilbertines, and Premonstratensians*. British Library.

BELL, David N., (1995). *What Nuns Read: Books and Libraries in Mediaeval English Nunneries*. Kalamazoo, Cistercian Studies Series 158. Michigan: Medieval Institute Publications.

BENSKIN, M.. LAING, M., KARAISKOS, V. & WILLIAMSON, D. K., (2013). *An Electronic Version of a Linguistic Atlas of Late Mediaeval English*. University of Edinburgh, eLALME. http://www.lel.ed.ac.uk/ihd/elalme/elalme.html

BETSON, Thomas (before AD 1517) *Notebook*; St John's College, Cambridge. MS 109 (E.6).

BETSON, Thomas. *Registrum bibliothece de Syon*. '*The catalogue of the Library of Syon Monastery, Isleworth.*' xv-xvi c. Latin on vellum. Cambridge, Corpus Christi College, Parker Medieval Manuscripts MS 141. Catalogue to the Brothers' Library. See also Bateson (1898) and Gillespie (2001).

BETSON, Thomas, (1500). *A Ryght Profytable Treatyse Drawen out of Dyuerse Wrytynges to Dyspose Men to Be Vertuously Occupied in Theyr Myndes and Prayers*. Westminster: Wynkyn de Worde. STC 1978.

BILDHAUER, Bettina, (2005). *The Secrets of Women* (c.1300): *A Mediaeval Perspective on Menstruation*, in *Menstruation, a Cultural History*, Edited by SHAIL, Andrew, and HOWIE, Gillian, Palgrave MacMillan.

BISHOP, Louise M., (2007). *Words, Stones, & Herbs: The Healing Word in Medieval and Early Modern England*. Syracuse University Press.

BLUNT, Wilfrid & RAPHAEL Sandra, (1994). *The Illustrated Herbal*. Thames and Hudson.

BODARWÉ, Katrinette, (2003). *Pflege und Medizin in mittelaterlichen Frauenkonventen ('Care and Medicine in Medieval Nuneries')* in the Medizin Historisches Journal (Medicine and the Life Sciences in History), Urban & Fischer Verlag, 3-4, Band 37, 2003.

BOTFIELD, B., ed. (1838). *Catalogi veteres librorum Ecclesiæ Cathedralis Dunelm. Catalogues of the Library of Durham Cathedral at various periods from the Conquest to the Dissolution, including catalogues of the Library of the Abbey of Hulm, and of the MSS. preserved in the Library of Bishop Cosin, at Durham.* Surtees Society, Volume 7.

BOWN, Deni, (1995). *The Royal Horticultural Society Encyclopedia of Herbs and their Uses.* Dorling Kindersley.

BRIDGET (BIRGITTA), Saint. *Reualaciones Extrauagantes.* Chapter 28, Sections 1-10. https://riksarkivet.se/Media/pdf-filer/SanctaBirgitta_Reuelaciones_Extrauagantes.pdf

BRIQUET, Charles Moïse, (1907). *Les Filigranes. Dictionnaire historique des marques du papier des leur apparition vers 1282 jusqu'en 1600.* A facsimile of the 1907 edition with supplementary material contributed by a number of scholars. Edited by Allan Stevenson. (The New Briquet. Jubilee edition).

BRODIN, Gösta, (1950). *Agnus Castus, A Middle English Herbal.* Essays and Studies On English Language and Literature, VI, edited by SB Liljegren.

BYNUM, Caroline Walker (c.1987). *Holy Food, Holy Fast, the significance of food to mediaeval women, c. 1480-1533.* Berkeley, University of California Press.

CAIUS, John. (1552). *A Boke or Counseill Against the Disease Commonly Called the Sweate, or Sweatyng Sicknesse.* Richard Grafton, London.

CANUTI, Benedictus, Bishop of Väseras, Denmark (1485?). *A litil boke...for the ...Pestilence.* Manchester University Press facsimile, 1910.

CAREY, H. M. (1992). *Courting disaster: astrology at the English court and university in the later middle ages.* New York: St Martin's.

CATHERINE OF SIENA, (1519). *The Orcherde of Syon*, Wynkyn de Worde, London.

CATTO, J., (2003). *Bibliographical Notes: Thomas Betson of Syon Abbey.* English Historical Review, Apr 2003; 118: 487 - 488.

CLARK, John Willis (1897). *Observances in use at the Augustinian Priory of St Giles and S Andrew, at Barnwell Cambridgeshire.* Macmillan and Bowes, Cambridge.

CLENDENING, Logan, (1960). *Source Book of Medical History.* Courier Dover Publications.

COATES, Alan (1999). *English Medieval Books: The Reading Abbey Collections from Foundation to Dispersal* Oxford: Clarendon Press.

COLLINS, Minta (2000). *Medieval Herbals: The Illustrative Traditions.* British Library Studies in Mediaeval Culture, British Library, London.

CROSSLEY, Fred. H., (1949). *The English Abbey, Its Life and Work in the Middle Ages*, Batsford, London.

DAEMS, W. F. (1993). *Nomina simplicium medicinarum ex synonymariis Medii Aevi collecta. Semantische Untersuchungen zum Fachwortschatz hoch- und spätmittelalterlicher Drogenkunde.* Studies in Ancient Medicine 6. (Leiden, Brill).

DARWIN, Tess, (2008). *The Scots Herbal: The Plant Lore of Scotland.* The Mercat Press.
DAWSON, Warren R., (1934). *A Leechbook or Collection of Medical Recipes from the Fifteenth Century.* The text of Medical Society of London MS No. 136. MacMillan and Co, London.

de HAMEL, C. (1991). *Syon Abbey: The Library of the Bridget Bridgettine Nuns and their Peregrinations after the Reformation, with the Manuscript at Arundel Castle: an Essay.* Otley. Privately printed at Smith Settle for the Roxburghe Club.

DE VRIEND, Hubert Jan (1984). EETS *The Old English Herbarium and Medicina de quadrupedis* No OS 286. Oxford University Press.

DEANESLY, Margaret (1920). *The Lollard Bible and other medieval Biblical versions*, Cambridge University Press.

DEANESLY, Margaret, (1915). The *Incendium Amoris of Richard Rolle of Hampole* (Manchester University Press). http://lollardsociety.org/pdfs/Rolle_IncendiumAmoris.pdf

DENDLE, P., & TOUWAIDE, A., (2008). *Herbs and the Medieval Surgeon*, in *Health and Healing from the Medieval Garden.* Woodbridge, The Boydell Press, Woodbridge.

DOBSON, M. J. (1989). *History of Malaria in England.* Journal of the Royal Society of Medicine, Supplement No 17, Volume 82, 1989.

NEBBIAI-DALLA GUARDA, Donatella (1994). *Les Livres De L'infirmeries dans les Monastères Mediaévaux._*Revue Mabillon 66, pp57-81.

DOYLE, A. I. (1956a). *Thomas Betson of Syon Abbey*, The Library, 5th series, 11 (1956).

DOYLE, A. I. (1956b). *The Durham University Catalogue for Cosin V, III, 16,* in *The Library*, 5th ser. 11 (1956) 115-118.

DOYLE, A. I. (2004). *"A Letter Written by Thomas Betson, Brother of Syon Abbey"* in *The Medieval Book and a Modern Collector: Essays in Honour of Toshiyuki Takamiya.* DS Brewer & Yushodo Press, Cambridge and Tokyo.

DUGDALE, W.,(1692). *Monasticon Anglicanum* VI, (1), 540. R. Midgley.

DUKE, James A., (2003). *The Green Pharmacy.* Rodale.

DYER, Alan (1997). *The English Sweating Sickness of 1551: An Epidemic anatomised.* Medical History. July 1997; 41(3): pp362–384.

EARLE, J. (1880). *English Plant Names From The Tenth To The Fifteenth Century.* OUP.

ERLER, M. C. (1992). 'Pasted-in embellishments in English manuscripts and printed books, c.1480–1533', The Library, 6th ser., 14 (1992), 185–206.

EVERETT, Nicholas, (2012). *Alphabet of Galen*, University of Toronto Press.

FECKENHAM, J. (c.1570). *The Book of Sovereign Remedies* in LALOR, Daphne, (1995). MS X3346 (Alexander Turnbull Library Wellington NZ). University of Auckland Ph.D Thesis 1995. PDF: https://researchspace.auckland.ac.nz/handle/2292/2281

FITTER, R., FITTER, A., & BLAMEY, Marjorie (1974). *The Wild Flowers of Britain and Northern Europe*. Collins.

FLETCHER J. R., (1930-1940). *Manuscripts relating to the history of Syon Abbey*, Exeter University.

FLETCHER, J. R,, (1933). *The Story of the English Bridgettines of Syon Abbey*. South Brent, Devon: Syon Abbey.

FORREST, R., (1831). *Alphabetical catalogue of the plants of Syon Garden 1831*. A & R Spottiswoode.

FRANCIA Susan & STOBART, Anne, Editors. (2014). *Critical Approaches to the History of Western Medical Medicine from Classical Antiquity to Early Modern Period*. Bloomsbury.

FRIBORG, Jeppe T., YUAN, Jian-Min , WANG , Renwei, KOH, Woon-Puay, LEE, Hin-Peng and YU, Mimi C., (2008). *Incense use and respiratory tract carcinomas* in Cancer, 113: 1676–1684. doi: 10.1002/cncr.23788. http://onlinelibrary.wiley.com/doi/10.1002/cncr.23788/full

FRIES, S., 'De Svenska Växtnamnen i S.A. Forsius' *Physica*, 1611' (1979). *Festskrift till Björn Pettersson, 29.12.1979* (1979), 21-6.

FRISK, Gösta, (1949). *A Middle English Translation of Macer Floridus de Viribus Herbarum*. Essays and Studies On English Language and Literature, III, edited by SB Liljegren. A.-B Lundequistska Bokhandeln, Upsala.

GASK, G. E., (1926). 'The Medical Staff of King Edward the Third' in The Proceedings of the Royal Society of Medicine, 1926; 19 (Sect Hist Med): 1–16.

GEOGHEGAN, D., (1957-58). '*A licence of Henry VI to practise alchemy*'. Ambix, 6 (1957–8), 10–17.

GETZ, Faye (1990). '*Medical practitioners in medieval England*', in Social History of Medicine, 3 (1990), 245–83, esp. 278–9.

GETZ, Faye (1992). '*The faculty of medicine before 1500*', in *Hist. U. Oxf. 2: Late med. Oxf.*, 373–405.

GETZ. F. M. (1991). *Healing and Society in Medieval England: A Middle English Translation of the Gilbertus Anglicus*. Univ. of Wisconsin Press.

GETZ, Faye, (1998). *Medicine in the English Middle Ages*. Princeton University Press, Princeton, New Jersey, USA.

GILCHRIST Roberta, (1994). *Gender and Material Culture: The Archaeology of Religious Women*. Routledge, London & New York.

GILCHRIST, Roberta & SLOANE, Barney (2005). *Requiem, The Monastic Cemetery in Britain*. Museum of London Archaeology Service.

GILLESPIE, Vincent, Ed., (2001). *Corpus of British Mediaeval Library Catalogues, Volume 9, Syon Abbey*, with *The Libraries of the Carthusians*, edited by AI Doyle. Published by the British Library in association with The British Academy.

GILLESPIE, Vincent. (2002). '*Syon and the New Learning.*' (2002) in *The Religious Orders in Pre-Reformation England*, edited by James G. Clark, 75-95. Woodbridge.

GILLESPIE, Vincent (2010). *Syon and the English Market for Continental Printed Books: The Incunable Phase* in *Syon Abbey and Its Books, Reading, Writing and Religion, c1400 – 1700*. Boydell Press, Woodbridge.

GILLESPIE, Vincent & POWELL, Susan, (2014). *A Companion to the Early Printed Book in Britain, 1476-1558*. Boydell & Brewer Limited.

GORDON, George (attributed. 1849). Manuscript Catalogue of trees at Syon.

GRADWOHL, Alex (2013). *Herbal Abortifacients and their Classical Hertage in Tudor England*. Penn History Review Volume 20, Issue 1 Spring 2013, Article 3. (Online PDF resource).

GRAHAM, Rose, (1903). *Saint Gilbert of Sempringham and the Gilbertians*. London, E. Stock.

GREEN, Monica H. (2000a). *Books as a Source of Medical Education for Women in the Middle Ages: Female Religious Institutions Owning Medical Books*. Dynamis. Acta His. Med. Sci. Hist. Illus. 2000, 20, 331-369. PDF: http://www.ugr.es/~dynamis/completo20/PDF/Dyna-11.PDF

GREEN, Monica H., (2000b). *Women's Healthcare in the Mediaeval West*, Ashgate, Variorum VII.

GREEN, Monica H., (2005). *Flowers, Poisons and Men: Menstruation in Mediaeval Western Europe*, in *Menstruation, a Cultural History*, Edited by SHAIL, Andrew, and HOWIE, Gillian, Palgrave MacMillan.

GREEN, Monica (2008). *Making Women's Medicine Masculine : The Rise of Male Authority in Pre-Modern Gynaecology*. Oxford University Press.

GREEN, Monica H. (2010). *Bodily Essences: Bodies as categories of difference* in *A Cultural History of the Body in the Middle Ages*. Berg, Oxford and New York.

GREEN Monica H., Editor, (2011). *The Trotula: An English Translation of the Medieval Compendium of Women's Medicine*, University of Pennsylvania Press.

GREEN, Monica H. (2013). *The Antidotarium magnum : A Short Description*. Revised draft: 2 November 2013, Arizona State University.

GRIGGS, Barbara, (1982). *Green Pharmacy: A history of herbal medicine*. London : Jill Norman and Hobhouse.

GRIGSON, Geoffrey (1958). *The Englishman's Flora*. Readers Union, Phoenix House, London.

GRINWIS, Marjan, (2007). *Reading Faces: Translation of a Latin text and translation and edition of a Middle English text concerning physiognomy.* Universiteit Utrecht.
Web resource: http://dspace.library.uu.nl/handle/1874/24993

HAINES, C. R., (1927). *The Library of Dover Priory: Its Catalogue And Extant Volumes.* The Library, (1927) s4-VIII (1): 73-118.
HALES, Mick, (2000). *Monastic Gardens.* Stewart, Tabori and Chang, New York..

HAREN, M. J., (1978). *Calendar of Papal Registers: Papal Letters,* XV, no. 76. Dublin.

HARGREAVES, Henry (1981). *Some problems in Indexing Middle English Recipes* in Edwards and Pearsall eds, *Middle English Prose, Essays on Bibliographis Problems,* New York, Garland.

HARTLEY, P. H.-S. & ALDRIDGE H. R., (1936). *Johannes de Mirfeld of St Bartholomew's, Smithfield: his life and works.* Cambridge, C.U.P.

HARRISON, Walter (1775). *A new and universal history, description and survey of the cities of London and Westminster, the borough of Southwark.* London. p. 127. (Cited by Wikipedia).

HARVEY, B., (1993). *Living and dying in England, 1100–1540: the monastic experience.* Oxford, Clarendon Press.

HARVEY, John, *John Bray.* ODNB. *Oxford Electronic Dictionary of National Biography,* Oxford University Press, 2004 [http://www.oxforddnb.com/view/article/3294, accessed 14 June 2014]

HEDLUND, Monica, HÄRDELIN, Alf & NILSEN, Anna. (1990). *Vadstena klosters bibliotek, Ny katalog och nya forskningsmöjligheter (The Monastic Library of Mediaeval Vadstena, A new Caralogue and New Potentials for Research.)* Almqvist & Wiksell International, Stockholm, Sweden.

HEINRICH, Fritz, (1896). *Ein Mittelenglisches Medizinbuch.* Halle, Max Niemeyer.

HELLINGA, Lotte & TRAPP, J. B., Eds. (1999). *The Cambridge History of the Book in Britain, Volume III, 1400-1557.* Cambridge University Press.

HENSLOW G. (1899).*Medical Works of The Fourteenth Century, together with a List of Plants recorded in Contemporary Writings, with their Identifications.* London, Chapman and Hall, Ltd.

HEWE, N., (1947). *Välsignade Växter: Skrock och Fakta om Hundra Läkeörter* . Stockholm, Sweden.

HILTON, Walter, (1494). *Scala Perfectionis (The Ladder of Perfection)* Wynkin de Worde, Westminster 1494, STC 14042. (The Rosenbach Foundation H491 copy).

HOGG, James, (1980). *The Rewyll of Seynt Sauioure Volume 3: The Syon Additions for the Brethren and The Boke of Sygnes From the St Paul's Cathedral Library MS.* Institut Für Anglistik und Amerikanistik, Universität Salzburg, Austria.

HARTLEY, Percival Horton-Smith Hartley & ALDRIDGE, Harold Richard, (2013). *Johannes de Mirfeld of St Bartholomew's, Smithfield: His Life and Works.* Cambridge University Press, 2013 (and 1936).

HUGHES, Muriel Joy, (1943). Petri Abelard *Opera* I, 176, cited in *Women Healers in Mediaeval Life and Literature,* Books for Libraries Press, Freeport New York.

HUNT, T. (1986-87). "*The Botanical Glossaries in MS London BL Add. 15236,*" *Pluteus* 4-5 (1986-67).

HUNT, Tony, (1989). *Plant Names of Medieval England.* Woodbridge.

HUNTING, P., (1998). *A History of the Society of Apothecaries.* London, Society of Apothecaries.

JACKA, H. T., (1917). *'Dissolution of the English Nunneries',* (London University M.A. Thesis, 125pp.)
JACKSON, A. BRUCE (1910). *Catalogue of Hardy Trees and Shrubs at Syon House, Brentford.* pp. ix. 38. West, Newman & Co.: London. Copies are in the London Library in St James's Square, and in the Library at Kew but not the British Library.

JACQUART, Danielle (1992). *The Introduction of Arabic Medicine into the West: The Question of Etiology, in Health Disease and Healing in Mediaeval Culture.* Macmillan.

JAMES, M. R., (1903). *Descriptive Catalogue of the Manuscripts in the Library of St John's College, Cambridge.* Cambridge University Press.

JAMES, M. R., (1913). *The Ancient Libraries of Canterbury and Dover.* Cambridge University Press.

JAMES, M. R., (1925). *Abbeys.* Great Western Railway, Paddington Station, London.

JAMES, Montague Rhodes, (1926). *Greek Manuscripts in England before the Renaissance.* The Library, Fourth series, Vol. VII. No. 1, June 1926.

JONES, E. A. & WALSHAM, A., (2010). *Syon Abbey and Its Books: Reading, Writing and Religion, C.1400-1700.* Boydell and Brewer.

JONES, Peter, (1984). *'Secreta Salernitana', Kos* (1984), 33-50.

JONES, P. M. (1994). *'John of Arderne and the Mediterranean tradition of scholastic surgery'* in *Practical medicine from Salerno to the black death,* ed. L. Garcia-Ballester.

JONES, Peter Murray (1999a). *Medical Libraries* in LEEDHAM-GREEN & WEBBER, Teresa, Eds. (2006). *The Cambridge History of Libraries in Britain and Ireland, Volume I, to 1640.*

JONES, Peter Murray (1999b). *Medicine and science* in HELLINGA, Lotte & TRAPP, J. B., Eds. (1999). *The Cambridge History of the Book in Britain, Volume III, 1400-1557.* Cambridge University Press.

JONES, W.R.D. (2004). *Turner, William (1509/10 - 1568).* Oxford Dictionary of National Biography (web resource). Oxford University Press.

JUSTE, David & BURNETT, Charles. *Bibliotheca Astrologica Latina.* The Warburg Institute website. http://warburg.sas.ac.uk/library/digital-collections/bibliotheca-astrologica/#c968

KEISER, George R., (1999). *Practical Books For The Gentleman,* p.474-477, In Hellinga, Lotte & Trapp, J. B., Eds. (1999).

KER, N. R., (1964 -1987). *Medieval Libraries of Great Britain*. Volumes I-V, and Supplement to the Second Edition (1987), edited by Andrew G. Watson. London, The Royal Historical Society.

KERBY-FULTON, Kathryn, HILMO, Maidie, and OLSON, Linda, (2012). *Opening Up Middle English Manuscripts. Literary and Visual Approaches*. Cornell University Press, Ithaca and London.

Klostermedizin Forschungsgruppe: www.klostermedizin.de Website of the University of Würzburg.

KRÄMER, Sigrid, & BERNHARD, Michael, (1989). *Mittelalterliche Bibliothekskataloge Deutschlands und der Schweiz*. C.H. Beck'sche Verlagsbuchhandlung, München.

KRUG, Rebecca, (2008). *Reading Families: Women's Literate Practice in Late Medieval England*. Cornell University Press.

LALOR, Daphne, (1995). *The Book of Sovereign Remedies*: MS X3346 (Alexander Turnbull Library Wellington NZ), by John of Feckenham DD, c.1570. University of Auckland Ph.D Thesis 1995. PDF: https://researchspace.auckland.ac.nz/handle/2292/2281

LANG, S. J., (2004). 'Bradmore, John (d. 1412)', *Oxford Electronic Dictionary of National Biography*, Oxford University Press.

LEHMANN, Paul, (1928). *Mittelalterliche Bibliothekskataloge Deutschlands und der Schweiz*. C.H. Beck'sche Verlagsbuchhandlung, München. Volume 2, pp.435-440.

LEEDHAM-GREEN & WEBBER, Teresa, Eds. (2006). *The Cambridge History of Libraries in Britain and Ireland, Volume I, to 1640*.

LATHAM, R. E., (2008). *Revised Medieval Latin Word-List from British and Irish Sources, with Supplement*. Published for the British Academy by Oxford University Press.

LAUNERT, Edmund, (1981). The *Edible and Medicinal Plants of Britain and Northern Europe*. Hamlyn.

LELAND, John. (1549) *The laboryouse journey [and] serche of Johan Leylande, for Englandes antiquites*. [London: Printed by S. Mierdman for John Bale, 1549]. STC 15445.

LE STRANGE, Richard (1977). *A history of herbal plants*. Angus and Robertson, London.

LIDDELL, J. R., (1939). *Leland's lists of manuscripts in Lincolnshire monasteries*. English Historical Review, Volume 54, 1939, pp88-95. The source is BL Ms. Roy., Appendix 69.

LINDEBLAD, Karin (2010). *Lavendel, hjärtstilla och svarta vinbär (Lavender, Motherwort and Blackcurrants)*. The Museum of National Antiquities, Stockholm Studies, 14.

LOEN-MARSHALL, Maria-Helena (2005). *An Edition of the English Texts in the British Library MS Sloane 3285, Practical Medicine, Sussex Dialect and the London Associations of a fifteenth century Book*. Ph.D Thesis for the University of Glasgow. Weblink: http://.gla.ac.uk/3128/

LOUDON, J. C. (1838 onwards in eight volumes). *Arboretum et Fruticetum Britannicum, with 3489 species of plants at Syon*.) Henry G. Bohn, London.

MACGILL, Elizabeth Rawson, (1990). *"This Booke of Sovereign Medicines"* . . . *Collected of Maister Doctour ffecknam late Abbott of Westmynster.* An edition of Folger MS V.b.129 (ca. 1570), with Introduction, Transcript, and Annotation, and Plant List with Identification. Ann Arbor, Mich.: UMI, 1990.

MACKINTOSH, Angus, SAMUELS M. L. & BENSKIN, Michael, (1986 & 2013). *Edinburgh University Electronic Linguistic Atlas of Late Mediaeval English.* http://www.lel.ed.ac.uk/ihd/elalme/elalme.html

MAKOWSKI, Elizabeth (2011). *English Nuns and the Law in the Middle Ages. Cloistered Nuns and their Lawyers, 1293-1540.* The Boydell Press.
MATTHEWS, Leslie G. (1967). *The Royal Apothecaries.* Wellcome Historical Medical Library, New Series Volume XIII.

MCSPARRAN, Francis, Chief Editor, (2013). *The Middle English Compendium,* web resource comprising *The Electronic Middle English Dictionary, The HyperBibliography of Middle English* and *The Corpus of Middle English Prose and Verse.* University of Michigan: http://quod.lib.umich.edu/m/med/

MENGIS, Simones & *de* GRUYTER Walter, (2013). *Schreibende Frauen um 1500: Scriptorium und Bibliothek des Dominikanerinnenklosters St. Katharina, St. Gallen.* (There is a list of MSS on pp274-376, but no index to this text.)

MEYVAERT, Paul, (1986). *Medieval Gardens,* in *"The Medieval Monastic Garden,".* Dumbarton Oaks.

MOFFATT, Dr Bryan, (1987-1998). *Sharp Practice, Reports 1-6: Researches into the Mediaeval Hospital at Soutra, Lothian.*

MORGAN, N. , THOMSON, R.M. (2008). *'University books and the sciences, c.1250–1400',* in *The Cambridge History of the Book in Britain,* vol. II (1100–1400). Cambridge University Press.

MORRIS, Bridget, (1999). *St Birgitta of Sweden.* The Boydell Press, Woodbridge.

MOWAT, J. L. G., (1882). *Sinonoma Bartholomaei & Synonyma Antidotarii Nicholai.* Oxford, Clarendon Press.

NIELSEN, H., (1978). *Läkeväxter Förr och Nu.* Stockholm, Sweden.

NEDDERMEYER, Uwe (1998). Von der Handschrift zum gedruckten Buch, Band 61, Teil 1 & 2, Buchwissenschaftliche Beiträge aus dem Deutschen Bucharchiv, München. Harrasowitz Verlag, Wiesbaden, Germany.

NORTH, J. D. (1986). *Horoscopes and history.* Warburg Institute Surveys and Texts, 13. Warburg Institute, University of London.

NYBERG, Tore (1965). *Birgittinische Klostergründungen des Mittelalters.* (Bibliotheca Historica Lundensis, xv.) Lund, Sweden: C W K Gleerup; Munich, Germany.

OESTMANN, Günther , RUTKIN, H. Darrel, STUCKRAD, Kocku Von (2005). *Horoscopes and Public Spheres: Essays on the History of Astrology.* Walter de Gruyter.

Ó CONCHUBAIR, Mícheál (1988). *Uisce Beatha.* Studia Hibernica, No. 24, 1984-8, pp64-65.

ODY, Penelope, (1993). *The Herb Society's Complete Medicinal Herbal*. Dorling Kindersley.

OGDEN, M. S., (1971). *The Cyrurgie of Guy de Chauliac*. EETS Vol 265.

O'MALLEY, C. D., (1968). *Tudor Medicine and Biology* in Huntington Library Quarterly Vol. 32, No. 1 (Nov., 1968), pp. 1-27 University of California Press.

OPSOMER-HALLEUX, Carmélia, (1986). *The Mediaeval Garden and its Role in Medicine* in *Mediaeval Gardens, History of Landscape Architecture Colloquium*, edited by MACDOUGALL Elisabeth B., Dumbarton Oaks.

PÄCHT, O., & ALEXANDER, J. J. G., (1973). *Illuminated Manuscripts in the Bodleian Library*. Clarendon Press, Oxford.

PAGE, William, ed. (1907). *A History of the County of Oxford, Volume 2*. Victoria County History. Archibald Constable & Co.

PAVORD, Anna, (2005). *The Naming of Plants: The Search for Order in the World of Plants*. Bloomsbury.

PEPLOW, Elizabeth & PEPLOW Reginald (1988). *In a Monastery Garden*. David & Charles.

PHILLIPS, Elaine (1999). *A Short History of the Great Hospital, Norwich*. Jarrold.

PLINY (1963). *Natural History* Books XX to XXVII trans. By WHS Jones. Loeb Classical Library. Harvard University Press.

POLUNIN, Oleg. (1972). *The Concise Flowers of Europe*. OUP.

PORMANN, Peter E. (2013). *The Mirror of Health: Discovering Medicine in the Golden Age of Islam*. Published by The Royal College of Physicians.

POWER, D. A., & SOUTH, J. F., eds. (1886). *Memorials of the craft of surgery in England*. Cassell & Co.

POWER, Eileen (1922). *Mediaeval English Nunneries c.1275 – 1535*. Cambridge University Press.

RAMAZZINI, Bernardo (1713). *De Morbis Artificum Diatriba*. Geneva.

RAMSAY, Nigel & WILLOUGHBY, James L, (2009). *Hospitals, Towns and the Professions*: Corpus of Medieval Library Catalogues 14. British Library.

RAWCLIFFE, C., (1984). '*The hospitals of later medieval London*', Medical History, 28 (1984), 1–21.

RAWCLIFFE, C., (1988). '*The profits of practice: the wealth and status of medical men in later medieval England*', Social History of Medicine, 1 (1988), 61–78.

RAWCLIFFE, Carole, (1998). '*Hospital Nurses and their Work*', in *Daily Life in the Late Middle Ages*, Richard Britnell, ed. Stroud: Sutton Publishing.

RAWCLIFFE, Carole, (1999). *Medicine for the Soul: The life, death and resurrection of an English Medieval Hospital, St Giles, Norwich, c.1249-1550* . Stroud: Sutton.

RAWCLIFFE, Carole, (2002). *'Passports to Paradise: How English Medieval Hospitals and Almshouses Kept their Archives'*, *Archives*, Volume 27.

RAWCLIFFE, Carole, (2002). *'Written in the Book of Life': Building the Libraries of Mediaeval English Hospitals and Almshouses;* The Library, Vol.3:2 (2002).

RAWCLIFFE , Carole, (2006). *Leprosy in Medieval England,* Woodbridge, Boydell and Brewer.

REEDS, Karen, (1980). *Botanical Books in Mediaeval Libraries* in *Res Publica Litterarum* III, 1980.

REEDS, Karen, (2012). *St John's Wort (Hypericum perforatum L.) in the Age of Paracelsus and the Great Herbals: Assessing the Historical Clims for a Traditional Remedy.* Chapter 9 in VAN ARSDALL, Anne & GRAHAM Timothy, Eds *Herbs and Healers from the Ancient Mediterranean Through the Medieval West,* Ashgate Publishing, Ltd.

REYNOLDS, Susan, (1962). *A History of the County of Middlesex.* Volume 3, Victoria County History, Oxford University Press.

RIDDLE, John, (1965). *'The Introduction and Use of Eastern Drugs in the Early Middle Ages'*, Sudhoffs Archiv für die Geschichte der Medizin 49 (1965), 185-98.

RIDDLE, John, (1974). *Theory and Practice in Medieval Medicine.* Viator 5.

RIDDLE, John, (1992). *Contraception and abortion from the ancient world to the middle ages.* Cambridge, Mass., Harvard U.P.

ROBBINS, Rossell Hope, (1970). *Medical Manuscripts in Middle English,* Speculum, Vol XLV, Number 3, July 1970. Mediaeval Academy of America, Cambridge, Mass.

RODRIGUEZ, María Victoria Domínguez, (2010). *Constructing Anatomical Terminology in Middle English: The Case of British Library MS Sloane 3486.* In SELIM, Journal of the Spanish Society for Mediaeval English Language and Literature, No 17, Oviedo, 2010: University of Oviedo.

ROHDE, Elanour Sinclair, (1922). *The Old English Herbals.* Longmans, Green and Co. London.

Rule of Our Most Holy Saviour (1914) which includes The Syon Additions and The Rule of St Austin. 'From the British Museum and St Pauls' Manuscripts'. In modern English. No publisher or Author given, but approved by the *Censor Deputatus* and the Bishop of Plymouth. See:
http://www.archive.org/stream/ruleofourmosthol00briduoft#page/10/mode/2up

RZIHACEK-BEDÖ, Dr. Andrea (2005). *Medizinische Wissenschaftspflege im Benediktinerkloster Admont bis 1500.* R. Oldenbourg Verlag, Wien, München.

SARGEANT, William, (1961). *Battle for the Mind, A Physiology of Conversion and Brain-Washing,* Baltimore, Maryland and Hammondsworth, England: Penguin Books.

SCARBOROUGH, John, (1984). *Early Byzantine Pharmacology*, Dumbarton Oaks Papers, Vol. 38, Symposium on Byzantine Medicine, (1984).

SCARBOROUGH, John, (2002). *Herbs of the Field and Herbs of the Garden* in *Byzantine Garden Culture* Dumbarton Oaks Research Library and Collection. Washington DC.

SEYMOUR, Michael, Ed., (1988). *Bartholomaeus Anglicus, trans. John Trevisa. On the Properties of Things, De Proprietatibus Rerum, A Critical Text*, 3 vols. Oxford: Clarendon Press, 1975-1988.

SHARPE, Professor R. Editor, (1990-2013). *Corpus of British Medieval Library Catalogues*, Volumes I to XV, July 1990 to November 2013. British Academy and British Library, London. Web resource, November 2013. http://www.history.ox.ac.uk/research/project/british-medieval-library-catalogues.html

SHARPE, R., CARLEY, J.P., THOMSON R.M., WATSON, A.G., (1996). *English Benedictine Libraries: The Shorter Catalogues*. The British Library in association with the British Academy.

SIM, Alison, (1997). *Food and Feast in Tudor England*. Sutton Publishing.

SINGER, C., (1916). "*Thirteenth Century Miniatures Illustrating Medical Practice,*" in *History of Medicine, PRSM* 9.

SINGER, Charles, (1927). *The Herbal in Antiquity and its Transmission to Later Ages*, Journal of Hellenic Studies 47 (1927), 1-52.

SMITH, Eliza (1753). '*The Compleat Housewife or Accomplish'd Gentleman's Companion.*' London.

SPENCER-HALL, Alicia, (2013). *Textual Authority and Symbolic Capital: Birgitta of Sweden's Inclusion in Walter Bower's Scotichronicron.* Journal of the North Atlantic. Special Volume 4 (107-119).

STONEMAN, William T., (1999). *Dover Priory Vol 5: Corpus of British Medieval Library Catalogues.* British Library.

STRACKE, Richard J. ed. (1974). *The Laud Herbal Glossary*. Rodopi N.V. Amsterdam.

STREHLOW, Wighard. (1988). *Hildegard of Bingen's Medicine*. NM: Bear and Co.

STRUTT, Joseph, (1785) *Bibliographical Dictionary*. British Library shelfmark G.4421.

TAAVITSAINE, Irma, PAHTA, Päivi, MÄKINEN, Martti, HILTUNEN, Turo, MARTTILA, Ville, RATIA, Maura SUHR, Carla, TYRKKÖ, , Jukka, (2000-2010). *Corpus of Early English Medical Writing 1375–1800*, (EMEMT). John Benjamins Publishing Company. (A copy of this CD is available at the British Library).

TAIT, Michael (2013 & 1975). *A Fair Place, Syon Abbey 1415-1539.*

TALBOT , C. H., &. HAMMOND, E. A., (1965). *The Medical Practitioners In Medieval England: A Biographical Register* . Wellcome Historical **Medical** Library.

THOMAS AQUINAS *Summa Theologiae*, Lib XCI-C, II^a-IIae q. 95 a. 5 co.
http://www.logicmuseum.com/authors/aquinas/Summa-index.htm

THORNDIKE, Lynn, (1946). *The Herbal of Rufinus, from the unique Manuscript.* Chicago, Illinois, University of Chicago Press.

THORNDIKE, Lynn & KIBRE, Pearl (1963). *A Catalogue of Incipits of Mediaeval Scientific Writings in Latin* (Cambridge, MA: Mediaeval Academy.) and supplements.

THROOP, Patricia (1998). *Hildegard von Bingen's Physica: the complete English translation of her classic work on Health and Healing.* Rochester, VT: Healing Arts.

TOUWALDE, Alain (2012). *Quid Pro Quo, Revisiting the Practice of Substitution in Ancient Pharmacy*; Chapter 2 in *Herbs and Healers from the Ancient Mediterranean Through the Medieval West*, edited by Anne Van Arsdall & Timothy Graham. Ashgate Publishing, Ltd.

TREASE, G. E., (1959). *The spicers and apothecaries of the royal household in the reigns of Henry III, Edward I and Edward II.* Nottingham Mediaeval Studies iii.

TURNER, William, (1538 & 1548). *Libellus de Re Herbaria & The Names of Herbs.* London: Ray Society Reprint (1965).

VAN ARSDALL, Anne & GRAHAM Timothy, Eds (2012). *Herbs and Healers from the Ancient Mediterranean Through the Medieval West*, Ashgate Publishing, Ltd.

VAN DE WALLE, Etienne, and RENNE, Elisha, editors (2001). *Regulating Menstruation: Beliefs, Practices, Interpretations.* Chicago: University of Chicago Press.

VITALIS, Johannes, (1260-1327). *Pro conservanda sanitate tuendaque prospera valetudine, ad totius humani corporis morbos et aegritudines salutarium remediorum curationumque liber.* First printed Mainz, 1531.

VOIGTS, Linda Ehrsam (1984). *'Medical Prose'* in *Middle English Prose, A Critical Guide To Major Authors And Genres*, edited by A. S. G. Edwards. Rutgers University Press.

VOIGTS, L. E., (1995). *'A doctor and his books: the manuscripts of Roger Marchall'*, in *New science out of old books*, ed. R. Beadle and A. J. Piper. Aldershot.

VOIGTS, L.E., & HUDSON R. P. (1992). *A drynke called dwale: a surgical anaesthetic from late medieval England.* In *Health, Disease And Healing In Medieval Culture*, Campbell S, Hall B, Klausner D, editors. New York: St Martin's Press.

VOIGTS, Linda E., & MCVAUGH Michael R. (1984). *A Latin Technical Phlebotomy and Its Middle English Translation*, Transactions of the American Philosophical Society, Volume 74, Part 2 1984, Philadelphia: Cambridge Gonville and Caius MS 176/97 attr. Henry of Winchester.

VOIGTS, Linda Ehrsam & KURTZ, Patricia Deery, (2000). *Scientific and Medical Writings in Old and Middle English: An Electronic Reference* CD. Ann Arbor: University of Michigan Press.
Website: http://cctr1.umkc.edu/search

WACK, Mary F., (1990). *Lovesickness in the Middle Ages: The Viaticum ad its Commentaries*. University of Philadelphia Press, Philadelphia.

WALLNER, B. (1964). *The Middle English Translation of Guy de Chauliac's Grande Chirurgie*, in *Acta Universitatis Lundensis* n.f., avd. 1, bd. 56, nr. 5 (1964).

WAY, A., (1857). *Bill of medicines Furnished for the Use of Edward I. 34 and 35 Edw I, 1306-1307*. Archaeological Journal 14.

WEAR, Andrew, FRENCH, Roger Kenneth & LONIE Iain M., ed. (1985). *The Medical renaissance of the sixteenth century*. Cambridge University Press.

WEBSTER, C., ed. (1979). *Health, medicine and mortality in the sixteenth century*. CUP.

WESSEX ARCHAEOLOGY, (2003). *Syon House, Syon Park, Hounslow - an archaeological Evaluation of a Bridgettine Abbey and Assessment of the Results , page 22,* prepared by Wessex Archaeology and issued by The Trust for Wessex Archaeology in October 2003, Document Reference 52568.05.

WILLARD, Charity Cannon, (1992). *The Writings of Christine de Pizan*. Persea, NY.

WILLIAMSON, Elizabeth M., (1988). *Potter's New Cyclopedia of Botanical Drugs & Preparations*. Saffron Walden: CW Daniel Company Limited.

WOLODARSKI, Anna (2011). *The Vadstena Library, Making New Discoveries* in *The Birgittine Experience* in *Papers from the Birgitta Conference in Stockholm, 2011.* Kungl Vitterhets Historie och Antikvitets Akademien, Stockholm.

WOODHAM, Anne & PETERS, David, (1997). *The Encyclopedia of Complementary Medicine.* Dorling Kindersley.

WORMALD, F., & WRIGHT, C.E., editors, (1958). *The English Library before 1700*. Athlone, London.

YOUNG, S., (1890). *The Annals of the Barber–Surgeons of London: compiled from their records and other sources*. London: Blades, East & Blades.

List of Manuscripts Consulted or Cited.

Aberdeen University Library, MS 134: *The Mirror of Our Lady.*

Alnwick Castle MS 758.

British Library MS Additional 5208, (fols 3v -18v by Betson). *The Rules of St Saviour and St Augustine.*

British Library Additional MS 22285: *Syon Martyrologium.*

British Library Additional MS 24661: Richard Rolle, *Incendium Amoris.*

British Library, Harvey MS 3: *Breviarium Bartholomaei,* (John Dee's copy).

British Library Royal MS 7 F XI; *'Liber qui intitulatur Florarium Bartholomei'.* Attributed to John Mirfield. 15th cent.

British Library, Sloane MS 282, fols. 167v–173v: *'sinonima de nominibus herbarum secundum magistrum Iohannem Bray'.*

British Library Sloane MS 521: ff. 128-159b, John Braye, *Practica medicinæ* & f. 159 b, John Braye, *Pillulæ ad omnia vulnera ubicunque.* 14th cent.

British Library, Sloane MS 1754: *'Medicina quam faciebat sibi Ypocras [Hippocrates].*

British Library, Sloane MS 3825: *Janua magicæ res*

British Library, Sloane 4031: Lydgate, *Dietarium rithmizatum in Anglicis.*

Cambridge University, Corpus Christi College, MS 141: *Registrum bibliothece de Syon.*

Cambridge University, Gonville and Caius MS 176/97: *on Phlebotomy.*

Cambridge University, Magdalene College, MS 12 (F.4.12): 'a devotional text'.

Cambridge, Magdalene College MS Pepys 1661 pp. 245-66; Bray's *Sinonima.*

Cambridge University Library Ms Hh. 6.8: Messhala, *Astrolabium.*

Cambridge University Library Dd.II.45; Bray's *Sinonima.*

Cambridge, St John's College MS 109, E.6: Notebook of T. Betson of Syon.

Cambridge Trinity College MS O. I. 13 (1037) ff. 37v-44r (incomplete); Bray's *Sinonima.*

Durham University Library: DUL MS Cosin V.III.11; Bray's *Sinonima. [not seen]*

Durham University Library MS Cosin V.iii.16, folio 118r. & v. A letter written by Thomas Betson.

Eton College MS 204: *de Herba Vettonica.*

Glasgow, University Library MS Hunterian 509 (V.8.12) : *Tractatus de medicinis in anglicis*: Gilbertus Anglicus *Compendium medicinae*.

Glasgow University Library, MS 185, ff. 1-6v.: Bray's *Sinonima*. *[not seen]*

London Metropolitan Archives: See St Paul's Cathedral below.

Medical Society of London, MS 136, edited by Dawson (1934), q.v. in Bibliography.

Oxford University, Bodleian Digby MS 29, Item 32, ff194b – 196, *Tractatus Brevis sed Perutilis de Constellacionibus*.

Oxford University, Bodleian MS Selden B35, amended by Mowat, with BL Sloane 284.: *Synonyma Antidotarii Nicolai* and *Sinonoma Bartholomei*.

Oxford University Bodleian 130: Pseudo Apuleius: *De virtutibus bestiarum in arte medicinae*.

Rosenbach Foundation H491: William Hilton, *Scala Perfectionis*.

St Paul's Cathedral MS 25,524, now in the London Metropolitan Archives: *Syon Additions for the Brethren* and *The Boke of Sygnes,* and other Syon material. Fols 3r-4v, and 56r-84v are written by Betson.

University of Uppsala UU C 28: Macer Floridus, *de Viribus Herbarum*.

Valor Ecclesiasticus Temp Henr VIII Auctoritate Regia Institutus (Volume I, 1810, British Library)

Extant Copies of Bray's Sinonima:

*British Library BL Sloane MS 282, ff. 167v-173v.
*Cambridge, Magdalene College MS Pepys 1661, pp. 245-66.
*Cambridge Trinity College MS O. I. 13 (1037) ff. 37v-44r (incomplete).
*Cambridge University. Library MS Dd. XI. 45 ff. 145-53.
 Durham as DUL MS Cosin V.III.11.
 Glasgow University Library, MS 185, ff.1-6v.

Underlined MSS above were consulted by Hunt.
Those marked with an asterisk (*) were seen by JS Adams.
Of those seen, BL Sloane 282 seemed the closest to Betson, but the two other unseen MSS may yet reveal more similarity.

INDEX

Note: This Index covers the Introduction, Herbarium, Remedies and Appendices, including both Latin and Middle English terms. The variety of spellings in Betson's text means that the Index may not be complete. It also does not contain most of the modern English and Linnaean names of plants (which are listed separately in Appendix 1 above).

Abrotanum, 84.
Absintheum, 84, 91, 301.
Acacia, 98, 134, 195, 304.
Acantium, 91, 188.
Acetosa, 88, 136.
Acetosum, 97.
Achalaffe, 83.
Ache merche, 84.
Acinalia, 187.
Acis, 92.
Acmalici semen, 93.
Aconite, 39.
Acus muscata, 92, 135.
Adarasta, 123, 319.
Additions to the Rule, 25, 56, 58, 62.
Adiantos, 82, 93, 293, 301.
Affoddillus, 90.
Agaldo, 91.
Agarwood, 239, 261, 274.
Agilon, Walter, Compendium urinarum, 59.
Agincourt, 20, 339.
Agnetum, 84, 192.
Agni lingua, 91.
Agnus Castus, 86.
Agnus castus, 49.
Agon, 93.
Agrediadema, 88.
Agresas, 204.
Agrimonia, 83, 186, 301, 303.
Agrimony, 83, 108, 186, 247, 251, 257, 285, 286, 301, 302, 303.
Agrimulatum, 92, 132, 150, 153, 162.
Ague, 52, 53, 235, 312.
Alacio, 93.
Album plumbum, 107.
Alexander, 91, 94, 295, 301, 343, 347.
Alexanders, 91, 94, 150, 165, 168, 171, 191, 227, 243, 261, 301.
Algea, 89.
Alipiardos, 90.
Alkanet, 100, 301.
Alla gallica, 90.
Alleluia, 80, 169, 170, 214, 301.

Alleuala, 94.
Alleum, 80.
Allium, 80, 81, 90, 94, 96, 109, 111, 194, 304, 306.
Allogallica, 90, 98, 132.
Almonds, 56, 162.
Aloes, 84, 96, 97, 231, 239, 257, 261, 273, 290, 292, 293, 301, 304.
Alphita, 40, 47, 77, 83, 94, 105, 113, 124, 125, 129, 159, 168, 171, 174, 179, 184, 185, 193, 194, 197, 201, 205, 206, 240, 254, 272, 289.
Altia, 81.
Amantilla, 80, 200.
Amaracus, 95, 151, 173, 183.
Amaricio cimbrium, 95.
Amaricom, 151.
Amarisca fetida, 94.
Amber, 42, 47, 290.
Ambergris, 47.
Ambra, 87, 97
Ambre, 87, 97, 261,87, 97.
Ambrosia, 87, 121, 147.
Amerok, 95.
Amictum dulce, 99.
Amidum agreste, 98.
Amiltus Datum, 120.
Amphoricon, 95.
Amydon, 195.
Anabulla, 144, 198.
Anacardus, 97.
Anacarus, 87.
Anagadum, 98.
Anagallicum, 85, 190.
Anagallis, 85, 137, 139, 140, 158, 175, 178, 190, 199, 306.
Anelitus, 226, 309.
Aniseed, 84,86, 111, 225, 226, 288, 289, 295, 296, 301, 307.
Annotana, 89.
Antale, 99.
Antidotarium Nicholai, 33, 46, 155.
Antifoly, 99.
Antiframacum, 96.
Apium amoraidarum, 84.

Apium domesticum, 83.
Apium ranarum, 84.
Apium risus, 84, 188.
Apostema, 220, 263, 275.
Appoplexia, 224.
Aqua Agrimonie: 268; -ardens: 36, 260, 272; -aromotica: 39, 268; aquamellis:266; -aurea: 266; - calamis: 275; -coporose: 268; -corrosiva: 269; -delabativa: 268; - Eufrasie: 257; -fabarum: 259; (de) -- floribus malve: 269; - (de) fumo terre: 239; -mirabilis: 57, 266, 267; -mirande virtutis: 275; -mundificativa: 259; -Nenufaris: 269; -nobilis: 39, 42, 270; -Rosarum: 258; -Sambuci: 260; -scribere in calibe: 270; -silicis: 265; -Tartari: 268; -Terebintine: 270; Violarum: 269; (de) -virgis Corulii: 258; -vite: 39, 42, 57, 260, 261, 264.
Aquileria, 85.
Arabic, 8, 46, 47, 48. Gum- 105, 129, 261.
Archaeology, 20, 26, 28, 29. 41, 50, 343, 353.
Archangelica, 83, 204.
Arderne, John, 39, 107, 346.
Ardillus, 96.
Argentaria, 197.
Arilli Kirnellis, 98.
Aristologia, 89.
Aritemis, 86.
Armfractus., 129.
Arnement, 250, 301.
Arnoglossa, 82, 89, 91, 118, 148.
Aron, 44, 85, 91, 138.
Artemisia pontica, 81, 152, 308, 319, 320, 327.
Asafoetida, 38, 40, 165.
Asedula, 88, 92.
Aspaltios, 89.
Assafetida, 241, 301.
Astula regia, 88.
Atramentum., 90, 98, 114.
Atriplex, 82, 88, 133.
Auricula leporina, 85.
Aurum calamentum, (potable gold) 301.
Autumn lady's tresses, 325.
Auxungia, 165.

Avelana, 146. 163.
Avence, 82, 131, 172, 242, 301.
Avencia, 82, 131.
Avens, 84, 131, 223, 226, 242, 257, 261, 273, 286, 301, 303, 307.
Averoyn, 114.
Avicenna (Abū ʿAlī al-Ḥusayn ibn ʿAbd Allāh ibn Al-Hasan ibn Ali ibn Sīnā), 28, 58, 60, 292.
Ayle, 81.
Ayson, 87.
Azarabaccara, 87, 103, 131, 204
Azizon, 83.
Baccara, 103.
Balanustia, 128. See also *Pomegranate.*
Balsamita, 101, 103, 191.
Barba Aaron, 44, 85, 91, 138, 188.
Barba iovis, 88.
Barba Ircina, 104.
Barbastus, 100, 103, 122, 127, 133, 136. 138, 142.
Bardona, 100.
Bariche, 100.
Basilica, 102.
Basiliscus, 119.
Battitura eris, 146.
Baucia. 103.
Baume, 101.
Bay Tree, 103, 116, 120, 144, 145, 240, 289, 293, 301, 305.
Bean ash, 214, 301.
Bear's breeches, 322.
Bedegar, 100.
Beer, 226, 240, 285.
Beeswax, 30. See also *Wax*
Bellewede, 173.
Bellirici marini, 104.
Benedicta., 102.
Berberies, 168.
Beth. Piper album, 129.
Betony, 52, 56, 192, 233, 234, 235, 244, 245, 246, 257, 267, 271, 287, 289, 301, 323, 327.
Betony, against drunkeness, 234.
Betson, Agnes, 26.

Betson, Thomas, at Syon Abbey: 2, 3, 5, 7, 9, 11, 13, 15, 21, 22, 23, 24, 25, 26, 27, 28, 30, 31, 33, 34, 35, 36, 37, 38, 39, 40, 41, 42, 43, 44, 45, 46, 47, 48, 49, 50, 51, 52, 53, 54, 55, 56, 57, 58, 59, 60, 62, 63, 64, 67, 68, 77, 78, 79. - Choice of Remedies: 216, 217, 218, 219, 221, 222, 223, 224, 225, 245, 246, 248, 249, 250, 252, 253, 254, 264, 282, 289, 294, 296. Other: 301, 305, 306, 309, 313, 316, 319, 320, 340, 341, 342, 354, 355.
Billericay, Essex, 7, 21, 25, 49, 50.
Binding, Notebook, 9, 67.
Binni robenet, 47, 105.
Birkbeck College, 29.
Birula, 100.
Bismalva, 81, 123, 152.
Blak berys, 157.
Blak Eleborum, 124.
Blak pepur, 129.
Blaunk plome, 128.
Bleddistong, 179.
Bleta, 192.
Blood-letting, 53, 57, 218.
Blood-sucker – *sanguisuga*, 58.
Bluebell, 324, 331, 332.
Blynde Netile, 83, 204, 294, 301.
Boneworte, 104, 125, 168.
Boniface VIII, Pope, and papal decree *Beata Clara*, 58.
Borage, 100, 102, 208, 226, 295, 301.
Brachios, 99.
Bramble, 110, 182, 199, 213, 301.
Branca urcine, 99.
Branca lauri, 103.
Brasica, 99, 195.
Bray, John, 8, 27, 34, 35, 36, 37, 39, 40, 41, 44, 45, 46, 47, 48, 49, 57, 79, 244, 246, 279, 291, 293, 319, 320, 345, 354, 355.
Breast cancer, 55.
Breviarium Bartholomaei, 36, 55, 77, 354.
Bridget (Saint, aso known as Birgitta), 19, 20, 22, 32, 62, 340, 342, 348.
Bridgettine Abbeys, foundation dates at Utrecht, Marbrunn, Mariendal, Maribo, Valencia, 32.
Broncus, 101.

Broom, 81, 102, 104, 125, 132, 157, 182, 213, 257, 302, 326, 329.
Broomrape, 322, 329.
Bruscus, 81, 102, 104, 125.
Bryony, 44, 62, 89, 99, 105, 111, 142, 186, 190, 259, 261, 277, 282, 293, 301, 302.
Buckshorn plantain, 323.
Bugle, 40, 102, 145, 285, 302.
Bugloss., 100, 148, 302, 304.
Burdock, 100, 122, 133, 138, 142, 245, 276, 296, 307, 308.
Burjuones of pepul, 164.
Burnet, 326.
Burning ague, 235.
Burns, Treatment of, 239. *Contra Usturas*.
Bursa pastorum, 104, 160.
Butalmon, 101.
Butts, Sir William, Royal Physician, 52.
Cabbage, 286, 302.
Caius, John, physician, 53, 54, 352, 354.
Calamint, 108, 163, 215, 290, 302.
Calcaticum, 114.
Calendula, 109, 110, 121, 139, 141, 157, 164, 193, 201, 307.
Calx Marinus, 86.
Camaleoncia., 115.
Camcattis, 114.
Camedreos, 52, 106, 179, 198.
Cameleon, 180.
Camelismete, 191.
Camely, 115.
Camlok, 181.
Camomile, 305, 328
Camomile, 52, 86, 94, 95, 111, 127, 180, 226, 235, 257, 283, 284, 301, 302, 303, 304, 305, 328.
Camophiteos, 114.
Campherata, 114.
Camphor Laurel, 239, 257, 261, 268, 274, 277, 290, 302.
Canabus, 108.
Canell, 142.
Caniclata, 107.
Cannabis sativa, 302.
Cantabrum, 106, 129.
Cantarides, 115.

Capability Brown, 13, 29, 321.
Cape gooseberry, 326.
Caper Bush, 261, 302.
Caper Spurge, 112, 302, 308.
Capillus veneris, 93, 110.
Caprificus, 153.
Caprifolium, 107, 152, 172, 204.
Caput monachi, 109.
Caraway, 78, 225, 227, 289, 296, 302.
Cardamom, 114, 116, 302.
Cardo, 115, 116, 142.
Carei Porcini, 116.
Caride miristice, 117.
Carpobalsamum, 206.
Carpocissi, 104.
Carthusians, 34, 61, 333.
Cashew nut, 97, 261, 301.
Cashew nuts (elephant lice), 47.
Cassanum, 106.
Cassia Fistula, 293, 302.
Castorium, 117.
Casum Capillorum, (hair loss), 243.
Catamatici, 116.
Catapucia, 112, 144, 198, 292, 302. See also *Spurge* and *Purge*
Catherine of Aragon, 21, 31, 52, 320.
Catholica, 80, 116.
Caticule, 109.
Catmint, 108, 161, 161, 243, 291, 305.
Cauda caballina., 137.
Cauda equina, 117.
Cauda porcina, 156, 169.
Cauda pulli, 117.
Cavvener, 111.
Celandine, 45, 54, 55, 86, 108, 131, 154, 177, 254, 256, 257, 271, 274, 301, 302.
Celsamus, 152.
Celsus amara, 117.
Cenerfole, 236, 302.
Centaurea, 47, 105, 107, 117, 126, 138, 141, 234, 242, 257, 302, 304, 305, 307.
Centenaria, 118.
Centerimsia, 91.
Centinodium., 109.
Centonica, 118.
Centrium Galli, 107.

Centrum grania, 109.
Centrum pulli, 118.
Centudina, 148.
Centum capita, 90.
Centum foramina, 194, 206.
Centum galle, 118, 130.
Cepa marina, 110.
Cepe, 111, 188, 244.
Cera, 176, 281, 283, 288. See also *Wax*
Cervisa, 106. See also *Beer*.
Ceteral, 226. See *Turmeric* and *Zedoar*.
Chancery Standard English, 50.
Charlok, 124, 180.
Charms or spells, 43.
Chastaynes, (for Chestnut) 48, 162.
Chekynworte, 137.
Chemerek, 80.
Chenet, 175.
Cherfole., 107.
Chevlange, 119.
Chikenmete., 140, 158.
Chimolia, 113.
Ciclamen, 105, 152, 170.
Ciclamen., 105.
Cicoria, 122, 139, 201.
Cicorie, 121.
Cicuta incubus, 135.
Cimbrium, 95, 151.
Ciminum dulce, 86, 111.
Cinnamon, 40, 141, 205, 225, 226, 239, 261, 268, 288, 289, 302, 303, 308.
Cinonima Correcta, 33.
Cinquefoil, 89, 103, 115, 180, 242, 271, 306.
Ciperus, 120.
Circa Instans, 33, 36, 55.
Citrago., 153.
Citraria, 153.
Clavis Sanitatis, 36, 47, 155

Clement VI, pope, 19.
Cliten, 182.
Clote, 100, 122, 133, 138, 142, 307.
Clover, 112, 151, 305.
Cloves, 13, 40, 54, 99, 130, 131, 242, 261, 268, 290, 296, 302, 303.
Clovetong, 124.

362

Cocnindium, 90.
Cocodrilla., 119.
Cokkill, 154.
Colamentum sanguinis, 35, 216.
Cold dropsi, 214.
Colera, 260, 292.
Colica, 224.
Colloquintida, 132.
Colophony, 106, 302.
Coloquinthida, 292, 302.
Coltsfoot, 48, 177.
Columbaria, 85, 172.
Columbrina, 112, 119.
Columbyn, 85.
Comfrey, 85, 110, 118, 190, 223, 302.
Common Centaury, 107, 117, 126, 226, 233, 234, 242, 246, 291, 293, 302, 303.
Compositiones Confectionum, 289.
Compositiones Siruporum, 286.
Concodium, 145.
Consolida, 85, 110, 118, 190, 306.
Constantinus Africanus, 59, 63.
Copiosa, 112.
Copper plate engraving of Betson, 25, 266.
Coriander, 94, 227, 302.
Corigiola, 170.
Corn Marigold, 155, 226, 230, 295, 304.
Corona Regia, 112.
Corpocissa, 129.
Corpus of Mediaeval Libraries, 24, 26, 34, 57, 59, 217, 340, 343, 348, 349, 351, 354.
Corpus Christi College, Cambridge, 26.
Cosmetics, 41.
Cotida, 94.
Couch Grass, 52.
Coule couell, 111.
Couslop, 101.
Crassula, 108, 202.
Cress, 114, 116, 149, 160, 189, 232.
Crisolocana, 82.
Cristos ladder, 117.
Crocus, 113, 134, 239.
Crouesope, 101, 111, 185.
Crowisfote, 174.
Cruciata major, 109.
Cucurbita agrestis, 99, 111.

Cudweed, 269, 286, 303.
Culrage., 172.
Cultor Dei Memento by Prudentius, 333.
Cumin, 40, 111, 162, 232, 246, 284, 302.
Cuscuta, 101, 112, 124, 177, 180, 302, 303.
Cuscuta, 101.
Custos librarie, 22, 24.
Custos Orti, 133.
Custos ortorum., 113.
Cutulus, 118.
Cypress, 29, 324.
Daisy, 85, 101, 109, 110, 111, 118, 164, 223, 253, 303, 306.
Dandelion, 48, 109, 119, 120, 226, 284, 303.
Darnel, 92, 107, 109, 118, 130, 132, 150, 153, 162, 271, 303.
Dascripta, 120, 121.
Daucus, 116, 119, 170, 303.
Daumocokci, 103.
De Urinalibus, 35.
Deadly Nightshade, 39, 44, 48, 158, 276, 307.
Deanesly, Margaret, 61.
Dematheam, 120.
Dendrolibani, 120.
Dens equi, 120.
Dens Leonis, 48, 109, 284, 303.
Dent de Lyon, 48, 109, 119.
Devil's Bit Scabious, 48, 158.
Diabetes, 60.
Diacatholicon, 46, 274, 303.
Diamargariton, 274, 303.
Diapenidion, 273, 306.
Dietarium rithmizatum in Anglicis, by John Lydgate, 27.
Dill, 84, 155, 192.
Dionisia., 121.
Dioscorides, 15, 44, 59, 194, 202, 327.
Diptanus, 178.
Diseases and Forms of Treatment, 50.
Dissolution of the monasteries, 11, 21, 26, 28, 30, 31, 32, 320, 339, 341, 346.
Ditany, 121, 242, 303.
Dock, 142, 143, 223, 243, 273, 304, 306.
Dodder, 101, 112, 124, 177, 180, 293, 302, 303.

Dodur, 101.
Dog's Mercury, 47, 96, 148, 155, 248.
Doyle, Ian, 7, 21, 25, 46, 49, 343.
Dragancia, 102, 112, 119, 180, 190, 214.
Dragantum, 119, 203.
Dragon Tree, 120, 156, 183, 293, 307.
Dragonwort., 102, 303.
Dropsy, 41, 208, 214, 215, 232, 233, 234, 236, 251.
Droptori, 121.
Dropwort., 127, 172, 306, 319, 325.
Dwale, 44, 352.
Dysentery, 249, 263. See also *Flux*.
Ebulus, 115, 303.
Edera, 121, 129, 204. See also *Ivy*.
Edward I, 39, 270, 352.
Edward III, 8, 19, 34, 39, 79, 270.
Edward IV, 20, 21.
Edward VI, 31, 319, 331, 332.
Eglenter, 100.
Elactorium, 122.
eLALME, 35, 49, 50.
Elder, 92, 114, 183, 215, 223, 241, 243, 276, 288, 293, 303, 308.
Elderflower, 260, 307
Eleboeris niger, 124
Eleborus Albus, 123.
Elecampane, 122, 135, 176, 303.
Elempnum., 122.
Elizabeth I, Queen, 21
Elotropia, 121.
Emathites., 122.
Emblicorum, 157.
Emigraniea, 224.
Endiva, 123, 199.
End of the World in AD 1500, on unnumberedpastedown board at rear of Betson Notebook, 297.
Enula campana, 122.
Epatica, 121, 293, 301.
Epatorium, 121, 147.
Epilencia, 224.
Epitimum, 124, 292, 303.
Eriscus, 124.
Erthe nuttis, 106, 152.
Eruca, 124.

Es ustum, 123.
Esbrinum, 122.
Esca camelorum, 191.
Euforbrium, 124.
Eutoporium, 87.
Everfern, 177.
Eviscus, 81, 123, 152.
Eyebright, 233, 245, 256, 257, 258, 267, 271, 303.
Eyeworte, 140.
Faba egipciata, 153.
Faba lupine., 153.
Fabaria, 125.
Fageria. Filix, 125.
Falkley, William, Confessor-General, 24.
False hellebore, 326.
Farina ordei, 94, 125.
Fasciculus Medicinae, 217.
Fatua, Sycamore Figs and lovesickness, 63, 192, 352
Febrifuga, 81, 126.
Fech, 167.
Feckenham, John, last Abbot of Westminster, 38, 43, 53, 347.
Fel terre, 107.
Feloun, 126, 227.
Feniculus porcinorum, 95, 126, 153.
Fennel, 78, 95, 98, 126, 155, 169, 171, 174, 208, 225, 226, 227, 233,236, 238, 242, 243, 259, 250 256, 257, 261, 267, 271, 274, 283, 291, 303, 305, 306.
Fenugrecum, 126.
Fern, 121, 125, 148, 149, 168, 177, 194, 223, 293, 303, 306.
Ferula, 40, 126, 130, 165, 301.
Fever, 52, 83, 219, 234, 236, 237, 251, 263, 296.
Feverfew, 37, 52, 81, 126, 226, 257, 284, 285, 303.
Fewterer, John, Confessor-General, 46.
Filago, 127, 303.
Filberdys nux, 146.
Fingerprint, 28.
Finicon Tamaides, 119.
Fisalidos, 127.
Fissh mente, 154.

Fistula, 263, 275, 276, 286, 316.
Five leved gres, 171.
Flammulus, 125.
Fleuma, 219, 226, 264, 265, 291, 292, 294, 292, 309.
Flint, 143, 224, 306.
Flos ciriacus, 127.
Flosmus pontfelyon, 136.
Flosmus tapsus, 127.
Floteworth, 89.
Flouris, 230. See also *Menstrua*.
Flux, 238, 242, 247, 263, 312.
Flyleaves, in Betson Notebook, 69, 73.
Forbiten, 181.
Foxglove, 15, 117.
Fragaria, 125.
Fragrum bruscus, 125.
Frankincense, 147, 165, 290, 305.
Fraximus, 125.
French Names for plants, 48.
Fuga demonum, 95, 135, 194.
Fulfulabia, 129.
Fulfules, 129.
Fumitory, Common, 128, 230, 239, 273, 303.
Furfur tritici, 106, 129.
Fyvelevedgres, 89.
Gagates, 131.
Galen, 28, 46, 57, 59, 187, 329, 342.
Galingale, 120, 130, 161, 191, 227, 261, 296, 303.
Gallicrista, 118, 130.
Gallitricum, 118, 130.
Gariofilata, 82, 87, 131, 185, 303.
Garlic, 40, 54, 80, 81, 90, 94, 96, 109, 194, 242, 238. See also *Tiriaca Rusticorum*
Gatherings,, in Notebook, 69 to 72.
Genest, 132, 157, 182. See also *Broom*.
Geniculata, 132, 170.
Gentian, 90, 96 98, 102, 132.
Gerarde, John, botanist, 29.
Germander, 52, 106, 114, 121, 132, 179, 198, 206, 261, 293, 302, 303.
Gersa, 132.
Gibbs, Elizabeth, Abbess of Syon, 24.
Gilbertus Anglicus, 43, 54, 59, 60, 343, 355.
Giles de Corbeil, 59.

Gillespie, Prof. Vincent, 7, 22, 23, 27, 31, 33, 34, 42, 217, 340.
Ginger, See *Zinziber*.
Gira solis, 122, 133.
Giro lapis, 134.
Giron, 133.
Gisasterios, 134.
Gith, 92, 132, 150, 153, 154, 162, 187, 209.
Gladden, 140, 187, 290, 303, 304.
Gladiole, 131, 140, 207, 290, 303, 304.
Glapes pulli, 93.
Glaucia, 131.
Glaucus, 134.
Glicida, 133, 319.
Gliconium, 133, 178.
Glis, 100, 133, 142.
Goatsbeard, 322, 323.
Gold, potable, 42, 110, 264.
Goldis boton, 155.
Golsough, 249, 253, See also *Jaundice*.
Goosefoot, 294, 305.
Gout, 13, 24, 37, 38, 39, 41, 224, 252, 263, 280.
Gramen amcastis, 131.
Grana solis, 131, 156.
Gratia Dei, 287
Greek Language, 8, 22, 24, 26, 45, 46, 47, 48, 79, 194, 329, 346.
Grenehalgh, James, Brother at Shene, 9, 61, 62, 63, 64, 333.
Grisanatana, 133.
Gromwell, 113, 131, 147, 156, 169, 171, 193, 225, 247, 283, 289, 304, 305.
Groundsel, 142, 189, 206, 225, 253, 304, 307.
Gum arabik, 134.
Gum Rockrose, 142, 290, 304.
Haemmoroids, 230.
Hair loss, 243, 309.
Hand signs, 25.
Harbell, 194.
Harefote, 82.
Harisworth, 85.
Harntraktat, der kurze, 35, 53, 60, 216, 217.
Harts tongue, 226, 304.
Hasilnott, 163.
Hastula regia, 88, 134.

Hastula Sancti Xtofori, 46, 88, 134.
Hawkisfote, 173.
Hawkweed, 53, 127, 175, 179, 253, 254, 285, 305, 306.
Hazel, 257, 269.
Health Warning, 15.
Hellebore, 39, 123, 124, 176, 282, 293, 303.
Hemlock, 39, 44, 102, 135, 139.
Hemp, 108, 285, 302.
Henbane, 43, 107, 138, 166, 190, 252.
Henbane, 37, 39, 43, 44, 45, 52, 107, 126, 138, 166, 190, 231, 254, 282, 304, 306.
Henry IV, 19.
Henry V, 11, 19, 20, 340.
Henry VI, 20, 343.
Henry VII, 53.
Henry VIII, 21, 26, 31, 52, 319.
Herb Bennet, 82, 102, 172, 257, 307.
Herb Robert, 92, 135.
Herba paradisi, 101.
Herba acetosa, 92, 168..
Herba benedicta, 135, 139.
Herba cancri, 109.
Herba cruciata, 136.
Herba fullonum, 136.
Herba hirca, 137.
Herba Iohannis, 95, 135, 139, 194, 206.
Herba luminaria, 127, 136. See also *Mullein*.
Herba medee, 136.
Herba muscata, 88.
Herba paralesis, 101.
Herba perforata, 95, 135, 139.
Herba Roberti, 135.
Herba Sancti Pauli, 137.
Herba Sancti Petri, 135.
Herba Veneris, 202.
Herba Walteri, 136.
Herbarium, 7, 8, 9, 22, 23, 28, 35, 36, 37, 39, 40, 41, 43, 46, 47, 52, 58, 64, 67, 78, 79, 80, 209, 239, 301, 312, 313, 316, 320, 342.
Hereve, 182.
Hertistong, 148, 194, 226.
Herworth, 88.
Heyhove, 121, 204.
Hindhal, 87.
Hiposeta, 137.

Hispia, 137.
Hog's Fennel, 306.
Hollyhock,.81, 82, 95, 243, 248, 294, 304.
Homelok, 139. See also *Hemlock*.
Honeysuckle, 107, 152, 153, 159, 172, 204, 236, 244, 247, 257, 263, 269, 271, 302, 308.
Horehound, 170, 259, 273, 291, 304, 305, 306.
Horse radish, 326, 328.
Horseheal, 122, 135, 176, 303.
Horself, 122.
Hortus Sanitatis, 42.
Horworth, 127.
Houndesfenell, 95, 127, 174.
Houndis tong, 148.
Houseleek, 87, 88, 141, 176, 188, 191, 198, 222, 242, 245, 256, 261, 282, 303, 304, 307.
Hurtene, 156, 201.
Hyndehale, 87, 121.
Hyssop, 32, 188, 226, 231, 238, 242, 243, 259, 260, 261, 291, 294, 308.
Iacia nigra, 138.
Iarus, 91.
Ictericia, jaundice, 219.
Ilapeas, 138.
Ill heryng, 244.
Illafeas, 133.
Impetigo, 209.
Incendium Amoris, by Richard Rolle of Hampole, 61, 63, 342, 354.
Incuba sponsa solis, 139.
Incubus cicuta, 139.
Indidictulus, 139.
Infirmaries, 29, 50.
Insana, 138. See also *Henbane*
Iovis barba, 141.
Iringi, 141.
Isaac Judeus, *Liber urinarum*, 59.
Iubarbe, 88, 222.
Iuniper, 129, 181, 279. See also *Juniper*.
Iusquiamus, 107, 138, 190. See also *Henbane*
Ivory, 193, 227, 249, 253, 307, See also *Spodium*.
Ivy, 88, 104, 121, 129, 204, 259, 273, 303, 308.

Jackson, A. Bruce, 29.
Jaundis, 227, 253.
John XXI, Pope, 36.
Jumelon, 139.
Juniper, 99, 129, 181, 186, 243.
Juse of sloue, 195.
Kakabre, 141.
Kalendula solsequium, 141.
Katariacum, 141.
Katherine of Aragon, 21, 31.
Kebuler Indorum, 157.
Knapweed, 37, 138, 226, 227, 257, 284, 304, 305, 307.
Knotgrass, 109, 132, 170, 274, 302.
Kokkill, 133, 209.
Kowisloppis, 135.
Kufordafin, 141.
Labanitidos, 120.
Lablis, 47, 155.
Labrum veneris, 116, 142.
Labrusca, 142, 203, 207.
Lactea, 218, 219, 220.
Lactuca domestica, 142.
Lambis tong, 118.
Lanceola, 80, 144.
Lanciolata, 180.
Lange de bef, 100.
Lapdanum, 142.
Lapis agapitis, 144.
Lapis Armenicus, 143, 292, 304.
Lapis calamiaris, 143, 163, 304
Lapis ematithes, 133.
Lapis iudiacus, 144.
Lapis Lazuli, 143, 144, 292, 293, 304.
Lapis linxcis, 47, 144.
Lapis magnetis, 134, 143.
Lapis sanguina, 122.
Lappa, 100, 122, 133, 138, 142, 243.
Lappatium, 142, 143.
Latin Galen, 40.
Laurel, 302, 306.
Laureola, 90, 116, 144, 198.
Laurus, 103, 116, 120, 144, 145, 239, 301, 302, 305, 306.
Lavendula, 145. 347.
Laxatives, 222, 238, 248, 288, 292, 296.

Lead, 15, 31, 38, 106, 128, 132, 176, 259, 265, 273, 277, 302, 304.
Lectoria, 146.
Leek, 81, 240, 306.
Lempnius, 145.
Lenticula aquatica, 145.
Lentigo, 145.
Lentiscus arbor, 145.
Leporina, 146, 186
Leprosy, 56, 264, 273, 314, 316, 350. See also *Oleum Leprosorum* 279.
Lettuce, 28, 123, 125, 142, 186, 196, 199, 226, 232, 276, 288, 304.
Leuco Piper album, 146.
Leveyis, 208.
Levisticum, 84, 145, 188, 305, 307.
Libanatidos, 147.
Libanum, 147, 165.
Libellus de Re Herbaria by Willima Turner, 46, 330, 331, 352.
Licoricia, 133. See also *Liquorice* below.
Licosoma, 147.
Lignum, Aloes 97; Iuniperi 181; Balsami 205; 304
Ligustrum, 147.
Lilifagus, 121, 147.
Lilium, Lilye, 147, 148, 161, 238.
Lily of the valley, 324.
Lingua agni, 118.
Lingua agnina, 148.
Lingua avis, 94, 149, 174.
Lingua bovis & bovina, 100, 148.
Lingua canis, 148.
Lingua cervina, 148.
Lingua ircina, 149.
Lingua passerum, 109.
Lingua silvana, 100.
Linilion, 147.
Linnaean plantnames, 9, 301.
Linseed, 164, 246, 304.
Lippotoma, 149.
Liquorice, 133, 225, 226, 227, 242, 288, 289, 296, 304.
Lisbon, 11, 21.
Litagiro, 273, 304.
Litargirio, 38.

Litaridos, 144.
Litodemonis, 147, 148.
Liverwort, 96, 97, 121, 257.
Lollium, 150, 202.
Longum piper, 150.
Loosestrife, 324.
Loquela, loss of speech, 243, 269, 316.
Lords and ladies, 44.
Lovage, 84, 145, 188, 235, 259, 305, 307.
Loveache, 145.
Lovesickness, 63, 192, 352.
Ludworte, 304.
Lumen Apothecariorum, 79.
Lupines, 150, 153.
Luther, Martin, 31.
Lydgate, 8, 27, 354.
Lye, 214, 228, 229, 243, 269, 273, 289, 304.
Lymphea aquatica, 148.
Lynarye, 149.
Lynochites, 148.
Lynsede, 147.
Lyons toth, 109.
Lyverworte, 121.
James, M.R., St John's College Cambridge Catalogue, 73.
Mabafematicon, 150.
Mace, 40, 261, 290, 304, 305.
Macedonium, 94, 171.
Macer Floridus, 28, 343, 355.
Macro peper, 150.
Macro piper longum, 150, 152.
Maculata trifolium, 151.
Madder, 195, 322
Madder, 182, 195, 231, 304, 308, 322. See also *Warence.*
Magnus of Sweden, 19.
Maidenhair fern, 45, 82, 93, 110, 173, 256, 293, 267, 301, 302, 304, 306.
Maiorana, 95, 151, 173, 183, 307.
Mala citorina, 152.
Mala coctaita, 151.
Malaria, 15, 51, 52, 53, 342.
Malewis, 193, 294, 304.
Malum granatum, 151, 320.
Malum macianum, 151.
Malum macidum, 151.

Malum punicum, 151, 320.
Malum terre, 106, 152, 170.
Malva viscus, 81, 123, 152.
Mandrake, 39, 88.
Manfocon, 149.
Maratrum, 126, 153.
Maraviscus, 95.
Marcilum lupynis, 150.
Marigold, 109, 110, 121, 139, 141, 157, 164, 193, 201, 241, 244, 257, 284, 307.
Maris, 104, 178, 235, 237, 318.
Marjoram, 95, 151, 167, 173, 183, 200, 227, 261, 267, 274, 301, 305, 307.
Marsilium, 153.
Martyrologium, (Syon), 24, 26, 54, 354.
Marubium, 170, 171.
Mary I, Queen, 21, 31.
Maslin, 305.
Masmaratrum, 95.
Mastix gum, 261, 305.
Mater herbarum, 81, 230, 305.
Mater silva, 107, 159. See also *matrisilva,* 152.
Matfelon, 138, 226, 227, 257, 284, 305.
Mather, 182.
Matricaria, 81, 152.
Matrisilva, 152.
Matrix, 64, 218, 220, 221, 222, 274, 275, 280, 318.
Maturella, 80.
Matyn, 95.
Maurus of Salerno, 58, 59.
Mecheworte, 183.
Melancium, 92, 132, 150, 153.
Melancolia, 259, 262, 292.
Meleum solis, 156.
Melissa, 85, 101, 136, 153, 173, 175.
Mellilotum, 112, 153, 175, 259, 305, 324.
Mellones, 153.
Meltrodatum, 156.
Menelata, 155.
Menesoun, 249. See also *flux.*
Menstrua, 60, 282, 318. See also *Flouris*
Menta aquatica, 103, 154.
Mental health, 60-63.
Mentastum, 154, 305.

Mentula episcopi, 154.
Mentula sacerdotis, 154.
Merchmawe, 82.
Merchsede, 188.
Merchworte, 151.
Mercurialis, 47, 89, 96, 148, 155.
Merica Brom, 132.
Merles, 155.
Mespilus, 155.
Methworth., 173.
Meu, 155.
Michigan (University) Middle English Dictionary (EMED), 44.
Michworth, 95.
Miconium, 156, 166.
Migraine, 241, 251, 293.
Migraine, 224, 290, 315
Milk, 42, 56, 200, 245, 246, 249; - of almonds. 295.
Millefolium, 13, 40, 156, 195, 201, 38, 242, 285, 305.
Mint, 237, 238, 243, 246, 261, 274.
Minutio, blood-letting, 53, 57, 218.
Mira solis, 139, 157.
Mirabulanes, 157.
Miracla, 133.
Mirfield, John, 8, 36, 40, 43, 47, 55, 79, 264, 354.
Mirica, 132, 157.
Mirra, 139, 157.
Mirror of Our Lady, 30, 354.
Mirtilles,156, 157, 201.
Mistletoe, 48, 203.
Moder, 213.
Moderwort, 181, 244.
Moleyn, 103, 127, 136, 169.
Moncton, Elizabeth, Sister at Syon, 30.
Mora celsi, 157.
Morell, 171, 158, 191, 201.
Morgan, Hugh, Apothecary, 32, 319, 321
Morphew, 223, 249.
Morsus demonis, 158, 181.
Morsus galline, 137, 139, 158, 207.
Morum nigrum, 201.
Moushere, 175, 179, 253, 305.

Mugwort, 39, 81, 95, 113, 152, 169, 230, 243, 248, 257, 284, 301, 305.
Mulberry trees, 29, 63, 157.
Muliebria, 45, 280, 318.
Mullein, 43, 48, 103, 127, 136, 158, 169, 178, 196, 293, 308.
Mulsa, 159.
Muscata woderofe, 158.
Mushroom, field, 293, 301.
Musk, 92, 158, 261, 274, 290, 305.
Muston, Elizabeth, Abbess of Syon, 24, 56.
Myrobalan, 157, 293, 303, 304, 305.
Myrrh, 157, 166, 239, 261, 272, 302, 305.
Myrtle, 201, 223, 305.
Narcha fish, 47.
Narcissus, 325.
Nardostanchium, 161.
Nasturtium agreste, - aquaticum, - ortulanum, - porcinum, 160.
Nedderworth, 112, 120, 190.
Nenuphar, 205.
Nepta calaminta minor, 161.
Nettill, 82
Nettle, Nettle seed and var.,53, 60, 82, 83, 91, 113, 169, 188, 204, 207, 235.
Nigella, 92, 132, 150, 154, 162.
Nigrum piper, 152.
Nimphea, 161.
Northumberland, Ninth Earl of. 'The Wizard Earl', 28.
Not muges, 117. See also *Nutmeg*.
Notebook of Thomas Betson,St John's College MS109 (E.6), 2, 7, 21, 22, 23, 25, 26, 27, 30, 44, 50, 51, 60, 64, 67, 340, 354.
Nutmeg, 40, 117, 162, 258, 261, 268, 273, 290, 304, 305.
Nux Coruli, 146, 163. See also Hazelnut.
Nux longa, 162.
Nux maior walnote, 162.
Nux muscata, 117,162, 305. See also *Nutmeg*.
Nux pina, 163.
Nux pontica, 146.
Nux terre, 106.
Nux Vomica, 305.

Oath of Supremacy, (to King Henry VIII), 21.
Obtalmiam, 163.
Obtaratium, 163.
Oculus bovis, 101, 164.
Oculus Lucii, 152.
Oculus populi, 164.
Oculus Xpi (Christi), 274, 305.
Ole de lynsede, 164.
Oleum Benedictum, 27, 43, 279.
Oleum de sinapio, 280, 305.
Oleum leprosorum, 279.
Oleum Ovorum, 223, 278.
Oleum Pulegii, 280.
Oleum rosarum, 182, 278.
Oleum Urticarum, 280.
Oleum Violarum, 279.
Olibanum, 147, 165, 199.
Olium de Luthion, 164.
Olium benedictum, 172.
Olive oil, 164, 213, 261, 305.
Olixatrum, 165.
Olus colex, 99.
Opium, 40, 165, 166, 169.
Opopunus, 166.
Origonum, 167.
Orobus, 167.
Orpement, 145.
Orpoba, 167.
Orpyn, 85, 108.
Osmunda, 125, 168.
Ossis de corde cervini, 306.
Ox appull, 130.
Oxencia, 119.
Oxford English Dictionary, 44, 77.
Oxifencia, 127, 139, 167
Oxilapacium, 136, 168.
Oyle de Beff, 101.
Oyle of Tartary, 229.
Oynons, 191.
Ozimum, 91, 168, 207.
Ozonpill, 92.
Padokpipe, 117.
Palma Xpi, 113, 169, 171.
Palma Xpī, 113, 133, 169.
Pampiris, 169.

Panifiligos, 169.
Panis cuculi, 80, 169.
Panis porcinus, 106, 152, 170.
Papaver album, 169. See also *Poppy*.
Paritaria, 171, 203, 274, 306.
Parsley, 52, 91, 94, 150, 155, 171, 191, 227, 236, 238, 242, 243, 246, 247, 261, 263, 291, 301, 306, 308, 325.
Parsnip, 93, 103, 116, 119, 170, 284, 290, 303, 305.
Passarla, 170.
Passerina Lingua, 170.
Pastinaca, Pastnepe, 93, 103, 116, 119, 170, 303, 305.
Pediculus, (lice) 36, 97, 282, 314.
Peletre of Spayne, 37, 175, 176.
Pellitory of the Wall, 171, 175, 203, 244, 251, 261, 274, 306, 308.
Pennyroyal, 39, 133,134, 167, 176, 178, 200, 246, 256, 261, 280, 288, 291, 293, 304, 306. See also *Pulegium regale*.
Pennywort, 45, 132, 187, 203, 293, 302.
Pentadactulus, 133, 171.
Pentafilon, 89, 103, 115, 127, 171, 180, 208.
Peony, 133, 271, 306, 329.
Pepper, 56, 129, 146, 150, 152, 172, 179, 246, 261, 263, 296, 306. See also Black and White -.
Peribit omnis caro per ignem. 297, See End of the World in AD 1500.
Perilose kogh, 56, 246. See also *Tuberculosis*
Periplimonia, 55, 224.
Peristerion, 172, 202.
Persa maiorana, 173.
Persicaria, 109, 132, 170, 172, 179, 302.
Pes ancipitris, 171.
Pes columbe, 135, 174.
Pes corvi, 173.
Pes leporis, 82, 131, 172, 185.
Pes nisi, 82
Pes pulli, 93, 174, 177.
Pes vituli, 85, 91, 138, 173.
Pestilencia, 37, 226, 241, 239, 284.
Petrocillum, 94, 171. See also *Parsley*.
Petrolium olium, 172.

Petrus Hispanus, 36, 267.
Peucedanum, 95, 98, 126, 155, 169, 171, 174, 195, 306.
Phlebotomy, 53, 58. See also *blood-letting*.
Phlegm, 208, 238, 249, 255, 263, 265, 294.
Pigaminis, 172.
Pigla. Lingua avis, 174.
Pigmentaria, 153, 175.
Pilioreal, 167.
Piloile riall, 134.
Pimpinella, 86, 93, 111, 137, 158, 175, 178, 187, 301, 306, 307. See also *Scarlet Pimpernel*.
Pinchbeck, John, Brother at Syon, 58.
Pionia, 133. See also *Peony*.
Piper nigrum, 129, 146, 152, 306.
Piretrum, 175.
Pisse, 215, 243, 247.
Pistasie. 174.
Pitarye, 203.
Pix greca, 106.
Plaga, 285, 318.
Plague See: Pestilencia.
Plantago, 148.
Plantago, 82, 89, 91, 118, 144, 148, 149, 170, 175, 176, 179, 180, 208, 230, 234, 243, 259, 269, 288, 304, 306, 308, 323, 327.
Platearius, 33.
Pliny, Natural History, 48.
Podagra lini, 112, 177.
Policaria, 135, 176, 179.
Poligonia, 132.
Polipodium, 121, 177, 292.
Politricum, 82, 293, 306.
Pollicaria, 135, 176.
Pollitricum, 82, 93, 173.
Polypody, 121, 125, 168, 177, 306.
Pomegranate, 31, 48, 151, 320, 324.
Pomfilion, 178.
Pomum Ambre, 42, 290.
Pomum citrine, 177.
Pomum quercinum, 130, 177.
Pomum silvestre, 151.
Poppy, 122, 156, 166, 169.
Portulaca, 86, 93, 177, 306.
Potell, 214, 215, 228.

Potentilla, 80, 89, 96, 103, 115, 128, 136, 138, 171, 180, 197, 199, 200, 272, 305, 306, 308.
Potters clay, 197.
Powder of Holland, 44, 225.
Practica Medicinae, 35.
Praemunire, used by Cromwell against Syon Abbey, 21.
Prassium, 170, 306.
Precentor, role in monastery, 24.
Pregnancy, 15, 31, 42, 60, 220, 221, 224, 310, 317.
Primrose, 147, 245, 306.
Propoleos, 176. See also *Wax*.
Proserpinia, 170.
Psalm 90: 333, 334.
Psidia, 175. See also *Pomegranate*.
Psillium, 175, 208.
Pulegium regale, 134, 167, 176,178.
Purges, various, 40, 46, 149, 162, 222, 232, 244, 246, 263, 274, 285, 292, 293. See also *Spurge*.
Purslane, 86, 93, 177, 276, 306.
Pygamen, 174.
Pyliol montayning, 176.
Pyntill, 248. See also *Yerde*.
Quartan fever, 41, 52, 53, 219, 312.
Quche grasse. 131.
Quencys, 152.
Quercula maior, 179.
Quercus, 179.
Quinconervia, 144.
Quinquefolium, 89, 115, 171, 180.
Quinquerina, 179.
Quinquiracium, 39, 40, 165.
Quotidian fever, 52, 53.
Radish, 119, 124, 180, 189, 291, 306.
Ramazzini, Bernardo, 55.
Ramsons, 81, 90, 94, 96, 109, 194, 282, 293, 304.
Raphanus, 119, 124, 180, 189, 306.
Red Dead Nettle, as diagnostic., 60, 83, 113, 204, 301.
Regement of Princes, 19.
Registrum, Syon Abbey Library catalogue, 7, 23, 24, 27, 31, 33, 42, 43, 217, 340, 354.
Reisyns, 200.

Repontiphus, 182.
Reremous, (bat) 202. See also *Vespertilio*.
Resta bovis, 181.
Resta lini, 180.
Resuris, 181, 292, 307. See also *Rhubarb*.
Revelationes, of St Bridget, 19, 20.
Reynolds, Richard, 26, 30, 339.
Reynolds, Edith, 26.
Rhubarb, 46, 181, 222, 292, 293, 307, 307.
Ribwort, 144, 180.
Richard II, 19.
Richard III, 21, 24.
Richard Reynolds, 21, 26, 33, 339.
Robelia, 182.
Rodaxigrou, 182.
Roden, 110, 157, 193, 201.
Rolle, Richard of Hamploe, 63.
Rosa rubea, 182.
Rosas caninas, 140.
Rose, 41, 55, 100, 120, 127, 147, 182, 188, 199, 222, 239, 256, 257, 259, 267, 271, 283, 288.
Rosemary, 120, 127,, 213, 261, 307.
Rosina, 181.
Rostrum porcinum, 48, 182.
Rubarbe, 64, 181, 222. See also *Resuris*.
Rubea maior & minor 182.
Rue, 39, 56, 172, 173, 174, 213, 233, 243, 244, 246, 247, 249, 256, 257, 267, 271, 274, 283, 294, 307.
Rule for the Brothers, 24.
Rules of St Saviour and St Augustine, 24, 354.
Ryght Profytable Treatyse, 5, 25, 28, 30, 50, 340.
Sacanus, 154.
Saffron, 40, 113, 134, 261, 307, 353.
Sagapium, 183.
Sage, 56, 87, 121, 122, 147, 183, 236, 238, 243, 245, 246, 261, 263, 271, 274, 288, 293, 295, 303, 307.
Sal alkali, 184.
Sal Capodoxitum, 184.
Sal Armoniacum, 241, 307.
Sal armoniak, 184.
Sal catercutie, 184.

Sal gemme, 184, 307.
Sal matelli, 184.
Sal nitrum, 184.
Sal ponsinus, 184.
Sal sacerdotale, 184.
Sal tartari, 184..
Sal traceatum, 184.
Saliunca, 196.
Salix, 86, 183, 193, 207.
Salt gumme, 184..
Salvatelle veins, 57, 189.
Salvia, 87, 107, 109, 118, 121, 122, 130, 147, 164, 183, 263, 303, 307.
Salvia agrestis, 87, 121, 147.
Sambucus, 92, 114, 183, 303, 304, 307, 308.
Samphire, 44.
Sana munda, 82, 131.
Sandarica, 185.
Sandix, 185, 195.
Sandonicum, 185.
Sanguinaria, 104, 160, 185, 307.
Sanguinem Draconis, 293, 307.
Sanguis draconis, 156.
Sanguis draconis, 120, 183.
Sanicle, 40, 87, 185, 271, 285, 307.
Sankdragon, 183.
Sansucus, 95, 151, 173, 183.
Sapa, 185.
Saponaria, 100, 111, 136, 185, 195.
Sarcocolla, 186
Satercia, 186.
Saturion leporina, 186.
Sauffleme, 214.
Saunders, Stephen, Confessor-General, 24.
Saundres, 185.
Savina, 99, 186. See also *Juniper*.
Saxifrage, 306, 327
Saxifrage, 93, 137, 147, 158, 175, 178, 187, 261, 289, 307, 327.
Scabius, 233, 307.
Scabwort., 122, 135, 176, 274, 303
Scala Perfectionis, by Walter Hilton 2, 61, 64, 333, 334, 345, 355.
Scammony, 187, 222, 231, 307.
Scariole, 196, 199.

Scarlet Pimpernel, 137, 175, 178, 230, 240, 257, 271, 287, 306. See also *Pimpinella*.
Sciatica, 225, 263.
Scicida, 89, 99, 190.
Scolopendria, 98, 148, 194.
Scopa regia, 95, 194
Scopia regia, 95, 139, 194, 206.
Scordion, 81, 194.
Scoriola silv., 186.
Secaul, 141.
Secretum Philosophorum, 23.
Seholin, 187.
Self-heal, 326.
Selfhele, 138, 178.
Semibrium, 154.
Semperviva, 88, 188. See also *Houseleek*.
Senecium, 189, 226, 307.
Senegrene, 141.
Senna, 46, 189, 295, 307
Senygrene, 88. See also *Houseleek*.
Sepha, 188
Serapion's Synonyms, 33.
Serapium, 183..
Seripigo, 209.
Serpentaria, 119, 190.
Serpentina., 102.
Serpillum pelege, 190.
Setacul, 141, 187.
Setwale, 208.
Sewarmede, 185.
Sewell, Joanna, Sister at Syon, 9, 61, 62, 63, 64, 333, 334.
Seynt John Worte,, 96, 135.
Seynt Mary bery, 158.
Seynt Mary flour, 191.
Sheen or Shene, 20, 34, 61, 62, 319, 319, 321, 322, 323, 324, 325, 326, 327, 328,329, 333.
Shepherd's Purse, 104, 160, 247, 274, 302, 304, 307.
Shingles, 248.
Sicidon, 130.
Sicla,192.
Sicomorus ficus, 192.
Sigillum Ste Marie, 191.
Signa Arietis, 91.

Siler montanum., 192.
Silicis nigre, pulvis, 224, 306. (powdered black flint).
Silium, 188.
Silverweed, 136, 138, 197, 199, 226, 257, 272, 284, 285, 305, 308.
Simon of Genoa, *Clavis Sanitatis*, 36, 47, 155.
Simphitum, 190.
Simphonica, 107, 126, 190
Simphonica., 107, 126
Simphonitum, 85
Sinabrium, 193
Sinamomum, 142
Sinicopis, 149.
Sinonoma de nominibus herbarum, by John Bray, Physician to Edward III, 34.
Siriarca, 193.
Sisinbrium mente, 103.
Sisoleos, 192.
Sistra, 192.
Sizinbeum, 191.
Skirewite, 124,
Sleveworth, 125,
Smallage, 84, 246, 247, 271, 289, 301.
Smallpox, 59.
Smerworth, 89.
Snake, *serpens*, 62, 241, 279, 333.
Soap, 51, 229, 243, 269.
Solerata, 188.
Solsequium, 110, 122, 141, 193, 243
Somerset, Protector, & Duke of, 9, 28, 29, 31, 32, 319, 320, 321, 332.
Sore eyes, 41, 78, 215, 233, 235, 245, 250, 256, 312.
Sorrel, Souredok, 88, 02, 119, 136, 168.
Southernwood, 114, 249, 307.
Soutra Aisle, Midlothian, 29, 40.
Sovereign Medicines, by John Feckenham, Abbot of Westminster, 38, 53, 343, 347.
Sowthistle, 48, 109, 115, 116, 123, 142, 169, 171, 199, 207, 256, 267, 271, 274, 295, 303, 307.
Sparowisfote, 93.
Spatula fedida, 140.
Spatula fetida, 187, 207.

Speech, loss of., 41, 49, 50, 243, 269. See also *Loquela.*
Speedwell, 323.
Speragon, 187.
Sperhaukesfote, 82, 93, 173.
Sperma cete, 87.
Sperorgle, 137.
Spewyngworth, 103.
Spica celtica, 183, 191.
Spikenard, 161, 191, 196, 225, 239, 251, 261, 307.
Spinach, 192, 295, 307.
Spleen, 52, 57, 233, 295, 315.
Spodium, 193, 307. See also *Ivory.*
Sponsa solis, 110, 122, 193.
Spurge, 90, 112, 122, 124, 137, 144, 186, 198, 246, 254, 261, 273, 288, 293, 302, 303, 306, 308.
Spurge Laurel, 90, 144, 198, 246, 254, 304, 328.
Sqillis, 110.
Squinatum, 191.
St Bartholomew's Priory and Hospital in London, 79.
St John's Wort, 37, 38, 43, 44, 95, 135, 139, 206, 241, 304, 322, 350.
St Michael's Mount in Cornwall, 20.
Stafisatis, 186.
Stanche, 104.
Star of Bethlehem, 325.
Statumcellus, 187.
Sternutatorium, 163.
Stevenwort, 80.
Stitchwort., 94, 149, 174, 295, 308.
Stomach problems, 41, 44, 53, 218, 220, 260, 262, 274, 276, 279, 280, 283, 284, 289, 293, 309, 317.
Stone, (in kidney), 226, 230, 235, 242, 247
Stonecrope, 202.
Stonewort, 127.
Stonhore, 108, 171.
Storax liquida, 193.
Streberiwise, 125.
Strignum, 158, 191, 201.
Strutt, Bibliographical Dictionary, 2, 25, 64, 335.

Stunci, 192.
Sturtium, 195.
Stynk of the mouth, 242.
Styrax officinalis, 193, 261, 273, 290, 308.
Succus prunellarum, 195.
Sugar. See *Zuccarie.*
Sulphur vivum, 194, 198.
Supercilium veneris, 45, 156, 195, 201,
Suppositoria et Pessaria, 203, 287, 295, 311.
Sutirion, 146.
Sweating Sickness, 53, 54, 342.
Swoyning, 149.
Swynesgrece, 110, 170.
Swynestaile, 171.
Syngles, (Shingles) 248.
Synonum, 191, 209, 238, 308.
Syon Abbey,-Care of the Sick: 50-63; Deacons, 25; 26; - Gardens, 28 to 30; 31; - History and Foundation, 19, 21; - Library and Medical Books, 33-36; 41, 42, 49; - *Martyrologium,* 24, 26, 54, 354; Other; 77, 217, 319, 333, 339, 340, 341, 342, 343, 344, 346, 351.
Syon House, 7, 9, 13, 20, 26, 29, 32, 103, 319, 320, 321, 339, 346, 353.
Syon Abbey *Martyrologium,* 24, 26, 54, 354.
Syon Abbey Pardon at Lammastide, 25.
Syphilis, 59.
Tamarind, 118, 139, 167, 168, 293, 294, 308.
Tanacetum agreste, 197, 241, 272, 308.
Tapsus barbastus, 136, 158, 178, 196.
Tarascon, 196.
Tartar, 277, 305.
Tartarii Argoil, 196.
Ten Commandments, Betson text of, 49.
Termonde, 21.
Terpentina, 197.
Terra Sarazenica, 197.
Terra sigillata, 113, 197, 308.
Tertian fever, 41, 52, 53, 312.
Testiculus muris, 199.
Tetereworth, 86.
Theodoricum, 222.
Thisic, 55.
Thomas Cromwell, Syon, *Praemunire,* 21.

Thomas, Comes Southamptoniensis – Thomas, Earl of Southampton, 67.
Thyme, 124, 167, 176, 178, 200, 256, 261, 288, 293, 303, 304, 306, 308.
Tibapirum, 198.
Timbria, 200.
Tingewick, William of, See *Tynechewik*
Tiriaca, -de Boys, 288;-rusticorum, 81, 94.
Tisik, Thisik, 55, 236.
Titimall, 198.
Toothache, 54.
Tormentill, 96, 200, 243, 259, 271, 289, 308.
Toteseyn, (Tutsan), 49, 86.
Touncras sede, 189.
Toxima, 199.
Tragacanth, 273, 303.
Transcription conventions, 78.
Treatyse of Fysshynge Wyth an Angle, 27
Tribulus ruby, 199.
Trifoliium, 112.
Trowell, John, Confessor-General, 24.
Tuberculosis (TB), 55.
Tumbra, 198.
Tunhove, 121.
Turmeric, See *Ceteral* and *Zedoar*.
Turner, William, 7, 8, 9, 29, 31, 32, 44, 46, 49, 63, 285, 302, 319, 320, 321, 322, 327, 328, 329, 330, 331, 332, 346.
Turpentine, 197, 213, 261, 270, 308.
Turpeth, Turbit, 291, 292, 293, 308.
Tussis, 227.
Tutsan, 49, 86.
Twickenham, 20, 51.
Thyme, 124, 231.
Tynechewik, William of, Royal Physician, 39, 42, 270.
Ulex, 140, 196.
Umbilicus veneris, 45, 187, 203.
Ungula caballina, 161, 205
Urina, 35, 53, 216, 218, 219, 220, 221, 223, 224, 311, 317.
Urina citrina, 218.
Urina lucida, 53, 219.
Urina pallida, 218.
Urina rubea, 218
Urina rufa, 216, 218, 219

Urina subrufa, 218, 219
Urina viridis, 218.
Urine, 35, 53, 60, 64, 216, 254, 310, 317.
Uroscopy, 35, 42, 59, 60, 67, 216
Urtica, 82, 83, 91, 168, 188, 204, 207, 243. See also *Nettle.*
Usifur vivum, 202.
Uterus, 213, 318.
Uva Lupina, 201.
Uva passa, 170, 200.
Uve Acerbe, 200.
Vaccicinium, 201.
Vadstena Abbey, 7, 19, 20, 27, 32, 39, 58, 339, 345, 353.
Valerian, 80, 128, 191, 19, 200, 239, 251, 307.
Vellum leaves in Betson Notebook, 9, 67, 69.
Venter apis, 195, 201.
Verdigris, 128, 249, 308.
Vermicularis,108, 201
Vermilion, 193, 202
Verucaria, 122, 139, 201
Vervain, 45, 52, 167, 172, 202, 235, 243, 244, 256, 257, 267, 269, 271, 287, 308.
Vespertilio, 202.
Viaticum, tr. by Constantinus Africanus, 63, 352.
Vicetoxicum, 96.
Vine leaves, 169, 199, 270, 271, 303.
Vinegar, 54, 55, 168, 239, 240, 247, 248, 255, 261, 282, 284, 301.
Violet, 139, 203, 223, 235, 247, 269, 294, 304
Virga pastoris, 202, 205
Vita, Pro Conservanda by Johannes Vitalis, 36, 60, 216, 217, 218, 219, 220, 221, 222.
Vitriole., 90, 203.
Vitriolum, 114, 203, 241, 308.
Volubilis, 153, 172, 204.
Vomiting, 282, 318.
Vulnerary, 236, 239, 240.
Walnut, 162, 259, 305.
Walworte, 115, 198.
War of the Roses, 21.
Warenyce, 182, 231, 308. See also *Madder*
Water cress, 160, 189, 252, 296, 308.
Water Lily, 148, 161, 177, 205, 269, 305, 308.

Watermarks, Notebook, 9, 67, 68, 69, 70, 71, 72.
Wax, 30, 176, 181, 213, 237, 253, 283, 287.
Weibrede, 82. See also *Plantain*.
Willow, 183, 207. See also *Salix*,
Wermode, 86, 118, 233, 308. See also *Wormwood*.
Westhaw, Thomas, Confessor-General, 22.
Whete, 129, 130, 294, 308 *(Wheat)*.
White piper, 129.
Whyte Elebo(ore), 123.
Wild carrot, 327.
Wild Celery, 56, 83, 84, 188, 227, 235, 242, 246, 253, 294, 307.
Wildetasill, 202, 205.
Wildnep, 89, 99. See also *Bryony*.
Wildsauge, 87.
Wildvyne, 89.
Wimbish, Essex, and Betson, 21, 31, 42, 49.
Wodebrounien, 102.
Wodebynde, 107, 153, 172, 247.
Wodecrabbis, 151.
Wodemadur, 195.
Wodemerch, 87, 185.
Woderove, 88, 134, 158.
Wodesour, 80, 170, 214, 308.
Womb, 230, 232, 235, 237, 246, 309, 317.
Women's illnesses, 31.
Wood Sorrell, 80, 169, 170, 214, 301, 308.
Woodbind, 204, 236.
Woodruff, 136, 158, 258.
Worms, 115, 234, 235, 245.
Wormwood, 84, 86, 91, 118, 185, 226, 230, 234, 243, 244, 248, 249, 253, 274, 284, 291, 296, 301, 308, 327.
Wounds, Treatment of,15, 43, 285.
Wrenging-worth, 110.
Wymawe, 82, 123.
Wine, 226, 233, 235, 236, 237, 242, 247, 248, 249, 252, 257.
Wynkyn de Worde, 5, 25, 50, 68, 340, 341.
Wyot, Richard, Brother at Syon, 58.

Xantos, 205.
Xillobalsamum, 205.
Xpīana, 206.
Yalow evell, Jaundice, 230, 314.
Yarrow, 45, 54, 156, 195, 201, 238, 242, 268, 285, 305, 308.
Ydromel, 207.
Ydropisis, 224, 238.
Yeksterys, 85.
Yellow flag, 131, 222, 290, 303, 304.
Yelowsought, jaundice, 231, 253.
Yerde, 45, 252.
Ygia. Netil sede, 207.
Ypericon, 95, 135, 139, 206.
Ypia, 139, 158, 207.
Ypomaratrium, 208.
Ypoquintides, 104, 140, 207.
Yposarcan, 208.
Ypoxanto, 205.
Yreos, 140.
Yriana vitis agrestis, 207.
Yris, 140, 207.
Ysalgar, 241, 308.
Ysope, 188, 206, 226, 231, 238, 242, 243, 259, 260, 261, 308. See also *Hyssop*.
Ysyon, 141.
Ytea, 207.
Zacaton, 208.
Zedoar, 208, 261, 274, 302, 308.
Zertia impetigo, 209.
Zhebreer, 100.
Zima, 208.
Zima Fermentum, 208.
Zinziber (Ginger), 208, 226, 261, 288, 289, 291, 292, 308.
Zodarium, 208.
Zuccarie, Zuccarra, (sugar),193, 208, 226, 259, 288-292, 308.
Zyrungen, 208.
Zyzania, 209.